KNOWLEDGE ENGINEERING

Volume II   APPLICATIONS

KNOWLEDGE ENGINEERING

Volume II   APPLICATIONS

Hojjat Adeli, Editor
Department of Civil Engineering
The Ohio State University

McGraw-Hill Publishing Company

New York St. Louis San Francisco Auckland Bogotá Caracas
Hamburg Lisbon London Madrid Mexico Milan Montreal New Delhi
Oklahoma City Paris San Juan São Paulo Singapore Sydney Tokyo Toronto

This book was set in Times Roman by the College Composition Unit
in cooperation with Ruttle Shaw & Wetherill, Inc.
The editors were B. J. Clark and John M. Morriss;
the production supervisor was Leroy A. Young.
The cover was designed by Carla Bauer.
Project supervision was done by The Total Book.
R. R. Donnelley & Sons Company was printer and binder.

KNOWLEDGE ENGINEERING

Vol. II, Applications

Copyright © 1990 by McGraw-Hill, Inc. All rights reserved. Printed in the
United States of America. Except as permitted under the United States Copyright Act
of 1976, no part of this publication may be reproduced or distributed in any form or
by any means, or stored in a data base or retrieval system, without the prior written
permission of the publisher.

3 4 5 6 7 8 9 0 DOC DOC 9 5 4 3 2 1 0

ISBN 0-07-000357-2

Library of Congress Cataloging-in-Publication Data

Knowledge engineering / [edited by] Hojjat Adeli.
    p.   cm.
  Includes index.
  Contents: v. 1. Fundamentals—v. 2. Applications.
  ISBN 0-07-000355-6 (v. 1)—ISBN 0-07-000357-2 (v.2)
    1. Expert systems (Computer science)   I. Adeli, Hojjat, (date).
QA76.76.E95K577   1990
006.3'3—dc20   89-8338

For information about our audio products, write us at:
Newbridge Book Clubs, 3000 Cindel Drive, Delran, NJ 08370

EDITOR'S BIOGRAPHY

Currently professor of civil engineering at The Ohio State University, Hojjat Adeli received his Ph.D. from Stanford University in 1976. He is the editor-in-chief of the international journal, *Microcomputers in Civil Engineering,* and the author or editor of nearly 200 research publications including several books in the fields of knowledge engineering and expert systems, computer-aided design, parallel processing, mathematical optimization and simulation, applied mechanics, and structural engineering. He is also the editor-in-chief of the forthcoming Marcel Dekker book series *New Generation Computing.* The first two volumes of series, *Supercomputing in Engineering Analysis* and *Parallel Processing in Computational Mechanics* are scheduled for publication in late 1990. He is listed in twelve *Who's Who*'s and biographical listings including *Who's Who in the World, Men of Achievement,* and *International Directory of Distinguished Leadership.*

CONTENTS

	Contributors	ix
	Preface	xiii
1	**Integrity Constraints in Knowledge-Based Systems** J. Grant and J. Minker	1
2	**Symbolic Decision Procedures for Knowledge-Based Systems** J. Fox	26
3	**Applications of Automated Reasoning** L. Wos	56
4	**Robot Problem Solving** T. Dean	84
5	**Autonomous Mobile Robots** R. C. Arkin	116
6	**AI Techniques in Computer-Aided Manufacturing Systems** S. G. Tzafestas	161
7	**AI Techniques in Software Engineering** G. E. Kaiser	213
8	**Knowledge-Based Vision Systems** M. G. Rodd	245
9	**Linguistic Knowledge and Automatic Speech Recognition** S. L. Lytinen	277

10 Knowledge Processing and Its Application to Engineering Design
S. Ohsuga   300

Index   341

CONTRIBUTORS

Ronald C. Arkin is an assistant professor in the school of information and computer science at the Georgia Institute of Technology. He received his Ph.D. from the University of Massachusetts in 1987. Between 1977 and 1985 he taught at Hawthorne College in Antrim, New Hampshire, where he was recognized as the faculty member of the year in 1983. Dr. Arkin's research interests are centered upon intelligent action and perception, particularly as evidenced by mobile robots and computer vision. He is listed in *Who's Who in the World, Who's Who in the East,* and *Who's Who of Emerging Leaders in America.*

Thomas L. Dean received his Ph.D. from Yale University in 1986. He is currently an assistant professor in the department of computer science at Brown University. His research interests include logic programming, deductive retrieval methods, and robot problem solving.

John Fox is head of the biomedical computing unit at the Imperial Cancer Research Fund, London, United Kingdom. He is editor of *The Knowledge Engineering Review,* an international journal. He has published extensively in the area of decision theory and technology.

John Grant received his Ph.D. from New York University in 1970. He is currently professor of computer and information science at Towson State University and visiting professor of computer science at the University of Maryland. He has published extensively in the area of databases and logic. He is the author of *Logical Introduction to Databases,* a textbook for advanced undergraduates.

Gail E. Kaiser is an assistant professor of computer science at Columbia University. She received her Ph.D. from Carnegie Mellon University in 1986. She was selected as a U.S. National Science Presidential Young Investigator in 1988. Her research interests include programming environments, application of AI technology to software development and maintenance, object-oriented languages and databases, and distributed systems.

Steven L. Lytinen is an assistant professor of electrical engineering and computer science at the University of Michigan. He received his Ph.D. from Yale University in 1984, where he wrote a knowledge-based machine translation system. One focus of his research has been on the interaction of different levels of linguistic knowledge in natural language analysis, and recently he has begun extending this work to speech recognition. Other research interests include language acquisition and acquiring knowledge from instructions.

Jack Minker received his Ph.D. from the University of Pennsylvania in 1959. He is currently a professor in the department of computer science and Institute for Advanced Computer Studies at the University of Maryland. He is on the editorial board of the *Journal of Logic Programming, Information Systems, IEEE Expert, Encyclopedia of Artificial Intelligence, Computing Reviews, Expert Systems: Research and Applications, International Series in Logic Programming,* and the *Journal of Academic Proceedings of Soviet Jewry.* He was the first chair of the department of computer science at the University of Maryland from 1974–1979 and served as chair of the Advisory Committee on computing to the U.S. National Science Foundation from 1980–1982. He has numerous publications in the areas of artificial intelligence, automated theorem proving, deductive databases, and logic programming. He has edited several books on deductive databases and logic programming, the most recent of which is *Foundations of Deductive Databases and Logic Programming.*

Setsuo Ohsuga received his Ph.D. from the University of Tokyo in 1966. He is currently a professor in the Research Center for Advanced Science and Technology at the University of Tokyo. He is now the vice president of the Japanese Society for Artificial Intelligence. Professor Ohsuga is a regional editor of the journal of *Knowledge-Based Systems.* His research interests include artificial intelligence, knowledge processing, databases, and CAD.

Mike G. Rodd received his B.Sc., M.Sc., and Ph.D. degrees from the University of Cape Town before joining the University of the Witwatersrand as professor of electronics in 1978. He became head of the department in 1982. He is currently head of the department of electrical and electronic engineering at the University College of Swansea, Wales. He has published widely in the areas of distributed computer control systems, real-time operating systems, computer architecture, computer vision, and the social impacts of automation. He is editor-in-chief of the international journal, *Engineering Applications of AI.*

Spyros G. Tzafestas received his M.Sc. in automatic control from the University of London (Imperial College) in 1967. He received a Ph.D. in electrical engineering and D.Sc. for his published work in the systems and control field from Southampton University, England, in 1969, and 1978, respectively. From

1973–1984, he was professor of systems and control engineering at Patras University, Greece. He is currently professor of computer science at the National Technical University of Athens, Greece. He has published 12 books and over 200 technical papers. He is editor-in-chief of the *Journal of Intelligent and Robotic Systems,* associate editor of three journals, and editor of the Reidel book series *Microprocessor-Based Systems Engineering.* He is a fellow of IEEE and the Institution of Electrical Engineers (United Kingdom), and vice president of the International Association for Mathematics and Computers in Simulation. His research interests include distributed-parameter and large-scale systems, reliability and maintenance optimization, fault detection, robotics, and knowledge-based intelligent systems.

Larry Wos is a senior mathematician in the Mathematics and Computer Science Division at Argonne National Laboratory. He has published extensively on automated theorem proving and automated reasoning and has authored two books on the subject. He is editor-in-chief of the *Journal of Automated Reasoning* and has been president of the Association for Automated Reasoning since its inception in 1982. He (with a colleague) won the first awarded American Mathematical Society Automated Theorem-Proving prize in 1983.

PREFACE

The first volume of *Knowledge Engineering* presents state-of-the-art reviews and tutorials on fundamental aspects of knowledge engineering. The second volume complements the first by presenting applications of applied artificial intelligence (AI). The field of applied AI and knowledge engineering is very young. Students usually must refer to numerous sources to learn the fundamentals of the subject. The two volumes attempt to present summaries of the various subjects in a single document and are oriented toward practical applications. They are suitable as primary reference books in introductory courses on applied AI and knowledge engineering.

Leading and internationally recognized researchers have contributed to these volumes. We hope this effort becomes a continuing book series with future volumes concentrating on other aspects of knowledge engineering and new applications of AI.

Hojjat Adeli
Editor

CHAPTER 1

INTEGRITY CONSTRAINTS IN KNOWLEDGE-BASED SYSTEMS

JOHN GRANT
JACK MINKER

1 INTRODUCTION

A database system is a system used for the storage and manipulation of facts. Deductive database and knowledge-based systems can be used for the storage and manipulation of knowledge that consists of facts and rules. We distinguish between a deductive database and a knowledge base by allowing function symbols in the latter but not in the former. An expert system may then be defined as a meta-interpreter over a knowledge base or deductive database that provides facilities such as a natural language interface or an explanation of the reasoning used in obtaining answers.

Both database and knowledge-based systems include integrity constraints, which are statements that must be satisfied by the database or the knowledge base. Much of the literature about knowledge-based systems emphasizes the facts and rules but deals with integrity constraints as a minor matter. In fact, the knowledge-based systems of today consider the facts and rules as the knowledge base. Our point of view is quite different: we consider integrity constraints as the essence of knowledge for a knowledge-based system. The reason is that the inclusion of integrity constraints provides semantic information about the data in the database. This semantic information more precisely defines what may exist in the database.

Consider the following example. In a deductive database, it is possible to write a rule to define a grandparent in terms of parent as follows: X is a grandparent of Y if X is a parent of Z and Z is a parent of Y. In a geometric database, a syntactically identical definition can be given for parallel lines in terms of perpendicular lines. That is, X is parallel to Y if X is perpendicular to Z and Z is perpendicular to Y. However, in the first case, there is an integrity constraint on parents: any individual may have no more than two parents. There is no corresponding integrity constraint for perpendicular lines. Thus, semantic considerations may distinguish between syntactically identical facts and rules.

The theme of this chapter is the application of knowledge, in the form of integrity constraints, to problems as diverse as update validation, query optimization, and informative answer generation. Researchers have previously developed special-purpose methods, using integrity constraints, to study these problems individually. Some of these will be reviewed later in the proper context as we describe each topic. Our emphasis will be on the presentation of a unified framework for representing the interaction of integrity constraints with the facts and rules of the knowledge base and on showing how this approach provides solutions to those problems.

Section 2 contains a formal definition of a knowledge-based system. We use the language of first-order logic to describe the contents of a knowledge-based system. First-order logic provides a very useful formalism for dealing with knowledge-based systems, because it is a uniform language for expressing facts, rules, integrity constraints, and queries. The uniform technique used in this paper for the application of integrity constraints in knowledge-based systems is called *partial subsumption*. Section 3 contains a description of this method. In a knowledge-based system, partial subsumption of the integrity constraints can be performed at an initial stage, before the processing of queries and updates. The result of partial subsumption is a set of residues that are then attached to the predicates and are used for various purposes during data manipulation.

The topic of Section 4 is update validation. This was, in fact, the initial and primary reason for the introduction of integrity constraints into database systems. Whenever a database is updated, the integrity constraints must remain true. This concept carries over to knowledge bases. We will show in this section how the generation of residues from the integrity constraints facilitates the validation of updates.

A query optimizer chooses a sequence of operations that translate the original query into an efficient program. Traditional query optimization uses the properties of various relational operators and the physical representation of data such as sizes of tables and indexings but does not use semantic knowledge about the application domain, that is, the integrity constraints. In Section 5 we show how semantic query optimization, that is, the optimization of query translation by the use of integrity constraints, can be applied to knowledge-based systems.

A knowledge-based system should respond to a questioner in an intelligent and cooperative manner. In Section 6 we will show that integrity constraints, via the residues, are highly useful in providing a knowledge-based system with a cooperative and informative answer. In particular, integrity constraints often provide the reason for the answer to a query. Communicating the reason for the answer to the user may be much more informative than the answer by itself. The last section, Section 7, summarizes the chapter.

2 DEFINITION OF A KNOWLEDGE-BASED SYSTEM

Since knowledge-based systems are commonly formalized in logic, we start this section by providing some terminology and concepts of first-order logic. For general information on the applications of logic to databases see Gallaire et al. (1984). The syntax of first-order logic is based on a class of languages and the formulas that may be written in these languages. Each language contains a set of logic and non-logic symbols. The logic symbols are the same for each language and contain variables, logical connectives and quantifiers, and punctuation symbols; the non-logic symbols are constants, predicates, and functions. The rules for constructing formulas are the same for all first-order languages.

The symbols of a first-order language are as follows.

1. Logic symbols:

   Variables: $x, y, z, x1, y1, z1, \ldots$ (infinitely many)
   Connectives: $\neg$ (not), $\vee$ (or), & (and), $\rightarrow$ (implies)
   Quantifiers: $\forall$ (for all), $\exists$ (there exists)
   Punctuation: parentheses and comma
   Equality: =

2. Non-logic symbols:

   Constants: a, b, c, susan, prof,...(as many as needed, possibly 0)
   Predicates: P, R, Teach,...(at least one)
   Functions: f, g, plus,...(as many as needed, possibly 0)

The presence of functions distinguishes knowledge-based systems from deductive database systems. Thus, deductive database systems are a special (but important) case of knowledge-based systems.

The symbols of a language are combined in a standard way to produce terms and formulas. We refer the reader to standard books in logic (Enderton, 1972; Mendelson, 1978) and theorem-proving (Chang and Lee, 1973; Loveland, 1978) for details. As is usual in work on theorem proving, we deal primarily with clauses, where all variables are universally quantified and which have the general form

$$\neg A_1 \vee \ldots \vee \neg A_k \vee A_{k+1} \vee \ldots \vee A_n$$

where $k \leq n$ and each A_i is an atomic formula. We use a Prolog-like notation where in most cases such a clause is written as

$$A_{k+1}, \ldots, A_n \leftarrow A_1, \ldots, A_k$$

with the atoms $A_1, \ldots, A_k$ in the *body* and $A_{k+1}, \ldots, A_n$ in the *head* of the clause. A *ground* clause contains no variables. A *Horn* clause has at most one atom in the head, that is, $k \leq n \leq k + 1$. A *definite* clause has one atom in the head, that is, $n = k + 1$. A clause is *range-restricted* if every variable that appears in the head also appears in the body. Range-restricted clauses are very useful because their truth or falsity does not depend on the set of constants in the language, only on the constants in the clause. A clause is *recursive* if a predicate appears in both the head and the body.

The presence of recursive definitions gives great power to knowledge-based systems over relational database systems. Consider a definition such as the one for Ancestor in terms of Parent:

Ancestor(x, y) ← Parent(x, y)
Ancestor(x, y) ← Parent(x, z), Ancestor(z, y)

The second clause is recursive, and the simple query

← Ancestor(joe, x)

finds the ancestors of *joe*. However, Ancestor cannot be defined by using the standard relational algebraic operations on Parent.

We mentioned earlier that clauses are usually written in such a way that both the body and the head of a clause contain only positive atoms. However, there are cases where it is useful to define rules using one or more negated atoms in the body. For example,

Backordered(x) ← Ordered(x), ¬Instock(x)

defines the predicate Backordered in terms of a negated atom in the head of the clause.

While both recursion and negation in the clause body are important and powerful concepts for knowledge bases, substantial problems may arise when they are combined. Consequently, usually a limitation is placed on the combination of recursion and negation by not allowing recursive definitions via negation. For example,

$P(x) \leftarrow \neg Q(x)$
$Q(x) \leftarrow P(x)$

would not be allowed. The idea is that in defining a predicate, negation should be applied only to already known predicates. That was the case for the definition of Backordered, as the Instock predicate was assumed to deal only with facts. But in this case, Q does not have a prior definition as far as P is concerned; in fact, Q is defined in terms of P. A knowledge-based (or deductive database) system that applies this restriction is said to be *stratified* [see Apt et al. (1988), Van Gelder (1988), and Przymusinski (1988) for the complete definition and many results about stratification].

Now we come to the definition of the knowledge base component of a knowledge-based system. Not all of the restrictions that we give are essential for our results, but these restrictions simplify the presentation and proofs of results, and, in any case, most knowledge bases in practice either satisfy the assumptions or can be transformed into such a form. A *knowledge base* $K = \langle TH, IC \rangle$ consists of two components: a theory TH and a set of integrity constraints IC. In this chapter we consider TH to consist of two distinct sets of clauses and a metarule:

$$TH = \langle EDB, IDB, NFF \rangle$$

EDB, the extensional database, is a set of ground atoms; these represent the facts of the knowledge base. The predicates that appear in EDB are called extensional predicates. IDB, the intensional database, is a set of deductive laws (axioms) that are range-restricted Horn clauses that satisfy the property of stratification. We also assume that no predicate is both intensional and extensional. NFF, negation as finite failure, is a metarule used for proving negated clauses as follows: If P is a ground atom, then $TH \vdash \neg P$ if not$[TH \vdash P]$, that is, if all attempts to prove P terminate in failure. In order to handle equality correctly, we assume that TH also contains $x = x \leftarrow$. Finally, in this chapter we restrict IC to be a set of nonrecursive range-restricted clauses containing only extensional predicates.

A *query* is a conjunction of atoms, $Q: A1 \& \ldots \& Ak$. We write Q as $Q(x1,\ldots,xn)$ if $x1,\ldots,xn$ are all the variables in Q. An *answer* to $Q(x1,\ldots,xn)$ is a sequence of constants, $\langle a1,\ldots,an \rangle$, such that $TH \vdash Q(a1,\ldots,an)$, where $Q(a1,\ldots,an)$ stands for the simultaneous substitution of ai for xi in Q. This definition carries over to the case where $n = 0$; such a query is a yes-no question.

We illustrate the notion of a knowledge-based system by providing an example. This example has only a few predicates, no functions, no recursion, and no negated atoms in the body, but it illustrates important concepts and techniques that can be applied in a similar way to large and more complex knowledge bases. First we write the extensional and intensional predicates and provide the attributes for each. The attributes are not used specifically later, but they are helpful in understanding the meaning of the predicates. We do not actually write the facts in the EDB because typically the number of facts is large. We also write each integrity constraint both as a clause and in English.

Example.

Extensional predicates:

Schedule(Teacher Name, Department Name, Course Number)
Registration(Student Name, Department Name, Course Number)
Catalog(Department Name, Course Number, Credits)
Instructor(Teacher Name)

Intensional predicate:

    Teacherof(Teacher Name, Student Name)

Extensional database:

    Schedule, Registration, Catalog, Instructor

Intensional database:

    Teacherof$(x, y) \leftarrow$ Schedule(x, u, v),Registration(y, u, v)

Intensional constraints:

IC1. Baker teaches only history courses.

    $y = $ hist $\leftarrow$ Schedule(baker, y, z)

IC2. Course numbers in the computer science department are less than 600.

    $y < 600 \leftarrow$ Catalog(cosc, y, z)

IC3. No one is a teacher and a student for the same course.

    $\leftarrow$ Schedule(x, y, z), Registration(x, y, z)

IC4. Davis is registered only for economics courses.

    $y = $ econ $\leftarrow$ Registration(davis, y, z)

IC5. Every teacher's name in the Schedule relation appears in the Instructor relation.

    Instructor$(x) \leftarrow$ Schedule(x, y, z)

3 PARTIAL SUBSUMPTION AND RESIDUES

In order to apply integrity constraints in knowledge-based systems, we use a technique called *partial subsumption*. This method is applied to predicates before data manipulation. Partial subsumption yields fragments of integrity constraints, called *residues,* which are then attached to the predicates and are used later during query processing and updates. The process of partial subsumption, residue generation, and residue attachment to predicates is called *semantic compilation.* This process can be performed at an initial stage and need not be modified after standard data manipulation. Only changes to the IDB or the IC would force a semantic recompilation. In this section we define and illustrate semantic compilation. A formal treatment, including proofs of theorems asserting the correctness of the process, may be found in Chakravarthy et al. (1988).

    Partial subsumption is a modification of subsumption, so we start with the latter. Subsumption is a relationship between two clauses.

Definition. A clause *C* *subsumes* a clause *D* if there is a substitution σ such that *C*σ is a subclause of *D*. For example, if

$$C = R(x, b) \leftarrow P(x, y), Q(y, z, b)$$

and

$$D = R(a, b) \leftarrow P(a, z), Q(z, z, b), S(a)$$

then *C* subsumes *D* by the substitution {*a*/*x*, *z*/*y*}.

To understand partial subsumption, we need to look at the basic subsumption algorithm in Chang and Lee (1973), testing to see if *C* subsumes *D*. We explain this algorithm by illustrating its effect on the clauses *C* and *D*. First, *D* is instantiated to a ground clause by using new constants, not present in *C* or *D*. We will use $k1, \ldots, kn$ for these constants and call the substitution θ. Here, θ = {*k*1/*z*}, so that

$$D\theta = R(a, b) \leftarrow P(a, k1), Q(k1, k1, b), S(a)$$

Then *D*θ is negated; ¬ *D*θ is a set of literals. In this case,

$$\neg D\theta = \{ \leftarrow R(a, b), P(a, k1) \leftarrow , Q(k1, k1, b) \leftarrow , S(a) \leftarrow \}$$

Next, the algorithm tries to construct a linear refutation tree with *C* as the root, using at each step an element of ¬ *D*θ in the resolution. The result is that *C* subsumes *D* if and only if at least one such refutation tree ends with the null clause. Here we obtain the tree shown in Fig. 1-1.

The essence of partial subsumption is the application of the subsumption algorithm to an integrity constraint and the body of an IDB clause (which defines the intensional predicate). As we need to do this process for extensional relations also, we write the trivial axiom $R \leftarrow R$ for each extensional relation, strictly for the purpose of applying the subsumption algorithm in this manner. In general, the subsumption algorithm does not yield the null clause, because the integrity constraint does not subsume the body of the axiom. However, a subclause of the integrity constraint might subsume the body of the axiom. This is

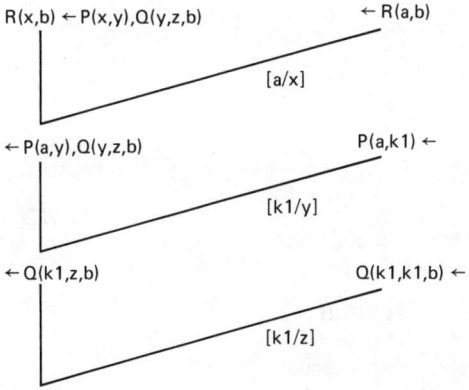

FIGURE 1-1
Linear refutation tree for subsumption.

the case where we say that the integrity constraint partially subsumes the body of the axiom. Instead of the null clause, a fragment of the integrity constraint remains at the bottom of a refutation tree. Such a fragment is called a *residue*.

Consider the following:

$$C' = R(x, b) \leftarrow P(x, y), Q(y, z, b), S(b)$$
$$D = R(a, b) \leftarrow P(a, z), Q(z, z, b), S(a)$$

As D is the same, we get

$$\neg D\theta = \{ \leftarrow R(a, b), P(a, k1) \leftarrow , Q(k1, k1, b) \leftarrow , S(a) \leftarrow \}$$

Applying the subsumption algorithm we obtain Fig. 1-2. The residue is $\leftarrow S(b)$.

It turns out that applying the subsumption algorithm to an integrity constraint and the body of an axiom may not lead to a useful residue even though there is an interaction between the two clauses. In our example from the previous section, consider IC1 and the axiom for Schedule, that is,

$$C: y = \text{hist} \leftarrow \text{Schedule}(\text{baker}, y, z)$$
$$D: \leftarrow \text{Schedule}(x, y, z)$$

Then,

$$\theta = \{k1/x, k2/y, k3/z\} \quad \text{and} \quad \neg D\theta = \{\text{Schedule}(k1, k2, k3) \leftarrow \}$$

Clearly, C and $\neg D\theta$ cannot be resolved, and no useful residue is obtained. The problem is caused by the constant *baker* in C. We get around this problem by placing C into a form called the *expanded form*, $C+$, so that resolution becomes possible. Expansion involves the substitution of variables for constants and repeated variables in the body of C as well as the addition of appropriate equalities. In this case,

$$C+ : y = \text{hist} \leftarrow \text{Schedule}(x1, y, z), x1 = \text{baker}$$

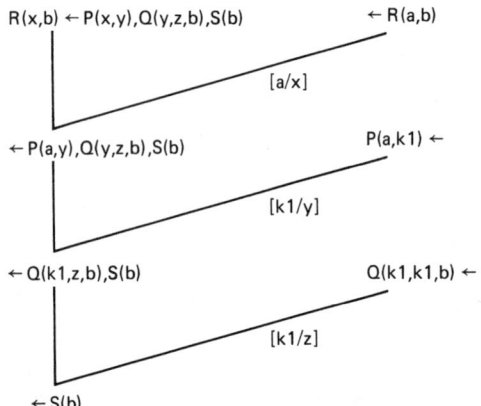

FIGURE 1-2
Linear refutation tree for partial subsumption.

Now, resolution is possible between $C+$ and $\neg D\theta$, as shown in Fig. 1-3. Recalling that $k1$ stands for x, we do a back substitution and obtain

$$y = \text{hist} \leftarrow x = \text{baker}$$

as the residue.

Next, we provide the steps for expanding a clause C.

Steps for expansion The expanded clause $C+$ is obtained from the clause C by modifying the body of C as follows:

1. An evaluable relation (such as $<$, $>$) that contains a constant and a variable is modified to two relations with the original relation containing two variables. For example, $(u > c)$ is replaced by $(u > x1)$, $(x1 >= c)$.
2. An extensional relation that contains a constant or a variable that has occurred previously (that is, to its left in the clause) is modified by changing the constant or the variable to a new variable and adding an equality consisting of the constant or the variable and the new variable.

We use x followed by an integer for the new variables and assume that the integrity constraint does not already contain such variables.

Now we are ready for the definition of partial subsumption.

Definition. An integrity constraint IC *partially subsumes* an axiom D if IC does not subsume the body of D but a subclause of IC+ subsumes the body of D.

As was shown in the last resolution example, the clause at the bottom of the resolution tree may contain some of the constants ki introduced for θ. The notion of back substitution is used to translate these constants into the variables of the integrity constraint. We write θ^{-1} for the inverse substitution. In the case above, where $\theta = \{k1/x, k2/y, k3/z\}$, $\theta^{-1} = \{x/k1, y/k2, z/k3\}$.

One more concept, *reduction,* is needed before defining formally the notion of residue. This process is used to reverse the effect of expansion at the end. The reduced form of a clause C is written as $C-$. C and $C-$ are logically equivalent.

Steps for reduction The reduced clause $C-$ is obtained from the clause C as follows:

1. Delete the head if it is a false atom.
2. In the body of C,

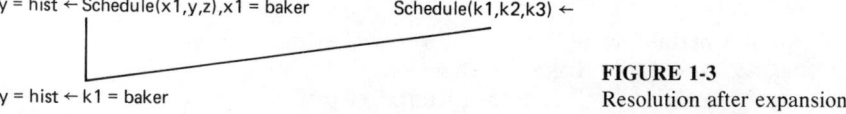

FIGURE 1-3
Resolution after expansion.

a. Delete every duplicate occurrence of an atom.
b. Delete every true atom.
c. Perform the reverse of step 1 in the steps for expansion.
d. Perform the reverse of step 2 in the steps for expansion.

Definition. Given an integrity constraint IC and axiom D, apply the subsumption algorithm to IC+ and the body of D until no more resolutions are possible. Let B be the clause at the bottom of a refutation tree. Then $(B-)\,\theta^{-1}$ is a *residue* of IC and D.

Note that there may be several different residues for an integrity constraint and an axiom. There are two types of residues that indicate no useful interaction between the integrity constraint and the axiom. If the residue is IC− (that is, no resolution steps were applied), we call it a *maximal residue*. A residue that evaluates to true, such as $a = a \leftarrow$, is called a *redundant residue*. [In the case of a redundant residue, we go up a level in the refutation tree and take B to be the clause above the previous clause named B and add $(B-)\theta^{-1}$ to the set of residues.]

Definition. An integrity constraint is *merge-compatible* with an axiom if at least one of the residues is nonmaximal and nonredundant.

The process of semantic compilation involves applying the partial subsumption algorithm for each axiom with each integrity constraint. The residues for the integrity constraints that are merge-compatible with each axiom are attached in braces to the axiom. This process is now illustrated for the example given in the previous section.

The Semantically Compiled Axioms

SCA1. Schedule(x, y, z) ← Schedule(x, y, z)
$\{y = \text{hist} \leftarrow x = \text{baker}; \leftarrow \text{Registration}(x, y, z); \text{Instructor}(x) \leftarrow \}$
(Note that only the integrity constraints IC1, IC3, and IC5 are merge-compatible with this trivial axiom. The residues may be understood in the following manner. Let $\langle x, y, z \rangle$ be a tuple in the Schedule relation. If $x = \text{baker}$, then $y = \text{hist}$. It is not possible for $\langle x, y, z \rangle$ to be a tuple in Registration. The Instructor relation contains the value x.)

SCA2. Registration(x, y, z) ← Registration(x, y, z)
$\{\leftarrow \text{Schedule}(x, y, z); y = \text{econ} \leftarrow x = \text{davis}\}$

SCA3. Catalog(x, y, z) ← Catalog(x, y, z)
$\{y < 600 \leftarrow x = \text{cosc}\}$

SCA4. Instructor(x) ← Instructor(x) $\{\ \}$
(None of the integrity constraints is merge-compatible with this axiom.)

SCA5. Teacherof(x, y) ← Schedule(x, u, v), Registration(y, u, v)
$\{u = \text{hist} \leftarrow x = \text{baker}; \leftarrow x = y;$
$u = \text{econ} \leftarrow y = \text{davis}; \text{Instructor}(x) \leftarrow \}$
(Note that according to the second residue, x may not be equal to y.)

4 UPDATE VALIDATION

Integrity constraints are statements that must remain true even after updates are made to the facts of the knowledge base. Therefore, a knowledge-based system must contain a component to verify that the integrity constraints are true. Queries cannot affect the truths of the integrity constraints, but updates must be validated. An update that would cause an integrity constraint to be false is erroneous and should not be executed. In this section we deal with update validation and show how residues are useful in this important process.

For relational databases and integrity constraints expressed in first-order logic, Nicolas proposed a method for integrity constraint checking (Nicolas, 1982). His method takes advantage of the fact that before an update the database is in a valid state satisfying all the integrity constraints. He derives simplified forms of integrity constraints, so that it suffices to check these simplified versions instead of the original constraints. The method of partial subsumption essentially reduces to Nicolas's method, but it has the advantage that residues can also be used for query optimization and cooperative answer generation, as we will show in the next two sections.

Several authors have extended the method of Nicolas to deductive databases. A simplification method for stratified deductive databases that allow general first-order logic formulas in the body of a clause is presented in Lloyd et al. (1986). Sadri and Kowalski (1988) use a special theorem-proving procedure to check for the validity of integrity constraints; simplifications can be simulated by applying certain theorem-proving strategies. Another recent paper (Bry et al., 1988) refines other techniques for integrity constraint checking and also deals with the checking of deductive database validity as constraints are updated.

The general idea of the method described here is the following. Assume that we are given the semantically compiled axioms for a knowledge base. Suppose that the update is an insertion into a table, such as

```
INSERT (a1,..., an)INTO T
```

Here T is the name of a table with n columns, whose defining axiom is

$$T(x1,\ldots, xn) \leftarrow T(x1,\ldots, xn)$$

Then the semantically compiled axiom is

$$T(x1,\ldots, xn) \leftarrow T(x1,\ldots, xn) \quad \{R1,\ldots, Rk\}$$

where the Ri are residues that may have xi as free variables. Let $\theta = \{a1/x1,\ldots, an/xn\}$. We claim that instead of checking $IC1,\ldots, ICm$ in the new database, it suffices to check $R1\theta,\ldots, Rk\theta$. That is, $R1\theta,\ldots, Rk\theta$ are all true in the updated database if and only if the original integrity constraints are all satisfied. We do not prove our claim here, but it is based on Nicolas's proof; in fact, the residues are logically equivalent to the simplified integrity constraints of Nicolas for insertion. Deletion is handled by semantically compiling negated relations, a technique discussed by Chakravarthy et al. (1989) and not treated in detail in this paper. We also consider transactions.

Now we show how to apply the method of residues for our knowledge base example. Our starting point is the set of semantically compiled axioms given at the end of the previous section. We deal with insertion first.

Consider inserting a tuple, say $\langle a, b, c \rangle$ into Schedule. The residues after the substitution $\{a/x, b/y, c/z\}$ are

$$b = \text{hist} \leftarrow a = \text{baker}; \leftarrow \text{Registration}(a, b, c); \text{Instructor}(a) \leftarrow$$

Thus the following checks must be done: (1) If the first element of the inserted tuple is *baker*, the second must be *hist*; (2) the Registration relation may not have the tuple $\langle a, b, c \rangle$ in it; and (3) the Instructor relation must contain the first element of the tuple. In a similar way, suppose that $\langle a, b, c \rangle$ is to be inserted into Registration. The residues are

$$\leftarrow \text{Schedule}(a, b, c) \quad \text{and} \quad b = \text{econ} \leftarrow a = \text{davis}$$

Thus two checks must be made: (1) The Schedule relation may not have the (same) tuple $\langle a, b, c \rangle$ and (2) if the first element of the inserted tuple is *davis*, the second must be *econ*. For Catalog, if the first element of the inserted tuple is *cosc*, then the second's value must be less than 600. Finally, an insertion into Instructor cannot violate any integrity constraints.

As mentioned above, residues for relations can be used to check the validity of insertions. For deletion, we can semantically compile negated relations by adding the new "axiom"

$$\text{not}(R) \leftarrow \text{not}(R)$$

for each relation R. This results in a difference in the partial subsumption algorithm by moving R to the right of the arrow from the left. In our example, a residue is obtained this way only for not(Instructor). The residue is

$$\leftarrow \text{Schedule}(x, y, z)$$

This is interpreted as follows: If an element a is deleted from Instructor, then there should not be any tuples in the Schedule relation whose first element is a. This method is also equivalent to Nicolas's technique.

A transaction is a sequence of updates that may contain both insertions and deletions. For the purpose of update validity, a transaction is treated as a single update. In other words, it is all right if during the transaction an integrity constraint becomes false, as long as at the end of the transaction all the integrity constraints are true. Nicolas (1982) showed how his method of integrity constraint simplification can be extended to transactions. The same principle works for us in terms of residues.

It is useful to make the following reasonable assumptions. Whenever a DELETE command is given, that tuple is in that relation in the knowledge base. Similarly, whenever an INSERT command is given, that tuple is not in that relation in the knowledge base. Finally, a transaction does not contain both an INSERT and a DELETE command for the same tuple in the same relation.

We illustrate the handling of transactions by giving several examples.

Transaction 1

```
INSERT (baker) INTO Instructor;
INSERT (cosc, 345, 4) INTO Catalog;
DELETE (smith, math, 610) FROM Registration;
```

In this case all the individual updates and the whole transaction preserve the truths of the integrity constraints. Consequently, this transaction is a valid update.

Transaction 2

```
INSERT (davis, econ, 430) INTO Schedule;
INSERT (davis, econ, 430) INTO Registration;
```

In this case each insertion, by itself, preserves the truths of the integrity constraints, but the combination does not. Recall now that for the first insertion (the one into Schedule)

$$\leftarrow \text{Registration(davis, econ, 430)}$$

is a residue. When we dealt with a single insertion, it was sufficient to search the Registration relation for the tuple (davis, econ, 430). But for a transaction, it is necessary to search the new Registration relation obtained by performing the second insertion (the one into Registration) in this case, and all insertions in the general case. Thus, this transaction is not a valid update.

Transaction 3

```
INSERT (johnson, cosc, 450) INTO Schedule;
INSERT (johnson) INTO Instructor;
```

For this transaction, the first INSERT does not preserve the truth of IC5. Hence, by itself, it is not a valid update. Note that the residue is

$$\text{Instructor(johnson)} \leftarrow$$

and *johnson* is not in the original Instructor relation. But because this is a transaction, it is necessary to search the new Instructor relation obtained by performing the second insertion also. Therefore, this transaction is a valid update.

Transaction 4

```
INSERT (tyson, hist, 330) INTO Schedule;
DELETE (tyson) FROM Instructor;
```

This is the counterpart to Transaction 3 where *tyson* is in the original Instructor relation. The residue is

$$\text{Instructor(tyson)} \leftarrow$$

which is false because the new Instructor relation (after the deletion) does not contain *tyson*. Therefore, this transaction is not a valid update.

Transaction 5

```
INSERT (baker, cosc, 400) INTO Schedule;
DELETE (baker, hist, 300) FROM Schedule;
```

This transaction represents a modification in a relation. The INSERT falsifies an integrity constraint. Hence, this transaction is not a valid update.

In conclusion, our method checks the truths of the residues on the new relations that result from performing all the insertions and deletions in the transaction. The transaction represents a valid update if and only if the residues are true for each individual update. There is another method to test the update validity of a transaction, one that does not require the list of all changes initially. Check one update at a time, each time on the new knowledge base, as if the transaction consisted of separate updates. If no integrity constraints are violated, the transaction is valid. Any integrity constraint violated at some time during the transaction must be retested on the entire knowledge base at the end to see if the violation has been erased by a later update.

5 SEMANTIC QUERY OPTIMIZATION

When relational database systems, the precursors of knowledge-based systems, were developed in the mid-1970s, performance was a major problem. The nonprocedurality of queries introduced the need for a translation phase into a procedural representation; this led to inefficient query processing. The problem was solved by the introduction of query optimizers, which can translate the original query into an efficient program. Traditional (standard) query optimization uses the properties of various relational operators and the physical representation of data such as sizes of tables and indexings. Knowledge-based systems require more sophisticated optimization techniques. In this section we show how integrity constraints can be applied in query optimization; as this method involves semantic knowledge about the knowledge base, it is called *semantic query optimization*.

Semantic query optimization has been studied for over a decade by several researchers. In McSkimin and Minker (1977) a semantic network model and typing of attributes is used in a deductive search process. In particular, a semantic well-formedness condition is applied to queries and data inputs to check for no solutions. The knowledge-based query process (KBQP) was presented by Hammer and Zdonik (1980). KBQP uses a knowledge base about the application domain and the database to replace subexpressions of a query by semantically equivalent expressions for more efficient query evaluation. The language is based on the lambda calculus. The QUIST (Query Improvement through Semantic Transformation) system is presented in King (1981). The query language is a subclass of Select-Join-Project queries for relational databases. The notions of semantic equivalence of queries and of merging an integrity constraint into a query are defined formally here.

The notion of partial subsumption for deductive databases using integrity constraints was introduced by Chakravarthy (1985). This forms the basis for the method of semantic query optimization presented in this section. Chakravarthy et al. (1990) contains additional historical remarks as well as many examples of semantic query optimization. A detailed account of the theory of semantic query optimization may be found in Chakravarthy et al. (1988).

Semantic query optimization assumes that the axioms have been semantically compiled, as we demonstrated in Section 3. A given query is then transformed, using the residues, into a semantically equivalent query. The semantic equivalence of queries is defined using integrity constraints: two queries are *semantically equivalent* if their answers are the same for all knowledge bases with the same intensional database and the same integrity constraints. Although updates may change the facts, since the knowledge base must satisfy the intensional axioms and integrity constraints, we may choose a query Q' over a query Q if Q' is easier to solve as long as Q and Q' are semantically equivalent.

Five types of transformations that may provide more efficient semantically equivalent queries have been identified.

1. Literal elimination refers to the elimination of a literal (an atom) from a query. This way the computation of a join of two relations is eliminated.
2. Restriction introduction refers to the addition to the query of a restriction that may make it possible to perform only a range search rather than the search of a relation.
3. Literal introduction involves the addition of an atom to a query. This is helpful in case the query evaluation involves the join of two large relations; the introduction of another join with a small instantiated relation can make query processing more efficient.
4. If there is a unique answer, a transformation may actually answer the query.
5. A transformation may detect an unsatisfiable condition, so that the existence of any answer would violate an integrity constraint. In such a case there are no answers.

Next we consider some queries on the example database whose semantically compiled axioms were given at the end of Section 3. For each query we also give the semantically constrained query obtained by adding the residue for each relation with the appropriate instantiation. Semantically equivalent queries are obtained using the semantically constrained query. We explained in Section 2 that a query is a conjunction of atoms, such as

Q: $A1$ &...& An

indicating that the atoms $A1, \ldots, An$ must be solved. When a query Q is to be solved in a knowledge-based system, the query is written in the form

$$\leftarrow A1, \ldots, An$$

We distinguish output variables by starring them.

Q1. Print the teacher name and course number taught for all courses in the Cosc department by teachers whose name appears in the Instructor table.

$$\leftarrow \text{Schedule}(x^*, \text{cosc}, z^*), \text{Instructor}(x^*)$$

The corresponding semantically constrained query is obtained by including the residue for each relation (none for Instructor in this case), using the appropriate instantiation in Schedule.

SCQ1: $\leftarrow$ Schedule(x^*, cosc, z^*)
{ $\leftarrow x^* =$ baker; $\leftarrow$ Registration(x^*, cosc, z^*);
Instructor(x^*) $\leftarrow$ }, Instructor(x^*)

The first residue for SCQ1 is obtained from the first residue in SCA1,

$$y = \text{hist} \leftarrow x = \text{baker}$$

by substituting cosc for y. The false head of the clause is then omitted. Essentially, this residue states that the x value cannot be *baker*; this is not a useful residue. The second residue for SCQ1, obtained from the second residue in SCA1, is also not useful. However, the third residue for SCQ1 is useful; it states that x^* must appear in the Instructor relation. But then it is not necessary to take the join of Schedule with Instructor, so the Instructor predicate may be eliminated. Hence the query

$$\leftarrow \text{Schedule}(x^*, \text{cosc}, z^*)$$

is semantically equivalent to Q1 and should be more efficient to evaluate. This query illustrates literal elimination.

Q2. Print the names of all the teachers of Davis.

$$\leftarrow \text{Teacherof}(x^*, \text{davis})$$

This query involves the intensional predicate Teacherof. Using SCA5 we obtain the corresponding semantically constrained query

SCQ2: $\leftarrow$ Schedule(x^*, u, v), Registration(davis, u, v)
{$u =$ hist $\leftarrow x^* =$ baker; $\leftarrow x^* =$ davis; $u =$ econ $\leftarrow$;
Instructor(x^*) $\leftarrow$ }

The first residue states that if x^* is *baker* then u is *hist*; this is not a useful residue. The second residue, stating that x^* is not *davis*, also does not appear useful. The fourth residue, which states that x^* is in the Instructor relation, also is not useful. The third residue is useful because it restricts the second value in both Schedule and Registration to *econ*. The semantically equivalent query is

← Schedule(x^*, econ, v), Registration(davis, econ, v)

This is an illustration of restriction introduction; the restriction is an equality in this case. An indexing on the second attribute of Schedule or Registration or a join support for these relations would speed up the processing of this query.

Q3. Print the course numbers for all computer science courses in the catalog.

← Catalog(cosc, y^*, z)

Using SCA3 we obtain

SCQ3:   ← Catalog(cosc, y^*, z)   {y^* < 600 ← }

as the head is deleted from the residue because it is true. The semantically equivalent query is

← Catalog(cosc, y^*, z), y^* < 600

This version is helpful if the Catalog table is sorted on course number, the second attribute, because it limits the search to y values less than 600. This illustrates restriction introduction also; here the restriction is an inequality.

Q4. Print all departments in which Baker teaches.

← Schedule(baker, y^*, z)

Using SCA1 we obtain

SCQ4:   ← Schedule(baker, y^*, z)
{y^* = hist ← ; ← Registration(baker, y^*, z);
Instructor(baker) ← }

The first residue states that y^* must be *hist*. Therefore, there is a unique answer, if there is one. The semantically equivalent query is

← Schedule(baker, y^*, z), y^* = hist

In this case we must still check to make sure that *baker* appears in the Schedule relation. This illustrates the case where the residue provides the answer to the query.

Q5. Print the names of all persons who are both a teacher and a student for a course.

← Schedule(x^*, y, z), Registration(x^*, y, z)

Using SCA1 and SCA2 we obtain

SCQ5:   ← Schedule(x^*, y, z)
{y = hist ← x^* = baker; ← Registration(x^*, y, z);
Instructor(x^*) ← }, Registration(x^*, y, z)
{ ← Schedule(x^*, y, z); y = econ ← x^* = davis}

Now note that the second residue for Schedule states that Registration (x^*, y, z) is not allowed, but Registration(x^*, y, z) is a conjunct in the query. This is an unsatisfiable condition, and hence there cannot be any answers. Note how the naive evaluation of this query might involve a large join. The semantically equivalent query in this case is the empty clause, $\leftarrow$.

We have demonstrated the usefulness of semantic query optimization on several queries for our knowledge base example. We end this section by giving a classification of residues and the types of transformations they provide. We classify residues into four classes: (1) the null clause, (2) a goal clause (clause with empty head), (3) a unit clause (Horn clause with empty body and nonempty head), and (4) a Horn clause with nonempty body and nonempty head.

When a null residue is obtained at any stage of semantic query optimization, the axiom/query has no answers. This is so because the axiom/query and the integrity constraints logically imply a contradiction for any possible answer. If a null residue is obtained during the semantic compilation phase, then the intensional relation, for which a null clause is generated, is empty. If it happens for an extensional relation, then the extensional relation is not consistent. Assuming that the database is consistent with respect to integrity constraints, the null clause for a query is derived on the basis of the instantiations in the query, signifying that there are no answers.

If the residue is a goal clause, there are two possibilities. If the residue subsumes the query, then, just as in the case of the null residue, the query cannot be satisfied for any constant, and hence there are no answers. This is what happened in Q5. When the residue does not subsume the query, it may be useful if it contains evaluable relations only. For instance, the residue $\leftarrow (y < 200)$ states that y cannot be less than 200. This information may be helpful if the relation on which y is an attribute is ordered on that attribute or has an index on it. An alternative way of handling this residue is to change the goal clause $\leftarrow (y < 200)$ to the unit clause $(y >= 200) \leftarrow$, thereby introducing a restriction.

When the residue is a unit clause, this clause may be asserted into the query, as it must be true in the database. If the clause is an evaluable relation, such as $(x > 150) \leftarrow$, a restriction is introduced, as for Q3. Even better is the case when the evaluable relation is an equality, as in Q4, where a unique answer is obtained. If the clause is not an evaluable relation, the possibilities are literal introduction (useful if it helps to avoid the computation of a large join) and literal elimination (as for Q1). The latter is possible if the residue subsumes a literal in the query, considered as a unit clause, and no output variables are lost in the process.

The last case is where the residue is a Horn clause with both a nonempty body and a nonempty head. When the body of the residue subsumes the query, say with substitution θ, then if C is the head of the residue, $C\theta$ may be treated as a unit clause. Another possibility occurs when the residue is used to limit the search in evaluating the query. A typical case involves a functional dependency constraint. Consider the following semantically compiled axiom for R:

$$R(x, y, z) \leftarrow R(x, y, z) \quad \{y = y' \leftarrow R(x, y,' z)\}$$

where the residue is obtained using the functional dependency $R: X \rightarrow Y$. If the query is

$$\leftarrow R(a, y^*, z)$$

the residue

$$\{y^* = y' \leftarrow R(a, y', z)\}$$

is interpreted as saying that a second y' value must be the same as any y^* value already obtained. Therefore, the search can be limited to a single value.

6 COOPERATIVE AND INFORMATIVE ANSWERS

In the previous section we showed how the processing of queries can be optimized by using the method of partial subsumption and residues. The answer to a query was taken as a list of tuples. But we would like a knowledge-based system to do more than just provide a list in every case; we would like such a system to provide an intelligent answer; one that is informative and cooperative for the questioner. This is particularly important when the system employs a natural language interface with the user. In this section we show how residues can be used for this purpose.

For motivation, consider the following English query for the knowledge base example of Section 2:

"List the number of credits for Cosc 630."

In logic, this query would be written

$\leftarrow$ Catalog(cosc, 630, x^*).

A knowledge-based system without cooperative answer facilities would return the empty list; a natural language version might return the answer

"Cosc 630 is not in the catalog."

This answer is unsatisfactory in the sense that it does not explain to the user the reason for the result. In particular, given such an answer, a user might assume that no catalog information has yet been entered for Cosc 630. Now consider the second answer,

"Cosc 630 is not in the catalog because there may not be a Cosc course with number 630."

This answer is certainly more informative than the previous one, but it is still not quite satisfactory. A user might believe that there could be a course Cosc 620, for instance. But consider the third answer,

> "Cosc 630 is not in the catalog because course numbers in Cosc are less than 600."

Note how the reason for this informative answer is obtained from an integrity constraint, IC2. This shows how an integrity constraint can be helpful in providing the reason for an answer.

The notion of cooperative and informative answers has been considered by several authors. In Kaplan (1979) the CO-OP system is described. This system detects false presuppositions. For example, Kaplan's query

> "How many students failed Cosc 400 last semester?"

would have "None" as the literal answer if Cosc 400 was not offered last semester. The problem is the questioner's presupposition that Cosc 400 was offered last semester. This is similar to the presupposition in our motivating example that there is a course Cosc 630. Kaplan's system provides an indirect cooperative answer when it detects a false presupposition.

The first paper connecting the detection of false presuppositions and the checking of integrity constraints in a database was that of Janas (1981). Janas divides queries into subqueries in such a way that an integrity constraint might make it impossible to have an answer in the database to a subquery and consequently to the query. He considers only integrity constraints that contain a single atom.

Webber (1986) gives a general review of much of the work studying information-seeking interactions between a user and a knowledge-based system, including the concept of cooperative answers. A recent paper (Cuppens and Demolombe, 1988) proposes to model the user's interests instead of the user's goals. For example, the query

> "List which flights from Paris to New York have departure times between 7 a.m. and 11 a.m."

may receive a response that relaxes the constraint about time (including a flight at 11:05 a.m.) or location (including departure from Brussels) and also gives the price of the ticket if it is very different from the average (such as for the Concorde).

We base our material on Gal and Minker (1988) and refer the reader to that paper for additional examples and details. In the rest of this section we analyze five cases that arise in the application of integrity constraints, via the method of residues, for obtaining cooperative and informative answers. These cases are as follows:

1. The residue is null or subsumes the query.
2. The residue instantiates a variable in the query.

3. The residue is true but does not affect the query.
4. The residue is present in the query.
5. The residue requires an extensional database search.

We continue to use the list of compiled axioms from Section 3. We also use some of the queries from the previous section.

First, suppose that the residue is null or subsumes the query. In both cases there cannot be any answers. Consider, for instance,

Q5. Print the names of all persons who are both a teacher and a student for a course.

As shown in the previous section, the residue for the atom Schedule(x^*, y, z) is

$\leftarrow$ Registration(x^*, y, z)

and that subsumes the query. Thus the informative answer is not "None" or "No such persons," but

"None, because no name may appear as both a teacher name and a student name for the same department name and course number."

Now consider

Q6. List all math course numbers taught by Baker.

The logic version is

$\leftarrow$ Schedule(baker, math, z^*)

The first residue is null because of the true hypothesis and false conclusion. The informative answer using IC1 is

"None, because Baker teaches only history courses."

The second case is where the residue instantiates a variable in the query. Our example for this case is

Q2. Print the names of all the teachers of Davis.

We showed in the previous section how the instantiation of the Department Name variable to *econ* introduces a restriction useful in query evaluation. This restriction is also relevant for an informative answer, which would list the teachers of Davis and state that Davis takes courses only in the economics department.

For the third case, the residue is true but does not affect the query. An example of this is the following:

Q7. Print all course numbers less than 500 for all computer science courses in the catalog.

The logic version is

$$\leftarrow \text{Catalog}(\text{cosc}, y^*, z), y^* < 500$$

Here the residue is $y^* < 600 \leftarrow$, which is already true for the query. It is not necessary in this case to add information about the residue; in fact, stating that Cosc course numbers must be less than 600 is not really relevant for this query. So the proper answer is simply the Cosc courses with number less than 500. A similar, but not identical, situation occurs for

Q3. Print the course numbers for all computer science courses in the catalog.

In the previous section we showed that the restriction introduced by the residue may be helpful in optimizing the query, but the extra information that all computer science courses have a number <600 is not one that would help the questioner. We want the answer to be informative but not verbose.

Q1 illustrates the fourth case, where the residue is present in the query.

Q1. Print the teacher name and course number taught for all courses in the Cosc department by teachers whose names appear in the Instructor table.

This query provides an example of literal elimination, as the Instructor literal is unnecessary for the query and can be eliminated. The user, in addition to being given the list of teacher names and course numbers, should be informed that all teacher names in the Schedule table must also appear in the Instructor table. Based on the wording of the question, the additional statement of the answer gives new and relevant information to the questioner.

The last case, where the residue is a formula requiring an extensional database search to be evaluated, can cover various situations. Consider

Q8. List all the courses taught by Smith.

The logic version is

$$\text{Schedule}(\text{smith}, y^*, z^*)$$

One of the residues is Instructor(smith) $\leftarrow$, and by literal introduction we may add this residue to the query. If the Instructor relation is much smaller than Schedule and our search does not find Smith in Instructor, then it is unnecessary to search Schedule. In this case, an informative answer is

"Smith teaches no courses; Smith is not an instructor."

Next, consider

Q4. Print all departments in which Baker teaches.

This yields another example where an extensional database search is necessary. But, by the residue, it is known that the only possible department is history. Hence, if history is the answer, then the informative answer would be

"Baker teaches only in the history department."

The interface developed by Gal and Minker (1988) works with a knowledge-based system as follows. A user enters a query in natural language. The interface transforms the query to a logic formula. A set of heuristics was developed to permit the system to select from the possibly many constraints relevant to the query the one or more to present to the user. Then the system responds to the query, giving the user a cooperative and informative answer, based on the concepts described here, in natural language. An additional interesting feature of this system is that the user may choose one of three levels of informativeness. The *prompt mode* is intended for the expert user; explanations are limited. The *explicative mode* provides a cooperative response but not information about how the query was processed. Finally, the *derivative mode* supplies, in addition to a cooperative response, all the deductive mechanisms applied to the query.

7 SUMMARY AND CONCLUSIONS

A knowledge-based system manipulates both facts and rules. Integrity constraints are statements that must be true for the knowledge base. We use first-order logic to describe the knowledge base as well as to write queries. We give in this chapter a method, partial subsumption, to attach fragments of integrity constraints, called residues, to the relations of the knowledge base. We apply these residues to three important problems: update validation, query optimization, and informative answer generation.

The original purpose of integrity constraints was to check for the consistency of the knowledge base. Later, various researchers discovered the application of integrity constraints to some other knowledge base problems. Their methods were special-purpose methods, intended for a particular application. The method of partial residues, on the other hand, provides a uniform technique to exploit the presence of integrity constraints in knowledge bases. An additional advantage of this method is that the residues need be obtained only once, before any knowledge base manipulation (query or update) takes place. We believe that in future knowledge-based systems, integrity constraints will occupy a more central role than they do today.

ACKNOWLEDGMENTS

We acknowledge the support given to us for this research by the National Science Foundation under grant numbers IRI-8714544 (both authors) and IRI-8609170 (J.M.), by the U.S. Army Research Office under grant number

DAAL-03-88-K0087 (J.M.), by the U.S. Air Force Office of Scientific Research under grant number AFOSR-88-0152 (J.M.), and by the Faculty Research Committee of Towson State University (J.G.). We also thank the editor, Dr. Hojjat Adeli, for his helpful comments on an earlier draft of this chapter.

REFERENCES

Apt, K. R., Blair, H. A., and Walker, A. (1988). Towards a Theory of Deductive Knowledge. In: *Foundations of Deductive Databases and Logic Programming* (J. Minker, Ed.). Morgan Kaufmann, Los Altos, Calif., pp. 89–148.

Bry, F., Decker, H., and Manthey, R. (1988). A Uniform Approach to Constraint Satisfaction and Constraint Satisfiability in Deductive Databases. In: *Advances in Database Technology—EDBT '88* (J. W. Schmidt, S. Ceri, and M. Missikoff, Eds.). Springer-Verlag Lecture Notes in Computer Science 303, Springer-Verlag, New York, pp. 488–505.

Chakravarthy, U. S. (1985). Semantic Query Optimization in Deductive Databases. Ph.D. Thesis, Department of Computer Science, University of Maryland.

Chakravarthy, U. S., Grant, J., and Minker, J. (1988). Foundations of Semantic Query Optimization for Deductive Databases. In: *Foundations of Deductive Databases and Logic Programming* (J. Minker, Ed.). Morgan Kaufmann, Los Altos, Calif., pp. 243–273.

Chakravarthy, U. S., Grant, J., and Minker, J. (1990). Logic Based Approach to Semantic Query Optimization. ACM *Transactions on Database Systems*. To appear.

Chang, C. L., and Lee, R. C. T. (1973). *Symbolic Logic and Mechanical Theorem Proving*. Academic Press, New York.

Cuppens, F., and Demolombe, R. (1988). Cooperative Answering: A Methodology to Provide Intelligent Access to Databases. In: *Expert Database Systems* (L. Kerschberg, Ed.). George Mason University, pp. 333–353.

Enderton, H. B. (1972). *A Mathematical Introduction to Logic*. Academic Press, New York.

Gal, A., and Minker, J. (1988). Informative and Cooperative Answers in Databases Using Integrity Constraints. In: *Natural Language Understanding and Logic* (P. Saint-Dizier and V. Dahl, Eds.). North-Holland, Amsterdam, pp. 277—300.

Gallaire, H., Minker, J., and Nicolas, J.-M. (1984). Logic and Databases: A Deductive Approach. *ACM Compu. Surv.* **16**:153–185.

Hammer, M. M., and Zdonik, S. B. (1980). Knowledge Based Query Processing. Proc. Sixth VLDB Conference, pp. 137–147.

Janas, J. M. (1981). On the Feasibility of Informative Answers. In: *Advances in Database Theory, Vol. 1* (H. Gallaire, J. Minker, and J.-M. Nicolas, Eds.). Plenum, New York, pp. 397–414.

Kaplan, J. (1979). Cooperative Responses from a Portable Natural Language Data Base Query System. Ph.D. Thesis, Dept. of Computer and Information Sciences, University of Pennsylvania.

King, J. J. (1981). Query Optimization by Semantic Reasoning. Ph.D. Thesis, Department of Computer Science, Stanford University.

Lloyd, J. W., Sonenberg, E. A., and Topor, R. W. (1986). Integrity Constraint Checking in Stratified Databases. TR 86/5, Department of Computer Science, University of Melbourne.

Loveland, D. (1978). *Automated Theorem Proving: A Logical Basis*. Elsevier/North-Holland, New York.

McSkimin, J. R., and Minker, J. (1977). The Use of a Semantic Network in a Deductive Query Answering System. Proc. 5th IJCAI, pp. 50–58.

Mendelson, E. (1978). *Introduction to Mathematical Logic*, 2nd ed. Van Nostrand-Reinhold, New York.

Nicolas, J. M. (1982). Logic for Improving Integrity Checking in Relational Data Bases. *Acta Informatica* **18**:227–253.

Przymusinski, T. C. (1988). On the Declarative Semantics of Deductive Databases and Logic Programs. In: *Foundations of Deductive Databases and Logic Programming* (J. Minker, Ed.). Morgan Kaufmann, Los Altos, Calif., pp. 193–216.

Sadri, F., and Kowalski, R. (1988). A Theorem-Proving Approach to Database Integrity. In: *Foundations of Deductive Databases and Logic Programming* (J. Minker, Ed.). Morgan Kaufmann, Los Altos, Calif., pp. 313–362.

Van Gelder, A. (1988). Negation as Failure Using Tight Derivations for General Logic Programs. In: *Foundations of Deductive Databases and Logic Programming* (J. Minker, Ed.). Morgan Kaufmann, Los Altos, Calif., pp. 149–176.

Webber, B. (1986). Questions, Answers and Responses: Interacting with Knowledge Base Systems. In: *On Knowledge Base Management Systems* (M. Brodie and J. Mylopoulos, Eds.). Springer-Verlag, New York, pp. 365–402.

CHAPTER 2

SYMBOLIC DECISION PROCEDURES FOR KNOWLEDGE-BASED SYSTEMS

JOHN FOX

In this tense, ever more crowded, ever more interdependent world, wise decision making is becoming more and more crucial. At present we are not very good at it.

Foreword, Hill et al. (1979)

The problem in the coming years is that of establishing meaning in a sea of neutral symbols.

David and Hersh (1986)

1 INTRODUCTION. DECISION MAKING AND AI

Decision making is a central, though surprisingly neglected, topic in artificial intelligence. Natural language systems need to be able to decide among alternative interpretations of utterances, such as ambiguities of syntax or meaning, or alternative intentions of other agents in a dialogue. Vision systems require analogous capabilities. Planning and design systems need to choose among alternative steps or components. Scientific theory formation requires choices among competing hypotheses and experiments. In general, all intelligent systems require a decision mechanism. In turn this must be supported by a systematic framework for representing decisions, for coping with uncertainty, for interacting with other agents who may be participating in the decision, for flexible control of the decision process, and so forth.

Nowhere is the need for a systematic decision framework more pressing than in knowledge-based systems. These have emerged as a distinct topic in

AI following the recognition that much of the knowledge required for intelligent behavior can be represented in an explicit symbolic form and that explicitness can lead to greater versatility. Expert systems (which can be viewed as a subclass of knowledge-based systems whose principal function is decision support) have been notable in attempting to exploit the benefits of explicit knowledge representations. Curiously, however, the decision procedures that use this knowledge have been left largely implicit in the control structure of most expert systems and/or in ad hoc procedural extensions.

A consequence of this is that a technology that specializes in decision making—and whose performance may be safety-critical in some applications—frequently uses decision procedures that have been developed pragmatically and may be difficult to isolate, understand, formalize, or test independently of their use in specific applications.

It has sometimes been said that knowledge-based systems *must* be developed pragmatically and empirically, since we lack general theories to underpin the design. So is this ad hoc character of the decision procedure inevitable given the knowledge-based approach?

The knowledge underlying nontrivial problem solving is highly heterogeneous. Systems that are designed to aid problem solving in knowledge-intensive domains must embody varied knowledge representations and multiple problem-solving methods. In the absence of well-understood design principles, knowledge engineers have responded with a eclectic approach, adapting a heterogeneous range of techniques from AI and symbolic computing to the details of their applications. Techniques have included semantic nets, propositional and predicate logics, and other representations for qualitative reasoning. Extensions to include numerical simulations and other algorithms as attached procedures, to exploit probability theory, fuzzy logic, and so on for the management of uncertainty, have been widely adopted. This was true of a late version of MYCIN, for example. Among the mechanisms used in that system were inference rules, the associated procedure for calculating certainty factors, frames for representing application parameters, attached LISP procedures for calculating drug dosages, and so forth. This pattern of combining many techniques remains commonplace.

There are many examples of expert systems of this heterogeneous kind that are reported to have been practically successful. Nevertheless there is reason to be seriously concerned about the empirical and pragmatic way in which this approach to knowledge engineering is justified, taught, and applied. Good engineering in any field demands a constant effort to achieve clarity, precision, reliability, and predictability in design. Heterogeneity tends to work against all of these goals. Although the last few years have seen significant developments in our formal understanding of many of the computational components of expert systems, there is still much controversy about how they can and should be combined, and precious little theory for guidance. In consequence, we have no accepted way of determining whether an expert system is sound or otherwise.

The aim here is a more systematic discussion of some of the knowledge engineering methods that have been used or proposed, focusing on the pivotal component, the decision process. In particular I shall discuss the concept of a *symbolic decision procedure,* an abstraction of general decision-making principles represented in a declarative but executable form. Decisions can be viewed as instances of a generic object, which specify the properties of particular kinds of decisions, when and how specific decisions should be dynamically constructed, and how the information required to make them can be collected and evaluated.

Before doing this, however, we must briefly review classical (numerical) decision procedures, which are well established and well understood, and the first-generation expert systems that have followed them.

2 CLASSICAL DECISION THEORY

A decision is a conscious choice between at least two possible courses of action.

Castles et al. (1971)

Decision: Settlement (of question etc), conclusion, formal judgement, making up one's mind.

Concise Oxford Dictionary

Formal procedures for decision making have been discussed for a very long time. Indeed the importance of being systematic in marshalling the pros and cons of a set of choices and applying a clear decision rule to select just one was discussed by Benjamin Franklin in a letter to the scientist Joseph Priestley in 1772 (see Fig. 2-1). Attempts to design and implement mechanical decision tools have had their most recent incarnation in expert systems, but these have been topics of active research for a long time—at least since World War II, when the need to optimize the use of resources in the light of uncertain present and future circumstances was paramount.

In modern times researchers have discussed many aspects of decision making. Sophisticated mathematical techniques for making rational decisions have been developed extensively in statistics and economics [see Lindley (1985) for an introduction]. Applications to assist human decision making have been discussed in medicine (de Dombal, 1972; Schwartz and Griffin, 1986), in business and politics (e.g., Hill et al., 1979), and in many other areas. Human decision behavior has been widely studied and modeled in psychology (e.g., Broadbent, 1972; Kahneman et al., 1982; Fischoff et al., 1983) where theoretical interpretations have often been based on the classical analysis (e.g., Hill et al., 1979; Hogarth, 1980).

> In the affair of so much importance to you, wherein you ask my advice, I cannot, for want of sufficient premises, advise you what to determine, but if you please, I can tell you how. When those difficult cases occur, they are difficult, chiefly because while we have them under consideration, all the reasons pro and con are not present to the mind at the same time; but sometimes one set present themselves, and at other times another, the first being out of sight. Hence the various purposes or inclinations that alternatively prevail, and the uncertainty that perplexes us. To get over this, my way is to divide half a sheet of paper by a line into two columns; writing over the one Pro, and the other Con. Then, during three or four days consideration, I put down under the different heads short hints of the different motives, that at different times occur to me, for and against the measure. When I have thus got them all together in one view, I endeavor to estimate their respective weights; and where I find two, one on each side that seem equal to some two reasons con, I strike out three. If I judge some two reasons con, equal to some three reasons pro, I strike out the five; and thus proceeding I find at length where the balance lies; and if, after a day or two of further consideration, nothing new that is of importance occurs on either side, I come to a determination accordingly. And, though the weight of reasons cannot be taken with the precision of algebraic quantities, yet when each is thus considered, separately and comparatively, and the whole lies before me, I think I can judge better, and am less liable to make a rash step, and in fact I have found a great advantage from this kind of equation, in what may be called moral and prudential algebra.

FIGURE 2-1
Excerpt from a letter written by Benjamin Franklin to Joseph Priestley in 1772. (*From MacCrimmon, 1973, p. 27, with permission.*)

Perhaps the most forthright statement of what should now be regarded as the classical theory of decision making is due to Lindley (1985).

> ...there is essentially only one way to reach a decision sensibly. First, the uncertainties present in the situation must be quantified in terms of values called probabilities. Second, the various consequences of the courses of action must be similarly described in terms of utilities. Third that decision must be taken which is expected—on the basis of the calculated probabilities—to give the greatest utility. The force of 'must,' used in three places there, is simply that any deviation from the precepts is liable to lead the decision maker into procedures which are demonstrably absurd.

This is probably the clearest account of what statistical theory is and of an influential position on what "rationality" demands. Two basic parameters, probability and utility, are identified. From these a range of measures for decision taking can be derived.

2.1 Probability

In some decision tasks, often called judgment tasks, all that is required is to assess the relative likelihood of a number of uncertain events as a basis for taking some action. An obvious example is medical diagnosis, where we may want to collect information about symptoms, signs, and test results and use these to compute the probabilities of a set of clinical conditions. This approach is illustrated in Fig. 2-2, which shows a plot of the a posteriori probabilities of two medical diagnoses. As more items of information are obtained, the probabilities provide an increasingly clear separation of the two alternatives.

The most widely known method for calculating posterior probabilities is Bayes' rule, shown here in one common form:

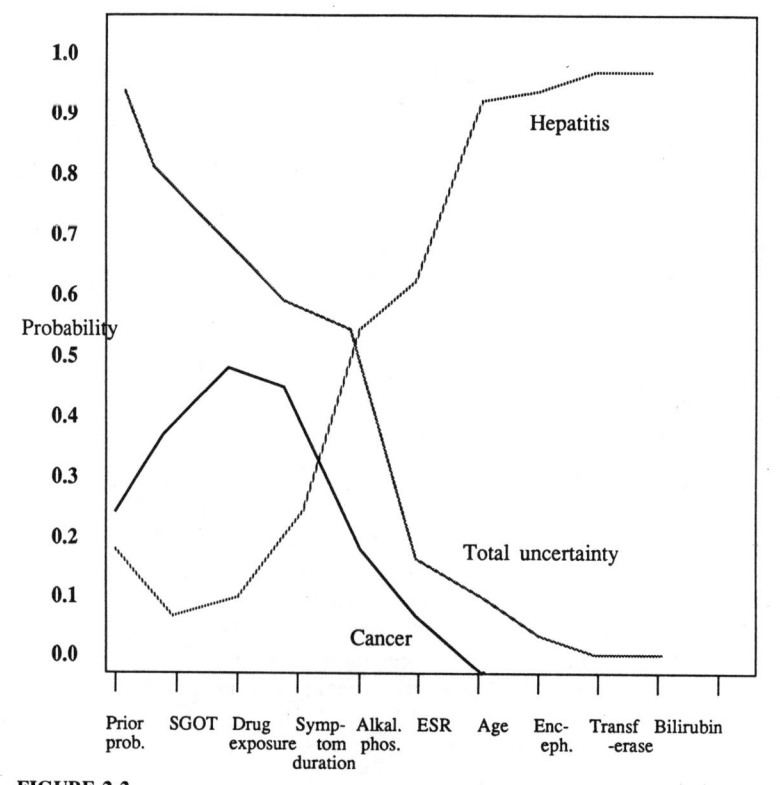

FIGURE 2-2
As information about symptoms, laboratory data, and so on are obtained, the probabilities of hepatitis and cancer are recomputed. In this case the probability of cancer quickly approaches 0.0 and hepatitis emerges as the most likely alternative. Since probabilities must sum to 1.0, the residual uncertainty (neither cancer nor hepatitis) is plotted separately.

$$p(H_i|e_j) = \frac{p(e_j|H_i) \cdot p(H_i)}{\sum_i p(e_j|H_i) \cdot p(H_i)}$$

Here H_i is a hypothesis and e_j an item of evidence. The posterior probability of each H_i is determined by weighting the prior probability of H_i with the conditional probability of e_j being present if H_i were true. Each revised value is normalized on the sum of the i weighted values.

A rational decision rule is to select the hypothesis for which the posterior probability is highest after all items of evidence have been acquired.

Probability theory is, of course, a well-developed field. Not only does it provide a clear and well-understood basis for decisions under uncertainty, it also offers opportunities for development of specialized extensions for different applications. One example [due to Lindley (1956)] provides a basis for choosing among procedures that yield information relevant to some decision. For example, we may wish to choose the most informative laboratory test to carry out in order to make a diagnostic decision. Lindley's method combines Bayes' rule with information theoretic ideas (Shannon and Weaver, 1959) and permits computation of the *expected information yield* of a test over all of the possible outcomes of the test weighted by their likelihood. In the case of tests that yield a yes/no or positive/negative answer, the expected information yield is computed by determining the entropy before and after all information outcomes, weighted by the likelihood of each hypothesis and each outcome x for the test. For the simple case of two outcomes, the expected information yield of the test is

$$\sum_i \{p(H_i|x) \log p(H_i|x)\} p(x) - \sum_i p(H_i) \log p(H_i)$$

where x takes the values "yes" and "no" and

$$p(x) = \sum_i p(x|H_i) p(H_i)$$

2.2 Utility

The second fundamental concept developed in classical theory is "utility," a quantitative expression of the values of different events. Utilities can be used to represent costs and benefits of alternative actions in objective or subjective terms. In choosing among alternative medical treatments, for example, one may wish to take into account the financial cost of alternative treatments, any side effects or distress they could cause, the value of decision outcomes, and so on. The normal decision rule associated with this approach is: Choose the action A from the set of alternatives that produces the outcome that maximizes the *subjective expected utility* (SEU) calculated by weighting the utility of each event by its probability:

$$SEU = p(A_i)U(A_i)$$

There are other decision rules, however. For example, we might choose the action that minimizes the possible cost (as when one avoids a treatment that has a significant likelihood of killing the patient, even though the selected treatment might have a lower probability of effecting a cure).

For decisions where it is possible to provide all the necessary probabilities and utilities, there is a well-developed discipline, decision analysis, for formalizing a decision process. Figure 2-3 shows part of a "decision tree" that addresses the decision of whether or not to treat a mother/infant with anticoagulants (drugs that under some circumstances can have either life-saving or fatal consequences). The squares represent "choice nodes" (over which the decision maker has control), and the circles are "chance nodes," where the probabilities of different outcomes are known but it is assumed there is no control. The full tree shows all routes through to the final possible outcomes of the initial decision, whether or not the mother/child will survive, and the decision is made to follow the route that maximizes the overall utility. The total expected utility of each decision (anticoagulation/no anticoagulation) is the sum of the SEUs of each outcome that it may give rise to. The SEU of each terminal outcome is the product of the probabilities of all contingencies in the path leading to the outcome, multiplied by its utility.

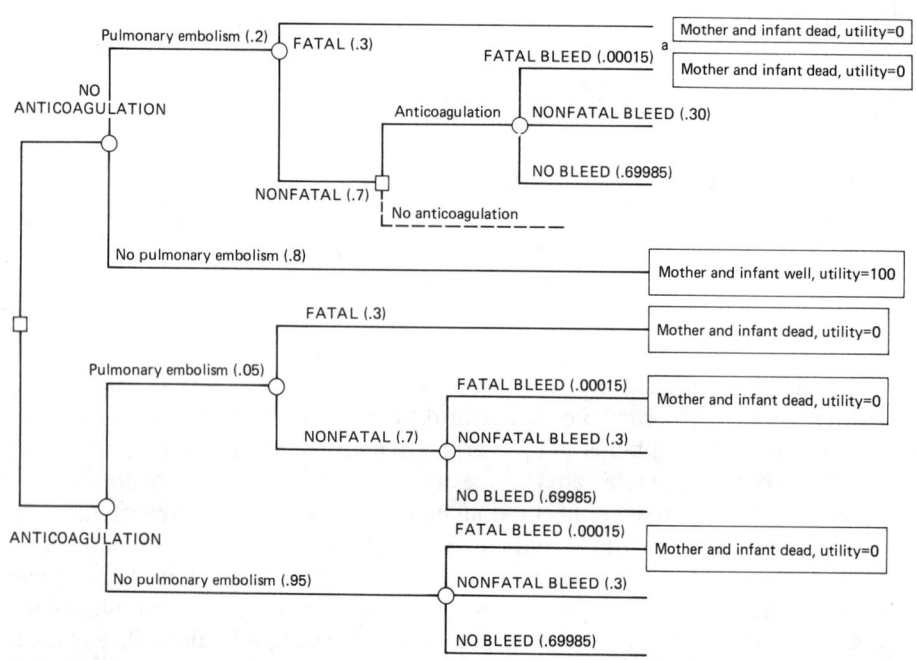

FIGURE 2-3

2.3 Discussion of Decision Theory

Although decision theory is well developed and has clear prescriptions for many aspects of decision making, it is not beyond criticism. For example, classical procedures make strong assumptions about the numerical data they need. They require that probabilistic parameters be unambiguous, and available (which they are frequently not); the notion of utility is problematic because costs and benefits are individualistic and subjective. Indeed, the utilities of outcomes (such as "quality of life" following surgery) may be almost impossible to determine. Psychological studies of uncertainty and expected utility give little comfort that these problems will be easily solved. As Fischoff et al. (1983) put it:

> The story of SEU research has...been a tale of deadends and hard-earned lessons. An enormous amount of effort was devoted to "capturing" decision strategies before it was realised that [people may not be] using an SEU decision rule at all. Many studies of how people estimate relative frequencies were conducted before researchers realized that such tasks failed to capture the sort of uncertainty found in most decision situations. For years, researchers derived satisfaction from the elicitation of consistent, reliable value judgments, before beginning to worry that such orderliness was a product of their methods.

Criticisms of statistical decision theory have also been made from an AI point of view. Numerical representations are impoverished of meaning (they are supposed to be; numerical representations are designed to be formal abstractions). They are difficult to understand, it is said, and they do not take advantage of the varied types of knowledge that human decision makers have access to. Such criticisms have been vigorously defended (e.g., Cheeseman, 1985).

Arguably, the most serious criticism of the numerical framework, however, is that it is a significantly incomplete account of what is involved in decision making. Figure 2-4 illustrates how decision making encompasses more than the bare mechanics of interpreting data to arrive at an assignment of probabilities or expected utilities. It emphasizes that decision making is a complex process, involving various steps and different types of activities. Important steps in the decision process are not addressed by classical procedures. The classical techniques do not say how to define the problem, how to identify decision alternatives, or how to select and control decision strategies. Consequently, classical decision systems depend heavily on having a (human) decision analyst to structure and control the decision process. From an AI point of view this is unsatisfactory, since advanced systems may need to operate autonomously.

Expert systems were AI's first attempt to address some of the problems of the decision support systems that were based on classical theory. Useful progress has been made, but many of the early aspirations have not been fully realized.

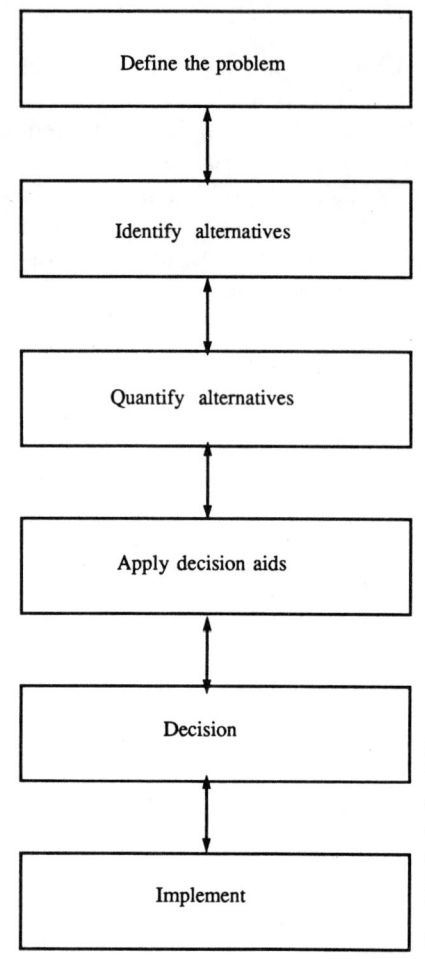

```
┌─────────────────────────┐
│    Define the problem   │
└─────────────────────────┘
            ↕
┌─────────────────────────┐
│   Identify alternatives │
└─────────────────────────┘
            ↕
┌─────────────────────────┐
│  Quantify alternatives  │
└─────────────────────────┘
            ↕
┌─────────────────────────┐
│    Apply decision aids  │
└─────────────────────────┘
            ↕
┌─────────────────────────┐
│        Decision         │
└─────────────────────────┘
            ↕
┌─────────────────────────┐
│        Implement        │
└─────────────────────────┘
```

FIGURE 2-4
The classical view of the decision process [from Hill et al. (1978)]. "The process begins with problem definition and ends with implementation of the decision. Iteration of steps occurs when there is insufficient information to complete a given step. The previous step must then be repeated until the necessary data are in hand."

3 KNOWLEDGE-BASED EXPERT SYSTEMS

I shall only review expert systems very briefly, in part because I assume that the reader has at least a basic knowledge of the area and in part because many good reviews already exist. We can raid a recent one for a clear opening statement:

> An expert system is a computer program that (a) reasons with domain-specific knowledge that is symbolic as well as mathematical; (b) uses domain-specific methods that are heuristic (plausible) as well as algorithmic (certain); (c) performs as well as specialists in its problem area; (d) makes understandable both what it knows and the reasons for its answers; and (e) retains flexibility (Buchanan and Smith, 1988, pp. 24–25).

To date, expert systems have been largely (though not exclusively) designed to provide decision support services (like the statistical programs before them). The typical, some would say defining, feature of the knowledge-based approach is that the knowledge required to solve a problem is stated explicitly (declaratively), rather than implicitly in the form of a procedure or abstractly in a numerical form. Figure 2-5 demonstrates the familiar style of rule-based knowledge representation in first-generation expert systems like MYCIN and PROSPECTOR, which combined explicit propositional knowledge and numerical "certainty factors."[1]

Expert systems directly addressed some of the criticisms of the earlier technology. Among the advantages claimed were that representing knowledge in rules and other symbolic forms made it easier to understand the processes of reasoning, that the modularity of rules permits progressive increases in functionality by incrementally extending the rules and facts in the knowledge base, and that symbolic representations easily encode different kinds of knowledge. Most important, the explicit representation of knowledge opens up the possibility of *metalevel* reasoning about reasoning itself. Rules can be used for purposes other than decision making, for example, as in explaining how a decision has been arrived at, reasoning about the knowledge that is available as opposed to that which isn't, or selecting alternative problem-solving methods.

3.1 Discussion of First-Generation Expert Systems

The idea of explicit symbolic knowledge representation and other innovations has had an irreversible impact on the design of decision support systems. However, many of the potential benefits have not been routinely realized. For example, expert systems were expected to be easy to understand and flexible in use. These expectations have not been as frequently achieved as was hoped. As Buchanan and Smith (1988) put it, following on from their description of expert systems quoted above: "Desiderata d [understandability] and e [flexibility] are less frequently cited and less frequently achieved than a–c. They...are included here to highlight their importance in designing and implementing any expert system." For example, the literal presentation of rules like those in Fig. 2-5 rarely offers a satisfactory explanation of a conclusion because one usually requires a deeper justification for such inference rules. Re-

---

[1] *Presentation note.* As far as possible the examples will be presented in the style of Fig. 2-5, showing a set of input data, a knowledge base fragment, and the output data that result from applying the fragment to the input data set, though minor technical details of the implementation have sometimes been omitted for clarity. All the examples are implemented in the Props2.5 knowledge engineering package, developed by the Imperial Cancer Research Fund and Edinburgh University AI Applications Institute. When reading the examples, bear in mind that data are normally interpreted by Props2 as they are acquired (by forward chaining). Additional properties of the package are introduced as necessary.

Input data

certainty of cancer is 0.1.
certainty of ulcer is 0.2.

symptoms include weight loss.
symptoms include haematemesis.

age is elderly.

Knowledge base

if symptoms include weight loss

    and age is elderly

then diagnoses include cancer, 0.5.

if symptoms include weight loss

    and symptoms include haematemesis

then diagnoses include ulcer, 0.6.

Output data

certainty of cancer is 0.05.

certainty of ulcer is 0.12.

FIGURE 2-5
Applying the knowledge base fragment (center) to the input data (top) yields the output data (bottom) as conclusions.

usability of knowledge bases has also often proved elusive. Some of the reasons for these difficulties are discussed later.

Knowledge base maintenance and development are also less easy than was first thought. Many designers have had difficulty scaling up from small demonstrations to comprehensive, convincing systems. Among the reasons for difficulty are that rules are frequently used procedurally and not just declaratively; in effect they are used as a programming language, which produces all the normal problems of programming and maintaining large software systems.

The example in Fig. 2-5 includes rules that incorporate numerical "certainty" terms. For each possible decision (the diagnosis is cancer; the diagnosis is an ulcer) we start with a prior expectation of the likelihood of each alternative and revise this using the conditional certainty coefficients associated with the rules. The scheme used for revising the likelihoods simply weights the prior certainties by multiplying them together with the conditional certainties. Note that the resulting certainty values are not normalized as they would be expected to be if they were interpreted as probabilities. Like many of the early schemes used in expert systems, this simplified revision procedure is *ad hoc* from the perspective of rigorous probability and decision theory. Such schemes have attracted much criticism.

However, the last few years have seen great efforts to develop sound procedures for propagating numerical uncertainty in symbolic inference systems [for recent reviews, see Bonissone (1987), Saffiotti (1988), and Clark (1989)]. Among the most developed probabilistic techniques are those due to Pearl (1986) and Lauritzen and Spiegelhalter (1988). Nonstandard techniques have also reached a high degree of refinement as in possibilistic reasoning (e.g., Dubois and Prade, 1988) and belief functions (e.g., Gordon and Shortliffe, 1986; Smets, 1988). We shall simply note this rather than pursuing technical questions of uncertainty management in detail, since many of the issues that have been studied so intensively in the last few years seem well on the way to being resolved. This progress is encouraging, but it should be remarked that while the clarifications achieved have been useful, the debate has had the effect of distracting research effort from questions of what tasks we want uncertainty management systems for, and traditional AI questions of how such concepts as goals, tasks, methods, and so on can be modeled (see also Fox, 1986, 1987; Saffiotti, 1988; Clark et al., 1988).

We have also observed that general decision theory acknowledges the costs and benefits associated with alternative actions. Most expert systems have been restricted to decisions under uncertainty, like diagnostic decisions. Decisions involving actions, such as planning and design decisions, have not generally been viewed in decision theoretic terms, and sound numerical or symbolic representations of utility have not yet been developed for them. The basic style of combining symbolic inference rules with numerical coefficients could presumably be extended to include utility coefficients, but there have been few attempts to develop this approach (but see Langlotz et al., 1987).

The promise of flexibility has not been realized. Knowledge-based systems were expected to be versatile because of the ability to reuse knowledge in different situations. It is now widely recognized that rules often implicitly encode knowledge of *purpose* (when and how they should be used), which limits their reusability. In practice, knowledge-based systems are "brittle." That is, the systems may operate acceptably under normal conditions but fail catastrophically with unusual data combinations, errors in the data, situations just outside the range of the knowledge base, and so on. Much discussion of the characteristics of "second-generation" expert systems focuses on this problem of brittleness and emphasizes the need for systems to have a deeper understanding of their subject matter if they are going to cope effectively with unexpected circumstances or degenerate data. If we are to achieve decision support systems that can help with more of the decision process (Fig. 2-4) or provide autonomous decision capabilities for AI systems, we need a deeper understanding of decision making and an appropriate decision theory.

4 SYMBOLIC DECISION PROCEDURES

Although Buchanan and Smith make the idea of symbolic processing central to the definition of an expert system, the early designs used symbolic processing in restricted and application-specific ways. The answer to many of the above criticisms is to radically extend the ensemble of symbolic techniques to explicitly cover representations of, and rationales for, decision making. More of the decision process can be automated than has traditionally been assumed, and important limits on early expert systems may now be surmountable. The remainder of this chapter sets out to show some important extensions and how symbolic techniques can significantly extend our understanding through the concept of a symbolic decision procedure.

> A *symbolic decision procedure* is an explicit representation of the knowledge required to define, organise and make a decision, and is a logical *abstraction* from the qualitative and quantitative knowledge that is required for any specific application. A SDP may include a specification of when and how the procedure is to be executed.

The critical step in adopting a symbolic decision procedure is to move away from propositional inference rules like those in Fig. 2-5 and use first-order inference systems such as the predicate calculus.[2] Judiciously used, first-order logics can provide sound, flexible inference methods while preserv-

---

[2] "Most fielded rule-based expert systems have used specialized rule interpreters, not based directly on logic...[this] reflects a need for more flexible styles of inference (in addition to a theorem prover's depth-first backtracking) and control over the strategies guiding the order of inferences" (Buchanan and Smith, 1988, p. 37). Our examples are implemented in Props2; this is a logic language but integrated with a variety of control and metaprogramming facilities.

ing the explicitness of application knowledge that is the strength of knowledge-based systems. Most important, we can carry out important decompositions of the knowledge base into specific application knowledge, generalized decision strategies, and knowledge of how to control the decision process. The following sections illustrate these characteristics.

4.1 Decomposition of Qualitative and Quantitative Knowledge

Figure 2-6 demonstrates a decomposition of qualitative information about symptoms and diseases from knowledge about how to revise the probabilities of diseases. It shows a knowledge base fragment containing six medical facts and a rule about the task of diagnosis. The first two facts encode the hypotheses that two diagnoses are possible—ulcer and cancer; the second pair, what the (current) probability of these is; and the final pair, the conditional probability of a particular symptom—weight loss—given each of the possible diagnoses.

The rule contains variables indicated by capitalized atoms. All variables are universally quantified over a class indicated by the variable name.[3] Suppose we enter the knowledge that a patient has lost weight into the input data. Variable S in the first clause of the rule is instantiated by "weight loss." With this finding it is possible to instantiate the remaining variables in the rule antecedents using facts already in the knowledge base, and the rule fires. The effect is that the probabilities of both diagnoses are revised by (trivially) multiplying them by the appropriate conditional probabilities. This yields the new probability values shown in the output data panel. (One or two implementation details have been omitted to emphasize principles.)

Some points about this revision procedure should be noted. First, the revision rule is defined separately from the specific facts that it uses. Also, it is not specified whether the probability refers to a causal link between a disease and a symptom or some other relation. The categorical component of the reasoning is modeled as a separate first-order theory (see next section). Second, since all variables are universally quantified, we may add more diagnosis or probability facts to the knowledge base, and the rule will automatically revise over the extended set. Indeed, it is easier to maintain a knowledge base of domain facts than a knowledge base of rules, because additions or deletions do not normally affect the logical or procedural characteristics of the knowledge base. Finally, the medical knowledge is liberated from a particular use and is available to be exploited in other ways (e.g., the probability facts could be used in calculating the expected information yield of a symptom, as discussed above).

---

[3] Props2 computes the full *forward closure* when any item is added to the knowledge base. That is to say, when an item is asserted into the knowledge base, then for all rules in the knowledge base all antecedents of the rules are instantiated to give a set of instantiated consequents; these consequents are asserted and propagated forward.

Input data

symptoms include weight loss

Knowledge base

possible diagnoses include cancer.
possible diagnoses include ulcer.

probability of cancer is 0.1.
probability of ulcer is 0.2.

conditional probability of weight loss | cancer is 0.3.
conditional probability of weight loss | ulcer is 0.2.

if symptoms include S
   and possible diagnoses include D
   and probability of D is P
   and conditional probability of S|D is Cp
   and Newval = P*Cp
then probability of D is Newval.

Output data

probability of cancer is 0.03.
probability of ulcer is 0.04.

FIGURE 2-6

4.1.1 DECOMPOSITION OF CONTROL KNOWLEDGE. Clancey (1982) pointed out that the rules in early expert systems frequently confounded control knowledge with the logical intention of a rule. Using our probability revision example we can also illustrate the explicit representation of control processes. In the revision rule in Fig. 2-6, which corresponds to the definition of Bayes' rule for probability revision above, the IF...THEN... form corresponds to the numerator of Bayes' rule, but there is no equivalent of the denominator. The latter is a normalization term that ensures that all the probabilities sum to 1. We can implement a normalization procedure in a similar style, but more information is needed. The missing information is *control* information, which constrains how the steps in the calculation should proceed sequentially; that is, *first* we must revise the raw probabilities, *then* compute the normalization factor by summing the raw values, and *finally* compute the set of posterior probabilities by dividing the revised values by the normalization factor. If we do not follow this sequence strictly, then we are likely to produce nonsense. This control information is implicit in the algebraic representation.

One way of making this sequencing information explicit is shown in Fig. 2-7. Here a control rule encodes the requirement that the steps must be explicitly queued.[4] Each step is explicitly named as a consequent in the control rule. (The procedures that carry out each step in the revision are defined by rules in much the same way as the revision rule. They are omitted for clarity.) The full symbolic revision procedure is clearly less succinct than the algebraic form, but this is the price of making explicit the procedure and its associated control information.

We can take these decompositions further. First, although the revision rule is defined for the specific task of medical diagnosis, the procedure can be further decomposed into medicine-specific parts and more general parts—more of this later. Second, we can decompose the control rule into a *general scheduling rule* and facts that define actions or *steps* in a procedure, and a set of *ordering constraints* on those steps. The declarative information yielded about medical diagnosis and the control information about how Bayesian revision is executed can then be used for other purposes (e.g., for explaining the current state of a task or the way the procedure is carried out). Again, more of this later.

4.2 Some Benefits of a Symbolic Decision Procedure

4.2.1 DEFINING AND ELABORATING THE DECISION. Classical decision theory has been concerned principally with valid probabilistic choice. Figure 2-4 acknowledges other processes in decision making as well as choice, including defining the problem and identifying the set of possible choices. Classical decision making only exploits theories that prescribe how probability and expected utility revisions can be carried out for a known set of decision options.

We can go further. Figure 2-8 illustrates how decision options can be *generated* using causal and structural knowledge and rules that embody

---

[4] Props2 provides an "agenda" structure for this purpose that can be executed sequentially, ensuring that each step is executed only after the previous step has been executed (and all forward chaining of the results has been completed).

Input data

symptoms include weight loss.

Knowledge base

if symptoms include F
then agenda update probabilities for F
    and agenda sum probabilities
    and agenda normalise probabilities
    and execute agenda.

Output data

sum of probabilities is 0.07.

probability of cancer is 0.428571.
probability of ulcer is 0.571429.

FIGURE 2-7

nonclassical models of causal and structural reasoning. We use an imaginary medical example again here, but the point is a general one.

The knowledge base in Fig. 2-8 contains several facts about the damage that certain disease processes can *cause* and some *structural* information. If we enter the fact "symptoms include pain in epigastrium," this satisfies the first antecedent of the first rule. The second antecedent requires the set of all possible causes of the symptom to be found. These could be stored explicitly and simply retrieved, but this would require that all such facts be explicitly

---

Input data

symptoms include pain in epigastrium.

Knowledge base

location of stomach is epigastrium.

causes of pain include cancer
causes of pain include ulcer.

disorders of stomach include cancer.
disorders of stomach include ulcer.

if symptoms include Symptom in Location
   and provable (possible causes of Symptom in Location include Disorder of Organ)
then supporting arguments for Disorder of Organ include possible cause of Symptom
                                                                  in Location.

if supporting arguments for Disorder of Structure include Argument
   and eliminated diagnoses do not include Disorder of Structure
then possible diagnoses include Disorder of Structure.

Output data

supporting arguments for cancer of stomach include
                            possible cause of pain in epigastrium.
supporting arguments for ulcer of stomach include
                            possible cause of pain in epigastrium.

possible diagnoses include cancer of stomach.
possible diagnoses include ulcer of stomach.

FIGURE 2-8

enumerated in the knowledge base. This may often be the case but is unlikely to be realistic in general. It would be preferable to generate such facts from causal or structural models.

Rule 1 embodies a simple first-order model that uses facts like "causes of pain include cancer" and knowledge of medical disorders and associated anatomy to generate sentences of the form "supporting arguments of Disorder of

Organ include possible cause of Symptom in Location."[5] The result is a set of *arguments* for considering new diagnostic hypotheses. Rule 2 completes the process of generating possible decision options in a way that is reminiscent of the "identity alternatives" box in Fig. 2-4. The rule detects that there are arguments in favor of a new diagnosis, checks whether there are any logical reasons to reject it, and, if not, explicitly adds the new possibility to the database.

Figure 2-9 extends the example to include *hypothesis propagation*. The rules introduce new options into the decision process on the basis of existing possibilities and knowledge of significant relationships between diagnostic concepts. The first rule expresses, in a general way, that if we suspect a patient has a peptic ulcer then it seems reasonable to consider both acute and chronic kinds of peptic ulcer as possible diagnoses (as well as all other subclasses).

The second rule can be instantiated by the fact that "ulcers are *caused* by cigarette smoking" (note that this example is oversimplified). If the patient smokes, then it is reasonable to introduce cigarette smoking as an important topic to pursue during the decision process; this rule is helping to *define the problem,* to use the terminology of Fig. 2-4 (or to expand the problem space, in AI parlance).

The process of identifying alternatives and problem definition have been traditionally assumed to be outside the scope of a formal decision process. As Lindley (1985) puts it, "The first task in any decision problem is to draw up a list of the possible actions that are available. Considerable attention should be paid to the compilation of this list because the choices of action will be limited to those contained within it." No hint here that the possible actions the decision maker can consider can, and often must, be defined progressively as new information is acquired.

One of the reasons for the classical restriction is that a nonclassical form of inference, which is neither probabilistic nor deductive, is required. The rules exemplify abductive reasoning—a form of reasoning that *generates new hypotheses* and that is *defeasible* (it can be withdrawn in the light of subsequent information). Rule 2 in Fig. 2-8 generates possible diagnoses as and when arguments in favor of the diagnoses arise, but does so on the defeasible assumption that there are no grounds for disregarding the diagnosis, which means that the decision maker can extend or revise its assumptions as more information is acquired. If a reason to reject the assumption is subsequently found, then the assumption is retracted and so is the possible diagnosis (and any other conclusion that depends directly or indirectly on the assumption).[6]

---

[5] In Props2 the prefix *provable* indicates to the interpreter that it should establish the set of all solutions for an antecedent condition. This is achieved using a backward chaining proof procedure that ranges over the entire knowledge base.

[6] Props2 automatically stores justifications along with all conclusions that it draws. Defeasibility is provided automatically by a mechanism that traces dependency paths over these justifications whenever a new fact is asserted into the knowledge base and retracting all unsupported inferences.

Input data

As in figure 2-8

Knowledge base

if possible diagnoses include Disorder of Structure
  and kinds of Disorder include Kind
then supporting arguments for Kind of Structure include kind of Disorder.

if possible diagnoses include Disorder of Structure
  and causes of Disorder include Cause
then consider Cause as possible cause of Disorder of Structure.

kinds of ulcer include acute ulcer .
kinds of ulcer include chronic ulcer.

causes of ulcer include cigarette smoking.

  Plus contents of knowledge base in figure 2-8

Output data

supporting arguments for acute ulcer of stomach include kind of ulcer.
supporting arguments for chronic ulcer of stomach include kind of ulcer.

consider cigarette smoking as possible cause of ulcer.

FIGURE 2-9

4.2.2 REUSABILITY OF KNOWLEDGE. The designers of early expert systems hoped that they would be able to improve on classical decision support techniques by being able to reuse knowledge for different purposes. In practice this was often found to be difficult (Buchanan and Smith, 1988). In fact, problems often arise because the problem-solving or decision-making knowledge has been insufficiently abstracted from strategic knowledge. The rules in Fig. 2-5, for example, not only contain knowledge about the symptomatology of diseases but also have the built-in assumption that they are to be used in diagnosis. If we abstract the information about symptoms and disease from the diagnostic inference rules, as in Fig. 2-8, then we can reuse the medical facts. For example, the second antecedent in the following rule reuses causal facts in the knowledge base of Fig. 2-8.

```
if confirmed diagnoses include Disease
   and causes of Symptom include Disease
   and subjective experience of symptom is unpleasant
then possible treatment decisions include prevention of
Symptom.
```

Previously the facts were used in an *object-level* role during the process of diagnosis; here they are used in a *metalevel* role for reasoning about treatment decisions that may have to be taken. Note that this rule can also be viewed as contributing to the process of *defining the problem,* which, as we have observed, lies outside the scope of classical techniques.

4.2.3 ACCOUNTABILITY AND INTELLIGIBILITY.
One of the early reasons for excitement about expert systems was their apparent ability to explain their behavior, a property uncharacteristic of traditional computer systems. Since knowledge was expressed in an intelligible and explicit form, this seemed to offer the possibility of providing explanations of their advice. It was subsequently realized that merely presenting rules to justify conclusions or explain why questions were being asked was unsatisfactory. Some of the reasons for this may now be clear.

First, propositional rules all deal with special cases, whereas good explanations frequently invoke general principles. The first-order inference rule that is defined over classes seems a more promising basis for explanation.

Second, traditional MYCIN-like rules are justified empirically—they do not appeal to any general theory about the world or how things depend upon each other (such as causal dependencies or anatomical constraints). First-order rules like those above embody deeper theories.

Third, reasoning models exist independently of the way in which they are to be used. As we remarked above, a rule may implicitly embody information about how and when it should be used. This has nothing to do with the logical intention of the rule. A MYCIN-like explanation mechanism cannot distinguish the two. Both may be needed for explanatory purposes but for quite different kinds of explanation—in one case to explain an argument but in the other to explain why a decision is proceeding in a particular way. Means and ends should not be confused. If we explicitly distinguish substantive conclusions and their justifications from control information, then appropriate explanation mechanisms can present both types without confusion. To illustrate, suppose the following hypothetical rule is used to reason about a medical treatment:

```
if possible diagnoses of the patient include cancer
   and the patient is not moribund
then chemotherapy is to be considered for the patient.
```

To explain the conclusion of the rule, one can do little more than list the antecedents. Suppose, in contrast, the conclusion had been arrived at by the following first-order rule, which reasons about *classes* of treatment and their justifications:

```
if diagnoses of Patient include Disease
and treatments of Disease include Treatment
and Treatment is not contraindicated
then Treatment is to be considered for Patient.
```

When instantiated in our hypothetical context, the rule is

```
if possible diagnoses of fred smith include cancer
and treatments of cancer include chemotherapy
and chemotherapy is not contraindicated
then chemotherapy is to be considered for fred smith.
```

This is a little more informative than the propositional rule, though not much. We can go further with this approach though, because it is possible to store much more information about the justifications of the rule antecedents than just their instantiating propositions, that is, whether the facts are explicitly known or deduced from other facts, whether they are demonstrably true or only defeasible assumptions, and so forth. Using this information we can construct the following explanation:

```
I have deduced that
  possible diagnoses of fred smith include cancer
    because
      dysphagia is a confirmed finding for fred smith and
      gastric-cancer is a possible cause of dysphagia
I know that
  treatments of cancer include chemotherapy and
since I cannot at this time show any reason that
  chemotherapy is contraindicated
I have concluded that
  chemotherapy is to be considered for fred smith.
```

There is also the potential for developing methods for explaining things in different ways here, since mechanisms for constructing explanations can themselves be first-order rules that exploit the explicit justifications within different explanatory frameworks.

4.2.4 REFLECTION AND METALEVEL REASONING. We have observed several times now that knowledge used at one time as object-level information *during* decision making may at another time be used for reasoning at the metalevel *about* the decision process. We have seen examples of the latter in strategic control and explanation. The need for metalevel capabilities pervades decision making. Among the more desirable abilities are the following.

1. *The ability to reflect on our knowledge:* It is advantageous to know whether or not there is knowledge available that is relevant to a decision, whether it is incomplete, whether it is unreliable, and if so why.
2. *The ability to reason about inference techniques:* Many decision techniques have similar purposes but are appropriate under different conditions.

For example, the idea has recently emerged that an eclectic view of uncertainty management techniques is useful; we may use different uncertainty representations and revisions procedures in the light of task constraints (Fox, 1986; Bonissone, 1987; Saffiotti, 1988; Clark et al., 1988). This can be done by reasoning about UMTs and their applicability conditions at the metalevel, selectively enabling the appropriate mechanisms. A practical demonstration of the approach is described by Fox et al. (1988).

3. *The ability to know how and why we arrived at conclusions:* Cohen (1985) argued the importance of reasoning about uncertainty as well as under uncertainty during problem solving. The reasons for believing or disbelieving things (Cohen calls them "endorsements") should be represented explicitly so that they can be examined, explained, questioned, corroborated, or withdrawn in the light of new information. We have seen several examples of this.

4. *The ability to reflect on the decision process:* A sophisticated decision maker needs to be able to examine its decisions—past, present, and future; to determine when a decision should be attempted; to plan and control decision processes; to decide how to identify decision options, when the decision can be taken, and so forth (Fox, 1984).

We shall develop points 3 and 4 in a little detail, because they are central to developing a symbolic theory of decision making and critical to the design of sound expert systems in the future. Point 4 demands that we ask, What is a decision? Classical theory replies that it is the action of choosing an option whose expected utility is maximal. Here we give a different type of answer, in the classic AI style: a decision can be viewed as a symbol structure that can be treated as *data* to be manipulated or the *specification* of a process to be executed.

This characterization of a decision may have an indefinite number of instances. In medicine alone, for example, physicians need to make diagnosis, treatment, investigation, referral, risk assessment, and even "do nothing" decisions. But what is the generic structure that underlies all these instances? Here we characterize a symbolic decision procedure as object-level *data* and *control* specifications and first-order rules for interpreting these specifications.

Computational procedures can be specified in terms of four control attributes. These are:

1. Conditions that evoke the procedure
2. Conditions that terminate it
3. Subprocedures that it is composed of, if any
4. Constraints on the order in which subprocedures must be carried out, if any

A control specification for a diagnostic decision is shown in the top half of Fig. 2-10, with rules for interpreting such specifications listed below. The initiation rule 1 is satisfied for a procedure if all the evoking conditions of that procedure are satisfied. Rule 5, on the other hand, will terminate the procedure if any of its termination conditions are satisfied. Rules 2, 3, and 4 embody a simple recursive scheduler that creates and maintains an ordered agenda of subprocedures where these are specified.

Part of control specification for diagnosis decision

evoking conditions of diagnosis include diagnosis is unknown.
evoking conditions of diagnosis include treatment is required.

termination conditions of diagnosis include diagnosis established.

steps of diagnosis include define problem.
steps of diagnosis include acquire evidence.
steps of diagnosis include review decision.

constraint of diagnosis is define problem precedes acquire evidence.

First order procedure for initiating, scheduling and terminating a task

if tasks include Task
  and not(evoking conditions of Task include Condition
      and not Condition)
then schedule Task in Task.

if schedule Operation in Task
  and steps of Operation include Step
then agenda schedule Step in Task.

if schedule Operation in Task
  and not steps of Operation include Step
then agenda Operation in Task.

if schedule Operation in Task
  and constraint of Task is Step1 precedes Step2
  and agenda Step2 precedes Step1
then agenda Step1 precedes Step2.

if termination conditions of Task include Condition
  and known Condition
then retract agenda Step in Task.

FIGURE 2-10

The diagnosis specification requires that the condition for initiating a diagnostic decision is that a treatment is required *and* the diagnosis is unknown. The termination condition for the procedure is, trivially, that the diagnosis is known. The procedure consists of three steps—define the problem, collect evidence, and review decision—with constraints that partially order the steps to indicate that the problem must be defined before evidence is collected. Note that this specification not only controls the decision procedure but is also available to be used by other first-order theories.

In contrast, the data specification defines *what kinds* of information the decision procedure uses rather than *how* it is to be carried out. Among the main types of information the data specification may provide are the following.

Input variables: What classes of information does the procedure take as input? For example, a diagnostic procedure may accept *findings* and *possible diagnoses* as input.

Output variables: A diagnostic procedure may deliver *possible diagnoses* as output.

Propagation relations: What relations should be used for propagating diagnostic options? In Section 4.2.1 we discussed the use of *causal* and *subclass* relations, for example.

Associations: Propagation rules can independently generate decision options that are not strictly independent. For example, we may have separate reasons for considering a diagnosis of peptic ulcer and a diagnosis of gastric ulcer, though one is simply a subclass of the other. The *associations* attribute informs the decision procedure what association relations apply among decision options.

Endorsement types: Adopting Cohen's (1985) term, the endorsements attribute specifies the types of reasoning that are relevant to "arguing the pros and cons" of the various decision options.

Figure 2-11 shows a procedure for generating endorsements, using relevant facts from the data specification of the diagnosis decision.

The rule is triggered by the availability of findings (a declared input class). In the example, the findings *weight loss* and *elderly* are notified to the rule, which establishes from the diagnosis specification that relevant endorsements include *supporting arguments* and that these include two subtypes: *possible causes* and *established associations*. Using appropriate models (not shown here), the set of all possible diagnoses and their associated endorsements are generated for the data set.

4.3 Overview and Example

I shall close by briefly describing one application that exploits developed variants of techniques outlined here. The *Oxford System of Medicine* (OSM) is designed to assist general medical practitioners with a variety of information retrieval, decision-making, and patient management tasks. A necessary design assumption is that the general physician has many tasks to carry out and the available facilities may be required unpredictably.

Figure 2-12 gives a schematic view of the decision-making elements of the OSM. The implementation can be viewed as consisting of a set of first-order theories or "specialist" knowledge bases composed of facts and univer-

---

Input data

decision is a diagnosis.

findings include elderly.
findings include weight loss.

Knowledge base (endorsement specification and model)

input variables of diagnosis include findings.

endorsements of diagnosis include supporting arguments.

supporting arguments of diagnosis include possible cause.
supporting arguments of diagnosis include established association.

if decision is a Type
  and input variables of Type include Inputs
  and Inputs include Item
  and endorsements of Type include Endorsements
  and Endorsements of Type include Arguments
  and provable Arguments of Item include Output
then confirmed Endorsements of Output include Arguments of Item.

Output data

confirmed supporting arguments of cancer include possible cause of weight loss.
confirmed supporting arguments of cancer include established association of elderly.

FIGURE 2-11

sally quantified rules. These specialists monitor and update a common data base defeasibly. Decision specifications for diagnosis, treatment, and other decisions can be evoked as required; these update beliefs about hypotheses, preferences for alternative treatments, and so on. Control knowledge is explicit and is used to evoke and manage the execution of all tasks in response to user requirements and the elicitation of patient data.

Other first-order specialists provide user interaction capabilities such as explanations, patient reviews, and decision summaries. These interface specialists have access to specific patient data and medical knowledge but also to the decision specifications as well as assumptions, justifications, dependencies, and so on.

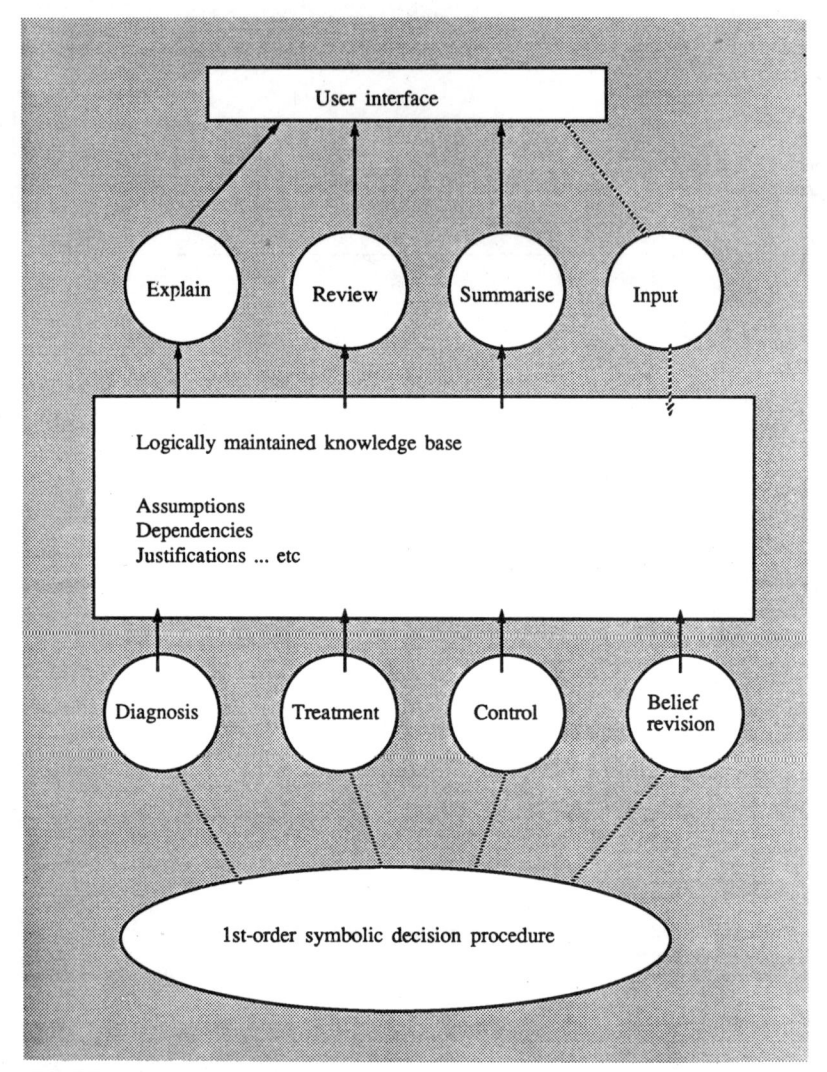

FIGURE 2-12

As more medical knowledge is acquired, the knowledge base of medical facts can be extended without altering the first-order components. As more capabilities are needed, additional first-order specialists can be added that exploit the symbolic decision procedure in new ways.

5 CONCLUSIONS

Decision making is a central topic for knowledge-based systems and applied artificial intelligence. In this chapter I have briefly outlined the classical statistical approach to decision theory and commented on some of its characteristics from an AI perspective. Knowledge-based expert systems introduced explicit symbolic techniques to overcome some of the problems of the classical approach. Although they have had success, this has been at some cost in an ad hoc growth of procedural and declarative techniques. The lack of a uniform approach has made the increased functionality, versatility, and opportunities for formalization promised by symbolic methods more difficult to achieve. These problems have been discussed and an approach based on first-order decision procedures that may restore the early promises and provide a more secure logical foundation for decision making in knowledge-based systems has been described.

Abstraction of principle from detail is fundamental. The theoretical benefit is that a clear statement of principle permits the analysis and formalization of the decision procedure(s) away from application complexities. The benefits of abstraction apply to the execution of a decision procedure as well as its organization. Description of control mechanisms in a first-order form gives a deeper insight into *how* decisions could or should be made as well as *why* they are organized the way they are.

These benefits of separating decision procedures from the details of their application are numerous:

1. The procedures can be stated in a succinct, generic form that permits formal analysis separate from the details of any domain.
2. Experience shows that generic decision procedures can be expressed by a small collection of inference rules, which makes a significant contribution to maintainability.
3. The application-specific knowledge base can be represented as an *extensional database* of propositions. These are easy to store and access, and the database can grow without limit to cover the domain without introducing unexpected logical difficulties in use.
4. The separation of extensional knowledge and first-order knowledge offers flexibility of use, because extensional knowledge can be used and reused by multiple first-order theories.
5. Instances of the generic decision procedure can be specified explicitly. Like any other knowledge, these specifications can be reused—to control the decision process, to give explanations, to guide knowledge acquisition, and so forth. When knowledge for a specific decision is not available, leading to brittleness, the decision procedure can fall back on more general procedures for reasoning about decision options or about the decision procedure itself.

Classical decision theory recognized that there is an underlying generic structure to decision making, which was captured in terms of SEU theory. This was an important contribution, but, as we have discussed, the approach is incomplete. It fails to model important parts of the decision process, and it makes no provision for intervention in the decision process by a human user. It is also rather inflexible, because the algebraic language within which it is normally discussed has insufficient expressive power to represent ideas of control, process, justification, quantification, and other metalevel concepts.

First-generation expert systems significantly extended the capabilities of decision support systems. However, they failed to address the need for a clear theory of decision making, which had been recognized in the classical approach. Such systems typically exploited some sort of propositional logic that required the explicit enumeration of large quantities of special-case knowledge, in which the decision procedure and other problem strategies were only implicit. First-order representations are likely to be the basis of second-generation expert systems because they clarify the regularities and principles that underlie decision making and other kinds of problem solving. They also offer a stronger basis for ensuring soundness in design, since they permit alternative decision procedures to be specified, formalized, analyzed, and tested outside the narrow confines of an application.

ACKNOWLEDGMENTS

I would like to thank Dominic Clark, Andrzej Glowinski, and Mike O'Neil, who have made important contributions to the ideas and techniques described in this paper and commented on drafts, and to Saki Hajnal, who made the software work, and the author work harder, in the service of clarity. Other aspects of the symbolic decision procedures discussed here have been described in more detail in Fox et al. (1988), O'Neil et al. (1989), and Glowinski et al. (1989).

REFERENCES

Bonissone, P. (1987). Reasoning, Plausible. In: *Encyclopedia of Artificial Intelligence* (S. C. Shapiro, Ed.). Wiley, New York, pp. 894–863.
Broadbent, D. E. (1972). *Decision and Stress*. Academic Press, New York.
Buchanan, B. G., and Smith, R. G. (1988). Fundamentals of Expert Systems. *Ann. Rev. Comput. Sci.* 3:23–58.
Castles, F. G., Murray, D. J., and Potter, D. C. (Eds.) (1971). *Decisions, Organisations and Society*. Penguin, Harmondsworth, U.K.
Cheeseman, P. (1985). In Defence of Probability. Proc. Int. Joint Conf. Artificial Intelligence, Los Angeles, pp.1002–1009.
Clancey, W. (1986). Heuristic Classification. *AI* 27:215–251.
Clark, D. A. (1989). Numeric and Symbolic Approaches to Uncertainty Management in AI: A Review and Discussion. *AI Rev.*, in print.
Clark, D. A., Baldwin, J., Berenji, H., Cohen, P., Dubois, D., Fox, J., Lemmer, J., Prade, H., Spiegelhalter, D., Smets, P., Zadeh, L. (1988). Discussion of paper by A. Saffiotti [see Saffiotti (1988).] *Knowledge Eng. Rev.* 3(1):59–92.
Cohen, P. (1985). *Heuristic Reasoning about Uncertainty: An Artificial Intelligence Approach*. Pitman, Boston.
de Dombal, T. (1979). Computers and the Surgeon: A Matter of Decision. *Surgery Ann.* 11:33–57.

Dubois, D., and Prade, H. (1988). An Introduction to Possibilistic and Fuzzy Logics. In: *Nonstandard Logics for Automated Reasoning* (P. Smets, E. H. Mamdani, D. Dubois, and H. Prade, Eds.). Academic Press, New York.
Fischoff, B., Goitein, B., and Shapira, Z. (1983). Subjective Expected Utility: A Theory of Decision Making. In: *Decision Making Under Uncertainty* (R. W. Scholz, Ed.). Elsevier/North-Holland, New York, 160–175.
Fox, J. (1984). Formal and Knowledge Based Methods in Decision Technology. *Acta Psycho*, pp. 330–331, reprinted in *Professional Judgement* (J. Dowie and A. Elstein, Eds.). Cambridge University Press, Cambridge, U.K.
Fox, J. (1986). Three Arguments for Extending the Framework of Probability. In: *Uncertainty in Artificial Intelligence* (L. N. Kanal and J. F. Lemmer, Eds.). North-Holland, Amsterdam.
Fox. J. (1987). Architectures for Decision Making. Proceedings of workshop on architectures for knowledge based systems, Mount Fuji, Japan (in press).
Fox, J., O'Neil, M., Glowinski, A. J., and Clark, D. A. (1988). Decision Making As a Logical Process. In: *Research and Development in Expert Systems*, Vol. 5. (B. Kelly and A. Rector, Eds.). Cambridge University Press, Cambridge, U.K.
Glowinski, A. J., O'Neil, M., and Fox, J. (1989). Design of a Generic Information System and Its Application to Primary Care. In: *Proceedings of 2nd European Conference on AI in Medicine* (J. Hunter, Ed.). Springer-Verlag, Berlin, 183–207.
Gordon, J., and Shortliffe, E. H. (1984). The Dempster-Shafer Theory of Evidence. In: *Rule-Based Expert Systems: The MYCIN Experiments of the Stanford Heuristic Programming Project*. (B. Buchanan and E. H. Shortliffe, Eds.). Addison-Wesley, Reading, Mass., 272–294.
Hill, P. H., Bedau, H. A., Chechile, R. A., Crochetiere, W. J., Kellerman, B. L., Ounjian, D., Pauker, S. G., Pauker, S. P., and Rubin, J. Z. (Eds.) (1979). *Making Decisions. A Multidisciplinary Introduction*. Addison-Wesley, Reading, Mass.
Hogarth, R. (1980). *Judgement and Choice: The Psychology of Decision*. Wiley, New York.
Kahneman, D., Slovic, P., and Tversky, A. (Eds.) (1982). *Judgement and Uncertainty: Heuristics and Biases*. Cambridge University Press, Cambridge, U.K.
Langlotz, C. P., Fagan, L. M., Tu, S. W., Sikic, B. I., and Shortliffe, E. H. (1987). A Therapy Planning Architecture That Combines Decision Theory and Artificial Intelligence. *Compu. Biomed. Res.* **20**:279–303.
Lauritzen, S. L., and Spiegelhalter, D. J. (1988). Local Computations with Probabilities on Graphical Structures and Their Application to Expert Systems. *J. Roy. Stat. Soc. B* **50**(2):157–244.
Lindley, D. V. (1956). On a Measure of the Information Provided by an Experiment. *Ann. Math. Stat.* **27**:986–1005.
Lindley, D. V. (1985). *Making Decisions,* 2nd ed. John Wiley, New York.
MacCrimmon, K. R. (1973). An Overview of Multiple Objective Decision-Making. In: *Multiple Criteria Decision Making* (J. L. Cochrane and M. Zeleny, Eds.). University of South Carolina Press, Columbia, S.C.
O'Neil, M., Glowinski, A. G., and Fox, J. (1989). A Symbolic Theory of Decision Making Applied to Several Decision Making Tasks. In: *Proceedings of 2nd European Conference on AI in Medicine* (J. Hunter, Ed.). Springer-Verlag, New York.
Pearl, J. (1984). *Heuristics. Intelligent Search Strategies for Computer Problem Solving*. Addison-Wesley, Reading, Mass.
Saffiotti, A. (1988). An AI View of the Treatment of Uncertainty. *Knowledge Eng. Rev.* **2**(2):79–98.
Schwartz, S., and Griffin, T. (1986). *Medical Thinking*. Springer, New York.
Shannon, C. E., and Weaver, W. (1959). *The Mathematical Theory of Communication*. University of Illinois, Urbana.
Smets, P. (1988). Belief Functions. In: *Non-standard Logics for Automated Reasoning* (P. Smets, E. H. Mamdani, D. Dubois and H. Prade, Eds.). Academic Press, New York.

CHAPTER 3

APPLICATIONS OF AUTOMATED REASONING

LARRY WOS

1 A BEGINNING

Less than 25 years ago, mathematicians and computer scientists generally believed there was only a remote possibility of designing a computer program to reason in the sense that scientists use the word. The obstacles of representing the problem to the program, of formulating sufficiently general ways of reasoning, and of devising strategies to adequately control the reasoning so that the program would function effectively appeared truly formidable. However, because of the potential value of successfully overcoming these obstacles, studying the possibility of having a computer reason was adopted as a long-range mathematical research area (Wos, 1987b).

In this chapter, using the quote above as the beginning, we shall focus on the rest of the story—a story that tells how the field of *automated reasoning* was founded, why it was extended, and what caused it to grow to maturity. In addition, we shall focus on various successes of this field, giving an up-to-date account of the kinds of assistance that a reasoning program can provide. The successful applications of automated reasoning include program verification, circuit design and validation, assembly line scheduling, and programming language (combinatory logic). To complete the picture, we shall also provide a rather extensive introduction to the elements of automated reasoning, a discussion of the obstacles still to be overcome, and a brief treatment of what the future offers. Since portable automated reasoning programs (discussed in Section 7) are now available—programs that in fact run on personal computers—

and since an easy-to-read book (Wos et al., 1984) exists that discusses in detail the way reasoning programs work and the successes achieved with their assistance, and another book (Wos, 1987a) offers specific research problems to solve, we conjecture that the future of automated reasoning is limited only by the time and energy that will be devoted to it.

1.1 The Objective of Automated Reasoning

The explicit objective of the field of automated reasoning is to design and implement a computer program that reasons logically and effectively. To possess each of these two vital properties—being logical and being effective—the program must have access to a variety of procedures. Although we shall discuss these procedures more fully in Section 2, let us briefly touch on them here.

To reach the objective of automated reasoning requires specific inference rules, ways of reasoning, that are *sound*. An inference rule is sound if its application always yields a conclusion that follows inevitably from the hypotheses to which the rule is applied. Without sound inference rules, the program cannot reason logically.

However, sound ways of reasoning are not enough. Indeed, to be effective, a reasoning program must also rely on the use of strategy. If strategy is not employed—to restrict the reasoning, and also to direct the reasoning—the program will draw entirely too many conclusions in most situations. An effective reasoning program must also rely on the use of rules—supplied by the user or found by the program itself—for rewriting information into the desired canonical form. Without such rules, called *demodulators* (Wos et al., 1967), a reasoning program will perform too poorly in most cases. The poor performance arises from the myriad of ways a fact or relationship can be stated. Finally, to be effective, a reasoning program must employ some means for discarding information that is captured by existing information; the procedure *subsumption* (Robinson, 1965) suffices.

Since attempting to reach the objective of having access to a computer program that reasons both logically and effectively might indeed be a formidable task—which was the opinion of scientists in the early 1960s—one might naturally ask for a practical justification for making such an attempt. The justification rests with the fact that one can easily list problems that would be very difficult to solve, or impossible to solve, without the power that a computer offers. Of course, because of the typical use of a computer, the problems one might think of first are numerical in character. However, with a little extra thought, if an appropriately powerful reasoning program were available, one can quickly suggest problems requiring deep reasoning, problems not only from mathematics and logic but also from the areas of program verification, circuit design, and real-time systems control. We thus have our practical justification—the desire to have access to an automated reasoning assistant and, if all goes as planned, access to an automated reasoning colleague.

1.2 The History of Automated Reasoning

The main effort directed toward producing a program that could reason logically was begun in the early 1960s at a small number of universities and laboratories. Each of these separate efforts focused on the area now known as automated theorem proving. As the name suggests, the essentially sole application in the early 1960s was that of proving theorems from various areas of mathematics and logic. The early programs, as one might expect, were unable to prove even the simplest of theorems. Nevertheless, some of the ideas on which those early programs were based did lead indirectly to important breakthroughs.

One of the groups that became interested in the area early in the game was based at Argonne National Laboratory. Using the problem of proving elementary theorems from algebra as a test application, researchers focused simultaneously on the formulation of strategies to control reasoning and the design of a computer program to reason subject to those strategies. In fact, it was this research that introduced the notion of strategy to the field then known as mechanical theorem proving. The introduction of strategy changed the entire course of this area of computer science. The first program that resulted from that early research proved to be far more powerful than any other program available at the time, and for years to come. Proofs of algebraic theorems from group theory and ring theory, two areas of abstract mathematics, were obtained in seconds with the Argonne program on an IBM 704, in contrast to being unprovable with other programs.

Fifteen years of research beyond that initial effort—years dedicated to extending the power of "automated theorem-proving" programs—culminated in 1980 with the introduction of the name "automated reasoning" and in the design and implementation of even more powerful automated reasoning programs. The name was introduced because no longer were reasoning programs essentially confined to proving theorems from mathematics. Such programs were being used for model generation, conjecture formulation, and hypothesis testing. The areas of application, originally mathematics and logic, had expanded to include program verification, circuit design and validation, robotics, and organic chemical synthesis.

Those 15 years of research, in addition to producing very powerful reasoning programs, also produced a number of very effective strategies and related procedures. Many of those strategies (for example, the set of support strategy) and procedures (for example, paramodulation and demodulation) have been adopted as fundamental features by other program developers in the rapidly expanding field of automated reasoning. Some of these deceptively simple strategies direct the reasoning effectively, while—even more important—others restrict the reasoning to paths relevant to the given assignment. The objectives of the various types of strategy are to cause the reasoning programs to give first priority to expressions with the least complexity, to focus on the more pertinent information about a problem rather than general background information, to retain more general conclusions in preference to more limited information, and to automatically produce and use a simplified form of each conclusion that is drawn. Without these strategies, reasoning programs will typically wander aimlessly through an enormous set of possible conclusions and, after far too much time, usually fail. For example, in problems from abstract algebra and set theory, a program without the set of support strategy can draw 20,000 conclusions yet fail to find a solution; but with the strategy, a program may draw only 200 conclusions before solving the given problem.

The final occurrence or, technically, set of occurrences we cite in the history of automated reasoning—the occurrence that brought the field to some maturity—concerns an unexpected success. Before this occurrence, with one exception, automated reasoning programs had not contributed *new* information to science. However, between 1978 and 1982, with heavy assistance from an automated reasoning program, open questions were answered. Even further, the questions were taken from three unrelated areas: ternary Boolean algebra, finite semigroups, and equivalential calculus. To have obtained the answers with an automated reasoning program marked a significant point in the history of automated reasoning. Indeed, the success with answering open questions was resumed in 1986, and still continues, in the field of combinatory logic. When in later sections we turn to applications of even greater interest, one might keep in mind that, were it not for those significant achievements at the end of the 1970s and during the early 1980s, perhaps the needed zeal to attack the other applications would have been lacking.

2 A REVIEW OF AUTOMATED REASONING

At this point, to provide readers with a feel for the subject, we turn to a rather extensive review of some of the pertinent aspects of automated reasoning, and show how an automated reasoning program can provide valuable assistance for various types of research. The elements to be covered in this review are representation of information (by use of the *clause language*), reasoning (the specific inference rule *binary resolution* and the specific inference rule *paramodulation* for building in equality), strategies (including the *set of support strategy*) of various types for controlling the reasoning, a procedure (*demodulation*) for rewriting information into a canonical form, a procedure (*subsumption*) for discarding trivial corollaries, and a means (*proof by contradiction*) for the program to determine that the given assignment has been completed. For a more complete treatment, see Wos et al. (1984).

As the name implies, automated reasoning focuses on the formulation and implementation of techniques that permit a computer program to reason. Although not implied by the name, the reasoning of main interest is logical in character. Even though automated reasoning programs have uses that do not focus on proof finding, the main use is in fact that of finding a proof. Of the applications for automated reasoning, that which has produced the greatest success concerns proving some theorem from mathematics or logic. Nevertheless, when we turn to a detailed discussion of applications, as we do in later sections, we shall focus on applications outside of mathematics and logic. However, at this point in the chapter—to avoid the continual addition of qualifying remarks—we shall talk mainly about theorems, noting that the observations we make naturally extend to problems and questions other than those that focus on proving some theorem.

The fields of mathematics from which a theorem may be taken include algebra, geometry, topology, set theory, and combinatory logic. The most widely used approach for proving theorems, or for solving any problem or answering any question, with a reasoning program focuses on searching for a proof by contradiction. Therefore, to enable a program using such an approach to attempt to prove a proposed theorem of the form **if** P **then** Q, one is required to define the field from which the theorem is taken, to give the special hypothesis (defined in Section 2.6) of the theorem, and to assume that the theorem is in fact false. If one is having a reasoning program attempt to answer some question whose form is not that of a theorem, then, predictably, one assumes that the desired answer is false and has the program seek a proof by contradiction. (In those cases in which one is not able to suggest an answer or prefers not to, the program can be used to draw conclusions that follow from the statement of the question, and the user can search among them for the desired answer.) To fulfill the requirement of setting the stage for seeking a proof by contradiction—whether attempting to prove a theorem or to answer a question—one writes a set of statements of the form P **and** (**not** Q), where P corresponds to the axioms of the underlying theory, the special hypothesis of the theorem, and any lemmas one might wish to supply, and where Q corresponds to the conclusion of the theorem. This set of statements is then given to the automated reasoning program in use, which applies logical reasoning in an attempt to complete the assignment of finding a proof by contradiction.

To reason logically—and thus begin its attack on the given problem—the reasoning program draws conclusions by applying one or more sound inference rules chosen by the researcher. The application of each rule is directed by one type of strategy and restricted by another type. When a conclusion is drawn, the program rewrites it into a canonical form by applying rules [*demodulators* (Wos et al., 1967)] supplied by the researcher or discovered by the program. The result is then tested [with the use of subsumption (Robinson, 1965)] to see whether it is a trivial corollary of information the program already has and should therefore be discarded. The result can also be tested to see whether it satisfies criteria, supplied by the researcher, for measuring significance; if the conclusion fails the test, it is discarded. The goal is to deduce some new conclusion that contradicts a conclusion drawn earlier or contradicts some input statement. When such a discovery is made, a proof by contradiction has been found, and the automated reasoning program in use "knows" that the given assignment has been completed.

Using the preceding summary of the program's actions as an outline for this section, let us sample each of the main areas, beginning with a discussion of how one specifies the problem to be considered.

2.1 Representation

In this section, we mainly use the notation that is consistent with that found in Wos et al. (1984) and in Wos (1987a), one that is an acceptable notation for the formal language—the *clause language*—most commonly used. Without doubt, the various languages of mathematics and logic are usually easier to read than the clause language. However, since one of our objectives is to introduce automated reasoning to mathematicians, logicians, and other scientists, we shall provide a limited treatment of the clause language, the language in which one usually converses with a reasoning program. Our first example will be a deductive database query, and then we shall turn to ordinary arithmetic for our next examples to show how a reasoning program can treat equality as if it is "understood".

The conventions require variables to be chosen from among terms whose first symbol is one of lowercase *u* through *z,* functions and constants to be written in lower case, and relations (predicates) to be written in upper case. Also by convention, each variable is implicitly universally quantified (meaning "for all"), and each variable is relevant only to the *clause* in which it occurs. In addition, by writing EQUAL for the equality relation, the program is able to treat equality as "understood" or "built in". Finally, the symbol ¬ means **not,** and the vertical bar symbol | means **or.** For the statements in which **or** occurs, the expressions separated by the vertical bar are called *literals*. As we shall see, existence is not represented with variables; but, instead, appropriate functions and constants are employed. In addition, we shall see that the logical operator **and** never occurs within a clause and is always assumed to be present implicitly between clauses. As for the operator **if-then,** its place is taken by the use of **not** and **or,** using the equivalence of **if** *P* **then** *Q* to **not** *P* **or** *Q*. Let us now turn to some examples.

We begin with an example that is representative of a trivial database query but that is also a very simple puzzle to solve.

> Roberta, who is unmarried, has the job of teacher or nurse,
> and the job of nurse is held by a male. What is Roberta's job?

A question of this type often contains hidden information. For example, people are female or male, and husbands are male, and Roberta is female. To submit the given question to an automated reasoning program, one typically selects a possible answer and assumes that the answer is false. This action sets the stage for the program to seek a proof by contradiction. Let us take the correct answer, Roberta is a teacher, and assume that she is in fact not one. The following clauses suffice.

Roberta is assumed not to be the teacher
(1) ¬HASAJOB(Roberta,teacher)

Roberta is a teacher or a nurse
(2) HASAJOB(Roberta,teacher) | HASAJOB(Roberta,nurse)

The job of nurse is held by a male
(3) ¬HASAJOB(x,nurse) | MALE(x)

Everyone is not female or not male
(4) ¬FEMALE(x) | ¬MALE(x)

Roberta is female
(5) FEMALE(Roberta)

We shall return to this simple puzzle when we study inference rules in Section 2.2, and again when we study proof by contradiction in Section 2.6.

Now let us turn to examples from ordinary arithmetic. To express the fact that

$$0 + x = x$$

for all x, we write

EQUAL(sum(0,x),x)

where x is treated implicitly as a universally quantified variable ranging over all numbers and 0 is treated as a *constant*; formally, 0 is a *Skolem constant*. To express the existence of an additive (right) inverse, for all x there exists a y such that

$$x + y = 0,$$

we write the clause

EQUAL(sum(x,minus(x)),0)

where x implicitly ranges over all numbers and where *minus* is an appropriate *Skolem function*.

A *Skolem constant* is used for expressing the existence of some element that does *not* depend on the universally quantified variables—for example, there exists a y such that for all x, $y + x = x$, which is, of course, closely related to the earlier example regarding 0. A *Skolem function* is used for existentially quantified variables that *do* depend on other universally quantified variables—for example, for all x there exists a y such that $x + y = 0$. A Skolem constant names the element in question, and a Skolem function names a function and, by its arguments, expresses the appropriate dependence. The respective equivalents, given earlier in which the predicate EQUAL occurs, of the two arithmetic laws are called *clauses*.

2.2 Inference Rules

A general-purpose reasoning program offers a wide variety of inference rules. We shall focus on two of them in this chapter. The first, *binary resolution* (Robinson, 1965), is in an important sense the least complicated to apply; the second, *paramodulation* (Robinson and Wos, 1969; Wos and Robinson, 1973), is the most complicated to apply, at least for a person. Paramodulation enables an automated reasoning program to treat equality as if it is "understood" in the sense that no axioms other than reflexivity ($x = x$) need to be included when a problem is submitted for consideration. In particular, when paramodulation is applied to two clauses satisfying the appropriate conditions, a conclusion is obtained in the spirit of equality substitution. Actually, as we shall see, paramodulation generalizes the usual notion of equality substitution.

For the actions of binary resolution and paramodulation to be easily understood, we need one concept, that of *unification* (Robinson, 1965; Wos et al., 1984; Wos, 1987a). This concept is also required for other aspects of automated reasoning presented later in this section.

To *unify* two expressions, the program must find terms to replace the variables in each such that the two resulting expressions are identical (possibly with the exception of sign). When unification is applied to two expressions that are both clauses, the program always treats the two expressions as having no variables in common; the program is allowed to take this action because a variable is relevant only to the clause in which it occurs. The most general replacement for variables is always preferred, as evidenced in the third example of paramodulation to be given shortly. The object is to maintain generality where possible, which adds markedly to the efficiency of the reasoning program.

An automated reasoning program's preference for generality is but one difference between computer-oriented and person-oriented reasoning. In particular, since people often prefer to use a specific instance of a general fact rather than the fact itself, we see that a typical reasoning program does *not* usually reason as a person does. Paramodulation, as we shall see, is an excellent example of the kind of reasoning used by reasoning programs that can hardly be said to imitate a person's reasoning. On the other hand, for the kind of reasoning a person often uses but that a typical reasoning program does not, we can turn to that area of mathematics known as group theory. For example, where the identity of a group is denoted by e, the reasoning that permits deducing

$$(yz)(yz) = e$$

from the hypothesis that

$$xx = e$$

is not used by such programs, although such reasoning is quite typical of mathematics. The view of many experts in the field of automated reasoning is that using this type of reasoning, called *instantiation,* would markedly decrease the efficiency of reasoning programs, even though mathematicians obviously use it very effectively.

Because unification is at the heart of so much of what occurs in an automated reasoning program, and because an understanding of the inference rule paramodulation does not come easily, let us first give an example of the inference rule binary resolution to illustrate unification and prepare the way for the discussion of paramodulation. As promised, we can use the simple puzzle given in the preceding section for our illustration, focusing on clauses (4) and (5).

>Everyone is not female or not male
>(4)   ¬FEMALE(x) | ¬MALE(x)

>Roberta is female
>(5)   FEMALE(Roberta)

From the two statements to which clauses (4) and (5) correspond, one can obviously conclude that Roberta is not male. A reasoning program can reach the same conclusion by applying binary resolution to clauses (4) and (5). To do so, the program unifies the first literal in clause (4) with the only literal in clause (5)—which it does by uniformly replacing the variable x in clause (4) by Roberta—and cancels the literal in clause (5) with the replaced literal in clause (4). The resulting conclusion

>¬MALE(Roberta)

is obtained.

2.2.1 PARAMODULATION DEFINED WITH EXAMPLES. Rather than giving a formal definition of paramodulation, we shall, as in the preceding section, rely on examples. The first example illustrates the use of the simplest and most familiar form of equality substitution. The second illustrates a slightly more complex form of substitution in that variables occur in one of the hypotheses. The third example, substantially more complex, is by far the most interesting, for it shows how paramodulation generalizes the standard notion of equality substitution.

For the first example, paramodulation applied to both the equation $a + (-a) = 0$ and the statement $a + (-a)$ is congruent to b yields in a single step the conclusion or statement 0 is congruent to b. In clause form, *from*

>EQUAL(sum(a,minus(a)),0)

into

>CONGRUENT(sum(a,minus(a)),b)

one obtains the clause

    CONGRUENT(0,b)

by paramodulation.

For the second example, since variables such as x mean "for all", one can show that the following example of equality-oriented reasoning is logically correct—*logically sound*. Paramodulation applied to both the equation $a + (-a) = 0$ and the statement $x + (-a)$ is congruent to x yields in a single step the conclusion or statement 0 is congruent to a. In clause form, *from*

    EQUAL(sum(a,minus(a)),0)

into

    CONGRUENT(sum(x,minus(a)),x)

the clause

    CONGRUENT(0,a)

is obtained. This example illustrates some of the complexity of paramodulation; in particular, the second occurrence of the variable x in the *into clause* becomes the constant a in the conclusion, but the term containing the first occurrence of x becomes the constant 0 in the conclusion. Although the unification of the first argument of the *from clause* with the first argument of the *into clause* temporarily requires both occurrences of the variable x to be replaced by the constant a, paramodulation then requires an additional term replacement justified by equality substitution. In particular, in this second example, paramodulation requires the replacement of $a + (-a)$ by 0.

Finally, for the third and complex example, paramodulation applied to both the equation $x + (-x) = 0$ and the equation $y + (-y+z) = z$ yields in a single step the conclusion $y + 0 = -(-y)$. In clause form, *from*

    EQUAL(sum(x,minus(x)),0)

into

    EQUAL(sum(y,sum(minus(y),z)),z)

the clause

    EQUAL(sum(y,0),minus(minus(y)))

is obtained by paramodulation.

To see that this last clause is in fact a logical sequence of its two parents, one unifies the argument sum(x, minus(x)) with the term sum(minus(y), z), applies the corresponding substitution to both the *from* and *into clauses*, and then makes the appropriate term replacement justified by the typical use of equality. The substitution found by the attempt to unify the given argument and given term requires substituting minus(y) for x and minus(minus(y)) for z. To prepare for the (standard) use of equality in this third example, a nontrivial substitution for variables in both the *from* and the *into clauses* is required, which illustrates how paramodulation generalizes the usual notion of equality substitution. In contrast, in the standard use of equality substitution, one does *not* apply a nontrivial replacement for variables in both the *from* and the *into* statements.

Summarizing, a successful use of paramodulation combines in a single step the process of finding the (in an obvious sense) most general common domain for which both the *from* and the *into clauses* are relevant and applying standard equality substitution to that common domain. The complexity of this inference rule rests in part with its unnaturalness if viewed from the type of reasoning people employ, in part with the fact that the rule is permitted to apply nontrivial variable replacement to both of the statements under consideration, and in part with the fact that different occurrences of the same expression can be transformed differently. As an illustration of the third cited property, in the third example of paramodulation, the (term containing the) first occurrence of z is transformed to 0, but the second occurrence of z is transformed to minus(minus(y)).

2.2.2 THE POWER OF PARAMODULATION. A single application of paramodulation can lead to the deduction of an interesting conclusion that the usual mathematical reasoning requires more than one step to yield. In contrast to paramodulation, the mathematician or logician picks the instances—the substitutions of terms for variables—that might be of interest and then applies (the usual notion of) equality substitution. Paramodulation, on the other hand, picks the (maximal) instances of the *from* and *into clauses* automatically and, rather than deducing intermediate conclusions by applying the corresponding replacement of terms for variables, instead combines the instance picking with a standard application of equality substitution. Avoiding the retention of intermediate conclusions can contribute markedly to the performance of a reasoning program. The instances that a person chooses may be far less general than those chosen by the reasoning program in its attempt to apply paramodulation. As a result, the program may deduce a conclusion that is far more general than a person might deduce. Again the program benefits, for its efficiency often increases by having access to general conclusions rather than specific ones; people do not require such generality in most cases. Summarizing, the inference rule instantiation—replacing variables by terms in a statement to deduce a corollary—is frequently used, and used wisely, in mathematics and logic. Instantiation is *not* an inference rule offered by the typical reasoning program, for no known strategy exists for wisely choosing appropriate instances even though mathematicians and logicians do have that ability.

To give a second illustration of the power offered by paramodulation—if combined with a procedure (demodulation) used by reasoning programs to simplify expressions—we consider the following example so typical of mathematics. In the example, the conclusion that is reached with a string of equalities—if one applies the usual type of reasoning that occurs in mathematics—is drawn by a reasoning program in a single deduction step.

$$z = 0 + z = (x + (-x)) + z = x + ((-x) + z)$$

This string of equalities comprises a proof of an obvious but useful lemma in arithmetic and in group theory, the lemma that asserts the equality of the first and last expressions in the string of equalities. In clause notation, we have that *from* the right inverse

```
EQUAL(sum(x,minus(x)),0)
```

into associativity

```
EQUAL(sum(sum(u,v),z),sum(u,sum(v,z)))
```

the program can deduce

```
EQUAL(sum(0,z),sum(x,sum(minus(x),z)))
```

which it can then automatically simplify (see Section 2.4) to

```
EQUAL(z,sum(x,sum(minus(x),z)))
```

without producing any intermediate results.

2.3 Strategy

Since, from the preceding section, we know that an automated reasoning program has access to individual inference rules, such as paramodulation, that combine a number of mathematical reasoning steps into one step, the need for strategy to control such reasoning may be puzzling. However, when one discovers that, from certain single axioms in combinatory logic, 16 conclusions can be drawn by applying paramodulation, then the puzzlement quickly disappears. In particular, the axiom for the combinator W with

$$(Wx)y = (xy)y$$

is just such an axiom. One can imagine how many additional conclusions would be drawn were we to continue reasoning by focusing on pairs of those 16 conclusions, which comprise the first generation of descendants of W with itself, and then reason by focusing on the second generation. To avoid the flood of conclusions that can result if reasoning is uncontrolled, an automated reasoning program can use various types of strategy. On the one hand, some types of strategy are designed to direct the reasoning; on the other hand, some types are designed to restrict it. From a different perspective, some types of strategy are general in the sense that they apply to all inference rules, and others are specific in the sense that they apply to only a single inference rule.

Of those of a general nature, the most powerful restriction strategy that an automated reasoning program can use is called the *set of support strategy* (Wos et al., 1965). That strategy restricts the program's reasoning with the intention of sharply retarding the generation of irrelevant conclusions. To use the set of support strategy, one is required to choose a subset T of the set S of clauses given to the program to describe the problem to be studied. The program then draws a conclusion only if it is recursively traceable to T. Therefore, at the beginning of the program's attack on a problem (from a procedural viewpoint) an inference rule is applied to a pair of clauses from S only if at least one of them is in T. Any clause that is retained is automatically given the power of the clauses that are members of T. For example, an inference rule can be applied to a pair of clauses if one of them is a clause not in S. Stated another way, with the set of support strategy, the program is not allowed to apply an inference rule to a pair of clauses that are both in $S - T$.

Of those of a specific nature—in addition to the set of support strategy, which can be used to restrict the application of any inference rule—an automated reasoning program can also use a number of strategies designed with the express purpose of restricting the application of paramodulation. First, the program can be restricted from paramodulating *from* or *into* a variable. This restriction prevents a myriad of conclusions from being drawn. Such a restriction strategy is, in most cases, mandatory. After all, paramodulating *from* or *into* a variable will always yield a conclusion, because the corresponding unification can never fail. Second, the program can be required to paramodulate only from a specified side of each equality. In some cases, all applications of paramodulation are required to be from the left side only; in others, all are required to be from the right only.

2.4 Demodulation

The next topic for this review of automated reasoning is that of canonicalization, which is available to automated reasoning programs through the use of demodulation (Wos et al., 1967). In many areas of mathematics and logic, one often rewrites each new item of information into a canonical form. In automated reasoning, a similar action can occur. A sharp difference, however, exists between mathematics and automated reasoning. In the former, one uses canonicalization when it seems convenient and appropriate. In the latter, one cannot in most cases exercise such freedom, because, if each conclusion is not required to be automatically rewritten into a canonical form, the program will drown in information. Of course, some conclusions will be unaffected by the particular choice of demodulators (Wos et al., 1967) in a given problem.

One other difference exists between the use of canonicalization by a mathematician or logician and its use by a reasoning program. When a person uses various equalities for canonicalization, the equalities are applied only to the expressions chosen by the person; when a program applies such equalities, all expressions to which the equalities are applicable are in fact rewritten into a canonical form.

Now, let us examine some typical uses of canonicalization.

One might, for example, uniformly replace $-(-t)$ by t for any term t, or replace $r(s+t)$ by $rs+rt$ for terms r, s, and t. For such term replacements, many automated reasoning programs offer the mechanism *demodulation*, referred to earlier, which automatically rewrites expressions into a canonical form based on some set of rewrite rules called *demodulators*. The demodulators can be included among the input clauses, or the program can be asked to find potentially useful ones. For the two given examples, the demodulators

```
EQUAL(minus(minus(x)),x)
```

and

```
EQUAL(prod(x,sum(y,z)),sum(prod(x,z),prod(y,z)))
```

can be used, respectively.

As one might predict, care must be taken in the choice of which equality clauses to attempt to use as demodulators. In particular, an unwise choice can cause the program to loop. To see how looping can occur, let us consider what will happen when the equation for W is used as a demodulator and when the program encounters a term of a certain type. In particular, when the clause

```
(W) EQUAL(a(a(W,x),y),a(a(x,y),y))
```

is used as a demodulator and the term *WWW* is encountered, this term will be transformed to itself repeatedly without ever terminating. For a more interesting example, let us consider the expression

$$\Gamma = a(a(W,a(B, x)),a(W,a(B, x)))$$

and what occurs when the two demodulators

```
(W) EQUAL(a(a(W,x),y),a(a(x,y),y))
```

and

```
(B) EQUAL(a(a(a(B,x),y),z),a(x,a(y,z)))
```

are applied to Γ with the object of producing a canonical form. Demodulation begins by successfully applying W, then B, to obtain

```
a(x,Γ)
```

which leads to another successful application of W followed by B to obtain

```
a(x,a(x,Γ))
```

which of course leads to yet another success and, in fact, to a nonterminating sequence of successful applications of W and B.

Nevertheless, as long as one is careful about the choice of demodulators, the use of demodulation can sharply increase the effectiveness of a reasoning program in its search for assignment completion. Even further, for many studies, without the use of demodulation the program will simply require an inordinate amount of computer time to complete rather simple assignments.

2.5 Subsumption

We now come to the next-to-the-last topic of this section, a mechanism that is almost always essential for a reasoning program to be effective. Although the use of various types of strategy does indeed contribute markedly to the efficiency of an automated reasoning program, such a program continues to deduce conclusions that are trivial and unneeded corollaries of existing clauses. For example, if the program paramodulates *from* the second argument of the clause equivalent of

$$(Wx)y = (xy)y$$

into the first subargument of the second argument of the clause equivalent of

$$(W(Wx))y = ((xy)y)y$$

the program deduces the clause equivalent of

$$(W(Wx))y = ((Wx)y)y$$

which is a trivial corollary, in fact an instance, of

$$(Wx)y = (xy)y$$

and is therefore immediately discarded. The procedure for discarding such deductions is *subsumption* (Robinson, 1965). The clause A *subsumes* the clause B if there exists a uniform replacement of terms for variables in A that produces a clause that is a subclause of B.

For a second example of subsumption, an example that might not be expected, let us consider the two clauses

```
P(x) | P(y)
```

and

```
P(x)
```

and recall that a variable is relevant only to the clause in which it occurs. That the second clause subsumes the first follows immediately from the definition of subsumption. However, as it turns out, the first also subsumes the second, as can be seen by replacing y by x in the first to produce

```
P(x)
```

since a clause, by definition, does not allow duplicate literals; technically, a clause is defined as a set of distinct literals. As an aside, if we wished to have our program use instantiation as an inference rule to permit the program to imitate the corresponding type of reasoning (discussed in Section 2.2) that is often used in mathematics, we would be forced to protect the instances that were deduced so that subsumption would not immediately discard them.

Of especial use is the role of subsumption for removing clauses that assert the equality of a term with itself; such an assertion is, needless to say, usually of little interest and seldom useful. To remove such trivial clauses, the clause

```
        EQUAL(x,x)
```

for reflexivity of equality subsumes many clauses that would otherwise be kept. This clause, which must be included in the input if paramodulation is the chosen rule of inference, is also important in that a proof often terminates with the deduction of a clause of the form

```
        ¬EQUAL(t,t)
```

for some term t.

2.6 Proof by Contradiction

In keeping with the introductory nature of this chapter, we give only a simple proof by contradiction. For far more interesting examples of such proofs, we recommend the two books cited earlier (Wos et al., 1984; Wos, 1987a). For our example, we return to the trivial puzzle.

> Roberta, who is unmarried, has the job of teacher or nurse,
> and the job of nurse is held by a male. What is Roberta's job?

An automated reasoning program can solve this puzzle by being given the assumption that asserts that the correct answer is in fact false. The inference rule binary resolution suffices for finding a proof by contradiction.

A Proof by Contradiction

(1)   ¬HASAJOB(Roberta,teacher)
(2)   HASAJOB(Roberta,teacher) | HASAJOB(Roberta,nurse)
(3)   ¬HASAJOB(x,nurse) | MALE(x)
(4)   ¬FEMALE(x) | ¬MALE(x)
(5)   FEMALE(Roberta)

from (1) and (2), canceling two literals,

(6)   HASAJOB(Roberta,nurse)

from (6) and (3), uniformly substituting Roberta for x and canceling two literals,

(7)   MALE(Roberta)

from (7) and (4), uniformly substituting Roberta for x and canceling two literals,

(8)   ¬FEMALE(Roberta)

Clause (8) contradicts clause (5), and the proof by contradiction is complete.

In addition to providing a specific example of proof by contradiction, the given proof also illustrates the use of strategy. In particular, this same proof would be found by an automated reasoning program using the set of support strategy in one of the recommended ways. One recommendation for the use of this strategy is to select for the set of support those input clauses that correspond to the union of the special hypothesis and the denial of the conclusion. By definition, the special hypothesis is the information (if any) that is added, to the underlying axioms and to the lemmas that are supplied, to form the hypothesis of the theorem. In other words, when a theorem is of the form **if** P **then** Q, the special hypothesis (if any) is that part of P that remains after one ignores the axioms of the underlying field and all the lemmas that have been supplied. In this simple puzzle, no special hypothesis exists, and the denial of the conclusion—the assumed false answer to the question—is represented with clause (1) only. A quick glance at the given proof shows that at no point is binary resolution applied to two clauses that are both from the input clauses, if clause (1) is ignored. Put another way, the entire proof is recursively traceable to clause (1), the only clause in the set of support when the program begins its attack on the question.

We have completed our review of automated reasoning. Therefore, we now turn to some of the applications of the field. As we shall see, an automated reasoning program has provided valuable assistance in a number of ways and in a number of areas.

3 PROGRAM VERIFICATION

Of the frequently cited applications of automated reasoning, we have received the greatest satisfaction from proving theorems in mathematics and logic. Nevertheless, many believe that program verification is the application that will have the greatest impact. To define program verification, we quote Boyer and Moore (1985): "Computer programs may be regarded as formal mathematical objects whose properties are subject to mathematical proof. Program verification is the use of formal, mathematical techniques to debug software and software specifications." (The article from which this quote is taken provides an excellent introduction to program verification and other applications of automated reasoning.)

Given the incentive for applying automated reasoning to the proof that computer programs satisfy the claims made for them—the application we refer to as program verification—one is immediately presented with two sharply opposite possibilities. On the one hand, since computer programs can be large, complicated, and highly disorganized, one might conjecture that, in general, it will never be possible to produce formal proofs establishing that computer programs fulfill their claims. On the other hand, in view of Boyer and Moore's quoted position, since automated reasoning programs have already succeeded in proving theorems that are clearly difficult to prove, one might conjecture that program verification is indeed a viable application.

Fortunately, to resolve the debate, we need not be content with mere speculation. Instead, we can cite a number of successes with existing algorithms and computer codes. Because of the impressiveness of some of these achievements, because of the obvious sharp increase in the power of automated reasoning programs, and because of the trend toward carefully written computer programs, we are now certain that program verification is far more than a viable application. To support this position, let us turn to specific successes. Some of these achievements are sufficiently impressive that we are convinced that, as the power of reasoning programs grows and as the style of computer programming improves, the interest in and the number of successes with automated reasoning will increase sharply.

Of the various efforts focusing on using an automated reasoning program for program verification, that of Boyer and Moore deserves the most acclaim. Their approach was to design and implement a program whose main purpose is in fact to verify algorithms and computer code. They refer to their program as a theorem prover, simply because its use is based on proving one theorem after another. The theorems submitted to the Boyer-Moore program (Boyer and Moore, 1979) are obtained from the attempt to prove that some given algorithm fulfills its intended purpose or from the attempt to prove that some given computer program satisfies the claims made for it. As the following list of successes shows, Boyer and Moore have indeed designed a powerful program, a program that demonstrates that automated reasoning can be and has been most useful for program verification.

Among the theorems proved by the Boyer-Moore theorem prover are the invertibility of the Rivest, Shamir, and Adleman public key encryption algorithm (Boyer and Moore, 1984), the soundness and completeness of a propositional calculus decision procedure, the soundness of an arithmetic simplifier (actually used in their program), the termination of Takeuchi's function, and the correctness of many elementary list and tree processing functions. They have also used their program to prove properties of many recursive functions. The Boyer-Moore theorem-proving program has also been used successfully to prove the correctness of various Fortran programs—more precisely, to prove the verification conditions for such programs. Among the Fortran programs proved correct are a fast string-searching algorithm, an integer square root algorithm using Newton's method, and a linear-time majority vote algorithm. These programs are each relatively small, requiring no more than a page of code. Nevertheless, the correctness arguments are fairly deep.

If, in contrast to the small Fortran programs that we have just cited, one wishes examples of rather larger programs that have been verified, they can be found among the successes obtained with two other reasoning programs. The two systems—the Stanford Verifier by David Luckham (Igarashi et al., 1973) and his students at Stanford University and the Gypsy Verification Environment by Don Good (1982) and his colleagues at the University of Texas at Austin—were designed for the express purpose of program verification.

These two verification systems present the user with an integrated set of tools and specially tailored programming languages designed to make verification more convenient.

The programming language supported by the Stanford Verifier is a variant of Pascal. The theorem prover used in the system is a rewrite-rule-based simplifier built on a decision procedure by Oppen and Nelsonn. The Stanford system was used to verify a compiler for Pascal by Polak consisting of approximately 3000 lines of executable code. The Gypsy Verification Environment (GVE) supports the programming language Gypsy, a derivative of Pascal, which provides concurrency and a somewhat cleaner semantics. The theorem prover used in GVE was adapted from a prover by Bledsoe (Bledsoe and Bruell, 1974). GVE was used to verify a communications interface to a computer network consisting of over 4200 lines of executable code; some 2600 verification conditions were proved in that effort. GVE has also been used to verify a "message flow modulator", which can be viewed as a switch on a communications line that shunts messages with certain properties to a branch line.

We close this section on the application of automated reasoning to program verification with one final citation. The success under consideration, obtained by Smith, Wojcik, Chisholm, and Kljaich (Chisholm et al., 1986; Kljaich et al., 1987, 1988), concerns the verification of software, hardware, and their interface in a system designed by Draper Laboratories to replace certain failing sensors in a nuclear reactor at Argonne National Laboratory. The reactor in question was designed in the late 1950s with the expectation of being used for approximately 15 years, and therefore the fact that its sensors are failing is no surprise. Since the reactor still provides much useful data, the software/hardware replacement system merits serious study. The automated reasoning program ITP (Lusk and Overbeek, 1984a, 1984b) played the key role in the verification of the fault-tolerant (replacement) system designed by Draper. In addition to proving that the appropriate properties are present in the Draper system—by examining the work performed by the reasoning program ITP—researchers found important simplifications that could be made to the design of the system. The success of Smith and his colleagues is, in an obvious sense, one of the best examples of the use of an automated reasoning program to verify the claims made, at the highest level, for a system.

4 CIRCUIT DESIGN AND VALIDATION

Because of the similarity of circuit validation to program verification, let us first focus on the use of an automated reasoning program for validation before focusing on its use for design. Hunt (1986), using the Boyer-Moore theorem prover, validated a 16-bit, microprogrammed microprocessor similar in complexity to a PDP-11. The proof that this microprocessor, named FM8501, possesses the appropriate properties involved approximately 100 proofs by induction about n-bit hardware devices. In addition, by induction, Hunt (1985) proved the correctness of wait loops in the microprogram used to control FM8501.

At this point—especially for those who have access to an automated reasoning program, but a program that lacks a mechanism for induction—one might wonder whether circuit validation is a viable application of automated reasoning without the use of induction. Indeed it is. For example, a 297-step proof validating the correctness of the design of a 16-bit adder was obtained (Wojcik, 1983) in less than 20 seconds of CPU time on an IBM 3033 by the reasoning program AURA (Smith, 1988), and without the use of induction. That proof would have been tedious, and perhaps out of reach, for a person working unaided.

In contrast to the close relationship that exists between circuit validation and program verification, the application of automated reasoning to circuit design presents sharply different obstacles to overcome. Fortunately, preliminary evidence strongly suggests that, despite these obstacles, circuit design is indeed a viable application. For an example, rather than again focusing on some problem selected from the real world, let us instead offer a puzzle to solve by discussing a problem taken from an exam given to engineers. The puzzle asks one to design a circuit that will return the signals not(x), not(y), and not(z), when x, y, and z are input to it. The task would be trivial were it not for one important constraint. One can use as many AND and OR gates as one wishes, but one cannot use more than two NOT gates. For those who are not familiar with circuit design and the various types of gates, we give the following equivalent problem, but phrased in terms of assembly language programming: One is asked to write a program that will store in locations U, V, and W the 1s complement of locations x, y, and z. One can use as many COPY, OR, and AND instructions as one wishes, but no more than two COMP (1s complement) instructions.

This circuit design problem (equivalently, programming problem) has been solved by the automated reasoning program ITP. Its solution and a discussion of circuit design and of circuit validation as applications of automated reasoning are given in Wos et al. (1984, Chapters 7 and 8). One of the distinct advantages offered by an automated reasoning program for circuit design is the program's ability to automatically apply rules of canonicalization. For those who might not be familiar with circuit design, a common practice is to rewrite expressions for a circuit into some preferred form where, for example, the NOT gates are migrated to the innermost possible place. Whatever one prefers, a reasoning program can effortlessly accommodate one's preference. One simply gives the program the appropriate rules—called demodulators (Wos et al., 1967)—for canonicalization, and the program applies them where they should be applied.

5 RESEARCH AID FOR FINDING PRACTICAL SOLUTIONS

One of the applications for automated reasoning that is seldom discussed concerns its use in finding some technique that serves as a practical solution to some given problem. To illustrate what can occur, we focus on an actual problem on which we worked, a problem posed by one of the major car manufacturers. The problem concerns assembly line scheduling.

The cars that come off an assembly line for a car manufacturer have a variety of options: air conditioning or not, sun roof or not, power windows or not, and others. Even more obvious, cars come in many colors. On any given day, the people responsible for running the assembly line know how many cars are expected to come off the line, and they also know the complete list of options and colors for each car. Those responsible must choose an order for the cars to be sent through the assembly line. If the sequencing of cars is poorly chosen, then the assembly line may fail to meet its quota, and fail badly.

One of the time-consuming operations appears to be the installation of air conditioning. If those who install this feature are asked to complete the corresponding job for, say, 10 cars in a row with no car passing their station without requiring air conditioning, the station may be incapable of meeting this heavy and continuous demand. Of course, because the appropriate information is not given out lightly, we can use only hypothetical figures. The important point is that, when the capacity of some aspect of an assembly line is exceeded, the line will not function as intended.

We were told of the scheduling problem in a general way by the car manufacturer and were asked whether we could find some way to produce a "good" algorithm for sequencing the day's cars, given the features required for each of those cars. Our response was to suggest that, since much of the pertinent data is proprietary and, more important, since technology continues to advance, what the manufacturer might actually desire is some means to experiment on demand with new algorithms. In other words, the solution that was most desirable, from a very practical viewpoint, was to find a means for the manufacturer to research various algorithms easily and to resume that research whenever improved technology called for it.

We did, in fact, provide such a means. We designed an approach for using the automated reasoning program ITP to take a given set of cars with assigned features and produce different sequences of those cars, where the sequence is determined by the user's choice of various parameters and the choice of the priorities for the various features (Parrello et al., 1986). The mechanism that ITP uses to determine a sequence is based on a number of parameters and on a penalty system. If the user wishes to experiment to see what would result from changing priorities or, in effect, changing the algorithm for assigning the order of cars for the assembly line, essentially what is required is to change the various parameter settings and penalties. When a good algorithm is found, then the suggestion is to take that algorithm and write a computer program in a high-level language to execute the algorithm. Even further, when and if the technology changes or when and if somebody has a new approach to try, all that is required is to again use ITP to conduct the appropriate experiments.

In other words, we designed an environment—whose main component is the use of an automated reasoning program—that enables the user to search for a practical solution to a given problem. Although the given problem that prompted our research was that of assembly line scheduling, one might easily imagine that—given an entirely unrelated problem to solve—the results of our research could be modified and imitated (where appropriate) to design a similar environment. From a larger perspective, we demonstrated that an automated reasoning program can indeed be used as a research aid for finding practical solutions.

6 PROGRAMMING LANGUAGE AND COMBINATORY LOGIC

To complement the preceding material, at this point we turn to material so current that it rests to some extent on supposition. We are in part motivated by our view that, when possible, a chapter covering a variety of topics stimulates inerest in a field when the chapter includes a challenge—a challenge in the form of questions that have just been posed. Therefore, we include the following discussion of the use of an automated reasoning program for the study of certain aspects of programming language. Because this chapter is but one of a number of chapters on a variety of subjects, only a taste of the subject can be given here. Nevertheless, we shall give sufficient evidence to support the position that the application of automated reasoning to the area of programming language—specifically, to combinatory logic—is indeed far more than a viable application.

One of the more interesting developments in the area of programming language is that focusing on the use of combinators as the basic instruction set. Of course, since programming with combinators is rather like programming with a Turing machine, the notion is not that of having a person use combinators directly. Rather, as David Turner (1979) explains, the intention is for the programmer to write code in some high-level language and then have that code compiled into combinators. In other words, combinators would comprise the instruction set for the computer. Such computers have in fact been designed and built, which brings us to the point of this section—to the discussion of an area that may be pure supposition.

The notion we have is that, if a computer is to use combinators as its instructions, then—as with any assembly language—one must make a choice about which combinators to use. In particular, just as with many sets of machine instructions, combinators have the property that one combinator can be expressed in terms of others, depending of course on the combinator to be expressed and on those available for producing the expression. The following simple example illustrates how it can work and at the same time provides a very small taste of combinatory logic.

Just as one specifies the actions of some machine instruction by saying what the instruction does to its arguments, one specifies the actions of a combinator by giving an equation that expresses its effect on other combinators. Let us consider the following three combinators, where the variables x, y, and z implicitly range over all combinators.

$$((Bx)y)z = x(yz)$$
$$(Wx)y = (xy)y$$
$$(Lx)y = x(yy)$$

Now let us consider how $(BW)B$ acts on other combinators. By using the given equations for B and W, we can prove that

$$(((BW)B)x)y = (W(Bx))y = ((Bx)y)y = x(yy)$$

for all x and y. In other words, $(BW)B$ acts exactly as L does. Therefore, from the viewpoint of programming language, if the computer offers as instructions B and W, then it also in effect offers the instruction L by using the combination $(BW)B$.

To complete the stage setting for presenting the challenge, stating the newly posed questions, and focusing directly on the application of automated reasoning to combinatory logic, we turn to the topic of fixed point combinators. By definition, if the combinator Θ satisfies

$$\Theta x = x(\Theta x)$$

for all combinators x, then Θ is called a *fixed point combinator*. Fixed point combinators are relevant to programming language because each can be used to remove recursion. As various logicians have informed us, the construction of fixed point combinators can be an extremely arduous task. The precise construction problem asks whether, given a set of combinators, one can find an expression purely in terms of those combinators such that the found expression is a fixed point combinator. If one can construct such a combinator for a given set P of combinators, then, by definition, the set P satisfies the *strong fixed point property*. In other words, using the given definitions, one can correctly conclude that the problem of determining whether a given set P satisfies the strong fixed point property can be very difficult to solve.

To illustrate how difficult the construction problem can be, let us first give a simple case to solve and then give its opposite. If we consider the set P consisting only of the combinator L and the combinator S with

$$((Sx)y)z = (xz)(yz)$$

we can easily prove that P satisfies the strong fixed point property. All we need do is focus on the combinator $\Theta = (SL)L$. Using the equations for L and S, we can quickly show that Θ is a fixed point combinator—in fact, one that is well known. On the other hand, if we instead consider the set P consisting of B and W alone, then a proof that P satisfies the strong fixed point property—which in fact it does—is far more difficult to supply. To gain some insight into how difficult this problem is to solve, one might pause immediately and try for, say, one hour to find an appropriate fixed point combinator; such a combinator does exist.

For those who have made an attempt to find such a combinator and for those who have continued on without pausing, we now give our favorite solution to the problem. We let

$$\Theta = ((B((B((B(WW))W))B))B)$$

We found this new fixed point combinator in late 1986, published the corresponding research in McCune and Wos (1987), and note that we would not have succeeded were it not for substantial assistance from an automated reasoning program.

We are now ready to issue the challenge, pose some questions, and focus directly on the application of automated reasoning to combinatory logic. The challenge is a friendly one. We wish to know of fixed point combinators with unusual properties, and we wish to know a number of other uses for such combinators. With regard to the newly posed questions—to be succinct—we simply ask, How useful would it be to have access to an automated procedure for searching for expressions that define one combinator in terms of some given set of combinators? For example, would such a procedure—which would rely heavily on the use of an automated reasoning program—be very useful for deciding which instructions to implement for a computer executing combinators as its instruction set?

As for the final aspect of this section—the excellence of using an automated reasoning program to study combinatory logic—we offer the following evidence. We have formulated (what appears to be) the first systematic method for searching for fixed point combinators (Wos and McCune, 1988). The method is especially effective when applied by an automated reasoning program. With its use, we have succeeded in answering a number of previously open questions.

We have also developed an approach that is very effective for a large class of problems whose object is to define one combinator in terms of some given set of combinators. With its use, we have succeeded in answering a number of previously open questions. Our success suggests that an automated reasoning program could be used, applying our approach, to study various possible sets of machine instructions for a computer using combinators. Such a study would be very useful—and this is supposition on our part—as an aid in deciding which combinators to implement.

7 PORTABLE AUTOMATED REASONING PROGRAMS

For a field to advance markedly, when it is essentially empirical, its technology must be tested under a variety of circumstances. Unfortunately, in many cases the needed variety of use has been hampered by inaccessibility. Such is not the case—now. Three portable automated reasoning programs are available. Boyer and Moore's program written in Lisp, whose main use is program verification, can be obtained electronically; for the appropriate details, either of these researchers can be contacted at the Computer Science Department of the University of Texas. The general-purpose automated reasoning program ITP and the library LMA of underlying subroutines, both written in Pascal and designed and implemented by Lusk, McCune, and Overbeek, can be easily obtained on tape; the precise details can be found in Appendix A of Wos (1987a). (Obtaining the codes electronically is impractical because of their size.) The third portable automated reasoning program, OTTER, written in C and designed and implemented by McCune in recent months, is expected to be available electronically or available on tape or diskette; details can be obtained from McCune in the Mathematics and Computer Science Division at Argonne National Laboratory.

For the following reasons, OTTER deserves particular attention. Although this program is not a replacement for the well-distributed program ITP, since the latter permits interactive use and automatic connection to Prolog, nevertheless it offers certain advantages over ITP. OTTER runs from eight to fifteen times faster than ITP and, for many problems, uses much less memory. OTTER runs on PCs, a feature not to be taken lightly, as many will agree. Even when run on a PC, this program has solved rather difficult problems. Finally, OTTER is the subject of a parallel-processing effort in automated reasoning within the Mathematics and Computer Science Division at Argonne National Laboratory; the results of that effort may be available by 1991.

8 THE FUTURE OF AUTOMATED REASONING

When one is a researcher in a field, the obvious expectation is that such a person will be optimistic. Since—to be candid—"optimistic" is too weak for our present state of mind, let us simply and quickly list the reasons for our view.

For fields like automated reasoning—which rely equally on theory, application, and implementation—progress occurs in direct proportion to the number of enthusiastic people who test and question the developments. The most significant test for this field rests with the results of using the reasoning programs that have been designed and implemented. For the appropriate amount of testing, questioning, and use of reasoning programs to occur—and, therefore, for advances to occur rapidly—certain items must be in place or nearly in place, and fortunately they are. There must exist material that is easily read, as in Wos et al. (1984); research problems presented with a means to test solutions to them, as in Wos (1987a); a journal in which to publish, such as the *Journal of Automated Reasoning;* an organization for exchanging information, such as the Association for Automated Reasoning; and, perhaps most important, a program with the appropriate attributes. The program must be portable, convenient to use, easy to modify, and very fast; and it must offer the main elements of automated reasoning. In addition, the desirable program must be continually updated to take advantage of new developments. We consider McCune's program OTTER to fulfill all the given requirements.

The other factors that produce our sharply positive view about the future of automated reasoning rest with the mounting successes and the work in parallel processing. Ever deeper theorems are being proved with a program playing the role of automated reasoning assistant. Markedly more involved computer programs are being verified with a reasoning program. In general, harder problems are being solved, and harder questions being answered, where the needed information is obtained from the use of an automated reasoning program. Finally, of all of the areas in computer science with which we are familiar, automated reasoning—more than any other—is amenable to parallel processing (Wos, 1987a, Chapter 7).

Of course, many obstacles still exist [see Wos (1987a, Chapter 2)] that prevent automated reasoning programs from being far more powerful. For example, too often a reasoning program strays from the relevant path, too many copies of the same conclusion are drawn, and too frequently the needed clauses for studying a new area are unavailable. With regard to the first of these three obstacles, a reasoning program can deduce 10,000 conclusions, using fewer than 20 in the sought-after proof. Although all of those 10,000 conclusions follow logically from the problem description, obviously almost all of them are unneeded. With regard to the second obstacle, we have examples of theorems from lattice theory with the property that the program, during its successful search for a proof, draws more than 3000 conclusions which are immediately discarded because they are already present. As for the study of new areas, frequently one finds that the needed axioms in clause form are unavailable, which presents a third obstacle to overcome. In addition to the three cited obstacles, too little is currently known about how to take full advantage of parallelism. For example, can one formulate a strategy that partitions the conclusions that are drawn into small subsets such that a reasoning program can focus its reasoning on the set of subsets in parallel and then pool its results to reduce the time to find proofs by a factor of 1000? But, despite many obstacles to overcome—even with the current state of the art—the number of successes continues to grow.

The necessary ingredients for a future that is brilliant and exciting exist now—except, possibly, for the most vital of all. That key ingredient is a vast amount of experimentation by inquisitive and eager researchers attempting to extend the power of automated reasoning programs and constantly seeking new applications. Since we conjecture that such researchers finally exist, and exist in growing numbers, we predict that within ten years, rather than functioning as automated reasoning assistants—as various reasoning programs do now—such programs will begin to function as automated reasoning associates and, eventually, as colleagues.

ACKNOWLEDGMENT

This work was supported by the Applied Mathematical Sciences subprogram of the Office of Energy Research, U.S. Department of Energy, under Contract W-31-109-Eng-38.

REFERENCES

Bledsoe, W. W., and Bruell, P. (1974). A Man-Machine Theorem-Proving System. *AI* **5**:51–72.
Boyer, R. S., and Moore J S. (1979). *A Computational Logic*. Academic Press, New York.
Boyer, R. S., and Moore, J S. (1984). Proof Checking the RSA Public Key Encryption Algorithm. *Am. Math. Monthly* **91**(3):181–189.
Boyer, R. S., and Moore, J S. (1985). Program Verification. *J. Autom. Reasoning* **1**(1):17–23.
Chisholm, G., Kljaich, J., Smith, B., and Wojcik, A. (1986). An Approach to the Verification of a Fault-Tolerant, Computer-Based Reactor Safety System—A Case Study Utilizing Automated Reasoning. NP-4924 and RP-2686-1 Final Report. Electric Power Research Institute, Palo Alto, Calif.
Good, D. I. (1982). The Proof of a Distributed System in Gypsy. Technical Report 30. Institute for Computing Science, University of Texas at Austin, Austin, Texas.
Hunt, W. (1985). FM8501: A Verified Microprocessor. Technical Report 47. University of Texas at Austin, Austin, Texas.
Hunt, W. (1987). The Mechanical Verification of a Microprocessor. In: *From HDL Descriptions to Guaranteed Correct Circuit Designs* (D. Borrione, ed.). North-Holland, New York.
Igarashi, S., London, R. L., and Luckham, D. C. (1973). Automatic Program Verification I: A Logical Basis and Its Implementation. Report ISI/RR-73-11. Information Science Institute, University of Southern California, Los Angeles.
Kljaich, J., Wojcik, A. S., and Smith, B. T. (1987). Formal Verification of Properties of Digital Systems, Using an Automated Reasoning System. In: *Proceedings of the Sixth Annual IEEE Phoenix Conference on Computers and Communications* (O. Friesen and F. Golshani, eds.). IEEE, New York, pp. 486–491.
Kljaich, J., Smith, B. T., and Wojcik, A. S. (1989). Formal Verification of Fault-Tolerance Using Theorem-Proving Techniques. *IEEE Trans. Compu.* **38**(3):366–376.
Lusk, E., and Overbeek, R. (1984a). The Automated Reasoning System ITP. Technical Report ANL-84-27. Argonne National Laboratory, Argonne, Ill.
Lusk, E., and Overbeek, R. (1984b). Logic Machine Architecture Inference Mechanisms—Layer 2 User Reference Manual Release 2.0. Technical Report ANL-82-84, Rev. 1, Argonne National Laboratory, Argonne, Ill.
McCune, W., and Wos, L. (1987). A Case Study in Automated Theorem Proving: Finding Sages in Combinatory Logic. *J. Autom. Reasoning* **3**(1):91–108.
Parrello, B., Kabat, W., and Wos, L. (1986). Job-Shop Scheduling Using Automated Reasoning: A Case Study of the Car-Sequencing Problem. *J. Autom. Reasoning* **2**(1):1–42.
Robinson, G., and Wos, L. (1969). Paramodulation and Theorem-Proving in First-Order Theories with Equality. In: *Machine Intelligence,* Vol. 4 (B. Meltzer and D. Michie, eds.). Edinburgh University Press, Edinburgh, pp. 135–150.
Robinson, J. (1965). A Machine-Oriented Logic Based on the Resolution Principle. *J. ACM* **12**:23–41.
Smith, B. (1988). Reference Manual for the Environmental Theorem Prover, An Incarnation of AURA. Technical Report ANL-88-2. Argonne National Laboratory, Argonne, Ill.
Turner, D. A. (1979). A New Implementation Technique for Applicative Languages. *Software—Prac. Exper.* **9**:31–49.
Wojcik, A. (1983). Formal Design Verification of Digital Systems. Proceedings of the Twentieth Design Automation Conference (Miami Beach, Fl.), IEEE, New York, pp. 228–234.
Wos, L. (1987a). *Automated Reasoning: 33 Basic Research Problems*. Prentice-Hall, Englewood Cliffs, N.J.
Wos, L. (1987b). Department of Energy brochure on Basic Energy Sciences accomplishments (to appear).
Wos, L., and McCune, W. W. (1988). Searching for Fixed Point Combinators by Using Automated Theorem Proving: A Preliminary Report. Technical Report ANL-88-10. Argonne National Laboratory, Argonne, Ill.

Wos, L., and Robinson, G. (1973). Maximal Models and Refutation Completeness: Semidecision Procedures in Automatic Theorem Proving. In: *Word Problems: Decision Problems and the Burnside Problem in Group Theory* (W. Boone, F. Cannonito, and R. Lyndon, eds.). North-Holland, New York, pp. 609–639.

Wos, L., Overbeek, R., Lusk, E., and Boyle, J. (1984). *Automated Reasoning: Introduction and Applications*. Prentice-Hall, Englewood Cliffs, N.J.

Wos, L., Robinson, G., and Carson, D. (1965). Efficiency and Completeness of the Set of Support Strategy in Theorem Proving. *J. ACM* **12**:536–541.

Wos, L., Robinson, G., Carson, D., and Shalla, L. (1967). The Concept of Demodulation in Theorem Proving. *J. ACM* **14**:698–709.

CHAPTER 4

ROBOT PROBLEM SOLVING

THOMAS DEAN

1 INTRODUCTION

A robot is a programmable device capable of sensing and affecting its environment. We are interested in the practical problem of programming such a device to do useful work. We need not get too technical concerning what it means to "sense" or "affect" an environment; for the applications we will be considering, the meaning of these terms will be clear. The hardware comprising the robot can be broken down into general-purpose computing machinery, sensors for extracting information concerning the state of the environment, and actuators for influencing the state of the environment. Figure 4-1 shows the general architecture of a robot as seen from a programmer's perspective. As far as the programmer is concerned, the sensors and actuators are just complex peripheral devices, like tape drives or terminals. We will assume that the architecture is fixed and that the task of the programmer is to write software that runs on the general-purpose computing machinery and controls the robot to achieve some particular purpose.

Robots of the sort we are concerned with in this chapter differ from the special-purpose devices that characterized automation in the 1960s in that they are meant to handle a range of industrial tasks with no change in hardware and only minor changes in programming. The idea is that the same basic hardware used to perform janitorial chores in an office building could, with some programming, be used to move appliances around in a warehouse or service farm machinery in the field. To achieve this flexibility, not only must the hardware be general purpose, but also the software must be sufficiently general to simplify the job of reprogramming the robot to perform a new task. You do not

FIGURE 4-1
General robot architecture.

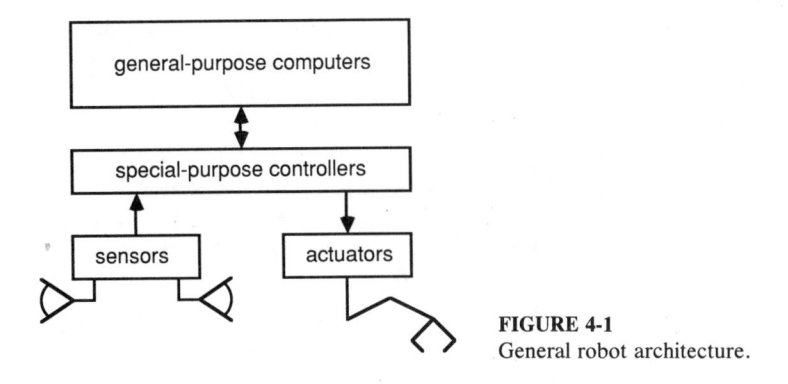

program the robot to change the oil filter on a specific model of farm tractor; rather, you program the robot to understand the assembling and disassembling of objects in somewhat general terms, and then have the robot figure out how to solve the particular problem of changing the oil filter on a 1987 International Harvester Model 4A by applying its general assembly/disassembly knowledge.

The sort of problem solving that a robot does is different from that employed in designing an automotive part or laying out a mask for a silicon chip; the robot is embedded in a complex environment, and it has limited ability to control and sense. The robot has to interact with other processes as they manifest themselves in space and change over time.

To get a robot to do what you want it to, the programmer has to tell the robot how and when to extract information about its environment and how and when to deploy its actuators to influence the environment. This process of telling the robot how to behave can be exceedingly complex. The programmer has to anticipate the situations in which the robot may find itself, ensure that the robot will be able to recognize those situations, and program the robot to respond in an appropriate manner. For any interesting application, it is impractical to list all situations in which the robot may find itself. Instead, the programmer tries to specify general classes of situations and advice about what the robot is to do when it is in a situation belonging to a particular class. When confronted with a specific situation, the robot tries to determine what class the situation belongs to and then uses the advice stored regarding that class of situations to determine what to do.

Sometimes the situation may be ambiguous, and it may not be clear what advice applies, or the situation may be recognizable but the advice offered is ambiguous or conflicting. This sort of problem is bound to arise in programming robots for complex environments. To cope with such problems, the robot is provided with a means of evaluating possible courses of action. Essentially the robot has a model of its environment that enables it to predict the consequences of its actions and those processes that are known to be active in that environment. Given a possible course of action, the robot can use its model to predict whether or not the course of action will have the desired effect.

To review, a robot is a programmable device embedded in a complex environment. We are interested in programming robots so that they can easily be set to perform new tasks or extended to handle increased possibilities. The basic idea for achieving this sort of flexible and extensible behavior is to provide the robot with general knowledge about its environment and general knowledge about solving problems, and then program it to apply this general knowledge in specific situations. Effective problem solving depends upon having a good predictive model that the robot can use to evaluate possible courses of action suggested as a result of problem solving.

The idea of robots having knowledge, understanding abstract concepts, and solving problems may be a little difficult to swallow, but we have in mind a very specific instantiation of these notions. We say that a robot solves a problem when, faced with a general sort of task to perform (e.g., empty all wastepaper baskets on the floor on which you are currently located) and a specific situation in which to perform that task (e.g, the robot is on the 14th floor of an office building in downtown Boston), the robot generates the appropriate commands to carry out the specified task. We say that a robot has a knowledge of an abstract concept if it has stored in memory information pertaining to a wide class of situations and is programmed to apply that information when appropriate.

A key issue in getting robots to solve problems concerns *representation*. How do we encode information about the robot's environment to facilitate programming the robot to perform useful work? In this chapter, we will be interested in general methods for representing and reasoning about space and time to support problem solving for applications in robotics. Before we get into details, we will describe a specific domain of application that will be used throughout the rest of the chapter to draw examples.

2 A DOMAIN FOR EXPLORING ROBOT PROBLEM SOLVING

The techniques that we will be describing in this chapter are quite general; they are, however, more appropriate for some applications than they are for others. The techniques of this chapter can be characterized by their explicit use of symbolic modeling in generating sequences of commands to control the behavior of a robot. Symbolic modeling techniques attempt to model the world in terms of logical relations between symbols corresponding to the objects of interest in a given domain. There are plenty of applications for which symbolic modeling techniques are more complex than is necessary and may, in fact, pose problems due to their computational overhead. For instance, it is possible to develop a symbolic model for predicting the behavior of a projectile for purposes of tracking; however, if the projectile's trajectory is simple (e.g., ballistic), a straightforward tracking method based on a technique from estimation theory called *Kalman filtering* is likely to provide perfectly acceptable performance. Moreover, given current state-of-the-art symbolic manipulation techniques, it may actually be difficult to implement a symbolic modeling approach that runs fast enough to provide acceptable performance.

In the Kalman filtering approach, the designer uses a model to develop the control algorithm, but, unlike the techniques described in this chapter, the control algorithm does not explicitly make use of the model. Symbolic problem-solving techniques are useful when the problem to be solved is complex, involving many different factors, and the resulting system is meant to be extensible or easily customized. The basic idea is that the problem-solving techniques are quite general and that all that is needed to extend or customize the system is to provide specific information about the application.

The application domain chosen for the examples used in this chapter is that of an automated materials handler—a computer-controlled forklift—given the task of filling orders and shelving stock in an industrial warehouse setting. Shipments of supplies (appliances in the examples provided) arrive in tractor-trailer trucks at the unloading dock, and their contents have to be catalogued and stored in the appropriate (predesignated) areas of the warehouse. Trucks arrive at the loading dock with stock orders. To fill an order, the robot must load the truck with the items specified on the order. Shipments and orders can arrive at any time. The numbers of orders and shipments over an interval of time can be predicted with a certain probability as a function of the current time and the current set of known orders and shipments. The sequence in which tasks are handled is up to the discretion of the robot controller. Orders have deadlines. If an order is not filled by its deadline, then there is a penalty that accrues as a function of the time that the truck picking up the order remains waiting in the loading dock. In addition, the warehouse is charged by the hour for any time over a set limit that a truck sits waiting to be unloaded.

All items stored in the warehouse are palletized: they are attached to special fixtures, called *pallets,* that facilitate picking the items up and moving them about with the use of a forklift. A pallet is a low hollow wooden structure open front and rear that supports an item so that a forklift can position its forks under the item in order to transport it from one place to another. The pallet is generally anchored to the item it supports so that the two move about as one unit. While pallets considerably simplify materials handling, there are still problems involved in positioning the forklift so as to insert the forks in a pallet: the robot has to be positioned front or rear facing the pallet and aligned so as to allow the fork to pass under the supported item without hitting the side of the pallet (see Fig. 4-2).

To complicate matters somewhat, orders may require certain assembly operations. In the warehouse domain, assembly involves installing options in stock items (e.g., adding an ice maker or decorative panel to a refrigerator). Installation requires taking the stock item and the parts for the options to a stationary robot, the *assembler,* which actually carries out the necessary modifications. The assembler, pictured in Fig. 4-3 has an input conveyor; an output conveyor; a control panel with on, off, and reset buttons; and a malfunction warning light. To install an option, the robot must turn the assembler off if it is

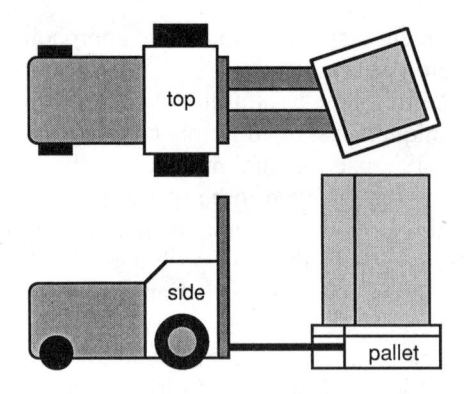

FIGURE 4-2
Two views of the robot lifting a palletized appliance.

on, place the stock item and the necessary parts on the input conveyor, and turn the assembler on. After a fixed amount of time depending on the options to be installed, the appliance with the options correctly installed will *usually* appear at the end of the output conveyor. Occasionally (i.e., with some probability) the installation will fail, the assembler will halt, and the malfunction light will turn on, signaling a problem. If the assembler malfunctions during an installation, the reset button has to be pushed before the assembler will attempt the installation again.

Figure 4-4 shows the basic layout of the warehouse used in the examples. The exact dimensions of the warehouse are not immediately important to our discussion, but, of course, how large the warehouse is and how fast the robot can travel will have important consequences in modeling this domain. Other factors will also have a significant impact on the performance of the robot. For instance, we will assume that the robot cannot determine whether or not the malfunction light on the assembler is on unless it is within the area designated the "assembly area" in Fig. 4-4 and it has correctly aimed its vision sensor to point in the general area of the malfunction light. Details concerning the robot's sensory capabilities, the domain, and the robot's ability to move about in that domain will be introduced in subsequent sections as required.

We have purposely chosen a domain that allows us to emphasize the strengths of the symbolic modeling techniques discussed in this chapter. The

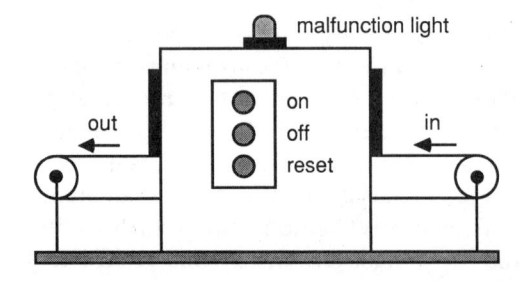

FIGURE 4-3
The assembly unit.

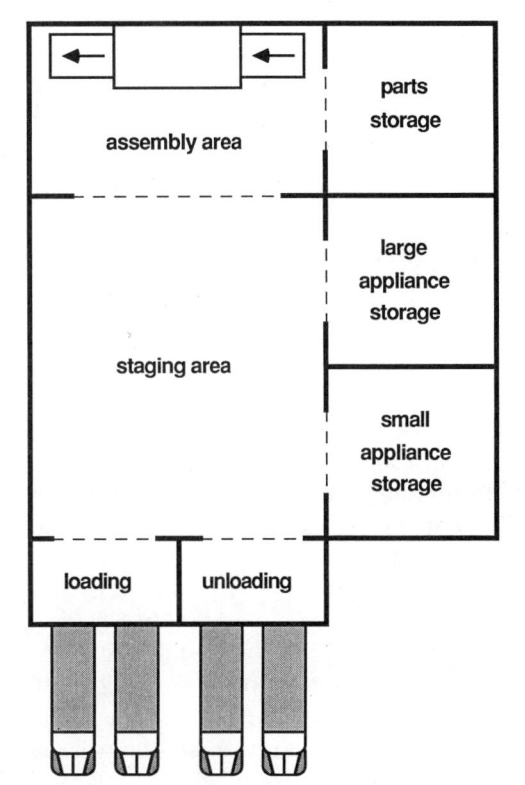

FIGURE 4-4
The warehouse layout.

fact that manipulation using palletized cargo is fairly simple allows us to ignore problems involving the recognition and manipulation of objects with arbitrary shapes. A domain for exploring robot problem solving is interesting from the perspective of symbolic modeling if it exhibits a diversity of phenomena requiring the use of clever abstractions to cope with the underlying complexity. Symbolic modeling techniques generally correspond to only one small part of a solution to a complex robotic control problem. We hope to communicate in this chapter some intuitions concerning where symbolic techniques are likely to play a role in solving control problems.

In the warehouse domain, reasoning about time and space figure prominently. The robot forklift's computational tasks include interpreting sensory information, scheduling loading and unloading activities, and reevaluating plans when new information becomes available (e.g., a new truck arrives or the assembler malfunction light goes on). Most of the robot's physical tasks involve moving about and manipulating objects. Given that the robot would like to minimize the penalties that result from letting trucks wait for loading and unloading, the robot has to reason about deadlines and make careful use of its time. We want the general architecture of our robot problem-solving system to allow for the incorporation of special-purpose (or domain-specific) knowledge, but time and space and the particular capabilities of the robot are common to all of its applications. In the following sections, we will explore methods for reasoning about time, space, and the consequences of actions performed by the robot. We begin by considering methods for reasoning about time, since time plays such a central role in planning and robot problem solving.

3 REASONING ABOUT TIME AND CHANGE

In order to act intelligently, it is important to be able to predict the consequences of events, both your own and those of the other agents and processes around you. By anticipating the actions of others and reasoning about the effects of your own actions, you can choose intelligently among various alternative courses of action. This section is concerned with temporal reasoning: the automatic prediction of the consequences of known or hypothesized events. Suppose that the robot places a refrigerator and an ice maker in the assembler and turns the unit on; it should be able to predict, given an appropriate model, that the ice maker will be correctly installed in the refrigerator in, say, half an hour. On the basis of such a prediction, the robot can schedule other activities (e.g., when to pick up the refrigerator in order to load it on a truck).

An important part of robot problem solving involves using models to analyze possible courses of action. These models either implicitly or explicitly make reference to time. In this section, we discuss a language for reasoning about events and propositions that change over time. In the next section, we will see how this language can be used as part of a strategy for generating robot plans.

We have to translate our intuitions concerning time and change into a precise framework for automating the process of prediction. We need notation (syntax) for describing the robot's knowledge about the state of its environment and its knowledge concerning how change occurs in this environment, and we need a calculus for mechanically generating the consequences of this knowledge in a manner deemed (semantically) correct. Rather than get bogged down in the details of describing a formal system, we will employ a variant of first-order predicate calculus syntax used in the logic programming language Prolog (Clocksin and Mellish, 1984; Maier and Warren, 1988). Conditional rules (i.e., Prolog Horn clauses) will be notated $A \leftarrow B$, where A is an atom (i.e., a predicate of zero or more arguments) and B is a conjunction of zero or more atoms. We will assume the standard semantics for logic programs augmented where needed with informal procedural semantics. The following is not intended as an introduction to logic or to Prolog; we assume some familiarity with both (see Volume 1 of this series).

First-order predicate calculus provides only the basic syntactic conventions for our language of time and change; we have to commit to specific objects of temporal reasoning and the relations that can hold between them. In everyday speech, we speak of events and propositions. Events are said to occur, and propositions hold, over various periods of time [e.g., ''Turning the assembly machine on" specifies an event, and "An ice maker is correctly installed in the refrigerator" specifies a proposition (or *fluent*) that is true at some times and false at others].

To speak about the structure of time itself, we refer to *points* (or *instants*) of time and *intervals* (or *periods*) of time. We distinguish between a general type of event or proposition (e.g., "I ate lunch in the cafeteria") and a specific instance of a general type (e.g., "I ate lunch in the cafeteria this afternoon"). The latter are referred to as *time tokens* or simply *tokens*. A token associates a general type of event or proposition with a specific interval of time over which the event is said to occur or the proposition hold.

Our calculus for reasoning about time will be concerned with manipulating time tokens. Given some set of initial tokens corresponding to events and propositions, we will want to generate additional tokens corresponding to the consequences of the events. First, we have to be able to enter new tokens into the Prolog database. We notate the general type of events and propositions using Prolog terms. For instance, the event type "truck #45 arrives at the loading dock" might appear as `arrive(truck45,loading_dock)`. To enter a new token, we assert an expression of the form, `token(type,symbol)`, where `type` is a term corresponding to a general type of event or proposition, and `symbol` is a term that will be associated with an interval of time. Asserting

`token(arrive(truck45,loading_dock),arrival14)`

adds a new token of type `arrive(truck45,loading_dock)` and interval `arrival14` to the database.

It is often convenient to refer to the points corresponding to the beginning and end of an interval. If `arrival14` denotes an interval, then `begin(arrival14)` denotes its begin point and `end(arrival14)` denotes its end point. Initially, the interval of time associated with a token is completely unconstrained (i.e., it could correspond to any interval). Intervals can be constrained using qualitative and metric constraints on their begin and end points. If `arrival14` and `departure23` are both intervals, then asserting

`precedes(end(arrival14),begin(departure23))`

constrains the first interval to end before the second begins. It is necessarily the case that

`precedes(begin(int), end(int))`

where *int* is any interval. Metric constraints allow us to bound the amount of time separating points. The notation `distance(`pt_1`, `pt_2`)` ∈ `[low, high]` is used to specify that the distance in time separating pt_1 and pt_2 is bounded from above by `high` and bounded from below by `low`, where time units are specified in the form *hours:minutes*. For instance, if `noon` is a reference point corresponding to 12:00 a.m. today, asserting

`distance(noon,begin(arrival14))` ∈ `[2:55,3:05]`

would constrain the interval associated with the arrival of truck 45 to occur at 3:00 p.m., give or take 5 minutes. If the upper and lower bounds are the same, we use = instead of ∈ and one number instead of a pair of numbers.

We treat events and propositions somewhat differently in our calculus. We assume that the durations of events are specified precisely. For instance, we might state that the event corresponding to the arrival of truck 45 took 1 minute:

```
distance(begin(arrival14),end(arrival14)) = 0:01
```

For tokens corresponding to propositions, we would like to predict how long the propositions persist once they become true. For instance, suppose we make the following assertions:

```
token(location(forklift,loading_area),location1).
token(location(forklift,staging_area),location2).
distance(noon,begin(location1)) = 1:15.
distance(noon,begin(location2)) = 2:30.
```

Assuming that the forklift can only be in one of staging_area or loading_area, we can conclude that the interval location1 should not persist past 2:30 a.m. In general, we require that the interval corresponding to a token persist no further than the first subsequent interval corresponding to a token of a *contradictory type*. For any type P, P and not(P) are said to be contradictory. Additional contradictory types have to be explicitly asserted. For instance, the assertion contradicts(location(: = ,: ≠)) indicates that any two tokens of type location(arg1,arg2) are contradictory if their first arguments are the same and their second arguments are different. The process of modifying the bounds on token intervals corresponding to propositions to ensure that tokens of contradictory types do not overlap is referred to as *persistence clipping*.

In the course of our discussions, we will be adding various capabilities to Prolog to support problem solving. We will call this extended logic programming language TEMPLOG in recognition of the central role of time. To begin with, we will assume that TEMPLOG automatically performs persistence clipping for all tokens stored in the database.

It will help in this and subsequent sections if we can display the contents of a TEMPLOG database graphically. To that end, we introduce the following graphical conventions. Time tokens are represented with a vertical bar indicating when the corresponding interval begins and either a second vertical bar providing some indication of when the interval ends or an arrow → indicating that the end of the interval is far enough in the future that it cannot be drawn in the diagram. The delimiters for tokens are connected by a horizontal arrow (e.g., |→). Each token is labeled with a symbol corresponding to its associated interval and a formula denoting its type. The tokens are laid out on the page so as to indicate their relative offset from some global reference point. Figure 4-5

```
location1  location(forklift,loading_area)
|——————————|
                    location2  location(forklift,staging_area)
                    |————————————————————→
```

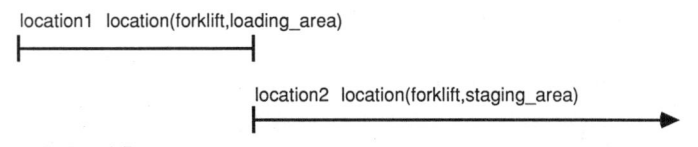

FIGURE 4-5
Tokens in the TEMPLOG database.

depicts the information stored in the TEMPLOG database as a consequence of the four assertions listed in the previous paragraph. In Fig. 4-5, the token interval location1 is constrained to end before the beginning of the token interval location2 by the process of persistence clipping.

Given a database of time tokens, one is generally interested in answering queries concerning what propositions are true over what intervals of time. A *temporal query* of the form holds(pt$_1$, pt$_2$, P), where P is an atom, should succeed just in case there is a token in the database of type P constrained to begin after or coincident with pt_1 and not constrained to end before pt_2. Complex temporal queries involving conjunctions and disjunctions can be defined in terms of atomic queries, using the standard Prolog convention for notating conjunctions and disjunctions [(P,Q) and (P;Q) are, respectively, the conjunction and disjunction of P and Q]:

```
holds(T1,T2,(P,Q)) ← holds(T1,T2,P),holds(T1,T2,Q).
holds(T1,T2,(P;_)) ← holds(T1,T2,P).
holds(T1,T2,(_;Q)) ← holds(T1,T2,Q).
```

We will assume that TEMPLOG processes temporal queries involving both atomic and complex queries efficiently. To get a better idea of how queries are processed in TEMPLOG, suppose that the following five queries are initiated in the database depicted in Fig. 4-6:

```
location1  location(forklift,loading_area)
|————————————|
                      location2  location(forklift,staging_area)
                      |——————————————————→
            location3  location(truck45,loading_dock)
            |————————————————————————————→
                  service1  routine_service(assembler)
                  |————|
                            service2  routine_service(forklift)
                            |————|
```

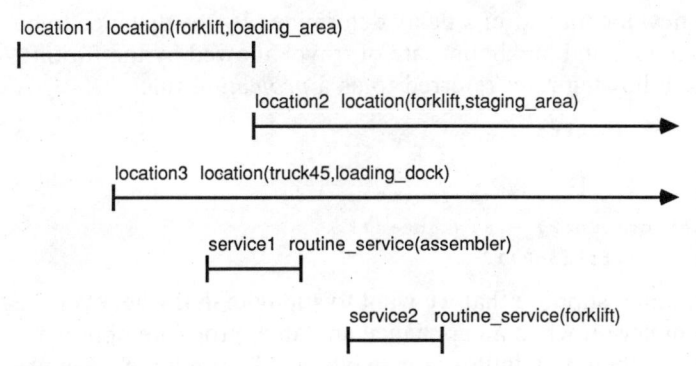

FIGURE 4-6
TEMPLOG database for illustrating query processing.

```
holds(begin(service1),end(service1),
      location(truck45,loading_dock)).
holds(begin(service1),end(service1),
      (location(forklift,staging_area);location(truck45,loading_dock))).
holds(begin(service2),end(service2),
      (location(forklift,staging_area)),location(truck45,loading_dock))).
holds(begin(service2),end(service2),
      (location(Object,staging_area),location(Object,loading_dock))).
holds(begin(service2),end(service2),
      (location(Object1,staging_area),location(Object2,loading_dock))).
```

The first three queries will succeed, the fourth will fail, and the fifth will succeed with `Object1` bound to `forklift` and `Object2` bound to `truck45`.

Persistence clipping is a type of routine inference important in reasoning about time and change. There is a second type of routine inference, called *projection*, that we would like TEMPLOG to perform for us. Projection is concerned with inferring the consequences of events based on a model specified in terms of the cause-and-effect relationships that exist between various event types. To notate such relationships, we use the following form:

```
project(antecedent_conditions, trigger_event, delay,
consequent_effects)
```

to indicate that if an event of type `trigger_event` occurs, and the `antecedent_conditions` hold at the outset of the interval associated with `trigger_event`, then the `consequent_effects` are true after an interval of time determined by `delay`. The trigger event is specified as a type, the antecedent conditions and consequent effects are specified as types or conjunctions of types, and the delay is specified as a pair consisting of a lower and an upper bound on the time between the end of the trigger event and the manifestation of the effects (if the upper and lower bound are the same, a single bound can be substituted for the pair).

To specify that whenever the forklift moves from one location to another it will appear in the new location after a delay determined by the distance to be traveled and the minimum and maximum rate of travel allowed by the forklift, we would assert the following rule, referred to as a *projection* rule:

```
project(location(forklift,Loc1),
        move(Loc1,Loc2),
        [(distance(Loc1,Loc2) ÷ max_speed),
         (distance(Loc1,Loc2) ÷ min_speed)],
        location(forklift,Loc2)).
```

As another example, suppose that we want to stipulate that whenever the robot turns the assembler on when an appliance and an appropriate option are on the input conveyor, then 30 minutes later, give or take 5 minutes, the appliance will appear in the output conveyor with the option properly installed. The following assertion will suffice:

```
project((status(assembler,off),
        location(Appliance,in_conveyor),
        instance_of(Appliance,home_appliance),
        location(Option,in_conveyor)
        instance_of(Option,option_for(Appliance))),
        push_button(on),
        [00:25,00:35],
        (installed(Appliance,Option),
        location(Appliance,out_conveyor),
        part_of(Option,Appliance))).
```

Projection is the process of generating new tokens from some set of initial tokens—roughly corresponding to the boundary conditions in a physics problem—using a set of projection rules. The basic algorithm for handling both projection and persistence clipping is quite simple. Whenever tokens or constraints are added to or deleted from the database, the system carries out the following steps:

1. Delete all tokens and constraints added the last time the algorithm was run.
2. Place all tokens in the database whose types correspond to events on the *open list*.
3. Let *token* be the earliest occurring token in the open list.
4. Find each rule whose trigger event type unifies with the type of *token*.
5. For each rule found in step 4 whose antecedent conditions are satisfied, add to the database tokens corresponding to the types specified in the consequent effects and constrain them according to the specified delay.
6. For each new token added in step 5 whose type corresponds to a fluent, find all tokens of a contradictory type that begin before the newly added token and constrain them to end before the beginning of the new token.
7. For each new token added in step 5 whose type corresponds to an event, place it on the open list.
8. Remove *token* from the open list.
9. If there are no tokens remaining on the open list, then quit, else go to step 3.

We will assume that TEMPLOG uses an algorithm similar to the one above to ensure that the database contains all and only those tokens warranted by the set of initial tokens, and the projection rules stored in the database.

There are many other rules that we would have to specify to model the operation of the assembler in enough detail to support useful prediction. We would have to state that pushing the on button when the assembler is off causes it to become on:

```
project(status(assembler,off),
        push_button(on),
        00:00
        status(assembler,on)).
```

and that a machine cannot be on and off at the same time:

```
contradicts(status(:= ,:≠ )).
```

In fact, there are potentially an infinite number of rules that would be required to correctly model the behavior of the assembler under every set of circumstances. Note that the assembler requires power, and the appliance and the options to be installed must be in some reasonable state of repair, and there cannot be anything blocking the output conveyor; all of these conditions and more would have to be made explicit in the rules if we required a model guaranteed to produce correct predictions in every conceivable situation. The causal rules that comprise a model are intended as an approximation. Greater accuracy can often be obtained by adding more rules, but there is a price to be paid in terms of computational overhead, and the increased accuracy may not result in a significant improvement in performance. The idea behind causal modeling is that an appropriate model will efficiently generate those commonsense predictions that are likely to have the greatest impact on the performance of the robot. It is up to the programmer to determine what rules are necessary to generate these commonsense predictions.

For a more detailed discussion of the representational issues involved in reasoning about time and change, the interested reader is encouraged to consult Allen (1983), McDermott (1982), or Shoham (1988). For more detail concerning the computational issues concerning projection and persistence clipping, see Dean and McDermott (1987). It should be mentioned that the simple projection algorithm described above is not guaranteed to work properly if the tokens corresponding to the initial conditions are partially ordered. The general problem of predicting the consequences of a set of partially ordered events is potentially intractable (Chapman, 1987). To deal with this potential source of complexity, partial decision procedures have been developed to avoid expending too much effort in performing projection (Dean and Boddy, 1988).

4 GENERATING PLANS OF ACTION

Given the techniques of Section 3, if the robot was considering a particular sequence of actions and possessed knowledge of the actions of other agents and processes in its environment, the robot could determine the consequences of carrying out that sequence of actions. In this section, we turn our attention to how such sequences of actions might be generated in the first place.

We begin with the notion of a *task,* which refers to an action that the robot is committed to performing. A task might correspond to an action or a queue of actions that the robot is executing, or it could be part of a plan that the robot has formed for dealing with a particular situation. Tasks come and go as the robot discovers information about its environment. If the robot enters the unloading area and notices a truck that was not there the last time the robot visited, then it will formulate a new task to unload that truck. Conversely, if the robot currently has the task of loading a refrigerator on truck 45, and it notices that truck 45 is no longer waiting, the robot will give up on that task.

Tasks are often abstract in the sense that they commit the robot to performing some general sort of action. Before an abstract task can be carried out, it has to be specified in enough detail that it can be executed directly by the robot hardware. One way of specifying more detail is to *reduce* an abstract task to a more specific task or a set of more specific tasks. This process of specifying more detail is called *task reduction*. In reducing an abstract task, the robot commits to carrying out the more specific tasks. A task that needs no further reduction before it can be executed by robot hardware is called a *primitive task*. Reduction continues until all tasks are either reduced or primitive. Reduction is complicated by the fact that at any instant the robot is likely to have many tasks and several methods for reducing any given one. It is quite possible that a choice for reducing one task may result in there being no choice for reducing one of the other tasks. The rest of this section describes a framework for generating plans of action based on the notion of task reduction.

As far as the robot is concerned, a task is just a special sort of time token. A new task is created by asserting an expression of the form task(type,symbol). We use the notation achieve(P) to denote the type of a task to make the proposition P true. If the query primitive(Q) succeeds, then Q is the type of task that can be directly executed on robot hardware. In the warehouse domain, we will assume that push_button(B) is primitive, where B is the label of a known push-button control switch. Being primitive does not guarantee that executing an action will succeed in achieving its intended results; the robot will have to see to it that certain prerequisites are met to guarantee that an action will have its intended results.

Planning knowledge is encoded in expressions of the form todo(what,when,how), where *what* is a task type, *when* is an interval, and *how* is either an alternative task type or the description of a plan specifying how to reduce the task type indicated by *what*. Perhaps the most common alternative task type corresponds to the no_op or do-nothing action. In general, when you have a task to accomplish something that is already true, the obvious action to perform is none at all. We can represent this simple strategy as

todo(achieve(P),T,no_op) ← holds(end(T),end(T),P).

where, in order to absolve the robot of its commitment to achieve P, all that is important is that P is true at the end of the interval T.

Plans are specified by expressions of the form plan(steps, constraints, protections, id), where *steps* indicates the new tasks involved in the reduction, *constraints* determines the order of those tasks, *protections* indicates how the various steps depend upon one another, and *id* serves to distinguish different instances of the same plan. The new tasks are referred to as *subtasks* of the task specified by the first two arguments of the todo expression, which is referred to as the *supertask* of the new tasks. Implicitly all new tasks are constrained to occur during the interval of the specified supertask. Protections are important in detecting problems that arise when one task interferes with another. Consider the following general method for making two propositions true at the same time:

```
todo(achieve((P,Q)),T,
    plan([step(task1(Id),achieve(P)),
          step(task2(Id),achieve(Q))],
         [precedes(end(task1(Id)),end(T)),
          precedes(end(task2(Id)),end(T))],
         [protect(end(task1(Id)),end(T),P),
          protect(end(task2(Id)),end(T),Q)],Id)).
```

Each step is specified by a unique name for the corresponding task's interval and a task type; we assume that TEMPLOG assigns Id a different integer each time the above expression is unified. The constraints are exactly as described in the previous section. The two protections stipulate that to achieve the conjunction of P and Q, achieve P and Q individually, and see to it that once each proposition is made true it remains so at least until the end of time interval T. A protection is said to be *violated* when the robot becomes committed to an action with an effect whose type contradicts the type of protection. Certain combinations of tasks can make it impossible to avoid violating protections. In some cases, it may be easy to detect such combinations as in

```
achieve(status(assembler,on),status(assembler,off))
```

In general, however, the interactions between tasks can be arbitrarily complex, requiring considerable effort to detect and resolve. We will return to discuss how protections are used to detect and avoid interactions in generating plans, but first we will consider some further examples of plans.

Most of the plans for a given application encode domain-specific strategies for reducing abstract tasks to more concrete tasks. The set of all such strategies is generally referred to as a *plan library*. In the following, we will provide examples of plans that might appear in the plan library for a robot operating in the warehouse domain. We will take the liberty to simplify the plans somewhat (e.g., by leaving out certain steps and constraints) in order to make the text more readable. Here is a plan for installing an option in an appliance:

```
todo(achieve(installed(Option,Appliance)),T,
    plan([step(task1(Id),achieve(location(Appliance,in_conveyor))),
          step(task2(Id),achieve(location(Option,in_conveyor))),
          step(task3(Id),achieve(status(assembler,on)))],
         [precedes(end(task1(Id)),begin(task3(Id))),
          precedes(end(task2(Id)),begin(task3(Id))),
          distance(end(task3(Id)),end(T)) ∈ [00:25,00:35]],
         [protect(end(task1(Id)),begin(task3(Id)),
                  location(Appliance,in_conveyor)),
          protect(end(task2(Id)),begin(task3(Id))
                  location(Option,in_conveyor)),
```

```
            protect(end(task3(Id)),end(T),status(assembler,on))]) ←
        holds(begin(T),begin(T),
                (status(assembler,off),status(malfunction_light,off))).
```

Take note of the role protections play in this plan. The first two protections serve to ensure that, once placed on the assembler's input conveyor, the appliance and the option to be installed will remain there until the robot starts the assembly. The third protection ensures that the robot does not inadvertently schedule some other activity that would result in turning the assembler off during the time that it is scheduled to carry out the installation. Note that the above plan explicitly constrains the amount of time separating the end of the task to start the assembler and the end of the installation interval.

The forklift robot will also need plans for changing the location of objects. The following rule specifies how to change the location of something other than the forklift:

```
todo(achieve(location(Object,Loc1)),T
    plan([[step(task1(Id),achieve(location(forklift,Loc2))),
           step(task2(Id),pick_up(Object)),
           step(task3(Id),achieve(location(forklift,Loc1))),
           step(task4(Id),set_down(Object))],
          [precedes(end(task1(Id)),begin(task2(Id))),
           precedes(end(task2(Id)),begin(task3(Id))),
           precedes(end(task3(Id)),begin(task4(Id)))],
          [protect(end(task1(Id)),begin(task2(Id)),
                   location(forklift,Loc2)),
           protect(end(task2(Id)),begin(task3(Id)),
                   holding(forklift,Object)),
           protect(end(task3(Id)),begin(task4(Id)),
                   location(forklift,Loc1))],Id)) ←
        holds(begin(T),begin(T),
                (location(Object,Loc2),Object ≠ forklift,Loc1 ≠ Loc2)).
```

The above plan assumes a somewhat implausible model of the forklift. In order to move an appliance onto the input conveyor, the forklift would have to move itself into the conveyor while holding the appliance and then set the appliance down in such a way that the appliance is resting on the conveyor. In the next section, we will consider the problem of reasoning about movement tasks in somewhat greater detail. For the time being, to plan for moving the robot about, we will use the following rule, and assume that the task type move(loc1,loc2) is primitive:

```
todo(achieve(status(location(forklift,Loc1))),T,move(Loc2,Loc1)) ←
    holds(begin(T),end(T),location(forklift,Loc2)).
```

Finally, the robot needs a plan for turning the assembler on or off:

```
todo(achieve(status(assembler,Stat1)),T,
    plan([step(task1(Id),achieve(location(forklift,assembly_area))),
          step(task2(Id),push_button(Stat1))],
         [precedes(end(task1(Id)),begin(task2(Id))),
         [protect(end(task1(Id)),begin(task2(Id)),
                  location(forklift,assembly_area))],Id)) ←
    holds(end(T),end(T),(status(assembler,Stat2),Stat1 ≠ Stat2)).
```

Now we are ready to consider how to go about reducing a set of abstract tasks to primitive tasks. In general, the reduction process can be quite complex. We will sketch an algorithm for performing the reduction, give an example illustrating the algorithm in operation, and then comment on where complications arise that are not explicitly handled by our algorithm. The reduction algorithm is listed as follows:

1. Find some task, `task(what,when)`, that is neither reduced nor primitive. If no such task exists, wait until a new task is added to the database.
2. Using the query `todo(what,when,how)`, try to find some method (*how*) for carrying out the task found in step 1.
3. If the query specified in step 2 fails, try adding constraints to restrict the ordering of the existing tasks.
4. If the query specified in step 2 fails even after trying various additional constraints, try removing one or more of the existing tasks.
5. If steps 2 through 4 fail to produce an applicable method, return to step 1 and try another task.
6. If *how* is an alternative task type, create a new task and add it to the database.
7. If *how* is a plan, create new tasks for each of the subtasks and add them to the database along with the specified constraints and protections.
8. Having added all of the new tasks, TEMPLOG will have updated the database using the projection and persistence clipping algorithm and the projection rules that describe the effects of the actions. Check to see if any protections are violated by the addition of the new tasks.
9. If any protections are violated, resolve the violation by either reordering or removing one or more of the existing tasks.
10. Go to step 1.

A concrete example should help in understanding the basic operation of the reduction algorithm. Figure 4-7 shows a TEMPLOG database containing one nonprimitive unreduced task to install an ice maker in a refrigerator. Figure 4-8 shows the TEMPLOG database resulting from applying the reduction algorithm, using the planning knowledge specified in this section and the knowledge of cause-and-effect relationships described in Section 3. (Only selected steps are depicted in Fig. 4-8 to keep the display readable.) The reduction illustrated in Fig. 4-8 is a particularly simple one; we now proceed to consider what sort of problems arise in more complicated situations.

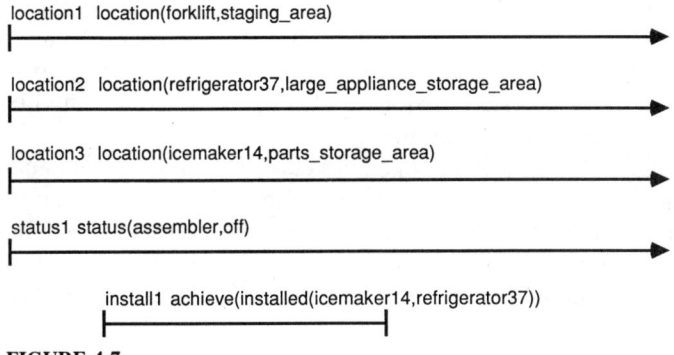

```
location1  location(forklift,staging_area)
├─────────────────────────────────────────►

location2  location(refrigerator37,large_appliance_storage_area)
├─────────────────────────────────────────►

location3  location(icemaker14,parts_storage_area)
├─────────────────────────────────────────►

status1  status(assembler,off)
├─────────────────────────────────────────►

           install1  achieve(installed(icemaker14,refrigerator37))
           ├──────────────────────────────┤
```

FIGURE 4-7
Database before reduction.

Returning to the previous listing of the reduction algorithm, note that there are a number of steps where choices are made. In step 1, the robot will generally have to choose from a number of unreduced nonprimitive tasks. In step 2, there are likely to be several methods for reducing the chosen task. If the todo query does not immediately succeed, the robot may have to consider several alternative orderings in step 3, or several reduced sets of tasks in step 4, before it is able to find a reduction strategy that works. If the robot is not clever, it can end up completely undoing all of its previous work. The loop involving steps 1–5 can cause the algorithm to loop indefinitely, and, if new tasks are continually added, the algorithm is not guaranteed to eventually reduce all tasks. The problem of resolving protection violations in step 10 can be particularly troublesome; sometimes involving numerous attempts at reorder

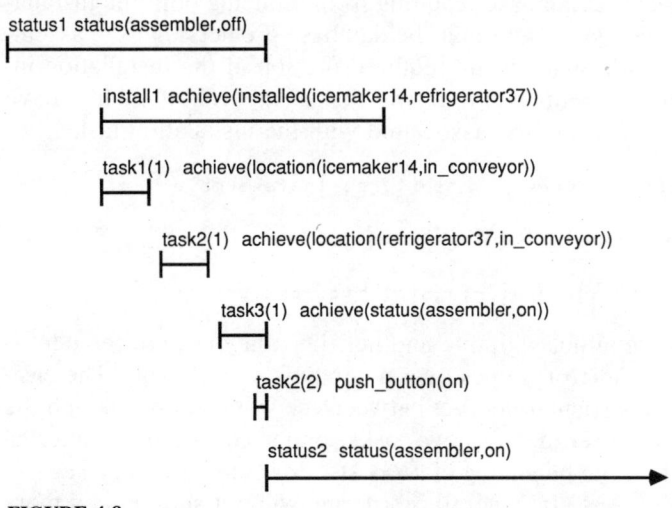

```
status1  status(assembler,off)
├────────────────┤

         install1  achieve(installed(icemaker14,refrigerator37))
         ├──────────────────────────────────────┤

              task1(1)  achieve(location(icemaker14,in_conveyor))
              ├───┤

                    task2(1)  achieve(location(refrigerator37,in_conveyor))
                    ├───┤

                         task3(1)  achieve(status(assembler,on))
                         ├───┤

                              task2(2)  push_button(on)
                              ├─┤

                                   status2  status(assembler,on)
                                   ├─────────────────────────►
```

FIGURE 4-8
Database after reduction.

ing or modifying the set of tasks. If the robot makes the wrong choice early in the planning process, it may expend a great deal of effort before it "backs up" and tries an alternative option. All of these problems and more have to be routinely solved by a robot control system that generates plans of action. The literature is full of methods for dealing with these problems.

To give one example of how interactions between tasks are detected and resolved, suppose that the TEMPLOG database depicted in Fig. 4-7 also contains a task committing the robot to perform routine service on the assembler. Suppose further that this routine service task is currently scheduled to overlap with the task to install the ice maker in the refrigerator. The plan for routine service is specified below:

```
todo(routine_service(assembler),T,
    plan([step(task1(Id),achieve(status(assembler,off))),
          step(task2(Id),lubricate(assembler)),
          step(task3(Id),replenish_coolant(assembler)),
          step(task4(Id),push_button(reset))],
         [precedes(end(task1(Id)),begin(task2(Id))),
          precedes(end(task1(Id)),begin(task3(Id)))],
          precedes(end(task2(Id)),begin(task4(Id))),
          precedes(end(task3(Id)),begin(task4(Id)))],
         [protect(end(task1(Id)),begin(task4(Id)),
              status(assembler,off))],Id).
```

Note that the routine service plan requires that the assembler be turned off before the lubrication and coolant-replacement tasks are initiated. The task to turn the assembler off conflicts with the plan that requires the assembler be on to complete the installation task.

Figure 4-9 depicts the database resulting from reducing both the installation and routine service tasks. Note that the database predicts that the assembler will not remain on throughout the required portion of the installation interval. In the course of reducing the two tasks, the robot should have generated two protections: the first associated with the installation task,

```
protect(end(task3(1)),end(installation1),status(assembler,on))
```

and the second associated with the routine service task,

```
protect(end(task1(3)),end(service1),status(assembler,off))
```

These two protections conflict with one another (i.e., they require the persistence of tokens of contradictory types over a common subinterval). The easiest way to resolve this particular conflict between the installation task and the routine service task is to reorder the two tasks: either constrain the interval service1 to end before the beginning of task3(1) or constrain service1 to begin after installation1. In general, reordering will not suffice, and more drastic measures must be taken.

```
status1  status(assembler,off)
├─────────────────────────┤

        installation1  achieve(installed(icemaker14,refrigerator37))
        ├─────────────────────────────────────┤

                task3(1)  achieve(status(assembler,on))
                ├──┤

                    task2(2)  push_button(on)
                    H

                        status2  status(assembler,on)
                        ├───────────┤

                            service1  routine_service(assembler)
                            ├─────────────────┤

                            task1(3)  achieve(status(assembler,off))
                            ├──┤

                                task2(4)  push_button(off)
                                H

                                    status3  status(assembler,off)
                                    ├──────────────────────→
```

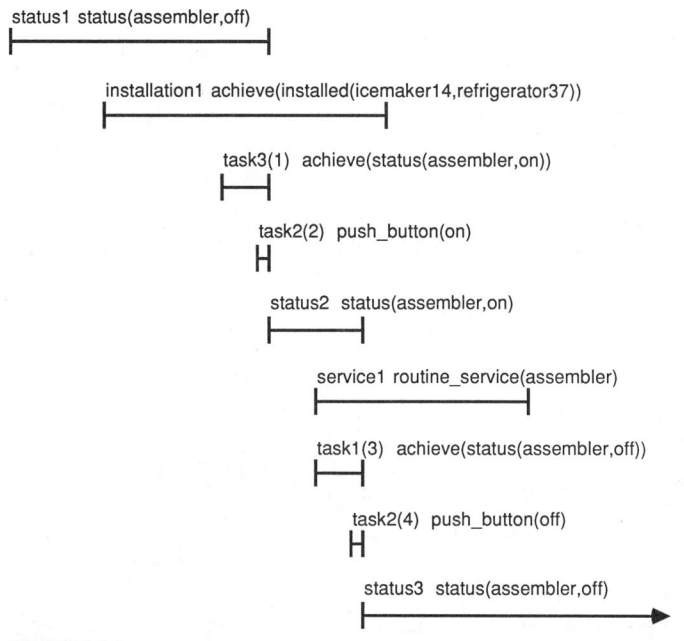

FIGURE 4-9
Database with a protection violation.

There are other problems that can arise besides protection violations. Many of the rules specifying reduction methods have conditions that must hold if the reduction method is to apply. We refer to these conditions as *reduction assumptions*. For instance, consider the general rule for avoiding unnecessary work:

```
todo(achieve(P),T,no_op) ← holds(end(T),end(T),P).
```

If the robot has a task, `task(achieve(status(assembler,off)), interval81)`, to turn the assembler off and the assembler is already off, then it will reduce the task to a `no_op`. The reduction assumption is that `status(assembler,off)` holds at `end(interval81)`. The robot will check at reduction time that the reduction assumption holds, but the assumption may become false during subsequent planning as additional tasks are added to the database. Reduction assumptions have to be carefully monitored in much the same way that protections are, and steps must be taken when the assumptions are found to be violated.

The general problem of reducing a set of tasks to primitive tasks so as to avoid violating any protections or falsifying any reduction assumptions is known to be very hard (i.e., it has been shown to be in the class of *NP-hard* problems). Deadlines and reasoning about resources are obvious sources of complexity, but even if we were to ignore deadlines and resources, most interesting planning problems remain in the company of those problems believed to be intractable. For certain versions of the problem, there is no effective method for generating plans (i.e., the problem is undecidable). For the problems that are decidable, it is fairly simple to write an algorithm that will find a solution if one exists and signal that no solution exists if that is indeed the case. Unfortunately, such an algorithm may take an enormously long time to return with an answer. While these observations are somewhat discouraging, we at least know that good approximate solutions are possible (e.g., humans perform reasonably well driving forklifts in warehouses). In artificial intelligence, planning problems are typically recast as search problems, and standard methods have been applied to develop heuristic algorithms that perform well in practice. In this chapter, we have not emphasized the underlying search problems so that we can concentrate on the basic problem of how a robot might use symbolic representations to guide its behavior. Before we move on to consider planning problems involving spatial reasoning, we will consider a couple of issues that were glossed over in the previous discussion.

The first step of the reduction algorithm mentions that if there currently are no reduced nonprimitive tasks, just wait until a new task is created. Exactly how are new tasks created? First, we assume that the robot knows certain things as a matter of course. For instance, we assume that the robot knows when it is in the loading or unloading areas. By "know that it is in the loading area" we mean that whenever the robot is in the loading area the temporal query

```
holds(now,now,location(forklift,loading_area))
```

succeeds in the TEMPLOG database, where now designates the current point in time. (This is actually a controversial assumption given the difficulty of visual recognition problems in the real world.) Next, we assume that the robot has rules—similar to the projection rules described in the section on temporal reasoning—that serve to add assertions corresponding to tasks to the TEMPLOG database. These rules are called *policies*. As an example, the robot has a general policy to keep track of the trucks waiting in the loading dock. Whenever the robot is in the loading area, a task is generated to scan the loading dock and note new arrivals and unexpected departures. Other policies would dictate that the robot create tasks for new arrivals and remove tasks associated with unexpected departures.

Some policies might be ignored in certain situations. For instance, whenever the forklift is in the assembly area and there is an assembly operation in progress, it should check to see if the assembler's malfunction light is on, and if so, generate a task to push the reset button. However, if the robot is in a hurry or has only recently checked the malfunction light, it might not generate the task to check. Policies provide one mechanism for the robot to react to the world around it.

Another issue that we avoided involves the representation of plans in which an action is repeated some number of times. For instance, how do you represent a plan to unload a truck containing seven appliances? Using the list manipulation routines in Prolog, this turns out to be relatively easy. A more difficult problem involves planning to unload a truck with some unknown number of appliances. We would like to be able to predict the type of the subtasks involved and how long the unloading is likely to take. We might specify a recursive plan such as

```
todo(achieve(empty(Truck)),T
    plan([step(task1(Id),unload_item(Truck)),
          step(task2(Id),achieve(empty(Truck)))],
         [precedes(end(task1(Id)),begin(task2(Id)))],[],Id) ←
    holds(end(T),end(T),not(empty(Truck))).
```

This gives us an idea of the subtask types involved, but we cannot determine how many tasks since it does not make sense to reduce the recursive (second) step until after some item is unloaded, and we are still left with the problem of estimating how long the unloading task will take. We could estimate how many items are likely to be on a given truck and expand a plan with this number of subtasks. We still cannot completely reduce the subtasks, since we cannot determine where the robot will have to travel until we know exactly what items are on the truck. Despite the complications involved in committing to tasks that may never be required, the basic idea of committing on the basis of expectations is important, and we will return to it briefly in the next section.

This section is a distillation of a great deal of research. For a more comprehensive treatment of protections and reduction algorithms, the interested reader is encouraged to consult Charniak and McDermott (1985). The notion of protections in planning was first mentioned in Sussman (1975). The basic idea of reduction interleaved with resolving interactions is derived from Sacerdoti (1977). The notion of policies was borrowed from McDermott (1978). For a discussion of issues in representing and reasoning about resources, see Wilkins (1984).

5 REASONING ABOUT SPACE

Much of a robot forklift's time is spent moving objects from one place to another in the warehouse. Grasping objects, picking them up, carrying them about, and setting them down comprise a fair amount of the robot's activities. In this section, we consider how a robot might plan routes from one place to another. We consider how symbolic modeling techniques can play a role in route planning in particular and spatial reasoning in general.

With Fig. 4-4, we described the layout of the factory using a labeled line drawing. The warehouse was divided up into areas corresponding to rooms designated for various purposes (e.g., storing large appliances or performing assembly operations) and subareas corresponding to specific locations or objects of interest within rooms (e.g., the input and output conveyors for the assembler). In the following, we show how a set of Prolog assertions can be used to capture a significant portion of the information in the labeled line drawing.

106 KNOWLEDGE ENGINEERING: APPLICATIONS

These assertions constitute a spatial representation that will serve for a number of spatial reasoning tasks including route planning.

As in our discussion of temporal reasoning, we need to develop an appropriate vocabulary for the objects and relations of interest. We will use the term *region* to refer to a connected piece of space. Regions are pretty much the spatial equivalent of temporal intervals. In this chapter, we will restrict our attention to regions corresponding to polygons in two-dimensional space.

To reason about space, we will define a number of relations on regions. We will be interested in specifying knowledge about one region containing, overlapping, or sharing a boundary edge with another region. It will be convenient to be able to divide up space according to different levels of detail. We use the term *partition* to refer to a specific scheme for carving up space into regions. A partition of a region consists of a set of nonoverlapping regions that completely cover the region. The seven regions corresponding to the seven rooms in Fig. 4-4 comprise a partition of the warehouse. We say that one region in a partition is *connected to* a second region in the same partition if the corresponding polygons share part or all of a boundary edge, and we notate this connected_to(r_1, r_2), where r_1 and r_2 denote regions. We say that one region is *contained in* another if the polygon corresponding to the contained region is completely enclosed in the polygon corresponding to the containing region, and we notate this contained_in(r_1, r_2), where r_1 and r_2 denote regions. Using assertions such as

```
connected_to(assembly_area,parts_storage_area).
connected_to(assembly_area,large_appliance_storage_area).
contained_in(out_conveyor,assembly_area).
```

we can capture a fair amount of the information in Fig. 4-4. Each assertion can be thought of as a labeled arc in a graphical representation of space. Figure 4-10 depicts the graph indicating the relations between the labeled regions in Fig. 4-4. We can now use standard graph-searching techniques to find a path from one region to another. The following rules employ a simple transitive-

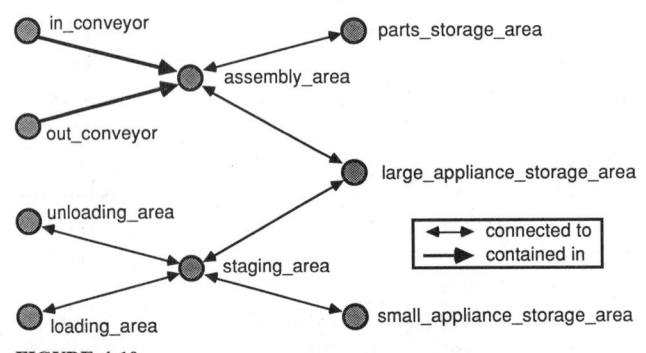

FIGURE 4-10
Graphical representation of spatial relationships.

closure algorithm for finding a path from one region to another within a given partition:

```
find_path(Region1,Region2,[Region1|Path]) ←
    trans(Region1,Region2,[Region1],Path).

trans(Region,Region,_,[ ]).
trans(Region1,Region2,PathSoFar,[Region3|RestOfPath]) ←
    Region1 ≠ Region2,
    connected_to(Region1,Region3),
    not(member(Region3,PathSoFar)),
    trans(Region3,Region2,[Region3|PathSoFar],RestOfPath).
```

where a path is represented as a list of connected regions. The Prolog negation-as-failure operator `not` and the membership predicate `member` are used to ensure that no region is visited more than once.

The partition of the warehouse region according to rooms is far too coarse a partition for planning useful routes. The forklift will usually have more information about its current location and anticipated destination than just "the forklift is in the staging area" or the "refrigerator is in the large-appliance storage area." To generate more accurate routes, we need a finer-grained partition of the warehouse. Figure 4-11 depicts such a partition. Notice that each room is partitioned by a set of regions. Given two partitions P_i and P_j, P_i is said to be a *refinement* of P_j if for any region r in P_j there is a set of regions in P_i that partitions r. The partition of the warehouse shown in Fig. 4-11 is a refinement of the partition shown in Fig. 4-4. If we need still more detail, we can further partition the regions shown in Fig. 4-11. In fact, we can define a hierarchy of partitions, $P_0, P_1, \ldots, P_n$, such that for $1 \leq i \leq n$, P_{i+1} is a refinement of P_i. Using such a hierarchy, we can specify a recursive algorithm for efficiently finding a *route* from a source location l_s to a destination location l_d where a route is a path in P_n, the most detailed partition available. Let r_s and r_d be regions in P_n containing, respectively, l_s and l_d. We assume that l_s and l_d are each contained in some region of P_n. To find a route from l_s to l_d, perform the following steps with $i = 0$:

1. Find $r_{s'}$ and $r_{d'}$ in P_i such that r_s is contained in $r_{s'}$ and r_d is contained in $r_{d'}$.
2. Find a path, $p = [r_{s'}, r_1, r_2, \ldots, r_k, r_{d'}]$, from $r_{s'}$ to $r_{d'}$ using the partition P_i.
3. If $i = n$, return p.
4. Plan a separate path through each region mentioned in p, so that we can combine these subpaths to form a single continuous path from r_s to r_d. In order for these separately computed paths to form a continuous path, we have to ensure that the region in P_n corresponding to the end of the path through $r_{s'}$ is connected to the region in P_n corresponding to the beginning of the path through r_1, and similarly for r_1 and r_2, r_2 and r_3, and so on up to and including r_k and $r_{d'}$. Suppose that we have identified these $2(k + 1)$ regions of P_n. Given that the regions corresponding to the beginning of the

108 KNOWLEDGE ENGINEERING: APPLICATIONS

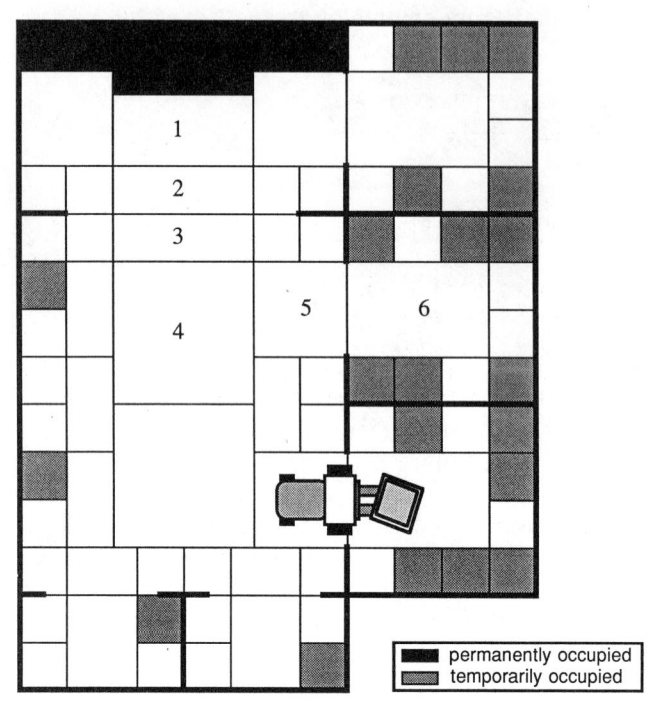

FIGURE 4-11
A spatial partition of the warehouse.

first path and the end of last are just r_s and r_d, we then have $k + 2$ paths to compute, and we do so by invoking this algorithm recursively with i bound to $i + 1$. The paths returned from these $k + 2$ recursive calls are then combined to form a continuous path from r_s to r_d.

As an example, suppose that we want to find a path from the region marked 1 in Fig. 4-11 to the region marked 6. There are just two partitions in our hierarchy: P_0, corresponding to the rooms shown in Fig. 4-4, and P_1, corresponding to the regions shown in Fig. 4-11. First the algorithm is invoked with the partition P_0 resulting in the following path composed of three regions in P_0:

`[assembly_area,staging_area,large_appliance_storage_area]`

Each of these three regions gives rise to a recursive call to the algorithm with the partition P_1. These recursive calls result in three subpaths in P_1, `[1,2]`, `[3,4,5]`, and `[6]`, which are combined to form the final path `[1,2,3,4,5,6]`.

Step 4 of the hierarchical find-path algorithm requires choosing begin and end points for the recursive calls. Even in the simple example described above, there are several possible choices. In general, making a good choice can be complicated; this is another situation where good search heuristics are needed to provide acceptable performance.

The above route-planning scheme has a number of problems that we neglected to mention. The most important problem has to do with the notion of the *traversability* of a region. Some regions may be occupied with large immovable physical objects, completely barring the forklift's passage, while other regions may be cluttered with small movable objects, making passage tedious and time consuming but still feasible. In a more detailed treatment, we would keep track of what objects were known to occupy what regions, and whether or not those objects could be moved to permit passage. Walls might be labeled as immovable objects and the regions of space they occupy as impassable, whereas doors would be labeled as objects that can often be manipulated to permit passage, and, hence, the regions they occupy potentially passable.

Some route-planning schemes employ an evaluation function for computing how difficult it is to traverse a given region or an edge corresponding to the connection between two regions. Each region or edge is assigned a single number as a measure of its traversability, and these numbers are used during route planning to choose between alternative paths. The problem of assigning useful numbers is complicated in domains in which space cannot easily be decomposed into nice neat partitions.

Several other problems that we have avoided stem from the fact that our representation is meant to deal with only a two-dimensional world. Extending the representation described here to handle three-dimensional space is nontrivial but is obviously necessary before the robot can reason about picking up objects and placing one object on another. Other issues concerning containment and support have to be addressed in order to reason correctly about the consequences of installing an ice maker in a refrigerator.

With a little effort, we could integrate our representation of space into the temporal inference scheme outlined in earlier sections. This would enable the robot to solve problems that required it to reason about being at a particular place at a particular time. For instance, by noticing that the assembler will have completed installing an option in a refrigerator at a time when the forklift will be returning empty-handed to the unloading area from the small parts storage area, the robot can merge two of its tasks: the task to return to the unloading area and the task to carry the refrigerator to the loading area. This sort of reasoning is complex as far as current robot planning systems go, but it is impossible without a solid representation scheme for reasoning about time and space.

It might be argued that, in the warehouse domain, as in most constructed environments, we have very accurate information about locations and configurations of objects and that to use the sort of reduced-resolution approximate methods described in this section is to throw away useful information and unnecessarily suffer a reduction in performance. The counterarguments are as follows. Having accurate information is not enough; you have to be able to infer interesting consequences from that information in a timely manner, and the sort of problems that we have been considering in this section (e.g., route-planning) are known to be computationally expensive. While the robot is solving problems, time is passing, orders are waiting to be filled, and stock is waiting to be shelved. In some cases, it is better to use a suboptimal strategy rather than wait for an optimal strategy and risk missing an important deadline. In other cases, it is possible to compute an optimal strategy and then not be able to follow it due to limitations in the robot's hardware. The world is uncertain and, to a large extent, unpredictable. It is important not to place too much faith in our predictive models—some things are better not planned for at all.

For a good discussion of symbolic spatial representations in artificial intelligence and robotics, see Davis (1986). The system described in Kuipers (1978) attempts to get by with as little metric information as possible. The methods described in Lozano-Perez (1983) provide a general framework for path planning and manipulator control. For examples of systems that integrate symbolic and metric information, see McDermott and Davis (1982) and Brooks (1981).

6 SENSING, FEEDBACK, AND CONTROL

This section attempts to address a number of important issues not covered in the previous sections. In particular, we are interested in how the robot extracts information about the state of the surrounding environment and how it uses this information to guide its behavior. We begin with the problem of interpreting the information returned by sensors.

How does our robot forklift know that there is a green side-by-side refrigerator freezer sitting in the back of a truck waiting in the unloading dock? How does the robot know that it is currently located in the assembly area of the warehouse? The answer is that the robot can never really know such things with certainty, but it can make more or less reasonable guesses on the basis of measurements made with its sensors. The main consequence of this observation is that a robot has to make complex decisions concerning what measurements are necessary to justify its decisions to act one way rather than another.

It is often comforting to think of the world as deterministic and predictable; propositions are either true or false, and with a little work, we can determine which. Unfortunately, the world is not always willing to divulge its secrets; information costs, and in some cases it costs dearly. The problem of determining the truth or falsity of a proposition on the basis of low-level sensor information has been referred to as the *pixels-to-predicates* problem ("pixels" being the term used to describe a single datum returned from an imaging device). Some researchers have argued that the sort of symbolic techniques described in the previous three sections are useful only for toy problems given that they depend upon a solution to the pixels-to-predicates problem. Their argument is based on a belief that the pixels-to-predicates problem cannot be solved for any interesting subset of the problem—the world is just too complex—and that by assuming it can be solved, the designer of a robot control system will build robots that make inappropriate and often dangerous commitments on the basis of poorly justified beliefs. The counterargument is simply that the robot has to commit to actions on the basis of its beliefs, and any useful application of the ideas described in this chapter will have to incorporate some method for collecting evidence to support certain propositions and for reevaluating certain decisions when new evidence becomes available.

All of the methods explored in this chapter can be seen as exercises in abstraction and concessions to complexity. We assume that the world is relatively simple and predictable at the level at which a robot has to understand it in order to achieve its goals. The idea of reducing complex tasks to simpler ones is central to dealing with complexity in control. This idea was explored first in the section on generating plans of actions and again in the hierarchical path-planning scheme described in Section 5. In basing a control strategy on this notion of task reduction, we assume that a robot's tasks tend not to interact with one another, but that, on those rare occasions when they do, the robot can use domain-independent knowledge to resolve the interactions.

Interactions between tasks occur at all levels in the control of robots. Consider the situation shown in Fig. 4-12. Suppose that the forklift has a single directional sensor used to judge distance between the forklift and nearby objects, and suppose that this sensor has a maximum range of 5 meters and a viewing angle of 10°. How can the robot manage to navigate the hall at a reasonable speed, avoiding obstacles on its right and left and detecting the doorway that serves as its current destination? The robot can be thought of as having several tasks (e.g., avoid running into the refrigerator, avoid falling down the stairs, find the first door leading into an office) that span overlapping intervals of time and compete for the same limited resource (i.e., information from the directional sensor). If the robot has reasonably accurate expectations regarding what objects it is likely to encounter in traversing the hall, it can use those expectations to plan out a strategy for aiming the sensor (e.g., look to the right and slightly forward until you notice a refrigerator, then move over to the opposite side of the hall and look to the left and slightly forward until you notice the edge of the stairway).

The notion of expectations is important in integrating a plan-generation scheme into a robot control system; even the most carefully formulated plans

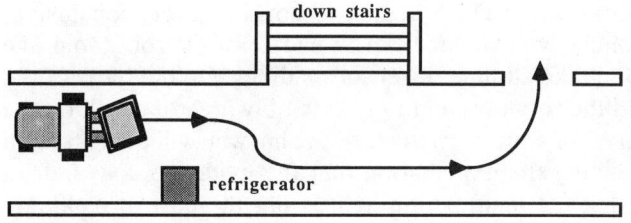

FIGURE 4-12
Forklift avoiding obstacles with limited sensors.

go awry. *Execution monitoring* refers to overseeing the execution of a plan by performing particular tests to determine whether or not certain steps in the plan are having their intended effects. After formulating the steps of a plan, the robot splices in additional steps that check to see if certain expected (and easily observable) consequences of the plan are manifest at appropriate times during its execution. If an expectation fails (i.e., the robot fails to observe a particular expected consequence), the robot enters into a replanning phase in which it tries to patch the plan or find a suitable alternative. Execution monitoring is one way of dealing with uncertainty; another way is to incorporate a model of change that represents uncertainty explicitly.

The predictive models that we described in the section on temporal reasoning employ simple if-then rules to model cause-and-effect relationships. Clearly, it is not always the case that when the robot pushes the on button the assembler immediately springs to life. Some events are less predictable than others, and there are situations in which a robot should take this unpredictability into account. The robot forklift can never be sure that when it returns to the loading area there will not be new trucks waiting to be loaded. If the predictive model captures this uncertainty, the plan-generation system can deal with it accordingly. There will be situations in which it will be worthwhile for the robot to postpone planning until it has some additional information; the robot will actually have to plan to gather the necessary information and then perform the required planning once the information is available. In some situations, the robot can determine what its options are in advance and generate what are called *conditional plans*: plans that incorporate tests that determine which of some set of available options is appropriate. Conditional plans complicate the process of planning, since the robot has to reason about all the different possible outcomes of the tests and all the resulting combinations of available options.

Of course, the robot's indecisiveness is not the only source of uncertainty. Sometimes, in predicting the outcome of a particular situation, the best that the robot can say is that 30% of the time it goes one way and 70% of the time it goes the other way. The use of probabilistic assessments extends not only to events external to the robot, but also to events pertaining to the functioning of the robot's own sensors and manipulators. For instance, suppose that the robot, while located in the staging area, is able to gather some evidence bearing on whether or not the malfunction light for the assembler located in the adjoining room is on. The evidence is not, however, conclusive, and the only way that conclusive evidence can be had is for the robot to move into the assembly area and take additional sensor readings. On the basis of the existing evidence, should the robot travel to the assembly area to check on the assembler? The question is, of course, rhetorical; the answer will depend upon a number of factors including the expectation that the evidence does indeed support the conclusion that the malfunction light is on, the cost of making a detour into the adjoining room, and the cost of ignoring a possible malfunction and thus delaying a delivery.

We could extend our model of prediction and plan generation to take into account probabilistic assessments, but there is a significant overhead in terms of computing the consequences of such an extended model. In terms of overall performance, it may be more appropriate to stick with a simpler deterministic model. The deterministic model will occasionally be wrong, but on average it will provide useful predictions. If a task is particularly critical, the robot's planning knowledge can be adjusted to have the robot employ conservative strategies to ensure that the task will be completed despite possible errors generated by the predictive model.

The topics discussed in this section cover areas of ongoing research. For a discussion of the power of robot control methods that do not rely upon the sort of plan generation and symbolic modeling described in this chapter, see Brooks (1985). For a discussion of execution monitoring issues, see Wilkins (1985) and Doyle et al. (1986). For a general discussion of probabilistic reasoning techniques in artificial intelligence, see Pearl (1988), and for a discussion of the application of probabilistic reasoning techniques to temporal reasoning, see Dean and Kanazawa (1989).

7 CONCLUSIONS

The techniques described in this chapter can be used as part of an effective strategy for controlling a robot. It would be misleading, however, to suggest that these techniques are sufficient for controlling a robot. A large part of controlling a robot involves interpreting the information returned by sensors and using this information in tightly coupled feedback loops to direct the behavior of actuators. Feedback loops can be implemented in a logic programming language, but the symbolic modeling techniques in this chapter are largely inappropriate for such tasks.

Neither is it the case that the techniques described in this chapter are necessary for controlling a robot. For many applications in robotics, symbolic modeling techniques simply are not needed and serve only to add unwarranted cost and complexity to a product. The engineer designing a control system has to decide whether or not the general techniques of this chapter are actually useful for the target application.

The predictive modeling techniques described in this chapter are appropriate in applications in which knowledge about the physical laws that govern the behavior of agents and processes in a particular domain can naturally be represented in terms of cause-and-effect rules *and* there is some advantage in actually predicting the behavior of these agents and processes. The techniques for generating plans of action are appropriate when the application requires that the control software be easily modified and extended to handle a particular set of tasks *and* it is convenient to encode the additional control knowledge in terms of domain-specific reduction rules. The techniques for reasoning about space are better suited to constructed environments, but there has been some success in extending highly qualitative and symbolic methods for reasoning about space to natural environments by Kuipers and Levitt (1988).

There is still a lot of research to be done in integrating high-level reasoning techniques of the sort described in this chapter with the low-level control algorithms necessary to deal with a complex and often unpredictable world. Hybrid control strategies that combine symbolic reasoning with special-purpose sensing-and-control algorithms are just beginning to have an impact on the field of robotics. For interesting accounts of such hybrid systems, see Andersson (1988) for a description of a Ping-Pong-playing robot that emphasizes the sensing-and-control aspect, and Chatila and Laumond (1985) for an account of a plan-generation program used as part of a system for directing the behavior of a mobile robot. As symbolic reasoning techniques improve and become more widely understood, we should see a significant increase in their use for applications in robotics and automation.

REFERENCES

Allen, J. (1983). Maintaining Knowledge About Temporal Intervals. *Commun. ACM* **26**:832–843.

Andersson, R. (1988). *A Robot Ping-Pong Player: Experiment in Real-Time Intelligent Control.* MIT Press, Cambridge, Mass.

Brooks, R. (1981). Symbolic Reasoning Among 3-D Models and 2-D Images. *AI* **17**:285–348.

Brooks, R. (1985). A Robust Layered Control System for a Mobile Robot. A.I. Memo No. 864. MIT Artificial Intelligence Laboratory, Boston.

Chapman, D. (1987). Planning for Conjunctive Goals. *AI* **32**:333–377.

Charniak, E., and McDermott, D. (1985). *Introduction to Artificial Intelligence.* Addison-Wesley, Reading, Mass.

Chatila, R., and Laumond, J.-P. (1985). Position Reference and Consistent World Modeling on Mobile Robots. IEEE International Conference on Robotics and Automation, St. Louis, MO, March, pp.138–145.

Clocksin, W.F., and Mellish, C.S. (1984). *Programming in Prolog.* Springer-Verlag, New York.

Davis, E. (1986). *Representing and Acquiring Geographic Knowledge.* Morgan-Kaufman, Los Altos, Calif.

Dean, T., and Boddy, M. (1988). Reasoning About Partially Ordered Events. *AI* **36**:375–399.

Dean, T., and Kanazawa, K. (1989). Persistence and Probabilistic Inference. *IEEE Trans. Syst., Man, Cybern.*

Dean T., and McDermott, D. (1987). Temporal Data Base Management. *AI* **32**:1–55.

Doyle, R., Atkinson, D., and Doshi, R. (1986). Generating Perception Requests and Expectations to Verify the Execution of Plans. Proceedings AAAI-86, Philadelphia, Pa., AAAI, pp. 65–69.

Kuipers, B., (1978). Modeling Spatial Knowledge. *Cogn. Sci.* **2**:129–153.

Kuipers, B., and Levitt, T. (1988). Navigation and Mapping in Large-Scale Space. *AI Mag.* **9**:25–43.

Lozano-Perez, T. (1983). Spatial Planning: A Configuration Space Approach. *IEEE Trans. Comput.* **32**:108–120.

McDermott, D. (1978). Planning and Acting. *Cogn. Sci.* **2**:71–109.

McDermott, D. (1982). A Temporal Logic for Reasoning About Processes and Plans. *Cogn. Sci.* **6**:101–155.

McDermott, D., and Davis, E. (1982). Planning Routes through Uncertain Territory. *AI* **22:**107–156.
Maier, D., and Warren D. (1988). *Computing with Logic: Logic Programming with Prolog.* Addison-Wesley, Reading, Mass.
Pearl, J. (1988). *Networks of Belief: Probabilistic Reasoning in Intelligent Systems.* Morgan-Kaufman, Los Altos, Calif.
Sacerdoti, E. (1977). *A Structure for Plans and Behavior.* American Elsevier, New York.
Shoham, Y. (1988). *Reasoning About Change: Time and Causation from the Standpoint of Artificial Intelligence.* MIT Press, Cambridge, Mass.
Sussman, G. (1975). *A Computer Model of Skill Acquisition.* American Elsevier, New York.
Wilkins, D. (1984). Domain Independent Planning: Representation and Plan Generation. *AI* **22:**269–302.
Wilkins, D. (1985). Recovering from Execution Errors in SIPE. *Comput. Intell.* **1:**33–45.

CHAPTER 5

AUTONOMOUS MOBILE ROBOTS

RONALD C. ARKIN

1 INTRODUCTION

Mobile robotics has a rich history within artificial intelligence. It has long been a pursuit of researchers in this area to endow machines with the ability to explore and understand their environment. Unfortunately the lay population tends to view mobile robotics as a solved problem. This is principally a result of the movie industry's successes in building seemingly intelligent machines that have appeared in many box-office smash hits. Compounding the problem are computer show robots that are capable of interacting with their audience and appear extremely intelligent but are actually radio controlled by a clever operator not far away. The reality of the state of the art lags far behind the glamorous veneer that Hollywood has produced.

Early work at Stanford Research Institute led to the production of Shakey, an intelligent reconnaissance robot (Nilsson, 1984; Rosen and Nilsson, 1966). By *intelligent robot* we mean a machine that is able to extract information from its environment and use knowledge about its world to safely navigate in a meaningful and purposeful manner. The research involving Shakey is remembered more for the planning system it produced (STRIPS) than for the robot itself and its navigational successes. The project, which extended from 1966 to 1972, used computer hardware that was pitifully underpowered by today's standards. Computer vision techniques were developed to support navigation. Predicate calculus was the means for knowledge expression. The path-finding strategy employed a breadth-first search algorithm. Shakey's world was well modeled and did not accommodate dynamic changes. Most of these techniques for navigation and sensing have since been abandoned in favor of new ones that are discussed later in this chapter.

After the early frustrations with Shakey, interest revived in the field with Moravec's Robot Rover project in 1980, which he completed for his dissertation at Stanford University (Moravec, 1981). With the development of specialized vision operators for use in more sophisticated algorithms, successful visual navigation was demonstrated. Although the representations for world modeling used in his dissertation are no longer used, Moravec's research group at Carnegie-Mellon University continues to make significant progress toward robot autonomy.

Marked changes in the underlying hardware supporting mobile vehicles, including the advent of VLSI technology and improved sensor capabilities, has enabled the field to make significant progress in the last several years. Part of the gains made are directly accountable to heavy funding as a consequence of the Defense Advanced Research Project Agency's (DARPA) Autonomous Land Vehicle (ALV) project. Through this funding effort, a consortium of academic and industrial centers has been formed to conduct basic research into the issues of intelligent mobility. Although the results obtained to date do not match DARPA's aspirations, significant progress has occurred in the areas of knowledge representation, intelligent sensing, route planning, and system integration.

Many research groups throughout the world are currently addressing the problem of intelligent navigation from a wide range of perspectives. There are few areas, if any, in which a general consensus has arisen, making this research area within artificial intelligence particularly stimulating and lively. Carnegie-Mellon, the University of Massachusetts, Stanford, MIT, and Georgia Tech constitute some of the major U.S. academic research centers in intelligent navigation that employ actual mobile vehicles. Many other universities are conducting research into subsidiary problems such as computer vision and spatial reasoning. Considerable industrial and governmental research is also being conducted by the National Bureau of Standards, the Jet Propulsion Laboratory, Martin-Marietta Corp., Oak Ridge National Laboratories, FMC Corp., and others. Outside the United States, there are major centers of research in Toulouse and Grenoble (France), Munich and Karlsruhe (West Germany), and several in Japan and elsewhere. The issues in mobility being studied range from planetary rovers and applications in flexible manufacturing systems and military scenarios to high-speed freeway driving.

Much of the research in mobile robotics has been performed only in simulation. Good simulation work can be likened to going to a wonderful restaurant, reading the menu, seeing many desirable choices, but never being allowed to order a meal. Although much of the work can be appealing, it is inherently unsatisfying until it is demonstrated on a real robot. Implementation of simulation ideas on real hardware can quickly invalidate many of the assumptions that were made by the designer of a simulation. With this in mind, this chapter will concentrate on those research efforts that have carried their ideas beyond simulation into actual implementation on real vehicles. It should be remembered, however, that simulation is an integral portion of the development cycle for mobile robot software. One should not try out complex software on expensive machines without carefully testing the underlying concepts first. Doing so can result in costly mistakes.

It is important to view mobile robotics not merely as a collection of isolated problems that need to be solved. Intelligent sensing (e.g., computer vision) should be considered in the context of both navigational needs and real-time performance. Planning systems that ignore the fact that the real world is constantly changing are doomed to failure. Route planning must be supplemented by dynamic replanning capabilities. The impact of the locomotion system on the robot's navigational capabilities must be taken into account (perhaps the robot can climb over an object rather than detour around it). We will study the unifying concepts that underlie mobile robot navigation in this chapter.

A systems approach to autonomous robot design can address the fundamental problems in intelligent navigation. Route planning, path execution, sensory data acquisition and processing, and motor control and locomotion all constitute important research areas within this field. An integrated system is the only effective way to capitalize on the advances made in each. How communication and control between the individual subsystems is conducted needs to be and is being addressed by several research groups throughout the world.

Despite the large amount of research being conducted in path planning, intelligent sensing, and locomotion systems, there are several areas that pertain to autonomous mobile robots that are not receiving as much attention as they deserve. Survivability in hazardous environments is one. One of the goals for robotics researchers is to place these machines in environments that are potentially hazardous to human beings, which include space, military, undersea, rescue, and certain manufacturing situations. It may be difficult or impossible for the robot to be serviced if it breaks down or is otherwise damaged when it is in these environments. As a consequence, it is important to endow a mobile robot with the ability to dynamically replan in light of changing internal conditions that threaten its very survival. Another area that warrants additional investigation includes studies of the mechanisms for biological mobility. Living animal systems have successfully solved the problems that researchers in mobile robotics are trying to conquer. Significant insights could likely be gained through serious studies into the means by which these biological systems solve the problem of navigation.

It should be seen from the onset that the study of autonomous mobile robots is strongly interdisciplinary. Mechanical engineering is required to address the problem of building effective machines to move through the world. Electrical and computer engineers can design the hardware required to support the computer and sensor systems needed for navigation. Computer scientists and artificial intelligence researchers need to develop the necessary software concepts and knowledge representations to conduct navigation and intelligent sensing. Cognitive psychologists can provide insights into the means by which perception and motor action are performed in humans and animals, and neuroscientists and ethologists can describe the underlying mechanisms for the implementation of motor behavior in living systems.

Space considerations will limit the development here of all the issues associated with intelligent mobile robot systems. We will concentrate on the issues of intelligent planning and perception for mobile robots, the knowledge required to conduct navigation effectively, and the progress made to date by various research teams around the globe. Nonetheless, we start, in Section 2, with a description of the interrelationship of action and perception abstracted away from any particular mobile robot system. It is important to discover just how dependent perceptual processing is on the notion of goal-oriented behavior.

Section 3 describes the nature of knowledge representation. It surveys the types of cartographic information that facilitate both path planning and world map making. A multiplicity of approaches have been used to address this issue. Additionally, the means by which motor behaviors and plans are embodied are also described in this section.

We next survey the techniques used for navigational planning. This includes the significantly different issues of planning amid that which is known a priori and, alternatively, amid that which is discovered via sensing.

Various sensors and sensing techniques are described in Section 5. These include computer vision, ultrasonic sensing, and three-dimensional scanners as the means by which a robot can obtain information about the world in which it moves.

Locomotion systems are described in Section 6. The issues of wheeled, legged, or tracked robots are addressed at this point. The impact of such design choices on the ultimate navigational ability of the vehicle are assessed.

Section 7 presents the rationale behind building survivable robot systems for dangerous operations.

Section 8 presents system issues through a case study of the Autonomous Robot Architecture.

This chapter ends with a commentary on the techniques available for autonomous mobile robot navigation, an assessment of the progress made to date, and what we can expect realistically in the near future.

2 ACTION AND PERCEPTION

We have an existence proof that intelligent navigation can be conducted. Many lower life forms, as well as humans, are capable of satisfying the needs of intelligent navigation. Animal perception has evolved to fit the motor demands of different organisms. As robotic researchers, we expect to make more rapid progress than would be found on an evolutionary time scale. It would be useful to extract insights from those working systems to apply wherever possible to mobile robot research. That is not to say that the goal of autonomous vehicle research should be to create artificial beings or creatures, although there are some who advocate this viewpoint (Brooks, 1986b; Moravec, 1985). Much can be gained, however, by studying the efforts to explain intelligent navigation at a variety of levels.

A useful place to start is by evaluating the action–perception cycle (Fig. 5-1) (Neisser, 1976). The goals of an intelligent entity affect the way in which it perceives the world. The action–perception cycle depicts the interplay between perception, cognition, and motor action. Perception gives rise to cognitive events, which drive the motor system to interact with the environment to produce new perceptual information. It is important to note that only the perceptual information necessary to conduct currently relevant motor behaviors need be extracted from the environment. Full-scale scene analysis is unnecessary. The motivations (plans) of an intelligent entity should influence the way in which it perceives the world. Similarly, the environmental perceptions afforded by the world can modify the plans of an intelligent agent.

It would be useful to develop representational strategies that present the opportunity to exploit this cycle. This can result in significant computational savings. Expectation-based perception is one such technique. Motor behavior specification also enables flexible interaction with the world. Brooks (1986a) advocates a layered "subsumption" architecture to implement this concept. Arkin (1988c) proposes a schema-based network in the Autonomous Robot Architecture (AuRA). Both of these methods are discussed in Section 4.2.

Work by modelers such as Arbib (1981) and Mittelstaedt (1985) can provide new insights into the issues of intelligent navigation. In particular, by abstracting brain models at levels above neural structures (i.e., behavioral or

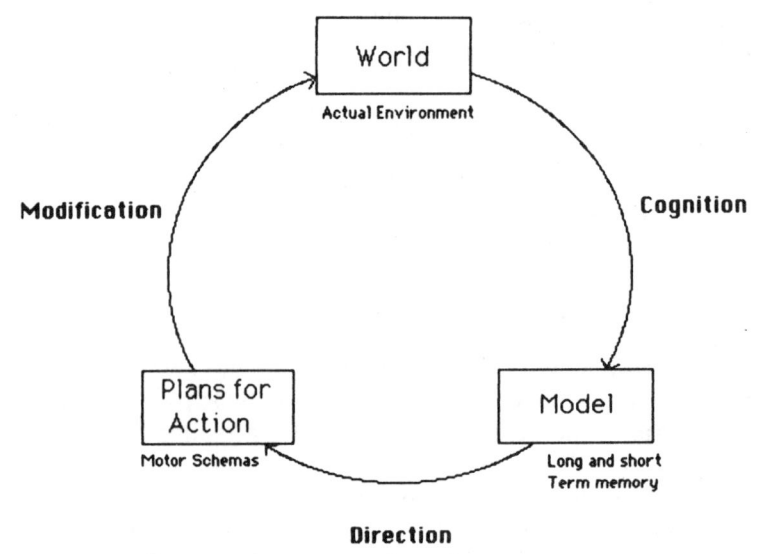

FIGURE 5-1
The action–perception cycle.

functional), a reasonable mapping can be made to mobile robot systems. The brain operates in a distributed, concurrent manner; mobile robot systems would do well to operate similarly. The amount of processing required to digest the tremendous quantity of sensory data from vision alone is staggering. By exploiting parallelism and expectation-based sensing wherever possible, the perceptual processing requirements can be made tractable.

3   KNOWLEDGE REPRESENTATIONS

In order for a robot to effectively interact with its environment, it must be provided with some knowledge of what the world is like. This knowledge can be of many different types. Cartographic knowledge encodes information regarding the world. Some of it may be a priori knowledge, such as static maps of the surroundings. Other cartographic knowledge can be acquired via sensing and built up dynamically as the robot moves through the world. Behavioral representations provide knowledge of how the robot should interact with the world.

3.1   Cartographic Knowledge

Cartographic information most typically represents knowledge of where the robot is free to travel. It may also include information regarding the location of landmarks and their models that can be used for recognition purposes. Other semantic information regarding the meaning or significance of particular locations or terrain types may also be embedded within the robot's internal maps.

Cartographic knowledge can be decomposed into two distinct classes. Long-term memory, information that is relative static and that can generally be relied upon to be true for navigational purposes, usually contains a priori knowledge. Short-term memory contains information that has been sensed in the recent past and cannot necessarily be relied upon for future navigational experiences.

Several characteristics that are important for a good cartographic representation are itemized below. A survey of the representational strategies will show that none of the techniques currently employed in mobile robot research fully satisfies all of these criteria. Nonetheless, these characteristics can be used as a metric upon which to evaluate the different cartographic representations available.

Efficiency: It is desirable for our robot to navigate as efficiently as possible within its world. By choosing appropriate representational strategies, the time required for planning can be minimized.

Uncertainty: A major characteristic of mobile robotics is the requirement to be able to cope with uncertainty. This uncertainty can take many forms: uncertainty in the robot's position relative to its modeled world; uncertainty in its perception; and uncertainty in the map itself. A good representation will support a means to represent these various aspects of uncertainty found in autonomous navigation.

Multiple frames of reference: How we express the interrelationships between the robot and its world poses a difficult question. An egocentric frame of reference for the robot, used for making its sensor observations, may need to be correlated against an absolute frame of reference obtained from blueprints, aerial maps, or mapping agencies. Perceptual processes may provide object-centered frames of reference for detected environmental objects. Transforms need to be provided to translate the knowledge encoded in one reference frame to another.

Sensor independence: In order to produce a flexible system, it is desirable to encode perceived knowledge in a sensor-independent format. Additional sensors can then be added, as new technology becomes available, with a minimum of system impact. This is no simple task, as different sensors generally provide different views of and information about the world. Careful thought must be given to the way in which detected features of the robot's world are represented.

Vehicle independence: Just as new sensor technology will become available, so will new robot systems. If the representational techniques employed are simply an ad hoc collection of information dependent upon a specific mobile platform, compatibility with new machinery as it becomes available is in serious doubt.

Semantic information: To take full advantage of expectation-based perception and goal-oriented behavior, it is important to be able to describe the nature of the world, not simply the places where the robot is free to travel. A representational strategy that facilitates the embedding of semantic knowledge is thus highly desirable and will be compatible with upward growth.

Facilitation of parallel processing: The ability to have representations accessed by multiple concurrent processes enables the robot to react more rapidly in situations requiring real-time response. Blackboard-like architectures are particularly well suited to fit this need. Of course, the issues of maintaining data integrity in such an environment are of paramount importance.

Support of localization: Representational techniques and mechanisms to correlate the robot's position relative to that of the modeled world must be available. This is particularly important to the exploitation of a priori knowledge of landmark location for expectation-based perception.

3.1.1 LONG-TERM MEMORY REPRESENTATIONAL STRATEGIES. Many techniques have been exploited as a means for representing a robot's world. Most of these are used specifically to support path-planning techniques. Four of the most significant representational strategies are described below followed by a summary of several other methods.

Meadow maps. A blend of two earlier representational forms has yielded the "meadow map"—a hybrid free-space vertex-graph representation. This model retains information concerning both the free navigable space and the bounding walls and obstacles that surround it. It was first developed by Crowley at Carnegie-Mellon University (CMU) (Crowley, 1984) and by Giralt and Chatila (Giralt et al., 1984) for the HILARE robot in France. It has recently been extended for use in multiple terrain types (Arkin, 1989a).

The basic representation consists of a collection of convex polygons networked in a connectivity graph (Fig. 5-2a). A basic property of convex regions guarantees that any two points found within a given region are to be free of collision with the modeled obstacles from which the region was produced. This simplifies the path-planning problem to finding a sequence of region traversals for the robot to undertake.

Several advantages are afforded by this approach. Semantic information that describes the nature of the regions themselves as well as the bounding obstacles that produced them can be readily embedded. A natural decomposition based on the nature of the space itself as opposed to overlaying a rigid grid is present. The ability to produce different types of paths (safe or short) dependent on the robot's mission is also available.

Regular grid. The regular grid representation (Fig. 5-2b) overlays a fixed spatial tesselation on the represented navigable space. Shakey (Nilsson, 1984) was

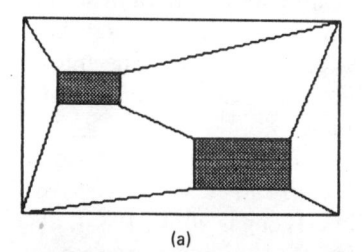

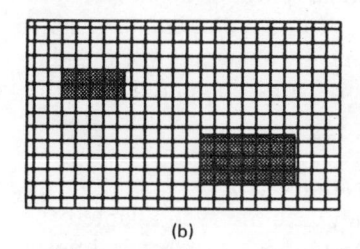

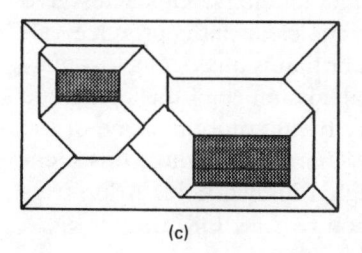

FIGURE 5-2
Navigational representations. (a) Meadow map; (b) regular grid; (c) Voronoi diagram.

the first system to use this approach, and its use persists today. Several systems (Mitchell and Keirsey, 1984; Parodi, 1985; Thorpe, 1984a) employ this representational methodology. A variant of the model, the quadtree representation (Kambhampati and Davis, 1986), uses a more efficient representation requiring significantly less memory. In the quadtree representation, free space is recursively decomposed into $2^n \times 2^n$ areas (areas whose borders are powers of 2). If larger blocks have uniform occupancy (vacant or occupied), the decomposition stops before reaching the lowest levels of resolution. Both methods suffer from a problem known as *digitization bias* (Mitchell and Keirsey, 1984), which causes less than optimal results to be produced. This problem is similar to the phenomenon of aliasing observed in computer graphics and can produce jagged, irregular paths. A major advantage of the grid method arises from the fact that much of the available data for map making (typically from the Defense Mapping Agency) is already present in a grid format.

Voronoi diagrams. Voronoi diagrams (Fig. 5-2c) are a variant of the free-space approach. This representational model is particularly amenable to the production of fast, safe paths. The Voronoi diagram is used to partition free space into equivalence classes. Typically, the space is represented very compactly as a series of connected straight-line segments. It is produced by the generation of a set of polygonal regions, each representing an enclosed area in which all contained points are closer to one particular point in a given point set than to any other point in the set. This set of polygons partitions the plane into a convex net. The resulting diagram or its straight-line dual can be used to compute the safest path for navigation of a mobile vehicle.

One interesting version of the Voronoi diagram (Miller, 1985) partitions the space according to the ability of the robot to localize itself via sonar. Another approach used by the HERMIES series robots (Iyengar et al., 1985), developed at the Oak Ridge National Laboratories for navigational experiments in nuclear power facilities, uses the more traditional Voronoi decomposition based on obstacle location. Although compact, the Voronoi diagram in general suffers from a limited ability to cope with a dynamically changing world and is somewhat restricted in its ability to generate short paths compared with the methods described above.

Potential fields. Potential fields have broad applications. Not only can they be used for path planning as described here, but they also are well adapted for sensor-driven reactive/reflexive navigation. A gravitational (or electrical field) analog is used for planning purposes with this methodology. Obstacles give rise to peaks, goals are viewed as depressions, while clear paths produce valleys. The robot's path can be computed in a manner that is analogous to a marble rolling through a course to its goal. A principal advantage of this technique lies in the ability to reflect perceptual uncertainty by altering the slope of the obstacle peaks and perceived goals. Krogh and Thorpe (1986) use this technique to produce paths for a mobile robot through a known field. Arkin uses this representation for reactive/reflexive navigation (Arkin, 1987a).

A major problem for this methodology lies in the existence of local maxima, minima, and cycles. Methodologies exist to cope with these problems but generally require additional planning and representational strategies. An advantage of this approach, in addition to handling uncertainty, lies in the smoother trajectories that can be produced with this technique.

Miscellaneous. A multiplicity of other methods exist for long-term memory representation. A few are briefly listed below.

Generalized cylinders: These (Kuan et al., 1985) partition free space into a collection of interconnected freeways. These freeways, represented as spines with information regarding their clearance to the left and right, are produced by sweeping a two-dimensional cross section through space according to a sweeping rule.

Vertex graphs: No express representation of the free space is present. Instead, the vertices of the obstacles to navigation are modeled (typically polygonal approximations). By using the configuration space approach attributed to Lozano-Perez (1982), the vertices can be grown by a distance equal to the radius of a circle enclosing the robot (more sophisticated techniques are also available). The path-planning problem is thus reduced to simply finding a sequence of grown vertices that produce the shortest path. Combining safe paths with short paths poses difficulties and requires regenerating the configuration space representation, a relatively costly operation.

Automaton representation: This technique represents landmark locations as states of an automaton. It has been used for the development of Meldog, a series of "guide dog" robots produced in Japan (Tachi and Komoriya, 1985). Inputs to the state diagram include directional commands, which when combined with internal state knowledge yield steering angles and the distance to travel to reach the next landmark, which corresponds to the next automaton state.

Other representational techniques are also used, but they have received less attention than those mentioned above. For a more comprehensive survey, see Arkin (1986).

3.1.2 SHORT-TERM MEMORY REPRESENTATIONAL STRATEGIES. The representational needs for short-term memory are considerably different from those associated with the storage of a priori knowledge in long-term memory. Sensor data must be readily integrable into these representations. Ideally sensor fusion should occur at or before this level in the quest to preserve our goal of sensor independence. The key factor is the ability to integrate perceived world information into a more long-lasting model.

There are cogent arguments against building up perceived world maps (Brooks, 1985). One such school of navigational thought advocates reacting to the perceived world rather than first building models and then planning in response to the model. Nonetheless, many researchers devote considerable effort to the production of dynamically acquired world models, where the robot explores, perceives, and learns information about its world. It then resorts to these representations for planning purposes. Some of the techniques used to model a dynamically acquired world model are described below.

Regular grids have been applied to the problem of sensor-acquired world modeling. Initially this approach was limited to ultrasonic data (Elfes, 1987), but it has recently been extended to include stereo vision (Moravec, 1988), dealing with the serious issues of sensor fusion. In essence, the grid forms a representation of free space in which sensor measurements are used to determine the occupancy of a specific area. Using appropriate sensor models, probabilistic interpretation of the raw data can be made. With the ability to recognize free space from cluttered areas, path-planning algorithms have been applied to produce successful navigation.

A three-dimensional short-term memory model, built from multiple stereo vision measurements, has been developed by Faugeras's group in the Institut National de Recherche en Informatique et en Automatique (INRIA) in France (Ayache and Faugeras, 1987). This method is capable of dealing with noisy sensor data. It exploits an important paradigm, the extended Kalman filter, which has found wide application in the fusing of sensory data collected from multiple locations. The resulting visual maps contain a geometric representation of the world (points, lines, and planes) in conjunction with an associated uncertainty measure for the values associated with these geometric primitives.

Work at SRI (Smith and Cheeseman, 1985) has provided an elegant framework, using Kalman filter theory and Monte Carlo techniques, for the combination of multiple sensor observations. Their techniques of compounding (combining a sequence of uncertain observations into a single transformation) and merging (combining multiple parallel uncertain observations of a single event into one observation) provide an important theoretical foundation for the combination of multiple sensor measurements. Kalman filters are also exploited for stereo navigation at CMU (Shafer and Mathies, 1986).

Brooks (1985) advocated the use of a relational map as the means to express the robot's perceived world. No world frame of reference is used. Instead multiple frames of reference (egocentric, object-centered, etc.) are represented, and the transforms to get from one to the other are modeled. Brooks has since taken the stance that the world itself is its own best representation (Brooks, 1988a).

3.2 Plan Representations

Another form of knowledge that must be encoded for effective navigation expresses the means by which the robot is to interact with its world. Some attempts have been made to use a rule-based approach (Weisbin et al., 1986), but in general this methodology is insufficient to produce the flexibility necessary for diverse environments.

A more common strategy is to encode the behaviors (or plans for interaction) in a form that can react to sensor data, draw on world models, and communicate its goals to the motor system of the robot. These behaviors can express knowledge regarding behaviors such as wandering, moving to a goal, exploring, and staying on a road. This general approach has had marked experimental success. Typically these plan units are formulated in terms of finite state automata (Brooks, 1986a) (a classical computer science formal model), schemas (Arkin, 1987a) (frame-like structures with associated processing capabilities), reflexive behaviors (Payton, 1986) (procedural units with stringent real-time demands), reactive adaptation packages (Firby, 1987) (flexible descriptions for enacting behaviors), or other related representations. The fundamental difference between the implementation of these ideas lies not in what the behaviors accomplish, but rather in the way in which the behaviors are initially chosen, interact with each other, and yield the final motor control commands to the vehicle.

High-level spatial and temporal reasoning is another important area of research that is intimately involved with the formulation of successful mission plans for a mobile robot. The reader is referred to *AI Magazine* (1988) for a discussion of this more general form of planning which is relatively far removed form actual robot navigation.

4 NAVIGATIONAL PLANNING

There are two major schools of navigational thought. These are represented by the hierarchical paradigm and the parallel paradigm. Considerable controversy rages between the proponents of these two different methodologies.

4.1 Hierarchical Planners

The hierarchical school predates the parallel school. It has been implemented in several systems (e.g., Keirsey et al., 1984; Koch et al., 1985) with varying degrees of success. Most of these systems use three to four levels in their planning hierarchy. The terms used to describe these levels (mission planner, helm, pilot, navigator, etc.) unfortunately do not have any well-defined semantics. The important distinction between these levels (Fig. 5-3) typically involves changes in spatial resolution, and as one progresses down the hierarchy the increased dependence on sensed data, the significance of response time, the greater importance of sensor information, and less dependence on previous knowledge. One dominant characteristic of hierarchical planners is the existence of well-defined interfaces between the levels, which offer predictable and predetermined control and communication between the modularized planning subsystems.

The National Bureau of Standards has formulated a decomposition of planning that it advocates as the correct methodology for robot planning in general. This approach is referred to as the NASA/NBS Standard Reference

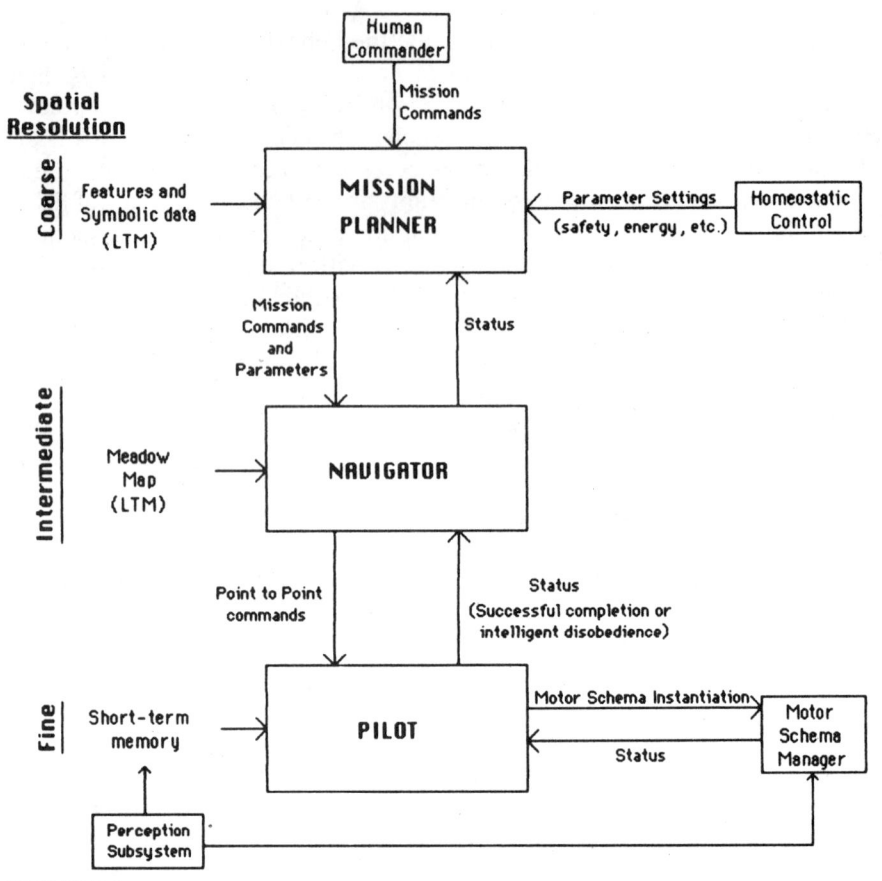

FIGURE 5-3
Typical hierarchical planner.

Model for Telerobot Control System Architecture (NASREM) (Albus et al., 1987). This architecture has been used in a project for the development of multiple autonomous undersea vehicles. This system is strictly hierarchical (Albus and Blidberg, 1987; Blidberg and Chappell, 1986; Herman and Albus, 1987). The highest level is mission control, which maps its commands onto various groups of undersea vehicles. The new goals are then mapped onto tasks for specific undersea robots, which are further decomposed into elemental moves and other low-level control layers prior to actuation by the thrusters. Two undersea vehicles were used in the undersea experiments of this work.

Meystel (1986) at Drexel University is evolving a theory of hierarchical planners that focuses on the issues of navigational scope. A nested hierarchical knowledge-based controller serves as the basis for much of this work. Key issues are centered upon the focus of concentration, which changes in planning from one level of the hierarchy to the next. The implications of representational adequacy (resolution of knowledge) for a particular hierarchical level are considered, especially in light of navigational scope. This work is one of the few efforts that concentrates on the theory of planning and gives major justification to the hierarchical school of navigational planning.

4.2 Parallel Planners

The primary strategy of parallel planners is to decompose a robot's task into an appropriate set of motor strategies. These are all then activated in parallel. The most significant demonstrations using actual robots that respond to a dynamically changing world have been achieved using this type of planners (Brooks and Connell, 1986; Arkin, 1987b).

Brooks's subsumption architecture is the first working example of this planning paradigm. This layered approach is built on the premise that more complex behaviors are built on top of existing simpler ones. These higher-level behaviors *subsume* the functionality of the lower ones. Using a finite-state automata model, specifications can be made for communication and control between these layers. This architecture, embedded in several robots whose goal is to emulate insect behavior, utilizes multiple concurrent task-achieving behaviors. The advantages are manifold. They include a more robust architecture, the ease of hardware retargetability (Brooks, 1987), and the ability to readily guide sensor processing to the points where it is needed. Although high-level planning was initially formulated within the subsumption architecture, the ability to integrate a priori world knowledge is considerably more difficult with this method. Brooks argues against the use of any such world representations as a potential stumbling block for researchers in navigational planning (Brooks, 1988a). His view is somewhat controversial.

Arkin's (1987a) schema-based plan execution system also exploits the parallel planning paradigm. Motor schemas (discussed further in Section 8) are similar to the subsumption architecture in that they represent primitive motor behaviors. Schemas, however, are configured in a dynamic network that is strongly dependent on the robot's current goals within the context of available a priori knowledge. The number of schemas and their interconnections changes as the robot moves through the world in response to perception, making this approach quite suitable for distributed computation. Each motor schema has one or more associated perceptual schemas that deliver the necessary sensor information to produce the correct motor action. A vector associated with a potential field is produced by each motor schema, which, after summation with the output of all active motor schemas, produces the motor commands for the vehicle. Typical primitive behaviors include move-to-goal, avoid-static-obstacle, stay-on-path, and move-ahead. It is usually the case that several of these are active in parallel. This schema-based methodology (Arkin, 1988c) is related to neuroscientific models of detour behavior (obstacle avoidance) in amphibians.

Payton (1986), Kadonoff (Kadonoff et al., 1986), and others also use variants of parallel planners to drive robot systems. The principal difficulty with this approach lies in the integration of previous world knowledge and incorporation of high-level reasoning. One method (Arkin et al., 1987a) uses a combination of hierarchical and parallel planning to exploit the best features of each paradigm. Although formal models exist for the definition and interconnection of various forms of parallel planners [e.g., finite-state automata, schema theory (Lyons, 1986)], it will probably be some time before a consensus arises regarding the relationship between the hierarchical and parallel navigational planning paradigms.

4.3 Route Planning

Quite commonly routes are generated before the mobile robot actually begins its motion. Generating the path from many of the representations described earlier poses a classic artificial intelligence problem, requiring the search of a possibly large state space. The representation used determines the nature and extent of the space to be searched. Some representations will require greater search effort than others.

In the vast majority of cases, the A* algorithm is the search technique used. This algorithm, developed over two decades ago (Hart et al., 1968), is central to much of artificial intelligence search techniques. The A* algorithm utilizes an evaluation function (f*) to assess which point (node) in the search tree should be expanded next. f* is equal to the sum of two components, g* and h*. Loosely speaking, g* is equal to the actual cost to get from the start to the current position on the search. h*, the heuristic component of the evaluation function, is an estimate of how much it will cost to get from the current position to the goal. It has been proved that with a properly chosen heuristic (h*) the optimal path is guaranteed to be found. The condition required to produce this optimal path is referred to as the admissibility condition and can be succinctly stated as follows: The Heuristic estimate (h*) must never overestimate the actual cost to the goal and must also be nonnegative. If a heuristic can be found that always returns the *actual* cost to the goal, it is a perfect heuristic, and the A* algorithm using this heuristic is guaranteed to find an optimal solution in optimal time.

Although Dijkstra's graph search is occasionally mentioned (e.g., Mitchell and Keirsey, 1984) for use in mobile robotics path planning, it is generally agreed that A* is the algorithm of choice. The basic question then becomes, Which heuristic should be used for the A* algorithm? Generally the most straightforward is employed: the remaining straight-line distance from the current position to the goal. This is sufficient to guarantee an admissible solution based on a distance metric for optimality. In several cases, however, criteria other than just straight-line distance are considered. Factors such as terrain and safety can be weighed when developing an appropriate cost function. It has been stated that the heuristics are developed largely on an ad hoc basis (Koch et al., 1985), and more theoretical research is needed to understand just what constitutes an optimal path for mobile robots. The question of how important an admissible solution is to this particular search problem also remains unanswered. Chattergy at the University of Hawaii has explored some other forms of heuristics that can be applied to mobile robot navigation (Chattergy, 1985). These include a probing technique for finding a target in the presence of barriers and an extension for avoiding backtracking in a cluttered world.

One interesting approach to path generation developed by Thorpe at CMU is based on a path relaxation process (Thorpe, 1984a). This planner develops a better path from the first-cut solution initially put forth by operations performed on the underlying grid representation. Subgoal nodes (produced from an A* search of the grid) are displaced according to specific constraints, and the cost function is recomputed. This process is repeated until convergence into a minimum cost path is observed. The net result is the removal of jagged edges as the path settles into a relaxed state. This idea of an iterative relaxation-type process for path refinement has been extended to the meadow-map representation as well (Arkin, 1989a).

In a few cases, dynamic programming techniques were exploited for path generation instead of pure heuristic search (e.g., Parodi, 1985). In the first case cited, dynamic programming is used in conjunction with standard AI search techniques. Based on the claims made by the authors, dynamic programming is a viable alternative to pure search, but it still appears to be the exception rather than the rule in generating paths in a mobile robot's world.

A novel technique using wave propagation through configuration space as the basis for path generation has recently appeared (Dorst and Trovato, 1988). Actually, a regular grid serves as the basic representation for this early work. The technique treats the start point as the place where waves are generated that subsequently radiate outwards. This propagation continues until the goal is encountered. The analog is the method by which waves are generated when a pebble is dropped into a still pond. The computed path is the direction normal to all the waves between the start and goal. Very smooth paths can be produced using this method, although the computation itself can be costly when compared to other methods.

5 INTELLIGENT SENSING

Without a doubt, the ability of a robot to interpret information about its immediate surroundings is crucial to the successful achievement of its navigational goals. The real world is quite hostile to mobile systems. Things move and change without warning, and only partial knowledge of the world is available. Additionally, any a priori information available may be incorrect or inaccurate. For these and other reasons, it is essential for the robot to be able to obtain sensor feedback regarding changes in the world as well as changes in its own position relative to the environment. Mobile robots are ultimately meant to operate in the natural world, with little to no restructuring available. Many computer vision techniques that exploit specialized lighting or scene constraints are worthless when applied to this difficult problem domain.

Sensor technology has advanced rapidly in the last several years. This has resulted in many low-cost sensor systems that can be deployed on functional mobile robots. Sensors are available in two forms: passive and active. Passive sensors use information that is already available in the environment and that is naturally directed toward the robot. Computer vision is perhaps the most typical mode of passive sensing. Passivity is particularly important in military applications where detection of the robot must be avoided. Active sensing, on the other hand, involves the emission into the environment of energy that is then reflected in some manner back to the robot. Ultrasonic sensing and laser range-finding are the two most common active sensor modalities used for mobile robot research.

A brief discussion of the operation of several representative sensor systems follows. This includes the use of shaft encoders for dead reckoning. Shaft encoders are not environmental sensors in the strict sense because they measure only the rotations of the robot's motors. Nonetheless, they are widely used for positional estimation and thus will be included in the following discussion. The remainder of this section is organized around the types of sensor tasks that are important for an intelligent autonomous robot to accomplish. These include (listed in approximate order of difficulty) obstacle avoidance, path or road following, goal or target identification, and landmark recognition for localization. After a brief discussion of the sensor systems themselves, the progress made toward achieving these tasks is presented.

5.1 Computer Vision

Video technology has been available for some time now. Only recently, however, has charge-coupled (CCD) camera technology advanced rapidly in terms of miniaturization and lowering cost. Color imagery is now available at relatively affordable prices.

Although some digital cameras are available, most mobile robot vision systems consist of one or two black-and-white or color analog-output CCD cameras, one or more digitizers, and an image processor. As mobile robots require real-time interpretation of incoming video data, the specialized architectures found in image processors are generally necessary for serious research.

The amount of video information received by the robot can be staggering. Typical image resolution is on the order of 512×512 pixels (picture elements), with each pixel consisting of 8 bits of information encoding 256 intensity levels. Multiply this value by 3 for color images (one image plane each for red, green, and blue), and then attempt to process at frame rate (30/second). You now have a receiving bandwidth of approximately 24 megabytes/second! Obviously, specialized hardware and software must be utilized to make computer vision applicable in this domain.

The real-time navigational needs of mobile robots tend to distinguish the research community's efforts from that of mainstream computer vision. Algorithms are generally designed to exploit action-oriented perception wherever possible. Adaptive techniques, which track features over multiple frames, are also commonly used. Full-scale scene interpretation is generally not required.

Two phases of perception can be readily distinguished in the application of computer vision to mobile robot navigation: the recognition phase, which extracts a recognizable feature (goal, landmark, path, obstacle) from an incoming image, and the tracking (or feedforward) phase, which uses information obtained from the recognition process to track the detected object in subsequent frames. This decoupling of recognition and tracking can be found in most of the successfully implemented computer vision strategies employed in current mobile vehicles and is clearly in evidence in the road-following strategies described below.

5.2 Ultrasonic Sensing

Sonar (ultrasonic sensing) involves active sensing. It operates on the same basic principle by which bats navigate through their environment. A high-frequency click of sound is emitted, which reflects off a nearby surface and returns at a measurable time later. The time for reflection can be used to compute the distance to the surface that reflected the sound. A typical ultrasonic sensor emits a beam that receives echoes from a region approximately 30° wide emanating from its source. These sensors can operate very rapidly, returning 10 or more depth data points per second. Accuracy for many working systems is typically on the order of 3 centimeters (0.1 foot) over a maximum range of up to 10 meters.

Ultrasonic sensing has decided advantages and disadvantages compared to computer vision. It is significantly lower in cost, provides three-dimensional information (distance to an object), and returns tractable amounts of data for interpretation. Its disadvantages are also substantial. These include much poorer discriminatory ability, a susceptibility to noise and distortion due to environmental conditions, the frequent production of erroneous data due to reflections of the outgoing sound waves, and spreading of the sonar beam. Sonar has found its best use in obstacle detection and avoidance at short range. Its inability to discriminate between what constitutes an obstacle and a goal, as a consequence of the fact that the return signal contains only distance information, limits its applicability to other tasks. Sonar cannot be used in outer space because it requires a medium for the transmission of sound waves. Progress has been made in the use of phased sonar arrays to provide greater information about the environment, but these currently have not been deployed for use on mobile vehicles.

5.3 Laser Scanners

Laser scanners are active sensors also. Instead of emitting sound, they emit a low-powered laser beam that is scanned over a surface. Through techniques such as phase amplitude modulation, the distance to the individual points can be computed. The net result is an array of image points that each have an associated depth. In effect, a three-dimensional image is obtained. Reflectance data are also generally available, providing data on the nature of the surface as well.

These machines provide a wealth of information that is unavailable from any other single sensor. As such, they hold the potential of yielding major advances in mobile robot research. They are not without their drawbacks, however. First and foremost is their cost. At the time of writing, this was approximately $100,000—beyond the reach of many research laboratories. Another problem arises from the mechanical instabilities associated with current implementations of these devices. More subtle intrinsic difficulties can be found as a result of the sparse data sampling found at longer distances (a consequence of the imaging geometry), which can cause certain objects to go undetected, and problems with range periodicities when using phase-modulated systems that force interpretation ambiguities on the incoming data.

5.4 Dead Reckoning

Dead reckoning provides information as to how far a vehicle is thought to have traveled, based on the rotation of its motors, wheels, or treads. It does not rely on environmental sensing. Two general methods for dead reckoning are available: shaft encoders and inertial navigational systems.

Shaft encoders are by far the most frequently used method of dead reckoning, because of their low cost. They operate by maintaining a count of the number of rotations of the steering and drive motor shafts (or wheel axles) and converting these data into the distance traveled and the orientation of the robot. Shaft encoders can be extremely misleading. If you have ever been stuck in mud or snow in an automobile, you can recognize that the information on how many times the drive wheels have turned does not correlate well with the positional changes of the car. As shaft encoders only measure changes in the internal state of the robot, they must be supplemented with environmental sensing to produce reliable results.

Inertial navigational systems (INS) do not measure the rotation of wheels or shafts but rather track the accelerations the robot has undergone and convert this information into positional displacements. This results in very accurate dead reckoning systems with one major penalty: extremely high costs. Inertial navigational systems are also prone to internal drift problems and must be recalibrated periodically to yield accurate information. The quality of these data makes INSs far more desirable than shaft encoders, but cost and power requirements frequently prevent their deployment.

Satellite navigational systems can also be used to provide geographic information. Geosynchronous satellites relay positional data whereby the robot can deduce its position relative to a world coordinate system. Satellite systems and other less sophisticated beacon systems (e.g., ground-based infrared) are really versions of landmark recognition where the perceptual task is greatly simplified by restructuring the environment in favor of the robot. Robots that rely on such systems are considerably less autonomous than those that try to extract information from an unstructured and more natural environment.

5.5 Perceptual Tasks

Now that we have described the typical sensor modalities by which a robot can acquire information from its environment, we will see how they can be exploited to solve the problems of intelligent navigation in a real and dynamically changing world. The four major perceptual tasks facing autonomous mobile robots are obstacle avoidance, road following, goal identification, and landmark recognition for localization.

None of these tasks is trivial, due to the inhospitability of the real world. Confounding factors are always present. These may take the form of shadows, reflections, occlusions, or specularities. Note also that the complexity of data interpretation is somewhat task-dependent. In some cases, an understanding of the meaning (the semantics) behind what the robot has sensed is required (e.g., goal recognition and landmark localization); for other tasks, the interpretation is less demanding (e.g., obstacle avoidance).

Several common threads run through many of the perceptual algorithms. As mentioned earlier, it can be seen that most perceptual tasks can be decomposed into two distinct phases: recognition and tracking. The recognition component, distinguishing the object from its surroundings for the first time, is considerably more difficult than tracking it subsequent to its discovery. The recognition phase must rely heavily on expectations produced by internal models of landmarks and how specific sensors would image the object to be recognized. Once recognized, however, the a priori models can be set aside in favor of using data from previous sensor data sets (e.g., earlier video images). These new expectations can then reflect changes in lighting, robot orientation, occlusion, and the like. Internal object representations must be constructed to reflect this inherent adaptability during the tracking phase. This is particularly important for goal recognition, landmark tracking, and road-following tasks.

Most representations currently used for recognition purposes in this domain are still developed on an ad hoc basis and in general are largely sensor-dependent. An important research problem lies in the development of sensor-independent models that can be transformed into specific sensor expectations. The use of discrimination nets (Burns and Kitchen, 1987) or aspect graphs as a means for tying together multiple views holds promise for a more coherent approach to goal and landmark modeling.

5.5.1 OBSTACLE AVOIDANCE. The task of obstacle avoidance is in many respects the easiest of the perceptual tasks the robot must undertake. It is also the most important. It is easy in the sense that we do not have to associate high-level semantic labels with objects in the environment; they need only be recognized as impediments to motion. It is important in the sense that if we cannot avoid crashing into things along the way, all the other navigational tasks become fruitless. Ultrasonic sensing, computer vision, and laser rangefinding have all been applied to this problem with varying degrees of success. Representative examples of how each sensor modality can be used to tackle this important perceptual need follow.

Ultrasound. Ultrasonic data, as mentioned earlier, are well suited for providing sensor information for obstacle avoidance purposes. In the simplest of systems, sonar echoes are used to detect the presence of an object within a given range in front of the robot. This in turn causes the robot to stop. More sophisticated systems use the information for navigation in one of two ways: path planning or reactive/reflexive navigation.

Path planning for obstacle avoidance yields a path for the robot based on environmentally sensed conditions. The scope of this path will typically extend for several meters. This approach is limited if there are moving obstacles present, as the path, generated at an earlier time, fails to take into account the motion of the obstacles and can thus become invalid. Reactive/reflexive navigation, on the other hand, does not compute a path per se but instead reacts immediately to perceived sensor information.

Actual working robots have been used to demonstrate both of these obstacle avoidance methods. The grid approach used for short-term memory described previously (Elfes, 1987) has been used to produce paths for a mobile robot after the ultrasonic sensors have filled the working grid model with information regarding the volumetric occupancy of the world (Fig. 5-4a). Potential fields have also been used for reactive/reflexive navigation using a repulsive force generated by ultrasonically detected obstacles (Brooks and Connell, 1986; Arkin, 1987b) (Fig. 5-4b).

Computer vision. The use of computer vision for the detection of obstacles can be more difficult. Even in well-defined environments, due to the absence of three-dimensional information regarding arbitrarily shaped objects in a two-dimensional video image, more sophisticated techniques must be used. It is easy to confuse a shadow or oil spot with an obstacle on a road when analyzing a single video frame. When certain assumptions are made to disambiguate these situations, the result is a decrease in the robustness of the vision algorithm and an increase in the likelihood of a collision.

Two major vision techniques have been used to recover three-dimensional information about the position of obstacles. The first utilizes stereo vision (Fig. 5-5a): two or more cameras separated by a known baseline. After features are matched in both incoming video frames, the distance to the object can be computed. This feature matching (the correlation problem) is the most difficult aspect of the technique. Early robot systems used stereo vision (Moravec, 1981; Nilsson, 1984), and its use is continually being refined in newer systems (Thorpe, 1984b; Ayache and Faugeras, 1987).

The second vision technique for recovering depth to objects involves the acquisition of multiple frames by a single camera mounted on the robot as it

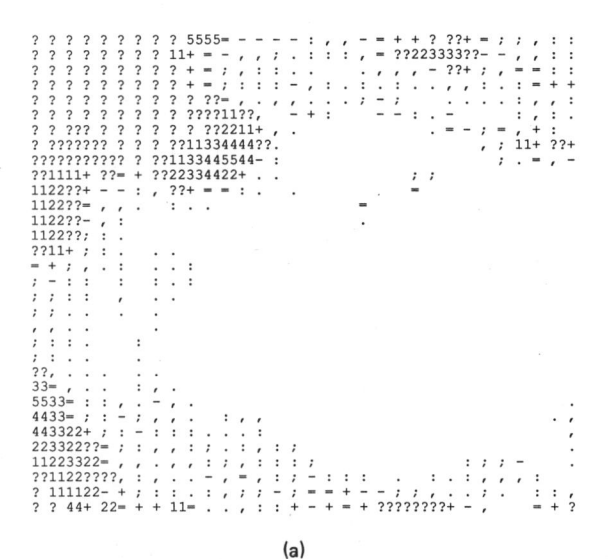

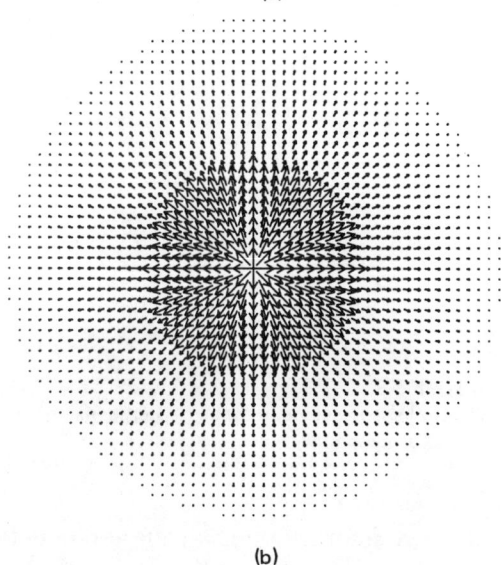

FIGURE 5-4
Ultrasonic obstacle representations. (a) Volumetric map; (b) potential field.

moves through the world (Fig. 5-5b). By measuring the distance between acquired frames and matching features between the images (yes, the correspondence problem is present here as well), an estimate of the distance to the object can be recovered. This method is considerably more difficult than stereo but requires only a single camera. Some systems have used this approach (Arkin et al., 1987b; Brooks et al., 1987) with limited success. A major disadvantage results from the presence of pitch, roll, and tilt errors that occur as a result of the robot's translation. Currently, this technique is not as robust as the stereo methods.

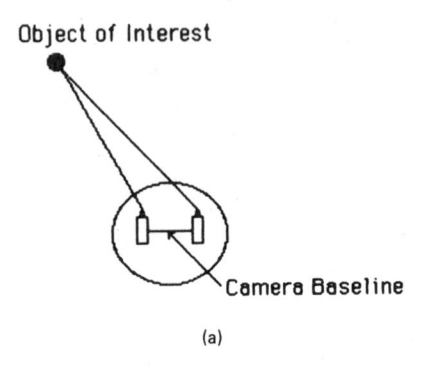

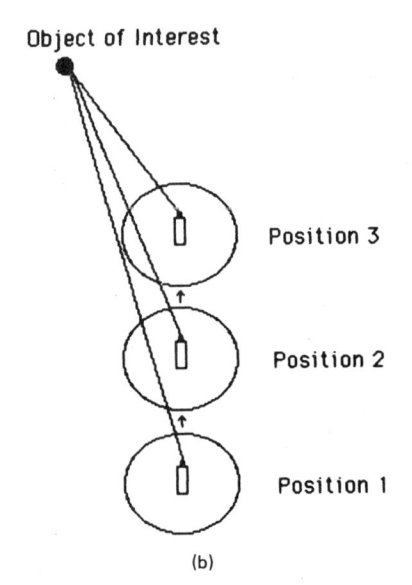

FIGURE 5-5
Visual obstacle detection (a) using stereo vision and (b) using motion vision.

Laser rangefinders. Three-dimensional range information is a natural product of laser scanning. It has been applied to obstacle avoidance (Whittaker et al., 1987) in a straightforward manner. Visual segmentation algorithms are applied to the depth data resident in the incoming scanner image, yielding regions (obstacles) that can be shown to violate the ground-plane assumption and thus can be declared obstacles. This ground-plane assumption, commonly used in much of mobile robotics, assumes that the region in front of the robot, at least locally, can be modeled as a plane and (in most cases) the robot is located and moving on that plane. Highly textured or bumpy regions, as well as hill crests or valley bottoms, can cause this assumption to be violated. Heuristics can be applied based on a priori topographical knowledge to take into account deviations from this assumption when such heuristic knowledge is available.

One problem with most of these obstacle detection techniques is their limited ability to detect pits and crevices (inverse obstacles) in the robot's path. These certainly are equally as dangerous as upstanding obstacles if not more so. Depressions in the path are not as readily discernible as upright obstacles due to the occlusion formed by the ground surface itself (Fig. 5-6). Additional research is required to find more robust techniques to detect these more obscure barriers to safe motion.

5.5.2 PATH AND ROAD FOLLOWING. Computer vision is particularly adept at providing information for road following. The depth sensors, ultrasound and laser rangefinders, generally do not provide the information required to find a road. Laser rangefinder reflectance data can be used, but this secondary information is really a modified version of computer vision data.

A variety of vision techniques have been applied to this problem. These try to find either the road edges or the road using line-finding or segmentation techniques. In almost all cases, information from previous images is used to modify the expectations of where the road is to occur and in some cases how it is to appear in subsequent images. Real-time navigation thus becomes pos-

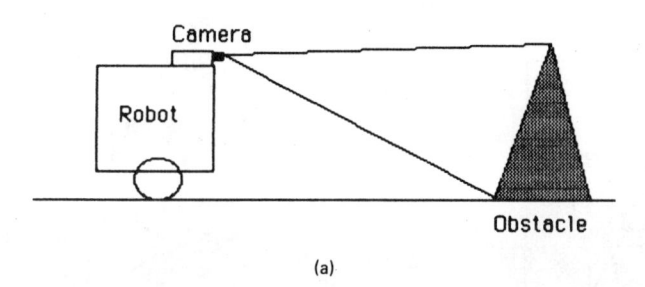

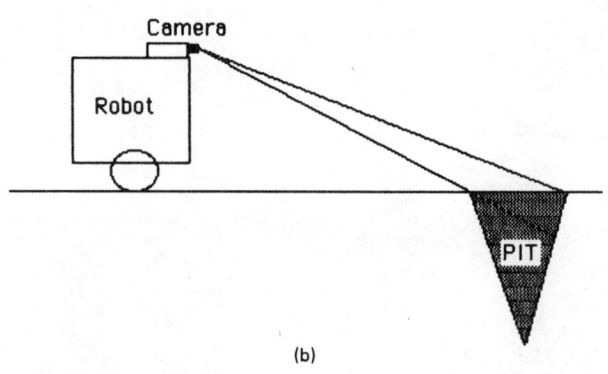

FIGURE 5-6
Obstacle versus pit detection. (a) Obstacle located on road; (b) depression in road (pit).

sible by restricting the amount of video information that must be processed. This is particularly important when one realizes how roads wind and may have shadows or other variations in their texture. If the assumption is made that these changes are gradual (i.e., the images are acquired at relatively small distances and at relatively short time intervals), reasonably robust video road following can be demonstrated (Wallace, 1987). This assumption forces a strong dependency on the processing of incoming frames and the velocity of the robot. The speed of the vehicle can safely increase only as the video processing speed increases.

Road and path edge extraction techniques typically use edge operators (Dickmanns and Zapp, 1985; Waxman et al., 1987) or straight-line finders (Arkin et al., 1987b). A common thread for all the algorithms lies in their use of predictive windows (focus-of-attention mechanisms) as a means of concentrating computational effort.

One edge-based technique (Davis et al., 1986) applies multiple windows (Fig. 5-7a) to the road edge area. An edge-finding algorithm is run within each window of the image. This is followed by thresholding based on gradient orientation and then the application of a model-based identification technique to determine the position of the road edge. This algorithm has been used successfully in visual navigation experiments on the Autonomous Land Vehicle man-

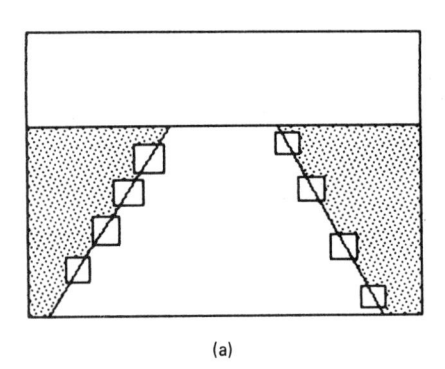

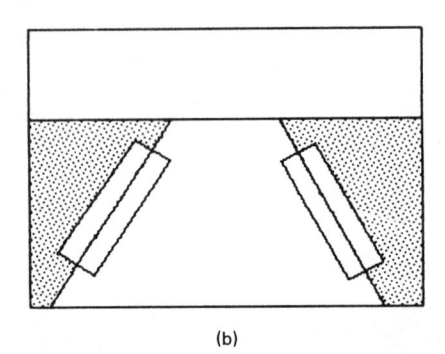

FIGURE 5-7
Road edge windowing. (a) Multiple windows for road edges; (b) single window for each road edge.

ufactured by Martin-Marietta Corp. A specialized image processor is used to obtain the high processing speeds necessary.

Another example of the use of edge-based methods for road following has been developed for use in high-speed navigation (65 km/hr and higher). A specialized machine architecture uses multiple windows as in the previous method but associates special microprocessors with each window, distributing the computation. This system additionally takes into account the actual dynamics of the vehicle and the constraints imposed by the domain (the German Autobahn) to restrict processing even further. Demonstrations of this system are impressive. It should be realized, though, that several aspects of this approach are not as general as the other methods in this section, due to the high reliance on the tight engineering constraints of the road system. Efforts are being made to relax these constraints.

Another system (Arkin et al., 1987b) extracts the path edge in a single operation (Figs. 5-7*b* and 5-8) as opposed to processing over multiple windows. This method does not rely on edge detectors but rather utilizes a straight-line-finding algorithm (Kahn et al, 1987) whose operation can be summarized as follows. Two windows are selected for the road boundaries, based on previous images, a priori knowledge, or other available sensor data. Within these regions the pixels are classified according to their gradient orientation. A connected components algorithm is then run, producing regions of similar orientation. Lines are then fitted to the resulting regions. A merging process is conducted using the candidate set of lines based on the expectation of the road boundary orientation, yielding a straight line associated with each path edge (Fig. 5-8*c*). This is then used to provide navigational information to the mobile robot and for updating the expectations to be used in subsequent video images. This system has been demonstrated on a working mobile robot (Arkin, 1987b).

All of the boundary detection methods are susceptible to occlusion of the path boundary by obstacles present on the road. Techniques must be available to cope with this eventual occurrence. Segmentation methods, described below, extract the body of the road as opposed to only the edges and are thus less susceptible to this problem.

The best example of visual segmentation for road following has been demonstrated to work on robots at CMU (Wallace, 1987). Adaptive techniques form the heart of this process. Color imagery is also used in contrast to the intensity-based methods typically employed for boundary detection. This algorithm first uses statistics gathered from previous images regarding the color intensity of road and non-road regions (including data about the sunny and shadowed characteristics). A connected components algorithm produces regions that are then approximated by polygons. The spatial extent of the road is determined, guided by domain knowledge, and a best fit of the road to the available data is produced. The color statistics inside the newly determined road area are reevaluated and used for subsequent images (as well as another iterative pass on the current image). Other systems using region segmentation for path following have also been effectively demonstrated (e.g., Arkin, 1987b; Turk et al., 1987).

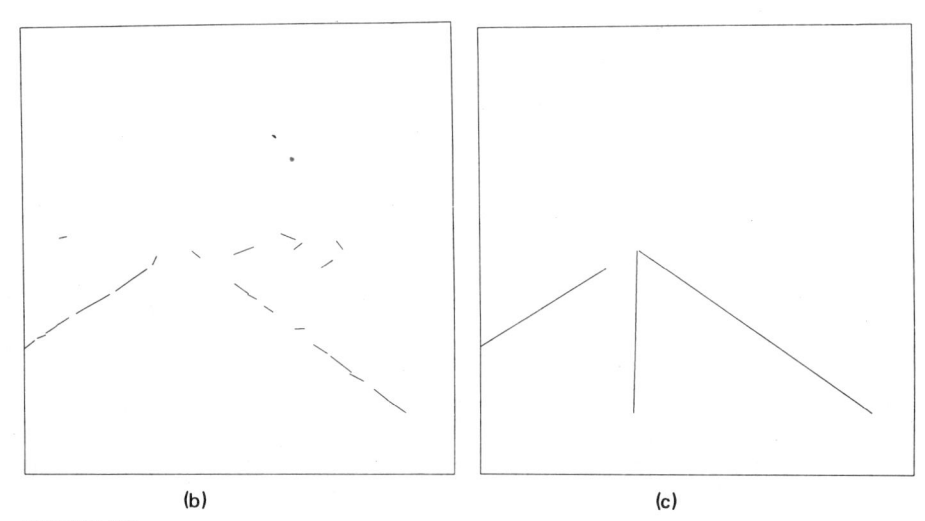

FIGURE 5-8
Road edge extraction using straight lines. (a) Original video image; (b) extracted straight lines; (c) road edges and computed centerline after grouping.

Integrated methods using both path boundary techniques and region segmentation methods hold promise for the future of successful road navigation. The issues of sensor fusion, even over a single sensor input device that uses multiple algorithms, comprise one of the most difficult areas of artificial intelligence. At times the algorithms are cooperative, confirming each other's hypotheses. At other times, however, they disagree and compete for credibility. Methods for the combination of evidence and the general issues of evidential reasoning require considerably more research before the sensor fusion question can be answered satisfactorily. This problem is only compounded when attempts are made to integrate different sensors that provide different types of information regarding the world.

5.5.3 GOAL IDENTIFICATION. Goal identification involves recognizing some readily discernible object of interest and then navigating toward it. In many respects, it is similar to landmark recognition, but it is a bit more restricted. In many instances the goals are deliberately chosen to be perceptually obvious.

Landmark recognition is used principally for orientation of the robot relative to its surroundings, which are typically represented in some world coordinate system. The purpose here is to maintain the bearings of the robot en route to finding its predetermined goal. Goal identification does not require correlation to an absolute frame of reference. The robot can navigate solely on the basis of its position relative to the goal and independent of any other reference frame.

The military targeting of missiles is an example of a goal-seeking mode of behavior. Much of the work done in this domain exploits infrared imagery, which relies on heat given off by the targeted object. If we make the assumption, for our more passive domains, that our goals (e.g., a sign) are not necessarily hotter than their surroundings, little can be gained by using infrared sensing. Nonetheless, the concept of exploiting the unique features of a target and designing specific perceptual strategies to recognize them can be of value.

General-purpose goal recognition (an arbitrary object in an arbitrary environment) requires a solution of the general vision problem that is well beyond our reach. Specialized objects in more constrained environments have been used with some success, however. The recognition of specialized objects (diamonds) (Fukui, 1981; Courtney et al., 1984) has provided the basis for some interesting navigational experiments in both localization and docking.

One approach to producing motor behavior from goal identification uses a potential field methodology. Upon recognition of the goal by a perceptual algorithm, a potential field is associated with it. This field can take the form of a coarse strategy (Fig. 5-9a) where the robot travels at a uniform speed at all points within the field, a coupled ballistic and controlled motor regime where uniform speed is enforced outside of a controlled region and a linear decrease in speed occurs as the robot approaches its goal within the controlled area (Fig. 5-9b), or a more sophisticated docking scenario (Fig. 5-9c), which in addition to ballistic and controlled motion incorporates approach and coercive regions, forcing the robot to follow a reasonable approach trajectory to the dock (Arkin, 1988a).

5.5.4 LOCALIZATION. Correlating the robot's position with an internal map of the environment is probably the most challenging aspect of perception in mobile robot research. These maps may either be acquired dynamically via environmental sensing or be created from a priori knowledge of the world. Fun-

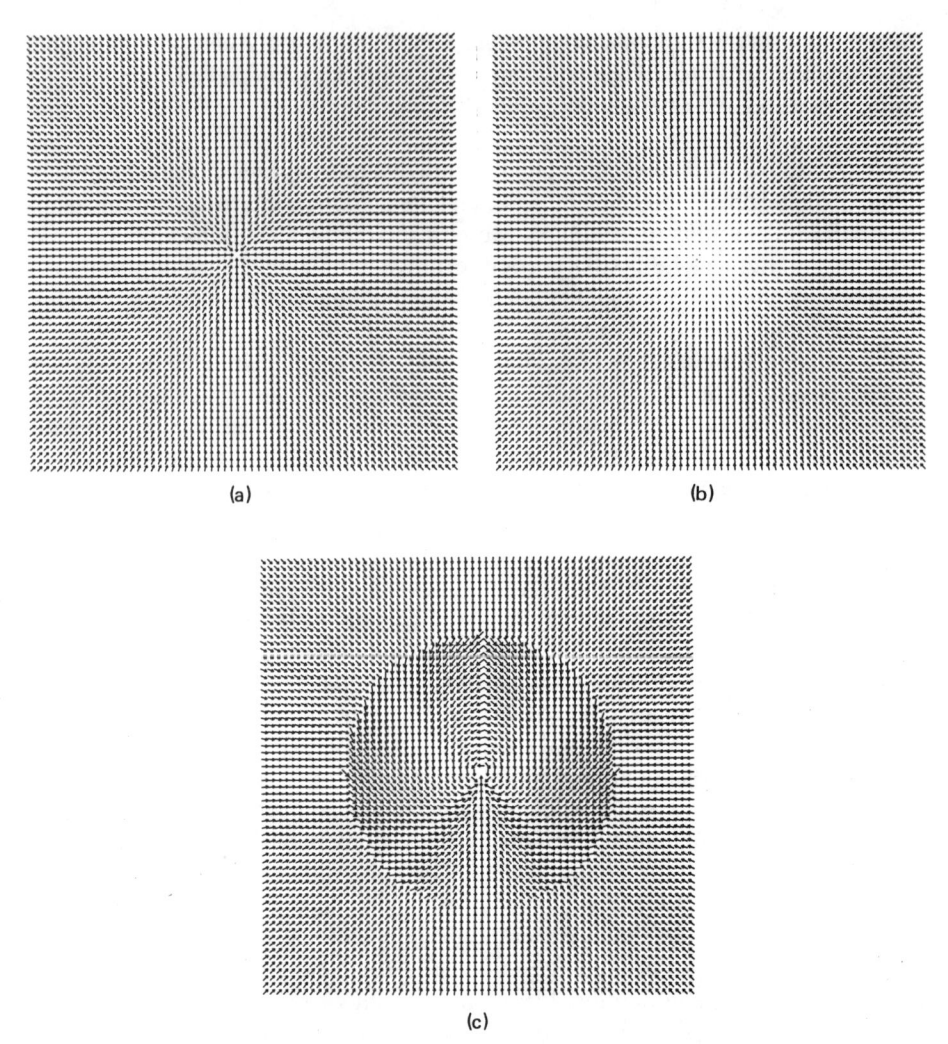

FIGURE 5-9
Goal seeking using potential fields. (a) Ballistic motion; (b) controlled (guarded) motion; (c) docking (preferred final orientation).

damental questions regarding the best representations for visual recognition of a landmark are yet to be resolved. Work in the area of visual discrimination graphs (Burns and Kitchen, 1987) is leading toward a better understanding of the representation problem. Research in perceptual organization (Lowe, 1985) is providing better clues as to what salient features are necessary for rapid recognition of an object.

Much research is proceeding in this area, particularly in the context of scene analysis. Mobile robotics, pursuing the premise of action-oriented perception, does not require full-scale scene understanding, but rather an interpretation of that which is necessary to achieve the motor task. With this in mind, two representative works for localization for mobile robots are described below, the first utilizing sonar data, and the second, vision.

Ultrasonic sensing as the basis for localization requires considerably different strategies than those used by vision. Research by Drumheller (1985) takes into account the inherent inaccuracies that are present due to reflectance, clutter, and the shape of the beam itself. Straight-line segments are generated from the received sonar data, and, using the generate-and-test paradigm, a collection of possible interpretations of the received data is produced from comparisons of the segments to individual modeled walls of the room. The individual interpretations are then tested against a global model of the room, which ultimately yields an answer as to where the robot is located, in terms of both translation and orientation, relative to its modeled surroundings. Work by Elfes (1987) using a certainty grid for sonar data has also been applied to the localization problem using correlation matching.

One of the more comprehensive vision-based localization systems has been developed at the University of Maryland (Andresen and Davis, 1984). Landmark representations are stored within a landmark database for use by the system, which consists of three major modules. The *Selector* chooses a set of landmarks from the database that would be most suitable for localization purposes given the robot's current position. The *Finder* actively directs the camera angle and focal length using a pan-tilt-zoom mechanism in an attempt to capture the entire landmark within the incoming video image. The *Matcher* establishes where a landmark may be located within an image and a measure of belief in its identification. A Hough transform is applied in an attempt to recognize the exact location of the landmark within the image, which in turn is then used to provide positional feedback for the robot. The system is still limited in the degrees of freedom available for recognition purposes (it assumes that the scale and orientation of the landmark are known) and has yet to be deployed on a working robot. Some simpler systems, using artificial landmarks for visual recognition, have already been used on working robot systems (e.g., Fukui, 1981).

6 LOCOMOTION SYSTEMS

A thorough discussion of locomotion systems belongs more in a mechanical engineering text than here. This section will describe some of the major design considerations of locomotion systems and the resultant impact on the planning aspects of mobile robot navigation. Three major issues are present: holonomic or non-holonomic vehicles, wheels (or tread) versus legged locomotion, and vehicle dynamics.

6.1 Holonomic versus Nonholonomic Vehicles

Holonomic robots are those robots whose axis of rotation coincides with the center of the robot. These robots have a turning radius of zero and can head off in any direction from a given position. Nonholonomic robots have a nonzero turning radius. If you have ever attempted to parallel park an automobile, you can quickly grasp the difficulties that nonholonomic vehicles have compared with their holonomic counterparts.

Holonomic vehicles can be made from wheeled vehicles (three-wheel synchronous steering systems), treaded vehicles (treads can move in opposite directions), and sophisticated legged vehicles. Not only is it easier to extract such a robot from tight quarters, but many of the representational issues in planning are simplified. As mentioned earlier, configuration space (C-space) approaches can be used for deriving navigational plans. This entails enlarging obstacles by a distance equal to the robot's radius, thus enabling the robot to be treated as a point thereafter for planning purposes. Nonholonomic vehicles require more sophisticated versions of C-space computation if worst-case analysis is not to be used (in worst-case analysis, turning radius is used instead of the robot's radius). The major difficulty is that C-space is dependent on the robot's orientation relative to the obstacles and must be recomputed on the fly. This is certainly inferior to systems that need only compute the C-space once and for all.

Aside from the C-space difficulty, more difficult sequences of commands must be issued to maneuver a nonholonomic robot through tight quarters. A single move for a holonomic vehicle might require three or more motor commands for its nonsymmetric counterpart. An interesting analysis of nonholonomic motion is given by Laumond (1987).

A considerable body of work is developing in the study of both types of vehicles. In general, vehicles whose domains tend to be indoors (and have tighter navigational circumstances) are frequently designed to be holonomic. Outdoor vehicles, where there is frequently more room for navigation, or where the navigational problem is constrained, such as road following, frequently use nonholonomic vehicles.

6.2 Legged Locomotion

Different drive systems can be built by constructing legs for robots as opposed to using rotational systems such as wheels or treads. Significant advantages can be gained through the use of legs, including the ability to step over obstacles, walk up stairs, and change the configuration of the robot from wide and stable in open areas to narrow (and less stable) in areas where tight navigation is required.

Many of the research issues involving legged robots dwell at levels far below artificial intelligence considerations. Low-level motor control of the leg joints, high-speed servo control, and the formulation of motor gaits can pose very challenging problems.

Robots have been constructed with one to six legs ranging in size from quite small to very large. Two representative examples of six-legged robots appear in Fig. 5-10. The interested reader is referred to Raibert (1986) for a general review of legged locomotion. We will quickly survey a few of the interesting efforts involving legged motor systems.

(a)

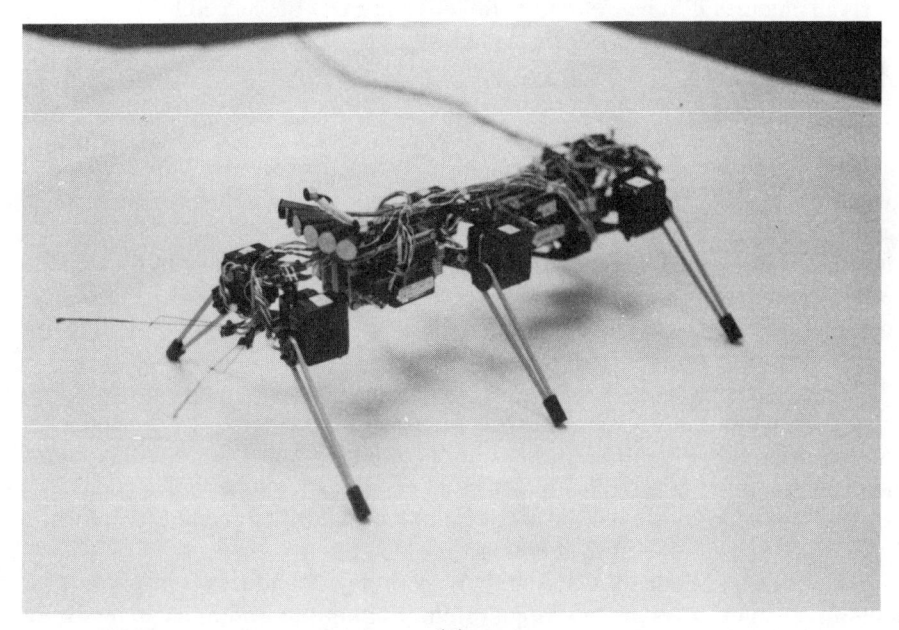

(b)

FIGURE 5-10
Various legged robots. (a) ODEX I—not autonomous (photo courtesy of Odetics, Inc., Anaheim, California). (b) Six-legged robot—autonomous (photo courtesy of Rodney Brooks, MIT AI Laboratory, Cambridge, Mass.).

147

Raibert's work in hopping and running machines initially involved one-legged hoppers. These robots are concerned with running as opposed to walking. His use of the inverted pendulum model for single-leg motion has been extended to biped and quadruped motion (Raibert et al., 1986). This research is centered on dynamic motion and does not exploit the stabilities available to slower-moving walking robots.

Many four-legged vehicles and six-legged robots exist with varying degrees of capability (e.g., Bartholet, 1986; Lee and Shih, 1986; Brooks, 1988b). Even a three-legged robot, Skitter, has been developed at the Georgia Institute of Technology. One of the largest legged machines ever developed is the Adaptive Suspension Vehicle (ASV or Hexapod) at Ohio State (Waldron, 1986). This machine, which is large enough to house an operator in its "head," has provided a test bed for many of the issues of low-level legged control and coordination. This vehicle is capable of walking under operator control, in a limited way, across open fields, where wheeled vehicles are likely to become mired in the terrain. Multiple gaits are being developed for the ASV to increase its navigational flexibility.

Most research in legged locomotion is currently preoccupied with the basic mechanics and control of safely moving the vehicle. The issues of intelligent planning and navigation are just beginning to be developed for these special systems. Many of the existing high-level planning systems will require nontrivial changes if they are to take full advantage of the legged robot's ability to climb and alter its basic configuration.

6.3 Dynamic Performance

Much of the research on mobile vehicles is concerned only with low-speed navigation. In much of this work, the dynamics of the vehicle itself can be safely ignored. If, however, we hope to be able to generalize to faster moving vehicles it is essential to take into account the mass and velocity of the vehicle itself in the equations of motion. This section describes some of the theoretical considerations and actual navigational experiments that have concerned themselves with this issue.

Sensory sampling is a major bottleneck in the navigational process, especially when computer vision is involved. Even when we exploit the concepts of action-oriented perception, if the robot is moving rapidly there will be times when it is traveling blind. This might be likened to moving about a room, periodically opening your eyes for a brief moment, and then using this information to plan your course until the next time you open your eyes.

How to avoid collisions during these periods of blindness is important for robots that travel fast. One working system, built at the Military University of Munich, is geared to drive a vehicle at high speeds (65 km/hr) on the German Autobahn. The use of specialized computer architectures (Mysliwetz and Dickmanns, 1986) to process the vision algorithm (described in Section 5.5.2) minimizes the time between "blinks" of the robot's eye. The navigational system (Dickmanns and Zapp, 1985) also takes into account the speed at which the robot is moving (it is a modified truck) to plan when to steer on curves. The robot's path is projected ahead into the modeled world and is heavily dependent upon the current velocity of the vehicle.

On a more theoretical note, the use of potential fields has been extended to include the motion of the robot itself. This formulation, called *generalized potential fields* (Krogh, 1984), holds promise for taking into account the dynamics of motion for a robot whose basis of navigation exploits the use of potential field methods.

Until sensory sampling rates improve and the current bottleneck associated with perceptual processing is relieved, a great proportion of mobile robot research will continue with the noted absence of dynamic considerations. This is a marked distinction from the robot arm research counterparts. The time will arrive, as robot perception improves, where the assumptions that are made by most current experimental systems will prove invalid at higher speeds for robot navigation. Then vehicle dynamics will play a greater role in the navigational process.

7 SURVIVABILITY

It has been a long-standing aim of robotics to place these machines in environments that are hazardous to human existence. Such locales include space, manufacturing, undersea environments, and battlefields. However, the fact that a robot can be placed in a location that is dangerous to people does not mean it is not dangerous to the robot itself. Engineers can only maximize component reliability; they cannot prevent failures from occurring. How can machines working in high or low temperatures, chemical-laden atmospheres, or high or low pressure environments protect themselves from failure? In certain cases, such as planetary exploration, it is almost impossible to send a technician out to repair a failed robotic component.

A basic question is, What do we really mean by autonomous? Do we simply mean the ability to get from one location to another in a safe and intelligent manner, or do we include the ability to monitor the conditions that are necessary to protect the survival of the vehicle itself? Robots have only limited available reserves and capabilities. This is reflected in the nature of their power source (even solar cells require time to recharge batteries) and the fuel consumption rates of their motors. How can these available resources be monitored effectively, and how can the results of this monitoring have an impact on high-level planning as well as other aspects of motor control?

Consider what happens when you go without food. At first, your activity continues in a normal manner. As time progresses, sensations and chemical messages from within your body both consciously and unconsciously begin to affect your behavior. You start to think more and more about food, and begin to devise plans to alleviate your perceived fuel reserve imbalance. In some cases you may do this opportunistically—for example, if you happen to see a cookie lying on a plate in front of you, which you might not have eaten if you were not so hungry. If you become sufficiently hungry, you start to actively seek out the food, first casually and then moving on to desperation as your total energy reserves become depleted by starvation. High-level conscious thought may affect your feeding behavior if some other goals might be better served at this time by fasting or dieting. Energy management is just one of the resources monitored by our bodies. Internal temperature, stress, emotion, and other related factors all contribute to the overall behavior of an intelligent entity.

One strategy for dealing with dangerous environments involves worst-case scenario analysis. Threat measures, available fuel, and other factors are all assessed at the onset of a mission. System parameters are then set based on this analysis and the robot enters its hazardous world protected by a prior situational assessment. Several systems use this method (Parodi, 1985; Shen and Signarowski, 1985).

There are at least two weaknesses with this approach. First, worst-case analysis may prevent the robot from carrying out a mission that is indeed possible. Second, environmental conditions change over time. It would be far better to endow the robot with the ability to change its behavior in light of both improving and deteriorating environmental factors.

One method used for dynamic replanning in hazardous environments is based on the use of knowledge structures called signal schemas (Arkin, 1989b). These schemas, which are associated with internal sensing devices (ammeters, thermistors, etc.) and active motor behaviors can provide sensory feedback necessary to modify both high-level plans and manifested motor behaviors at low levels. This method is based on a correlate of the endocrine system in mammals that uses similar communication mechanisms to effect global system changes in a living organism.

In any case, it may be premature to worry about the issues of making a robot survivable in dangerous environments when it still is so difficult to make them function in a robust manner in relatively safe and structured worlds. Nonetheless, it is important that this research be conducted in parallel, so we will be ready when research on intelligent perception and safe navigation has reached the point where robots may be deployed into these dangerous worlds.

8 A CASE STUDY

The integration of the many aspects of a mobile robot system is a formidable task. Nonetheless there are several systems that approach this problem. These include the NAVLAB system and architecture (Shafer et al., 1986; Goto and Stentz, 1987) developed at Carnegie-Mellon University, the MIT robots (Brooks, 1986a, 1986b, 1987; Brooks and Connell, 1986), and the Martin-Marietta Autonomous Land Vehicle (ALV) (Turk et al., 1987; Hennessy et al., 1988). In this section we will take an overview of the Autonomous Robot Architecture (AuRA), initially developed at the University of Massachusetts and subsequently at the Georgia Institute of Technology, as a representative example.

8.1 AuRA Overview

The Autonomous Robot architecture (Arkin et al., 1987a; Arkin, 1987b) (Fig. 5-11) consists of five major subsystems: the perceptual, cartographic, planning, motor, and homeostatic control systems. George (Fig. 5-12) is the current vehicle testbed for the system. The perceptual subsystem receives environmental data through the use of computer vision, ultrasonic, and shaft encoding sensors; structures the data in a form that is useful to other components of the system; and then runs interpretive algorithms (Arkin et al., 1987b) (line finding, region segmentation, ultrasonic interpretation, etc.) to solve the perceptual requirements of the currently active motor behaviors. Knowledge representations referred to as perceptual schemas are the basic program units of perceptual activity.

The cartographic subsystem consists of long-term memory representations, short-term memory, and uncertainty management processes. Long-term

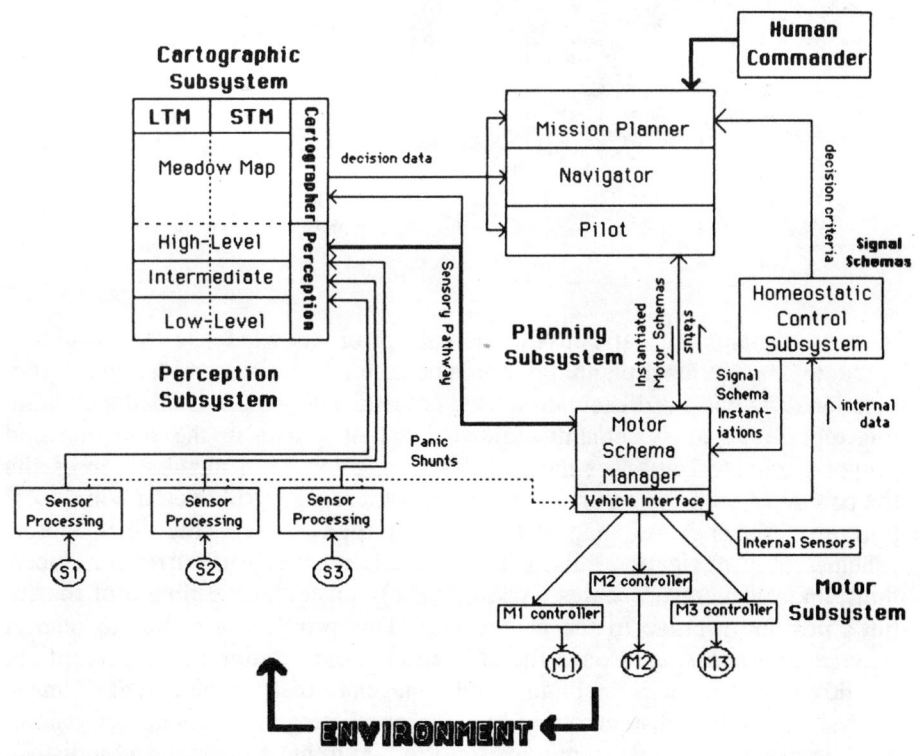

FIGURE 5-11
The Autonomous Robot architecture.

FIGURE 5-12
George, a Denning mobile robot.

memory contains the static environmental a priori knowledge of the world that facilitates navigational planning, motor behavior selection, and landmark recognition. The basic representation used is the meadow map. Embedded within this representation is semantic knowledge that assists in the selection and proper parameterization of motor behaviors. Short-term memory represents the perceived world and currently consists of a regular grid overlaid on a local portion of the meadow map. This representation is used only when motor-schema-based navigation fails, which is a relatively rare occurrence. Uncertainty management processes (Arkin, 1988c) correlate an estimate of the robot's position relative to the global map. This provides a means to restrict perceptual processing through the utilization of expectation-based perception. Windows are created in incoming video images to restrict the extent of image analysis and thus substantially reduce the processing requirements of vision.

The planning subsystem consists of a hierarchical planner and a distributed plan executor. The hierarchical planner is composed of a mission planner, navigator, and pilot. The mission planner's responsibilities include high-level reasoning and goal formulation and ordering. The navigator is charged with finding the point-to-point path for one particular component of the overall mission at a time. The pilot then analyzes an individual leg of the navigator's computed path, selects appropriate motor behaviors and perceptual strategies (schemas) to accomplish the task, and turns control over to the motor schema manager.

The motor schema manager is the execution arm of the pilot. Here the primitive behaviors selected by the pilot are activated in a distributed and concurrent manner. Each strives to achieve its goal by means of a potential field methodology, which may involve staying on a path, avoiding obstacles, moving toward the goal, and so on. These primitive behaviors react in a reflexive manner to perceived environmental sensor data and dynamically change the vehicle's path in response to the currently perceived state of the world.

The motor subsystem is the most vehicle-dependent component of the architecture. It is charged with establishing and maintaining communications with the robot and translating the velocity vector commands produced by the motor schemas into a format that is appropriate for the specific robot motor controllers and vehicle configuration.

Finally, the homeostatic control subsystem is concerned with robot survivability. It is currently implemented only in simulation, but these simulation studies clearly illustrate the effect of internal sensing and monitoring of fuel reserves on the path the robot takes (Arkin, 1989c).

AuRA is one of the few mobile robot systems that take into account cybernetic considerations (Arkin, 1988b). These aspects include the integration of schema theory (a cognitive psychological description of behavior and memory) into mobile robotics, consideration of the action–perception cycle as a basis for the design of the system, the use of expectation-based perception, and integration of homeostatic control as a means to enhance robot survivability. AuRA is an ongoing project and is undergoing continual development and enhancement. The reader is referred to Arkin et al. (1987a) and Arkin (1987b, 1988a) for more details on the operation and status of this particular system.

8.2 Navigation Scenario

To illustrate the many issues associated with navigation, we will run through an example scenario. The robot has available in long-term memory a model of its world—in this instance, a part of the college campus (Fig. 5-13). The navigational goal of the robot is to get from one building to another. This may be the result of the mission planner's determination that a package the robot is to deliver to Professor Jones must get to his office, which is located in the distant building. The navigator produces a path subject to the mission planner's constraints, which indicate that it is best to follow the gravel path because of current weather and traffic conditions (Fig. 5-14). The pilot selects appropriate motor behaviors and perceptual strategies for each leg of the journey. For the

154 KNOWLEDGE ENGINEERING: APPLICATIONS

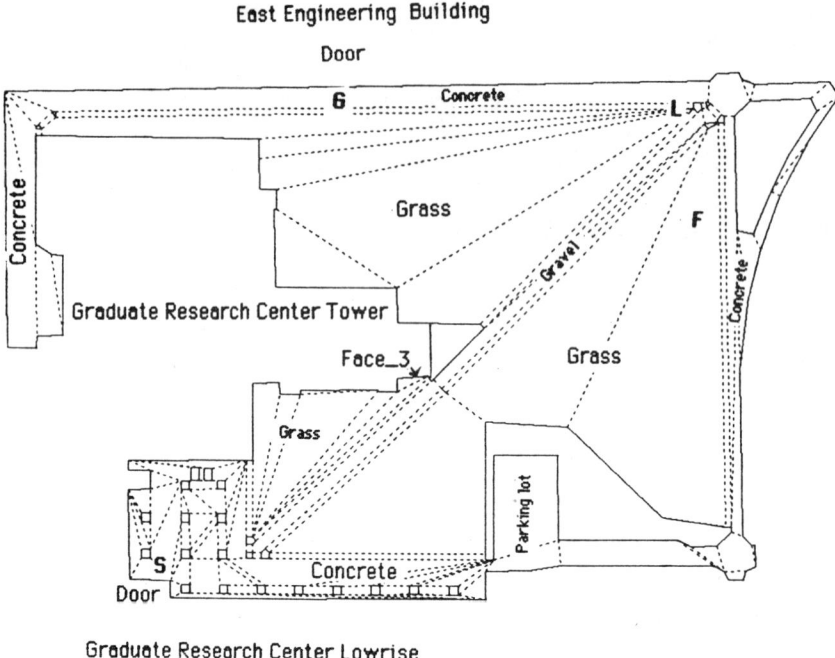

FIGURE 5-13
Long-term memory meadow map.

leg where the robot is traveling along the path, these would include motor schemas to stay on the path, avoid obstacles, and move in a particular direction. Associated perceptual schemas to use vision to detect the road, use ultrasonic sensors to find obstacles, provide information regarding landmark position for localization, and rely on the shaft encoders for approximate directional information are attached to each motor schema.

The robot then begins its journey, under the control of the motor schema manager, reacting to the sensed world as it travels. A view of the potential fields within which the robot might be located as it travels is depicted in Fig. 5-15. It should be remembered that the robot does not compute a path through the field but rather computes an instantaneous single velocity vector dependent solely on the immediately available sensor data. The robot continues along each leg of the overall journey until it recognizes, using specific perceptual cues, that it has satisfied the requirements of each navigational leg of the trip and ultimately accomplishes its mission.

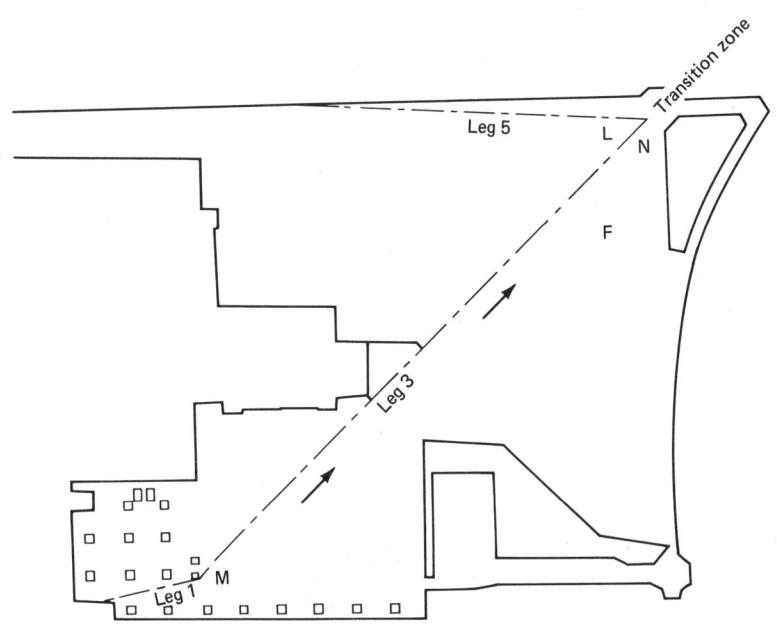

FIGURE 5-14
Navigator's planned path.

9 SUMMARY

Autonomous mobile robot research is a highly active and competitive area. It is filled with creative new ideas and approaches to a problem that is inherently important and challenging. Fortunately we know that the problem can be solved; humans and other animals conduct safe navigation routinely.

The potential applications of autonomous mobile robots are manifold: planetary rovers for use in space; service robots for applications in manufacturing and warehouses; domestic robots for home and office maintenance; and robots for supervision and repair of nuclear reactors, for similar activities in mines and other dangerous environments, and for use in military situations. We have come far in the last 30 years or so, but we still have a long way to go before truly autonomous, self-sustaining, intelligent robots are achieved.

Many aspects of knowledge representation are crucial to achieving this goal. Cartographic knowledge of both the robot's modeled world and perceived world models can provide information essential for navigation. A wide variety of representational strategies exist, each with its own particular strengths and weaknesses. The representations chosen to formulate plan activity are equally important, whether they be schemas, finite-state machines, rules, or whatever.

The difference between hierarchical planning and parallel planning is important to understand. Hierarchical planning offers predictable control and

FIGURE 5-15
Typical potential field as robot approaches goal.

communication between the planning agents and the ability to focus by changing the scope of the plan from one hierarchical level to the next. Parallel planners afford a greater responsiveness to environmental planning and a more natural decomposition for problem solving. Hybrid hierarchical-parallel planners afford hope of exploiting the advantages of both techniques.

Perception remains the major bottleneck to real-time navigation. Some sensor modalities such as sonar offer rapid but coarse environmental feedback. Computer vision holds great promise for robot navigation but requires specialized and costly machine architectures to even approach real-time navigation. Laser scanners, capable of returning a three-dimensional view of the world, are very expensive and are subject to their own set of idiosyncratic problems. Dead reckoning is useful only to a degree, as wheel slippage can cause significant disorientation to occur. Inertial navigation systems, though immune to this problem, are still too costly and are subject to drift over time. The major perceptual tasks for a mobile robot are obstacle avoidance, path following, goal identification, and localization. Some successes have been achieved in each of these areas, but more robust algorithms are required to ensure reliable and versatile performance of the robot.

Advances in locomotion systems will have an impact on future autonomous robots. More flexible holonomic robots, sophisticated legged vehicles with multiple gaits and even capable of running, and the injection into planning strategies of vehicle dynamics considerations for use at high speeds will increase the versatility of these machines.

True autonomy in the sense of self-sustaining robots can result from continued research into the impact of internal sensing on previously formulated plans. This is especially useful for hazardous or remote environments.

If the diversity of representation, control, and perception efforts reminds you of the early days of aviation, it is understandable. Perhaps a clearly superior approach to the problem of intelligent sensor-driven autonomous mobile robot navigation will become apparent. Until then we extend our best wishes to those daring researchers and their walking, creeping, crawling, rolling, and hopping machines.

REFERENCES

AI magazine. (1988). Special issue on spatial reasoning, Vol. 9, No. 2.

Albus, J., and Blidberg, D.R. (1987). A Control System Architecture for Multiple Autonomous Undersea Vehicles (MAUV). Robot Systems Division Report, National Bureau of Standards, Washington, D.C.

Albus, J., McCain, H., and Lumia, R. (1987). NASA/NBS Standard Reference Model for Telerobot Control System Architecture (NASREM). NBS Tech. Note 1235, Robot Systems Division, National Bureau of Standards, Washington, D.C.

Andresen, F., and Davis, L. (1984). Visual Position Determination for Autonomous Vehicle Navigation. Center for Automation Research TR-100, Univ. of Maryland, College Park, Md.

Arbib, M. (1981). Perceptual Structures and Distributed Motor Control. In: *Handbook of Physiology: The Nervous System II* (Brooks, Ed.). American Physiological Society, Bethesda, MD, pp. 1449–1465.

Arkin, R. (1986). Path Planning and Execution for a Mobile Robot: A Review of Representation and Control Strategies. COINS Tech. Report 86-47. Computer and Information Science Department, University of Massachusetts, Amherst.

Arkin, R. (1987a). Motor Schema Based Navigation for a Mobile Robot: An Approach to Programming by Behavior. Proc. IEEE Int. Conf. Robotics and Automation, Raleigh, N.C., pp. 264–271.

Arkin, R. (1987b). Towards Cosmopolitan Robots: Intelligent Navigation of a Mobile Robot in Extended Man-made Environments. Ph.D. Dissertation, COINS Tech. Report 87-80, Department of Computer and Information Science, University of Massachusetts, Amherst.

Arkin, R. (1988a). Intelligent Mobile Robots in the Workplace: Leaving the Guide Behind. Proc. the First Int. Conf. on Industrial and Engineering Applications of Artificial Intelligence and Expert Systems, pp. 553–561.

Arkin, R. (1988b). Neuroscience in Motion: The Application of Schema Theory to Mobile Robotics. In: *Visuomotor Coordination: Amphibians, Comparisons, Models, and Robots* (J.-P. Ewert and M. Arbib, Eds.). Plenum Press, New York, pp. 649–672.

Arkin, R. (1988c). Spatial Uncertainty Management for a Mobile Robot and Its Role in Expectation-Based Perception. Proc. Symposium on Robot Control '88 (Syroco), Karlsruhe, W. Germany, pp. 00–00.

Arkin, R. (1989a). Navigational Path Planning for a Vision-Based Mobile Robot. *Robotica*. 7:49–63.

Arkin, R. (1989b). Homeostatic Control for a Mobile Robot: Dynamic Replanning in Hazardous Environments. Proc. SPIE Conf. on Mobile Robots III, Cambridge Symposium on Advances in Intelligent Robotics Systems.

Arkin, R. (1989c). Dynamic Replanning for a Mobile Robot Based on Internal Sensing. 1989 IEEE International Conference on Robotics and Automation, Scottsdale, Ariz., submitted.

Arkin, R., Riseman, E., and Hanson, A. (1987a). AuRA: An Architecture for Vision-Based Robot Navigation. Proc. DARPA Image Understanding Workshop, Los Angeles, pp. 417–431.

Arkin, R., Riseman, E., and Hanson, A. (1987b). Visual Strategies for Mobile Robot Navigation. Proc. IEEE Computer Society Workshop on Computer Vision, Miami Beach, Fla., pp. 176–181.

Ayache, N., and Faugeras, O. (1987). Building, Registrating, and Fusing Noisy Visual Maps. Proc. Int. Conf. on Computer Vision, London, pp. 73–82.

Bartholet, S. (1986). Evolution of Odetics Walking Machine Technology. SPIE Conf. on Mobile Robots, Cambridge, Mass., pp. 25–31.

Blidberg, D. R., and Chappell, S. (1986). Guidance and Control Architecture for the EAVE Vehicle. *IEEE J. Oceanic Eng.* **OE-11**(4):449–461.

Brooks, R. (1985). Visual Map Making for a Mobile Robot. Proc. IEEE Int. Conf. Robotics and Automation, St. Louis, Mo., pp. 824–829.

Brooks, R. (1986a). A Robust Layered Control System for a Mobile Robot. *IEEE J. Robotics Autom.* **RA-2**(1):14–23.

Brooks, R. (1986b). Achieving Artificial Intelligence Through Building Robots. A.I. Memo 899, AI Lab., MIT, Cambridge, Mass.

Brooks, R. (1987). A Hardware Retargetable Distributed Layered Architecture for Mobile Robot Navigation. Proc. IEEE Int. Conf. on Robotics and Automation, Raleigh, N.C., pp. 106–110.

Brooks, R. (1988a). Intelligence Without Representation. Research paper, AI Lab., MIT, Cambridge, Mass.

Brooks, R. (1988b). A Robot That Walks; Emergent Behaviors from a Carefully Evolved Network. A.I. Memo, AI Lab., MIT, Cambridge, Mass.

Brooks, R., and Connell, J. (1986). Asynchronous Distributed Control System for a Mobile Robot. In: *Mobile Robots*. (W. Wolfe and N. Marquina, Eds.). Proc. SPIE Vol. 727. SPIE, Bellingham, Wash., pp. 77–84.

Brooks, R., Flynn, A., and Marill, T. (1987). Self Calibration of Motion and Stereo Vision for Mobile Robot Navigation. A.I. Memo 984, MIT AI Lab.

Burns, J., and Kitchen, L. (1987). Recognition in 2D Images of 3D Objects from Large Model Bases Using Prediction Hierarchies. Proc. IJCAI, Milan, Italy.

Chattergy, R. (1985). Some Heuristics for the Navigation of a Robot. *Int. J. Robotics Res.* **4**(1):59–66.

Courtney, J., Magee, M., and Aggarwal, J. (1984). Robot Guidance Using Computer Vision. *Pattern Recognition* **17**(6):585–592.

Crowley, J. (1984). Navigation for an Intelligent Mobile Robot. CMU Robotics Institute Tech. Report CMU-RI-TR-84-18.

Davis, L., Kushner, T., Le Moigne, J., and Waxman, A. (1986). Road Boundary Detection for Autonomous Vehicle Navigation. *Opt. Eng.* **25**(3):409–414.

Dickmanns, E., and Zapp, A. (1985). Guiding Land Vehicles along Roadways by Computer Vision. AFCET Conference, Toulouse, France.

Dorst, L., and Trovato, K. (1988). Optimal Path Planning by Cost Wave Propagation in Metric Configuration Space. Proc. SPIE Conf. on Mobile Robots III, Cambridge Symp. of Advances in Intelligent Robotics Systems.

Drumheller, M. (1985). Mobile Robot Localization Using Sonar. A.I. Memo 826, MIT AI Lab.

Elfes, A. (1987). Sonar-Based Real-World Mapping and Navigation. *IEEE J. Robotics Autom.* **RA-3**(3):249–265.

Firby, J. (1987). An Investigation into Reactive Planning in Complex Domains. Proc. Sixth AAAI Conference, Seattle.

Fukui, I. (1981). TV Image Processing to Determine the Position of a Robot Vehicle. *Pattern Recognition* **14**(1–6):101–109.

Giralt, G., Chatila, R., and Vaisset, M. (1984). An Integrated Navigation and Motion Control Sys-

tem for Autonomous Multisensory Mobile Robots. *Robotics Research: The First International Symposium.* (M. Brady and R. Paul, Eds.). MIT Press, Cambridge, Mass., pp. 191–214.
Goto, Y., and Stentz, A. (1987). The CMU System for Mobile Robot Navigation. Proc. IEEE Conf. on Robotics and Automation, Raleigh, N.C., pp. 99–105.
Hart, P.E., Nilsson, N.J., and Raphael, B. (1968). A Formal Basis for the Heuristic Determination of Minimum Cost Paths. *IEEE Trans. Syst. Sci. Cybern.* **SSC-4**(2):100–107.
Hennessy, S., Dunlay, R.T., Marra, M., Morgenthaler, D., and Seida, S. (1988). The 1988 Autonomous Land Vehicle Computer Architecture. Proc. ROBOTS 12 and VISION '88, Detroit, Mich., pp. 12.17–12.26.
Herman, M., and Albus, J. (1987). Overview of the Multiple Autonomous Underwater Vehicle (MAUV) Project. Robot Systems Division Report, National Bureau of Standards, Washington, D.C.
Iyengar, S., Jorgensen, C., Rao, S., and Weisbin, C. (1985). Learned Navigation Paths for a Robot in Unexplored Terrain. IEEE 2nd Conf. on Artificial Intelligence Applications, pp. 148–155.
Kadonoff, M., Benayad-Cherif, F., Franklin, A., Maddox, J., Muller, L., Sert, B., and Moravec, H. (1986). Arbitration of Multiple Control Strategies for Mobile Robots. *Mobile Robots.* (W. Wolfe and N. Marquina, Eds.). SPIE Proc. Vol. 727, pp. 90–98.
Kahn, P., Kitchen, L., and Riseman, E. (1987). Real-Time Feature Extraction: A Fast Line Finder for Vision-Guided Robot Navigation. COINS Tech. Report 87-57. Department of Computer and Information Science, University of Massachusetts, Amherst.
Kambhampati, S., and Davis, L. (1986). Multiresolution Path Planning for Mobile Robots. *IEEE J. Robotics Autom.* **RA-2**(3):135–145.
Keirsey, D., Mitchel, J., Payton, D., and Preyss, E. (1984). Multilevel Path Planning for Autonomous Vehicles. *Applications of Artificial Intelligence.* (J. Gilmore, Ed.) SPIE Vol. 485, pp. 133–137.
Koch, E., Yeh, C., Hillel, G., Meystel, A., and Isik, C. (1985). Simulation of Path Planning for a System with Vision and Map Updating. Proc. IEEE Int. Conf. Robotics and Automation, St. Louis, Mo., pp. 146–160.
Krogh, B. (1984). A Generalized Potential Field Approach to Obstacle Avoidance Control. SME-RI Tech. Paper MS84-484.
Krogh, B., and Thorpe, C. (1986). Integrated Path Planning and Dynamic Steering Control for Autonomous Vehicles. IEEE Conf. on Robotics and Automation, pp. 1664–1669.
Kuan, D.T., Zamiska, J., and Brooks, R. (1985). Natural Decomposition of Free Space for Path Planning. Proc. IEEE Int. Conf. on Robotics and Automation, St. Louis, Mo., pp. 168–173.
Laumond, J.P. (1987). Finding Collision-Free Smooth Trajectories for a Non- holonomic Mobile Robot. Proc. 10th Int. Joint Conf. on Artificial Intelligence, Milan.
Lee, T., and Shih, C. (1986). A Study of the Gait Control of a Quadruped Walking Vehicle. *IEEE J. Robotics Autom.* **RA-2**(2):61–69.
Lowe, D. (1985). *Perceptual Organization and Visual Recognition.* Kluwer Academic Publ., Boston.
Lozano-Perez, T. (1982). Automatic Planning of Manipulator Transfer Movements. In: *Robot Motion: Planning and Control.* (M. Brady, J. Hollerbach, T. Johnson, T. Lozeno-Perez, and M. Mason, Eds.). MIT Press, Cambridge, MA, pp. 499–535.
Lyons, D. (1986). RS: A Formal Model of Distributed Computation for Sensory-Based Robot Control. Ph.D. Dissertation, COINS Tech. Report 86-43, Dept. of Computer and Info. Science, University of Massachusetts, Amherst, Mass.
Meystel, A. (1986). Theoretical Foundations of Decision Making Processes for Design and Control of Intelligent Mobile Autonomous Robots. Tech. Report, Drexel University, Philadelphia, Pa.
Miller, D. (1985). A Spatial Representation System for Mobile Robots. CH2152-7/85, IEEE, pp. 122–127.
Mitchell, J., and Keirsey, D. (1984). Planning Strategic Paths through Variable Terrain Data. *Applications of Artificial Intelligence,* SPIE Vol. 485, pp. 172–179.

Mittelstaedt, H. (1985). Analytical Cybernetics of Spider Navigation. In: *Neurobiology of Arachnids* (F.G. Barth, Ed.). Springer-Verlag, Berlin, pp. 298–316.
Moravec, H. (1981). *Robot Rover Visual Navigation.* UMI Press, Ann Arbor, MI.
Moravec, H. (1985). Robots that Rove. Autonomous Mobile Robots Annual Report 1985. Robotics Institute, Carnegie-Mellon University.
Moravec, H. (1988). Sensor Fusion in Certainty Grids for Mobile Robots. *AI Mag.* 9(2):61–74.
Mysliwetz, B., and Dickmanns, E.D. (1986). A Vision System with Active Gaze for Real-Time Interpretation of Well Structured Dynamic Scenes. Proc. Int. Conf. on Intelligent Autonomous Systems, Amsterdam.
Neisser, U. (1976). *Cognition and Reality: Principles and Implications of Cognitive Psychology.* Freeman, San Francisco, Calif.
Nillson, N., Ed. (1984). Shakey the Robot. SRI International Tech. Note 323.
Parodi, A.M. (1985). Multi-Goal Real-Time Global Path Planning for an Autonomous Land Vehicle using a High-Speed Graph Search Processor. Proc. IEEE Int. Conf. Robotics and Automation, St. Louis, Mo., pp. 161–167.
Payton, D. (1986). An Architecture for Reflexive Autonomous Vehicle Control. IEEE Conf. on Robotics and Automation, pp. 1838–1845.
Raibert, M. (1986). *Legged Robots that Balance.* MIT Press, Cambridge, Mass.
Raibert, M., Chepponis, M., and Brown, H. (1986). Running on Four Legs as Though They Were One. *IEEE J. Robotics Autom.* **RA-2**(2):70–82.
Rosen, C., and Nilsson, N. (1966). Application of Intelligent Automata to Reconnaissance. First Interim Report, SRI.
Shafer, S., and Mathies, L. (1986). Error Modelling in Stereo Navigation. Carnegie-Mellon Tech. Report CMU-SC-86-140, Dept. of Computer Science.
Shafer, S., Stentz, A., and Thorpe, C. (1986). An Architecture for Sensor Fusion in a Mobile Robot. CMU Tech. Report CMU-RI-TR-86-9.
Shen, H., and Signarowski, G. (1985). A Knowledge Representation for Roving Robots. IEEE 2nd Conf. on Artificial Intelligence Applications, pp. 621–628.
Smith, R., and Cheeseman, P. (1985). On the Representation and Estimation of Spatial Uncertainty. Robotics Lab. Tech. Paper, SRI Projects 4760 and 7239. SRI International.
Tachi, S., and Komoriya, K. (1985). Guide Dog Robot. *Robotics Research, Second International Symposium* (H. Hanafusa and H. Inoue, Eds.). MIT Press, Cambridge, Mass., pp. 333–340.
Thorpe, C. (1984a). Path Relaxation: Path Planning for a Mobile Robot. CMU Robotics Institute Tech. Report CMU-RI-TR-84-5.
Thorpe, C. (1984b). FIDO: Vision and Navigation for a Robot Rover. Ph.D. dissertation, CMU Computer Science Tech. Report CMU-CS-84-168.
Turk, M., Morgenthaler, D., Gremban, K., and Marra, M. (1987). Video Road-Following for the Autonomous Land Vehicle. Proc. IEEE Int. Conf. on Robotics and Automation, Raleigh, N.C., pp. 273–280.
Waldron, K. (1986). Force and Motion Management in Legged Locomotion. *IEEE J. Robotics and Autom.* **RA-2**(4):214–220.
Wallace, R. (1987). Robot Road Following by Adaptive Color Classification and Shape Tracking. Proc. IEEE Int. Conf. on Robotics and Automation, pp. 258–263.
Waxman A., LeMoigne J., Davis L., Srinivasen, B., Kushner T., Liang, E., and Siddalingaiah, T., A Visual Navigation System for Autonomous Land Vehicles, *IEEE J. Robotics Autom.* **RA-3**(2):pp. 124–141.
Weisbin, C., de Saussure, G., and Kammer, D. (1986). Self Controlled: A Real-Time Expert System for an Autonomous Mobile Robot. *CIME—Computers in Mechanical Engineering* 5(2).
Whittaker, W., Turkiyyah, G., and Hebert, M. (1987). An Architecture and Two Cases in Range-Based Modeling and Planning. Proc. IEEE Int. Conf. on Robotics and Automation, pp. 1991–1997.

CHAPTER 6

AI TECHNIQUES IN COMPUTER-AIDED MANUFACTURING SYSTEMS

SPYROS G. TZAFESTAS

1 INTRODUCTION

Manufacturing involves many activities that can be monitored and controlled at several levels of abstraction. A manufacturing plant (shop floor) has a variety of work centers, each composed of many manufacturing cells, and a manufacturing cell consists of a group of individual machines, robots, and tools. Very broadly, activity planning in a manufacturing plant consists of selecting activities and allocating and scheduling resources at each level of abstraction so as to meet the desired production, quality, and economic goals. By nature, the manufacturing environment is dynamic, and so predictive planning does not lead to success. The manufacturing system has to be able to adapt to quick changes in its environment (Rembold and Dillmann, 1986; Ranky, 1986).

Modern shop floors have a hierarchical structure with at least three hierarchical levels (Fig. 6-1) (Koren, 1985). At the highest level there is a computer that supervises the various manufacturing functions (activities or operations). In a system of this type, which is called a *computer-integrated manufacturing* (CIM) system, there is a coordinated cooperation of computers in all phases of the enterprise—the design of a product, the planning of its manufacture, automatic production of parts, automatic assembly, automatic inspection, control of the flow of materials and parts through the plant, and so on. All these phases must be accommodated into a computer network, supervised by the CIM central computer, which controls the various interrelated tasks according to overall management policy.

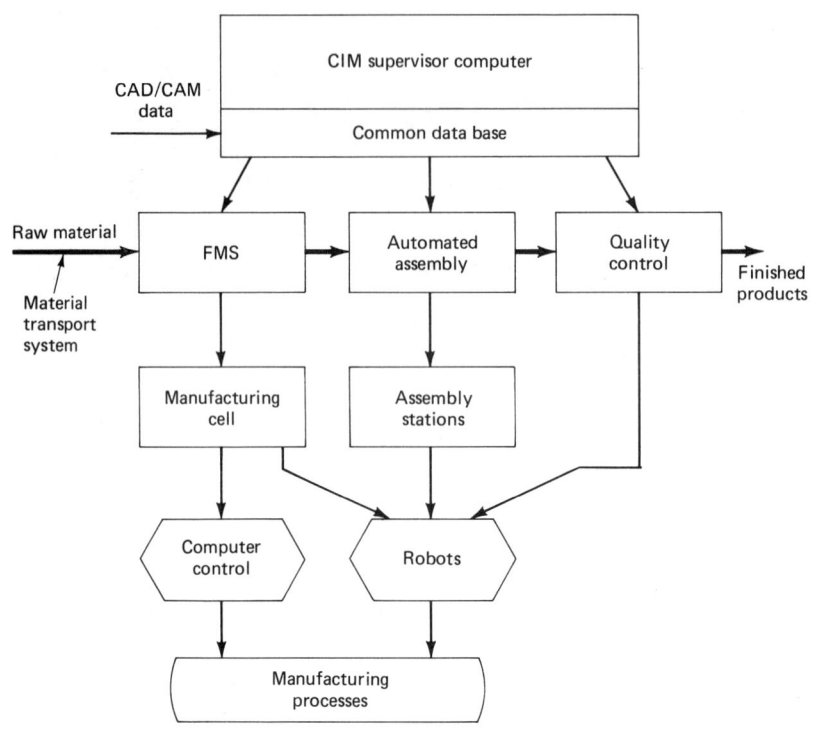

FIGURE 6-1
Hierarchical architecture of CIM system.

At the lowest level of this scheme there are stand-alone computer control systems of manufacturing processes and industrial robots (manufacturing cells). The operation of several manufacturing cells is coordinated by the central computer through a materials-handling system. This constitutes the intermediate level of the CIM system, which is known as the *flexible manufacturing system* (FMS). The products (final or semifinal) of the FMS are tested by appropriate automatic inspection stations. The integration of the design and manufacturing tasks of an FMS can be made with the aid of a CAD/CAM (computer-aided design/computer-aided manufacturing) system. This leads to substantial reductions of the factory's production cycle. It is remarked that robots and *computerized numerical control* (CNC) *machines* can only replace human power and skill. CIM systems can also replace human intelligence and achieve an incomparably higher efficiency.

But what actually is CIM—a concept, a philosophy, or a technology? CIM is much of a challenge like artificial intelligence (AI), and according to Appleton (1984) it is divided into three parts, three points of view:

1. The *demand for information*—the *user view* of CIM determined by the market environment of the system

2. The *supply of information*—the *technology view* of CIM, which is the outcome of pressures on the suppliers of technology
3. The *enterprise view* of CIM, which provides a control structure that can maintain alignment between the dynamic user and technology views and at the same time leads to the integration and consistency required by the enterprise as a whole.

The enterprise view of CIM involves planning and project management policies, data and technical standards, budgeting and performance controls, and so on, and specifies what will be shared, why, and how. Users' views have been driven by technology views of CIM. Now there is a tendency for user and technology views to drift apart. Vendors and software houses like to tell users what they need. But users like to come up with their own ideas. The traditional management policies are changing drastically to deal with new concepts such as the *just-in-time* and *full-service* concepts.

Only recently the AI discipline has arrived at the point where some of its applications have seen important practical results (Barr et al., 1981; Tzafestas, 1988a; Gerencser and Smetek, 1985). AI researchers attempt to construct computer programs that perform tasks that, at the moment, people perform better (Rich, 1983). AI technology offers the tools that enable us to:

1. Capture and retain expertise that was gained over many years of engineering
2. Amplify expertise that is needed to successfully deploy new methods and applications
3. Design systems that reason intelligently about necessary actions to take in real time, thus freeing operational staff

Manufacturing is one of the most attractive areas of application of AI techniques. However, considerable effort is required to capture and organize the accumulated knowledge of manufacturing engineers. There is a vast amount of knowledge here, extending over many processes, diverse situations, and an infinite array of parts and products. Particular attention should be given to representing this knowledge and adequately representing explicitly the characteristics of machines and processes (Fisher, 1985; King et al., 1985; Rayson, 1985; Snyder, 1984; Schneider, 1987; Warman, 1985; Meyer, 1987; Kusiak, 1987; Connor, 1984; Tzafestas, 1988b).

According to Nevins et al. (1987), two radically different approaches can be followed to automate manufacturing tasks:

- By duplicating (imitating) human actions (e.g., in spray painting, a robot is programmed to move a spray gun in exactly the same patterns as an expert painter)
- By studying the task's goal or expected functions and applying a convenient strategy that may bear little or no resemblance to human methods (e.g., automatic dishwashing or automatic sewing)

Both approaches have serious disadvantages. Today robots do not have sufficient intelligence and sensory capabilities to address very complex manufacturing tasks. On the other hand, manufacturing (e.g., inspection) tasks can require great skill acquired through many years of experience and in many cases through formal engineering training. Usually the underlying physics is very complex and very poorly understood. The classical pure expert system approach to these problems would embody the skill aspects in heuristics that implicitly, but not explicitly, capture physics. The combined approach, called the *engineering-based expert systems approach,* explicitly models the physics and provides the proper solution. Engineering-based expert systems capture algorithmically the capabilities of human experts and trained process operators in an efficient and cost-effective way. They use a blending of process modeling and identification, pattern recognition, hypothesis testing, and control systems techniques, as well as conventional AI tools and expert systems rules and heuristics. The engineering-based expert systems approach to automated manufacturing is at its very beginning and provides a challenging area for further work.

Our purpose in this chapter is to provide a survey of AI and knowledge-based expert systems techniques applied in the CIM environment. Special attention is given to the Petri net models of manufacturing systems and their marriage with knowledge-based systems. For completeness, we include a more detailed presentation of a few representative manufacturing expert systems, and start with a brief description of the basic CIM functions.

2 A LOOK AT COMPUTER-INTEGRATED MANUFACTURING FUNCTIONS

In this section we give some background material on the principal CIM functions that provide a challenge for AI and knowledge-based techniques and tools. These functions are:

- Product design and design for assembly
- CAD/CAM in terms of features
- Process planning, scheduling, and control
- Dynamic simulation of FMS
- Equipment selection
- Fault diagnosis
- Facility layout
- Quality assurance

Specific examples of expert and knowledge-based systems developed for some of these functions will be presented in Section 6.

2.1 Product Design and Design for Assembly

Product design is a complex task that requires intelligence and experience and is performed in several stages: definition of the product's functional structure, definition of physical principles, drawing of product (or part) shape, and specification of manufacturing data (detailing). The design of a product involves a preliminary design process, a refinement process, an analysis procedure, and finally the implementation process.

Computer-aided design (CAD) is a well-defined set of hardware and software methods and tools by which the product design is computer-automated. Very often, commercial CAD systems are turnkey systems that provide an integrated combination of both CAD hardware and CAD software for carrying out a specific design process. Many CAD systems consist purely of computer-independent CAD software packages that can work on a hardware system supported by appropriate workstations. A CAD system has to support the designer via a graphic-interactive communication technique together with appropriate processing tools such as geometry processing and graphics processing. The data that describe the technical solution as well as the results of the processing are stored in a database and form the computer *internal product model*. The purpose of the computer internal model is to provide data for the optimization and control of the product (tolerance analysis, control of correctness, completeness, etc.) as well as for other manufacturing functions such as the generation of production schedules, generation of numerical control programs for machine tools and robots, and simulation of manufacture and assembly operations.

Design for assembly (DFA) belongs to the more general field of *design for manufacturing* (DFM) (Stoll, 1986). DFM deals with understanding how product design interacts with the other parts of the manufacturing system. It also involves the problems of specifying product design alternatives that help to globally optimize the manufacturing system as a whole. DFA is concerned with the design of products with ease of assembly in mind. By using DFA, a product can be systematically designed to minimize the technological and financial efforts required for assembly and simultaneously satisfy all constraints on the product functionality. To facilitate the designers in this job, a *decision support system* (DSS) is needed that can take into account the knowledge of assembly requirements and help the product engineers in their task (i.e., in designing for easy manual and automated assembly, designing for assembly process planning, and reducing reworking). Such a system should, among other things, be able to:

- Analyze all decision relevant to assembly and point out if there is some fault
- Indicate the critical features in the design
- Propose possible changes of inappropriate design characteristics
- Suggest examples of design changes and check whether a design change will affect product functionality

Some available classical tools (not using expert systems techniques) for DFA that are not consistent with all the above objectives can be found in Gairola (1985, 1986) and Andreasen et al. (1982). These tools are tedious, costly, and time-consuming. Also, they do not guarantee success in all cases, since most of the knowledge on DFA exists only as experience that brings irreproducible results. But most of the DFA knowledge is available in a well-formulated form, which means that the greatest problem of knowledge acquisition is solved. Thus the DFA field is an ideal field for the application of expert systems.

In general there are three fundamental approaches to designing a product for assembly (Gairola, 1986):

1. Simplifying the assembly task
2. Improving assembly organization
3. Facilitating assembly execution

To simplify the assembly task, one has to minimize the number of parts, reduce the variety of parts, and select simple assembly methods. To improve planning performance in assembly through specific design features, one has the following alternatives:

- Allow arbitrary decomposition of the product in subassemblies.
- Use standard parts and subassemblies.
- Avoid compulsory assembly sequences in order to be able to solve easily the line balancing problem.

2.2 CAD/CAM in Terms of Features

A key link between design and AI techniques in manufacturing is the method of representing design geometry (Choi et al., 1984; Henderson and Anderson, 1984; Woo, 1982; Dixon and Dym, 1986). To obtain a true CIM system, a single database of the design aspects, especially geometry, should be accessible for all functions within the design and manufacturing repertoire. These functions include graphics, analysis, evaluation for manufacturability, process design, and process planning.

The representation of geometry in terms of features is one solution to the problem of obtaining a unified database. An identifiable geometric shape or entity is considered a feature of a design. Examples of such features are two- or three-dimensional corners, slabs, boxes, holes, and so on. The importance of this approach is that most of the knowledge required for evaluation of manufacturability, design, and process planning is expressed in terms of features or combinations of features. The creation of the desired design representations in terms of features is a promising and active area of CIM and knowledge engineering research. The link with the CAD system is natural, since information about features can be obtained from the boundary representation of points, edges, and surfaces of objects that are provided by CAD systems. Of course, another approach is to design with features from the very beginning. Some appropriate combination of feature extraction and design-with features would give the most general and successful solution. This can be best realized through AI/expert systems techniques.

Looking at the existing manufacturing systems and the related technical literature, we are persuaded that, within a CIM environment, CAD can and must do more than give a purely geometric database for production operations (Meister, 1985; Feder and Victor, 1980). The existing systems such as the Initial Graphics Exchange Specification (IGES) (Smith and Wellington, 1985), the Graphical Kernel System (GKS) (Anon., 1982) and the Product Definition Data Interface (PDDI) (Carringer, 1986) provide only part of the solution. These systems should be expanded using AI and knowledge-based techniques that take into account product requirements for interchangeable parts, time procurement, maintainability, logistics support, ergonomics, fault detection, and safety. The expert system(s) to be developed should include a *validation component*. The design engineer should be able to observe the impact of various product design enhancements using a set of given measurable criteria. CAD has a strong effect in many areas of the CIM environment. Therefore, application of AI/expert system tools to the CAD-generated product definition database can increase substantially the beneficial issues of this impact for both the manufacturer and the customer (Matsushima et al., 1982).

2.3 Process Planning, Scheduling, and Control

Computer-aided process planning (CAPP) is the computer-aided activity that determines the appropriate procedure to transform raw material (usually in some prespecified form) into a final product. It defines what has to be produced, how it should be manufactured, and what means should be used to meet competition and economic goals. *Process scheduling* determines how many items have to be produced, when and where they should be manufactured, and by whom. The correction of the observed deviations between actual product and planned output is achieved through appropriate *feedback control* (Weill et al., 1982; Spur and Krause, 1986; Chang and Wysk, 1985).

Process planning can be categorized as *variant* or *generative*. In variant process planning a plan is selected from among a set of standard plans. In generative process planning one uses information on product or part features (coming, for example, from a CAD system) for creating a process plan. Examples of available CAPP systems are AUTAP (Eversheim et al., 1980), CAPP (Link, 1976), CAPSY (Spur and Hein, 1981), CPP (Dunn and Mann, 1978), MIPLAN (Schaffer, 1980), and GENPLAN (Tulkoff, 1981). The real integration of CAD and CAM becomes possible with the introduction of a CAPP system in the chain through a connective information flow and a central database. CAPP systems reduce the deficiencies of traditional process planning systems realized by skilled planners; that is, they improve planning time and promptly prepare the information for decision-making and planning objectives. Knowledge-based CAPP systems can further improve the capabilities of CAPP systems by utilizing human experience and providing increased flexibility.

Process (production) scheduling determines a sequence (a schedule) of part lots to be machined in the FMS so as to meet the due dates of lots and minimize machine idle times, queues at machines, and so on. Process scheduling involves two basic tasks:

1. Production scheduling
2. Real-time rescheduling

The production scheduling is based on a medium-term horizon (e.g., 2–3 weeks) and determines the estimated starting times of lots to allocate auxiliary resources. The production scheduling must take into account several constraints such as planned maintenance periods for machines and raw materials availability times. Real-time rescheduling is needed when the planned schedule must be modified because of the occurrence of unexpected events (e.g., when raw material is not available when required or when a machine breaks down). Examples of conventional production scheduling systems can be found in Rolstadås (1977) and Alexander and Jagannathan (1983).

Process control involves control structures and algorithms that support planning and supervision tasks at various levels of the manufacturing system (production scheduling, materials flow, maintenance control, quality control, etc.). In general, CIM possesses three distinct control levels:

1. Highest-level control (management control)
2. Intermediate-level control (shop-floor control)
3. Lowest-level control (control of machines)

At the highest level, the processing of management data (production scheduling, operational management, etc.) takes place. Also, at this level, horizontal communication to other factories or plants and vertical communication to local production and control units are coordinated. Intermediate-level control relates to plant supervision and coordination, the disposition of materials flow, production process control, quality assurance, and the supervision of the lower-level controllers. Horizontal and vertical communication is again involved. The lowest level of control involves specific control algorithms (e.g., DDC algorithms and optimal control algorithms). Future systems will be characterized by increased intelligence located at different hierarchical control levels (adaptive control, rule-based control, intelligent control, and so on) (Dillmann, 1986; Williams, 1983; Conterno, 1987).

2.4 Dynamic Simulation of a Flexible Manufacturing System

Dynamic FMS simulation imitates the operation of the system through the use of some dynamic model. The objective of the simulation is to study the system behavior and evaluate alternative decision, design, and operation rules. The simulation must be dynamic because the system behavior and the results obtained are time-dependent and deterministic or stochastic. Appropriate models for the simulation are queuing models for the buffer stores or the automated storage and retrieval system. Of increasing use for manufacturing system simulation are the various types of Petri nets, which will be discussed in Section 5.

According to Ranky (1983, 1986a, 1986b) the FMS simulation models are classified as

- Graphical models
- Mathematical models
- Scaled-down physical models

Most present-day graphic systems and CAD packages provide not only three-dimensional solid graphics representations of models and animation techniques, but also high-level task description languages.

Mathematical models use functional expressions and appropriate simulation languages such as GPSS (general-purpose simulation system), DYNAMO, SIMSCRIPT, or SLAM. Simulation of a flexible manufacturing system needs appropriate data such as manufacturing time distributions, inspection time distributions, transportation times, fixturing time distributions, and unloading time distributions.

The scaled-down physical models are controlled by computers or microprocessors and are used in plant engineering for getting information about the layout and the behavior of the system. These models are static and are expensive to build.

2.5 Equipment Selection

The equipment selection problem is very important to the design of a manufacturing system, since it is a dominant factor in overall capital cost. A successful solution to this problem leads to (Heragu and Kusiak, 1987):

- Lower capital cost
- Lower operating and maintenance cost
- Increased utilization rate
- Improved layout facilities
- Increased total production efficiency

A survey and comparison of the available approaches to solving the equipment selection problem is provided by Miller and Davis (1977). Many of the assumptions made in these techniques are unrealistic. As Kusiak explains (Kusiak, 1987a), it is very difficult to precisely formulate the equipment selection problem to reflect practice accurately. To this end, it is necessary to use engineering-based expert system techniques (including quantitative and qualitative issues).

2.6 Fault Diagnosis

Fault diagnosis and maintenance and repair present a tough problem in all large and complex technological systems (Tzafestas, 1986, 1988c). Fault diagnosis requires pulling apart the interactions of components in order to isolate the presence of a fault to a particular component or interconnection. Fast fault diagnosis improves the availability of a manufacturing system, which is closely connected to its autonomy, its ability to run fully automatically without human interference. Actual automated manufacturing systems have facilities for prevention of damage via appropriate fault containment measures (e.g., by interrupting robot motion and calling the operator). High degrees of autonomy can be achieved using appropriate fault recovery schemes based on sensor signals. But independently of the desired degree of autonomy, fault detection and diagnosis are prerequisites.

The faults occurring in manufacturing systems can be caused by:

- Unsuccessful operation due to module misfunction (primary failure)
- Defective parts after an undetected primary failure (secondary failure)
- Program and operator faults

The diagnosis in an FMS can be at the *cell level,* for example, localize a particular equipment in the work cell, or at the *equipment level,* troubleshooting inside the equipment. The work on the application of AI and knowledge-based techniques for diagnosing faults in manufacturing systems is rather limited [see, e.g., Chiu and Niedermayr (1985) and Dungern and Schmidt (1987)]. However, the knowledge-based diagnostic field is one of the mostly developed applications of AI in medicine and other technological areas [see, e.g., Tzafestas et al. (1987); Singh et al. (1987); Tzafestas (1988c, 1988d)].

2.7 Facility Layout

The facility layout problem of manufacturing systems [for a review see Kusiak and Heragu (1987)] concerns the optimal location of each unit or facility to its corresponding site. The criterion for optimality is the minimization of the total materials handling cost. This problem can be put in the quadratic assignment form, or the set covering problem form, or linear integer programming form, and so on. For systems with 10 or more facilities it is extremely difficult, if not impossible, to find optimal algorithms for the solution. Kusiak and Heragu (1987) provided a survey of heuristic algorithms that can sometimes give a solution relatively quickly, but the solutions need further examination and cannot be applied directly. This is so because (1) the configuration for some facilities provided may be not acceptable and (2) the algorithms do not consider some important constraints (e.g., the space needed for materials-handling equipment and clearance between machines). Thus the application of expert systems techniques is absolutely necessary for effectively solving the facility layout problem.

Schmidt-Streier and Altenhein (1985) have implemented a procedure for the selection of appropriate handling devices, layout planning, and output calculation in a given FMS. The selection of the appropriate robot is based on a database for 170 industrial robots in the German market. This selection is made through dialogue. When an industrial robot is to be installed in a given workstation, usually the existing layout must be altered. The machines should be arranged so that all positions can be reached by the robot and sufficient output can be ensured. The selection of the optimum layout is again done by dialogue with the help of an interactive graphic screen. This includes modification of machine layout, definition of gripper type, planning of operation sequences, and the calculation of cycle time.

2.8 Quality Assurance

Quality control (QC) is a crucial operation in a manufacturing system that determines the amounts by which the quality of actual products deviates from the specified product quality. The quality standards are set by the market (customer standards, industrial acceptance), by legislation (producer liability, authorities, safety guards for workers), and by the enterprise (failure rates, costs, profit, image). Quality control has to be performed at many different levels of a manufacturing process. *Quality assurance* (QA) is the procedure that includes all phases of the life cycle of a product. It integrates all QC activities into one system. Quality assurance is performed in a hierarchical way according to the local network of operational data acquisition and the equipment configuration conceived for the various QC levels.

Quality control must be applied during every production cycle of the product and involves some or all of the following:

- Design quality (planning, development, layout design)
- Supply quality (purchasing, material reception)
- Manufacturing quality (manufacture, assembly)
- Delivery quality (acceptance, final test)
- User quality (sale, user installation, use of the products)

3 ARTIFICIAL INTELLIGENCE AND KNOWLEDGE-BASED ISSUES FOR CIM SYSTEMS

In this section we provide a short review of three AI areas (automatic planning, automatic learning, and qualitative simulation) and the basic knowledge-based issues that are used in CIM functions.

3.1 Automatic Planning

Automatic planning can be used for robot and manufacturing cell task planning. Planning is an important area of AI and is connected to general problem solving. A typical example of AI planning is the well-known "blocks world" problem. The planning consists of finding a path (or subgraph) in a graph in which the nodes represent situations (e.g., states in the blocks world) and the links between nodes represent the possible moves (e.g., the robot's elementary operations). The design of a state feedback controller can be formulated as an AI planning problem.

The initial state of the AI planning system consists of the open-loop system and the desired closed-loop characteristics. The final state consists mainly of the control law that leads the system to the desired performance or sufficiently near to it. Each node of the tree (or graph) represents a unique model of the process and/or a unique control law. Lines of reasoning about the design method are represented by branches of the tree (Bratko, 1988).

Daniel (1984) reviews two planning systems, STRIPS and NOAH [see also Sacerdoti (1977)]. STRIPS can also be found in Fikes and Nillson (1971). Other examples of AI-based planners are GPS (General Problem Solver) (Ernst and Newell, 1969), WARPLAN (Warren, 1974), AL 3 (Bratko, 1982), and SIPE (Wilkins, 1985). STRIPS is actually a Lisp implementation of GPS (Fikes et al., 1973), and WARPLAN is an improved version of STRIPS in Prolog.

STRIPS uses formal logic for representing domain knowledge, and so the current state is represented by a logical statement involving terms of relations among objects. Permissible operations actually remove some of the relations from the current state and introduce new relations to it. STRIPS is appropriate for robot planning systems. WARPLAN allows nonlinear construction of plans and is somewhat superior to STRIPS, but it possesses the drawbacks of the depth-first search strategy it employs. NOAH is a planner that can examine the nature of incomplete ordering for actions in plans. SIPE has the capability of replanning whenever some plan fails to achieve the desired goal. During the execution of a plan by a robot, some action in the plan may not lead to the desired goal. This can be detected by the robot sensors (e.g., visual or tactile), and the robot has to make a new plan. SIPE modifies the original plan so as to work well with the new, unforeseen conditions. Planning in CIM is needed not only for generating robot actions on the basis of sensory feedback, but also for planning the procedures of collecting information.

3.2 Automatic Learning

Automatic learning can be accomplished using the following approaches:

- Learning from instruction
- Learning by analogy
- Learning from examples (inductive learning)
- Learning by discovery

Of course, there are other styles of learning, such as learning, through visual imagery or through tactile sensing. So far, machine learning has mainly been connected with symbolic forms of learning.

Generally the learning problem is the following:

Given a set of objects specified in some description language and the classes to which the objects belong,

Find a general classification rule that "explains" the learning set of objects and can also be used for the classification of new objects.

Explaining a set of objects means classifying them correctly into classes as specified in the initial specification. Learning algorithms differ in their use of particular generalizing and specializing rules, rule selection criteria, whether negative instances are included in the training set, and whether a bottom-up or top-down learning strategy is used.

A useful collection of chapters on various approaches of learning is provided in Michalski et al. (1983). A discussion on the relation of machine learning techniques and expert systems is presented in Bundy (1984). Several examples of learning systems are given in Quinlan (1981), Shepherd (1983), Dechter and Michie (1984) and Dufay and Latcombe (1987).

3.3 Qualitative Modeling and Simulation

Qualitative modeling and simulation is based on symbolic processing techniques, in contrast with traditional modeling, which is based on differential equation models and numerical techniques. Qualitative models are more appropriate for performing the structural synthesis of a process and carrying out fault diagnosis.

Qualitative modeling and reasoning techniques:

- Can explain the past and predict the future
- Can be used to interpret measurement results
- Can be applied to detect analogies between different domains
- Are suitable for use as teachware

Qualitative reasoning systems use abstract models of their domain, employing the model and causal relationships between the model components to draw conclusions. The domain models are abstract in the sense that they do not use any numerical values to represent the objects, their properties, and their relationships.

Some benefits of the qualitative approach are:

Qualitative models can be developed much more easily than quantitative models.

Qualitative simulation needs less computational effort than quantitative simulation.

Qualitative simulation provides a basis for user-oriented explanation of the simulation process.

Examples of qualitative models are given in Bratko et al. (1988). A survey of qualitative modeling techniques of dynamic systems is given in Bürle (1987), where the techniques for qualitative modeling of time, space, and motion are described. A combination of qualitative and quantitative modeling and simulation is also provided in Bürle (1987) for performance-reliability modeling [see also O'Keefe (1986)].

3.4 Architecture and Design of Expert Systems

3.4.1 EXPERT SYSTEMS ARCHITECTURE.
The keys of AI expert system building tools are:

1. Symbolic representation of the knowledge (predicate logic, semantic networks, frames, production systems, etc.)
2. Symbolic reasoning using rules and methods able to deduce, examine, judge, determine, and so on
3. Graphic explanations using developer-oriented graphic means (knowledge-based graphs and rule graphs, etc.) and end-user-oriented graphic means to provide representations and reasoning to developers and users

Some of the benefits of the above AI issues are the following:

- Explicit representation of symbolic structures, performance, and reasoning and easy integration of various representation types
- Visibility, flexibility, and adaptability obtained from the declarative nature of the representation
- Reasoning in radically different ways from those tried by non-AI systems
- Intelligent interaction, based on the representation

AI/expert systems attempt to remove the programmers as problem translators and allow the expert to interact directly with the system to explore the problem space.

An expert system consists of the following clearly separated components (Fig. 6-2) (Forsyth, 1984; Hayes-Roth et al., 1983; Murphy, 1985):

- Knowledge base (general knowledge about the problem, i.e., facts and rules)
- Data base (information about the current problem, i.e., input data)
- Inference engine (methods for applying the general knowledge of the problem)
- Explanation component (which can inform the user on why and how the conclusions are obtained)
- User interface and knowledge acquisition component
- Work space (i.e., an area of memory for storing a description of the problem constructed from facts supplied by the user or inferred from the knowledge base)

3.4.2 RULE-BASED SYSTEMS.
First-generation expert systems use the knowledge representation in the form of if-then (the so-called production) rules. The basic form of a production rule is:

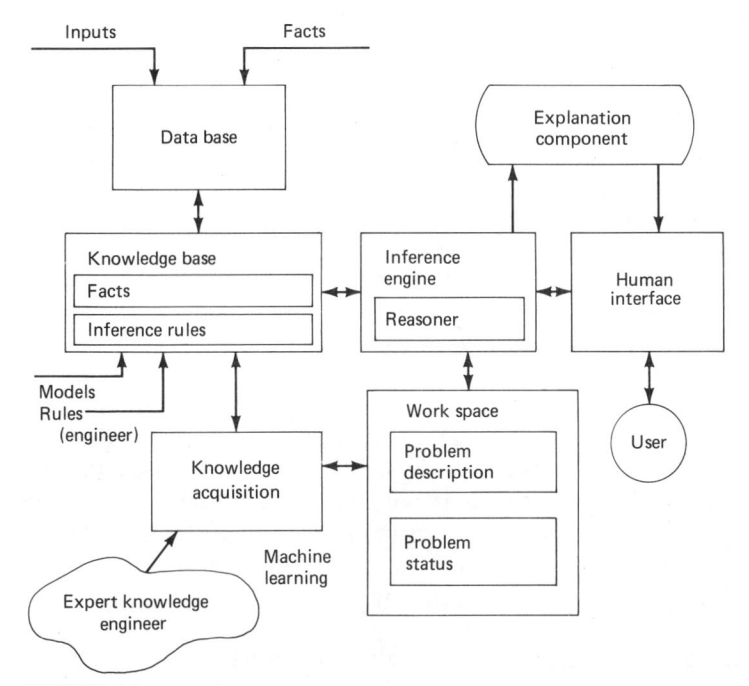

FIGURE 6-2
Expert system architecture.

```
RULE R_k
IF    c_1, c_2, ..., c_m
THEN  h_1, h_2, ..., h_n
```

where the c_i ($i = 1, 2, \ldots, m$) are predicates known as *conditions* (antecedents, premises, etc.) and the h_i ($i = 1, 2, \ldots, n$) are referred to as *consequents* (deductions or actions). The fundamental reasoning (syllogism) that applies here is: "If A implies B and B implies C, then A implies C." When all c_i are true, rule R_k is said to be *triggered*. The set of triggered rules is called the *conflict set*. A rule is selected from the conflict set using a *conflict resolution strategy*. A triggered rule is said to be *fired* when its consequences are performed.

Some strategies for selecting the rule for firing from the conflict set are:

- Rule ordering (Rule appearing earliest has highest priority.)
- Data ordering (Rule with highest priority data-condition has highest priority.)
- Size ordering (Rule with longest list of constraining conditions has highest priority.)
- Context limiting (Activate or deactivate groups of rules at any time to reduce the occurrence of conflict.)
- Specificity ordering (Arrange rules whose conditions are a superset of another rule.)

The conflict resolution strategy is selected ad hoc. Most popular are specificity-ordering and context-limiting strategies.

The *control* (or *interpretation*) mechanism used by synthesis systems is:

1. Find rules whose IF parts are triggered, and select a rule using a certain conflict resolution strategy.
2. Fire the rule (i.e., do what the rule's THEN part says).

In analysis systems, the antecedents of rules can be either observed or derived facts, and the consequents are new facts that are deducted. The above mechanism is known as a *forward-chaining inference* mechanism. In analysis systems the control mechanism can be either of the forward or backward chaining type. In the backward-chaining mechanism, a particular hypothesis is selected, and the rules are searched to see if the hypothesis is a consequent. If yes, the antecedents of the rule constitute the next set of hypotheses. The process is continued until some hypothesis is not true or all hypotheses are true based on the data. Forward and backward inference chaining resemble the bottom-up and top-down control in general computer algorithms (compilers).

Rule-based systems have many advantages. For example:

They provide a homogeneous representation of knowledge.

They allow incremental growth of knowledge through addition of new rules.

They allow unplanned but useful interactions.

A well-known example of a rule-based system is XCON, a synthesis expert system for configuring DEC's VAX computers. The main disadvantage of rule-based systems is that in their case the knowledge acquisition from domain experts is time-consuming and difficult. All possibilities have to be explicitly enumerated, and there is no capability of system generalization.

Rule-based systems can be efficiently implemented using various programming languages such as Fortran, Pascal, C, Lisp, or Prolog or expert system tools (shells) such as EMYCIN, KAS, ROSIE, OPS5, or M1, which possess built-in inference mechanisms. EMYCIN was derived from MYCIN by removing the domain knowledge. In the same way, KAS was derived from Prospector. OPS5 provides flexibility and generality in that it is easy to tailor the system to the domain, but unlike EMYCIN and KAS it does not have sophisticated front ends. ROSIE uses English-like syntax but does not possess a sophisticated database structure. M1 was developed by Teknowledge for the IBM PC and uses English-like syntax. Most first-generation production rule systems are written in Lisp dialects. For example, EMYCIN is written in Interlisp (Stanford University), OPS5 is written in Franzlisp (Carnegie-Mellon University), and ROSIE is again written in Interlisp (Rand Corporation).

Developing a rule-based expert system via an expert system tool reduces the need to program it directly in an AI language (Lisp or Prolog), but most expert systems tools presently available are not designed for real-time applications, that is, they do not support interrupts, nor do they accept on-line data (Gidwani, 1986; Kaemmerer and Christopherson, 1986; Moore et al., 1984). However, there is no reason why these properties cannot be added, particularly if the host computer allows access to its operating system. One point about employing Lisp-based systems for real-time control is that during execution, a Lisp system periodically carries out garbage collection of unused memory, and usually garbage collection is an automatic and uninterruptible process. Thus if interrupting procedures are needed during garbage collection, it may not be possible for the system to respond in time. This point (i.e., the way of handling garbage collection) should be carefully examined whenever one wants to develop a Lisp-based expert system. This problem always appears when the system makes use of linked lists and heap storage, no matter what language or expert system tool is used.

3.4.3 SYSTEMS USING SEMANTIC NETWORKS AND FRAMES. *Semantic networks* are based on the very simple and ancient idea that memory consists of associations between concepts. The associative memory concept has its origin with Aristotle and entered computer science work through the use of simple associations to represent word meaning in databases. A semantic network is a method of knowledge representation where *concepts* are represented as nodes (circles) and *relations* between pairs of concepts are represented by directed arcs (labeled arrows). Such pairs of related concepts may be thought of as representing simple facts. Node-and-link nets are not necessarily semantic nets—only when there is a way of associating meaning with the network. One approach to this, the so-called *procedural semantics,* is to associate a set of programs that operate on descriptions in the representation (Minsky, 1986).

The concept of *frame* is the result of organizing the properties of some object or event (or a class of objects) to form a prototype (structure). A frame, for example, can be used to represent a part of a manufacturing operation (e.g., drilling) or a controller or a class of vehicles. The power of frame representation is due to the fact that those elements that are conventionally present in a description of an object or event are grouped together and can be accessed and processed as a unit. A frame can be regarded as a collection of semantic net nodes and slots that together describe a prototypical (stereotypical) object or class of objects. A frame language has special constructs for organizing frames that represent classes into hierarchical taxonomies. Associated with this there are special-purpose reasoning procedures that use the structural characteristics of frames to carry out particular inferences that extend the explicitly held set of beliefs to a larger (virtual) set of beliefs.

Many systems combine frame representation with production rule languages. Such systems include KEE and LOOPS. KEE is written in Interlisp and was originally produced for the Xerox 1100 and Symbolics 3600 machines but is now available as a general-purpose system (knowledge engineering environment). KEE also supports procedure-oriented and object-oriented representation methods. LOOPS was developed at the Xerox Palo Alto Research Center and is appropriate for object-oriented, rule-based, access-oriented, and procedure-oriented representation methods. Its main feature is the integration of these four programming methods to permit the paradigms to be used together in system building. LOOPS is written in Interlisp-D and works on Xerox 1100 series workstations. Other systems for frame-based representation are KL-ONE, which possesses automatic inheritance and support for semantic nets using subsumption, and KMS, which consists of a collection of subsystems, each with its own knowledge representation and inference mechanism. KL-ONE operates on the DEC VAX, and KMS on UNIVAC 1100/40.

3.4.4 ENGINEERING-BASED EXPERT SYSTEMS. The traditional expert systems discussed above are well suited to problems that cannot be rigorously analyzed because of lack of understanding or inadequate analytic techniques. But as mentioned in Section 1, for many domains of the CIM field the development and use of an engineering-based expert system (EBES) is more appropriate. An EBES combines formal engineering analysis and mathematical processing techniques with traditional expert system techniques. The models resulting from the analysis are augmented by experiential heuristic rules. The models represent precise knowledge about the problem, and the heuristic rules capture the skills of the human expert. Thus the knowledge base for the EBES consists of both models and rules. The rules associated with the engineering-based expert system may be different and fewer in number than the heuristic rules used in a traditional expert system. The knowledge base can be richer than that of the conventional expert system, because the process models may contain information that is not explicitly known by the human expert or information that is only implicit in the expert's heuristic rules. Often the experts do not understand the underlying physics and mathematics. In the concept of "models" we also include optimization models, simulation models, and algorithmic models in general. Thus the EBES concept coincides with the so-called tandem expert system (Heragu and Kusiak, 1987) or hybrid (coupled) knowledge-based expert system.

Typical applications of EBES in manufacturing are in assembly (deterministic, nondeterministic), structural materials processing, and process operations (machine shop grinding, deburring, fettling or snagging of casting fins, etc.) (Nevins et al., 1987).

4 SURVEY OF MANUFACTURING KNOWLEDGE-BASED SYSTEMS

This section provides a brief survey of a number of knowledge-based expert systems for manufacturing functions that are available in the open literature. It is not intended to be exhaustive, but it is hoped that the reader will obtain a good picture of the present status of this area.

4.1 Product Computer-Aided Design

The product design task in manufacturing depends on whether the desired product (or part) is a typical one for which standard well-established design procedures exist or a new or rarely used part that needs the development of a new design procedure. If the product is a modification of an existing product, then one can accordingly design it by suitably modifying available design procedures (Tzafestas, 1988a; Heragu and Kusiak, 1987).

PROPLAN (PROcess PLANning) (Mouleeswaran and Fisher, 1986; Mouleeswaran, 1984) is a knowledge-based environment that integrates the design and planning phases for mechanical parts. Its main advantage is the reduction of human intervention between design and planning. To this end CAD data are automatically transformed into a symbolic form that permits automatic geometric feature extraction. At its current stage of development, PROPLAN uses the capabilities of a Lisp machine for graphics entry and part description. PROPLAN's current working domain is a repertoire of rotational parts produced by turning machines (lathes, screw machines, etc.). The system involves two principal subsystems, a design subsystem and a planning subsystem. The user can design a new part, derive a machine sequence plan for stored or new part designs, or merely retrieve a process plan.

In the design mode, the system provides a window with appropriate menu items for the graphical description of a part (Fig. 6-3). PROPLAN uses such part features as external profile, internal profile, line, arc, thread, and knurl, which are sufficient for describing a large repertoire of rotational parts. After locating the coordinate system at the center of the tool face of the workpiece, the user describes the external and internal profiles of the parts, selecting the appropriate symbolic menu items and arranging the profile segments in a sequence. Threads and knurls (pitch, depth, angle, etc.) can be specified during the selection process, and tolerances as well as surface finishes can be added after the segments have been laid out. Part descriptions can be modified by changing the internal symbolic representation (model) of the parts.

AIFIX (Ferreira et al., 1985) is an expert system suitable for designing fixtures for parts being produced on milling machines. It is an if-then rule-based system and involves Fortran routines that are called by Lisp functions. To design a fixture, all appropriate orientations for the part are at first generated and evaluated, and a number of them are retained. Then the fixture design around the part is carried out in three steps: fixture configuration proposal, fixture configuration realization, and final evaluation (including cost issues).

DOMINIC I (Dixon et al., 1987) is a rather domain-independent expert system (coded in Common Lisp) for iterative design of mechanical parts. Design and performance data are introduced through a knowledge acquisition module. The system asks the user to provide an initial design or generates such a design automatically. This design, which may be poor, is then improved iteratively by the expert system until an acceptable design is found. Otherwise the redesign process is terminated. The refinement process in DOMINIC I is

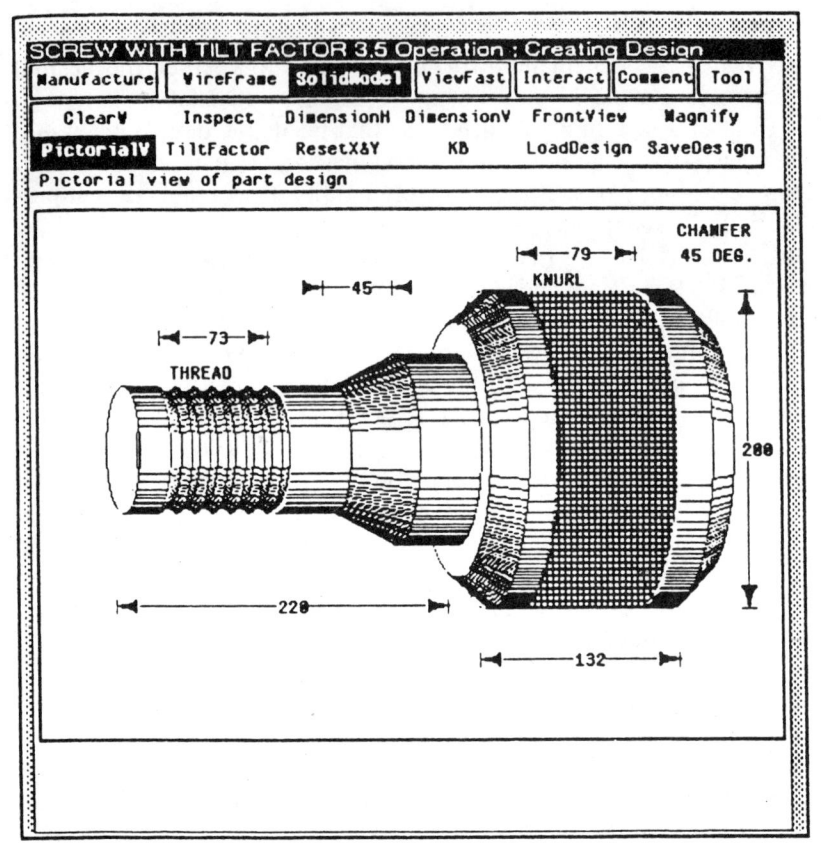

FIGURE 6-3
PROPLAN part window. Reprinted with permission from Mouleeswaran and Fisher (1986). © Springer-Verlag (Computational Mechanics Publications).

based on only one performance parameter at a time, and in some situations it exhibits serious difficulties. But it is still under improvement.

Other expert systems available for product design can be found in Mittal et al. (1985), Dixon and Simmons (1985), Dixon et al. (1985), Shah (1985), and Brown and Chandrasekaran (1983, 1986). In Brown and Chandrasekaran (1986) the design problem of mechanical parts is solved in a top-down way using a hierarchy of specialists. A prototype is described for the design of a small table that consists of a cylindrical support and a circular top. The expert system AIR-CYL presented in Brown and Chandrasekaran (1986) is suitable for the design of air cylinders. It is based on the same principles as that of Brown and Chandrasekaran (1983), that is, it follows a redesign/refinement process. It is coded in DSPL (Design Specialists and Plans Language), which is a task-level language.

4.2 Process Planning and Scheduling

This is the area for which many expert systems with important properties and features are available.

Fellenstein et al. (1985) describe a prototype knowledge base for manufacturing planning that is implemented using the expert system shell Syllog. This knowledge base is built with a combination of a relational database and an expert system shell. The Syllog system is written in Prolog, and its inference engine can perform many sets of recursive syllogisms that are outside the scope of pure Prolog (Walker, 1985). Knowledge in the Syllog shell is written as facts and syllogisms. Facts are similar to types in a relational table (although in Syllog a table has an English-like heading), and syllogisms are English-like rules for the use of facts.

Fellenstein et al. (1985) describe *tester capacity planning* and a *yield analysis task*, which are used in the Syllog shell. The manufacturing task of interest is that of testing electronic items in a production system before they are put into larger assemblies. The purpose of the plan is to determine the numbers of various types of testing machines that are needed to meet a production target. Estimating correctly the numbers of machines is important, since too little capacity can lead to production delays while too much is wasteful.

Descotte and Latombe (1984) describe an if-then rule-based expert system called GARI, which employs a general problem solver (GPS) and appropriate knowledge for planning the sequence of machining cuts for mechanical parts. The approach of iterative refinement is followed, and the part geometry is represented in terms of features. GARI together with other manufacturing expert systems such as TOM (Matsushima et al., 1982), PROPLAN (Mouleeswaran and Fisher, 1986; Mouleeswaran, 1984) and Hi-MAPP (Berenji and Khoshnevis, 1986) formulate the process planning problem as a sequence of actions by which the goal state (i.e., the finished parts) is obtained from the initial state (i.e., the raw material), a set of allowable actions (operations), and a group of available resources (robots, machines, tools, etc.).

TOM (Technostructure of Machining) is written in Pascal and generates a plan for a given finished geometry in the hole-making domain. It is again an if-then rule-based system with backward inference (alpha-beta) strategy. TOM provides a process plan with minimum machining time but must be used with care because sometimes its heuristic conflict resolution strategy leads to wrong results.

PROPLAN (Process Planning) involves a parts design subsystem and a process planning subsystem. The design subsystem has been discussed in Section 4.1. The process planning subsystem was designed to be generative in the prototype phase, but enhancements are under development to allow both variant and generative planning whenever appropriate. Presently, PROPLAN is implemented in Interlisp-D on a Xerox 1108 machine or in muLisp on an IBM personal computer. One of the potential applications of the variant approach in a hybrid generative/variant environment is the retrieval of existing plans, previously produced by generative planning methods, and then the editing of machining operation descriptions in order to tune the plans to specific shop-floor installations.

Hi-MAPP (Hierarchical Intelligent Manufacturing Automated Process Planner) is similar to GARI with regard to part presentation but differs in two respects: (1) it produces hierarchical plans and (2) it produces initially an abstract of a correct plan, whereas GARI generates initially a loosely constrained plan and uses a time-consuming refinement process.

Other examples of expert process planning systems are EXCAP (Darbyshire and Davies, 1984), OPEX (Sluga et al., 1988), SIPP (Nau and Chang, 1985), SAPT (Milačič and Urosevič, 1988), and those described in Preiss and Kaplanski (1983), Bourne and Fox (1984), Vancza (1988), and Gliviak et al. (1984).

EXCAP (Expert Computer-Aided Process Planning) is written in Pascal and provides process plans for rotational parts only. OPEX (Operation Sequence Planning) is an expert system appropriate for operation sequence planning and can be used either as a stand-alone shell or as a numerical control (NC) part programming tool. SIPP is a frame-based expert system for planning parts requiring metal removal processes. SAPT (System for Automatic Programming Technology) is a part designer/expert system consisting of a product designer segment, a manufacture designer segment, and a production planner/controller segment. These three segments employ the same engineering knowledge basis but are mutually independent with respect to modularity. The expert plan-producing system of Preiss and Kaplanski (1983) is suitable for production on a three-axis mill starting from a digitized part drawing, and that of Bourne and Fox (1984) is a constrained/governed scheduling system that does planning and scheduling and is supported by a language-oriented database.

Vancza (1988) follows the inductive learning approach for constructing a knowledge base that is appropriate for manufacturing process planning. The goal is to bridge the gap between variant and generative methods. It is shown how domain-specific a priori knowledge can direct the inductive reasoning process toward useful assertions. The approach taken is strongly based on *group technology,* and the key idea is that workpieces forming a family must bear common characteristic features that can be extracted and explicitly described.

Our discussion on process planning expert systems is closed with the system CEMAS (Cell Management System) (Gliviak et al, 1984), which was designed to supervise a manufacturing cell. It contains a database, a knowledge base, an inference engine, a knowledge acquisition block, and an explanation block. It is realized in Lisp supported by a data structure array. CEMAS has three activity levels: (1) the execution level, which controls the moves of the machine tools; (2) the information level, which records the actual state; and (3) the decision level, which schedules work to the workstations.

Regarding the process scheduling problem, the systems described by Szenes (1982), Fox and Smith (1984), Bruno et al. (1986), Mill and Spraggett

(1984), and Litt et al. (1988) are worth mentioning. Szenes (1982) presents a prototype tool for modeling planning decision support. This is more closely related to manufacturing than to computer algorithms. Fox and Smith (1984) describe the system ISIS, which is suitable for process scheduling in a job-shop facility. Bruno et al. (1986) propose a production scheduling system that combines the expert systems methodology with queueing network analysis for fast performance evaluation. The scheduler follows a simple guideline given by the priority of lots and was implemented in the rule-based domain-independent production system language OPS5. In Mill and Spraggett (1984) a rule-based expert scheduling system is described that includes the design of a database of part geometry. Finally, Litt et al. (1988) developed a rule-based forward-chaining expert system called FSAS (Furnace Scheduling Advisory System) to schedule a multipass glassing and furnacing operation for glass-lined vessels. This system captures the expertise of the shop-floor supervisor, attempting to satisfy all resource constraints on the basis of heuristics. The system is written in OPS5 and is implemented on a microVAX II. The resulting heuristic scheduler ensures a best solution that meets delivery date requirements, optimizes utilization of multiple furnaces, and minimizes energy consumption. The resource constraints include availability and capacity of the furnaces and availability of firing tools. Operational constraints include part mix, firing temperature, and allowed thickness difference.

4.3 Assembly and Equipment Selection Expert Systems

A large database for assembly operations (feeding, handling, orienting, and insertion times) is provided in Rembold and Dillman (1986) and Boothroyd and Dewhurst (1983, 1984). Other works in the assembly area using AI and expert system tools are those of De Winter and Van Brussel (1985), Jozefowicz and Urbanski (1984), Lee and Gossard (1985), Ambler et al. (1975), Kak et al. (1986), and Chang and Wee (1988). In Kak et al. (1986) the automated assembly cell developed at the Robot Vision Laboratory of Purdue University is described. It consists of five modules: supervisor, global knowledge base, current world model, motion controller, and sensory unit. The object representation is made using the slot-filler technique, which works well for objects with distinctive landmarks. For solid objects of high symmetry, the extended Gaussian image concept representation is used. Experimental results are included in parts mating using three-dimensional vision feedback.

Chang and Wee (1988) use a new approach to attack the problems of planning and mechanical assembly. They describe system knowledge types in detail and examine thoroughly the system's control structure, which functions in two separate phases (analysis and generation). A versatile system for computer-controlled assembly, using television cameras, a moving table, and an intelligent robot is proposed in Ambler et al. (1975). The operator places a number of parts in a heap on the table, and the machine has to separate them, recognize them, and then assemble them into a predetermined configuration. The system occupies about 50K of 24-bit words of POP-2 code in a 128K timeshared ICL 4130 machine. The program is written as two distinct subprograms, layout and assembly, which rely on common conventions. The layout subprogram uses tactile and visual information and has internal descriptions of parts and the tabletop. It can face failures, errors, and accidents. The assembly subprogram employs tactile data only and has no internal descriptions of parts. It can cope with small positioning errors but cannot recover from accidents.

The application of artificial intelligence in the domain of equipment selection is limited. A rule-based expert system for the selection of materials handling equipment, called MATHES (MATerial Handling Equipment Selection), is described in Farber and Fisher (1985). The domain of application is the transportation of material between facilities in a manufacturing environment. The conclusions are derived on the basis of four main parameters (path, volume of flow, size of load, and distance between facilities) and several minor ones concerning specific situations.

In Malmborg et al. (1987) a Prolog-based expert system for truck selection is proposed. Truck selection is very important in dock operations, unit load storage, order picking, in-process handling, yard operations, and elsewhere. The selection process is based on truck features, including type of engine, type of loading, type of tires, and capacity, as well as on the specific activities taking place in the application areas. The system provides a user–system interaction facility by means of which the user can ask for alternative truck selection if she or he is not satisfied with the current selection.

Two expert systems for industrial robot selection are presented in McGlennon et al. (1987) and Tzafestas and Tsihrintzis (1988). The first, called ROBOSPEC, has a knowledge base that includes information on several application areas (handling, manufacturing, assembly). The system is written in OPS5 and provides as a final result the specifications of the selected robot for the application area specified by the user.

The second robot-selecting expert system, ROBBAS (Tzafestas and Tsihrintzis, 1988), was realized with the expert system shell M1., which runs on the IBM PC. Sessions with M1. are divided into several cycles of dialogue, so that the user is able to modify the value of a robot characteristic without having to go through the entire session from the beginning. As usual, ROBBAS consists of two main components, one containing pure expertise (rules, facts, and metafacts) and one containing a database of commercially available industrial robots and their characteristics. Because of the shortage of available space in the central memory of the IBM PC, the system knowledge base was split into 10 knowledge bases with a total length of 205 bytes. The main knowledge base of ROBBAS is ROBBAS-0 and consists of all those knowledge base entries (facts, rules, metarules) that will collect information about the desired values of the characteristics of the robot, either directly (by asking the user) or indirectly (by posing a set of questions to the user and then using an associated set of rules and facts). The robot characteristics used in ROBBAS-0 are system cost, desired task, accuracy, repeatability, resolution, carrying capacity, standard grippers, positioning control, sensors supported, steps stored, mounting floor space, programming method, and language supported. The files ROBBAS-1 through ROBBAS-8 contain records of the characteristics of 81 robots. Through the use of the rules existing in these knowledge bases, M1. is guided to select a robot after the desired values of its characteristics are specified. The last knowledge base, ROBBAS-9, improves the system output. It provides the user with the name of the selected robot and the point of contact with its manufacturer. The system has the ability to present explanatory texts on the screen when the user so wishes. In case of uncertainty the system works by employing certainty factors. The user provides, together with the information asked, associated certainty factors, and the selection is also followed by a certainty factor. Example sessions can be found in Tzafestas and Tsihrintzis (1988).

Another expert system for the specification and selection of robots is presented in Fisher and Maimon (1987), which discusses the relative advantages of the expert system and integer programming approaches. The expert system identifies by forward inference the required technology alternatives that are needed to carry out the desired tasks, and selects by backward inference the best available robots that satisfy the technological requirements. Finally, ROKON 1, an expert system for selecting a suitable sensor and gripper configuration written in the Franzlisp version of OPS5 on a VAX 750 under UNIX, is presented in Doll (1988).

5 ARTIFICIAL INTELLIGENCE AND PETRI NETS IN MANUFACTURING SYSTEMS

5.1 General Issues

Petri nets (PNs) were devised by Carl Petri (Petri, 1962; Peterson, 1981) in the framework of his work on communication systems. Presently PNs find important applications in system engineering, with the manufacturing systems area being the dominant one (Kamath and Viswanadham, 1986).

Petri nets are very good tools for representing, analyzing, and simulating manufacturing systems because they have the following features:

They provide a graphical way of visually representing a manufacturing system.

They capture precedence relations and structural couplings among concurrent or asynchronous unpredictable discrete events.

They can easily model existing deadlocks, conflicts, and storage sizes.

There exist several extended PN models (timed PNs, colored PNs, stochastic PNs, fuzzy PNs, etc.) that cover a large variety of manufacturing situations and problems.

However, PNs possess a number of drawbacks. For example:

They become very large, particularly when the modeling is required at a detailed level (combinatorial explosion).

They are not suitable for modeling combinational aspects.

They provide an evaluative, not a generative, modeling tool; that is, they are appropriate for model and performance evaluation analysis but not for generating solutions.

Merging AI and knowledge-based tools with PNs leads to more descriptive and inferential power and eliminates some of these disadvantages.

5.2 Review of Basic Petri Net Concepts

A comprehensive study of PNs for manufacturing system analysis and modeling is provided in Kamath and Viswanadham (1986). The various objects (robots, machines, parts, jobs) are modeled with the aid of PNs, and their invariants are computed. Then a PN model for the entire system is found and analyzed with regard to deadlocks and overflows. This is a bottom-up modeling approach.

Formally, a Petri net N is defined as

$$N = \{P, T, U, Y\}$$

where P is a set of places, T is a set of transitions, U is the input function, and Y is the output function. The ordinary PN view of a system involves two concepts, *transitions* and *conditions*. Transitions represent the actions that occur in the system. The occurrence of these transitions is controlled by the state of the system, which is described as a set of conditions. Preconditions of a transition are the conditions that must be satisfied in order for a transition to occur. A condition is actually a logical description of the system's state. After the occurrence of a transition, some preconditions may be violated, but other conditions, called postconditions, may be satisfied.

A more practical way to represent a Petri net is by using its graph. A PN graph illustrates pictorially the concepts of PNs in an informal and understandable manner. A PN graph has two kinds of nodes: nodes corresponding to *places* of the PN structure (represented by circles) and nodes corresponding to *transitions* (denoted by bars). The input and output functions are represented by directed arcs (branches) from places to transitions and from transitions to places, respectively.

The places of a PN graph contain various numbers of tokens, which are moved during the execution of the PN. Thus the position and number of tokens residing in the places of a PN are controlled by the firing of transitions. The tokens are symbolized by solid dots inside the places (circles) of the PN graph. A transition can fire only if it is *enabled,* that is, if each of its input places contains at least one token. The components of the marking vector $\mathbf{m} = \{m_1, m_2, \ldots, m_n\}$ give the number of tokens residing at the places p_1, $p_2, \ldots, p_n$, respectively.

An example of a simple PN is (Duggan and Browne, 1988)

$$N = \{P, T, U, Y\}$$

where

$$P = \{p_1, p_2, p_3, p_4, p_5\}, \qquad T = \{t_1, t_2, t_3, t_4\}$$

$$U(t_1) = \{p_1\}, \qquad U(t_2) = \{p_2, p_3, p_5\}, \qquad U(t_3) = \{p_3\}, \qquad U(t_4) = \{p_4\}$$

$$Y(t_1) = \{p_2, p_3, p_4\}, \qquad Y(t_2) = \{p_5\}, \qquad Y(t_3) = \{p_4\}, \qquad Y(t_4) = \{p_2, p_3\}$$

This PN with the marking $\mathbf{m} = \{1, 0, 1, 0, 2\}$ is denoted as $N = \{P, T, U, Y, \mathbf{m}\}$ and has the marked PN graph of Fig. 6-4a. As is evident from this graph, the transition t_1 is enabled (one token resides in place p_1) but t_2 and t_4 are not enabled (because no token resides in p_2 and p_4). Thus t_1 can fire, and after its firing the PN graph of Fig. 6-4b is obtained. Note that one token has moved from p_1 to all outputs of t_1 (i.e., to the places p_2, p_3, and p_5) and thus no token now exists in p_1. Hence t_1 is now nonenabled and t_2 becomes enabled. The set of all markings of a PN is called "the state of the PN" and is changed after each transition firing.

One way to take into account the duration of activities in a PN is the following (see also discussion of timed Petri nets in Section 5.3). Consider an activity that needs τ time units to complete. If the starting time of the activity is s time units, then the end of the activity occurs at $s + \tau$. Thus the activity can be modeled by two transitions, the first transition occurring at time s (start activity) and the second transition firing at time $s + \tau$ (end activity). Hence, in order for the transition to fire, two conditions must be valid: its input place must have at

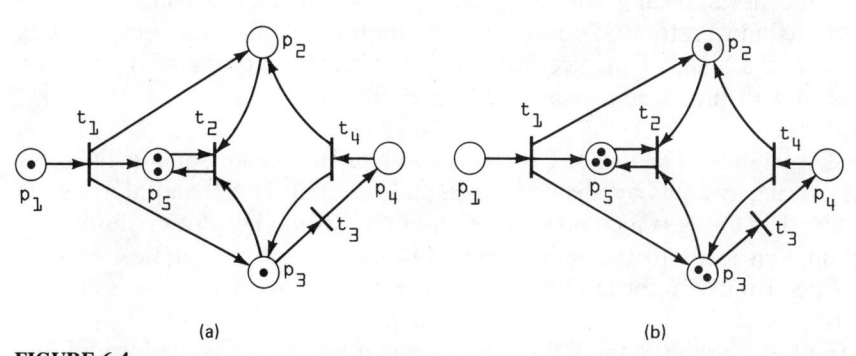

FIGURE 6-4
(a) A simple Petri net. (b) The Petri net after firing of transition 1.

least one token, and the transition should occur at time $s + \tau$ (current clock time) (Coolahan and Roussopoulos, 1983; Duggan and Browne, 1988). When all transitions scheduled for the current clock time have been fired, the current clock time is updated to the next scheduled firing of a transition.

5.3 Generalized Petri Nets

Petri nets are also called "condition event models" or "place transition nets." Ordinary (basic) PNs are useful for modeling local levels of a CIM system, but they are too simple for high levels. Thus various extensions have been proposed that have special features for certain applications or can be used as general models with precise mathematical representations.

Some of the PN extensions developed over the years are:

- Timed Petri nets (TP-N) (Stotts and Cai, 1988)
- Colored Petri nets (CP-N) (Viswanadham and Narahari, 1987; Martinez et al., 1986)
- Structured adaptive Petri nets (SAP-N) (Corbeel et al., 1985)
- Structured colored adaptive Petri nets (SCAP-N) (Gentina and Corbeel, 1987; Bourey et al., 1987; Gentina et al., 1988)
- Modified Petri nets (MP-N) (Beck and Krogh, 1987; Jaswinder and Valavanis, 1988)
- "Petrillo" nets (PR-N) (Rillo, 1988)
- Colored stochastic Petri nets (CSP-N) (Zenie, 1987)
- Fuzzy Petri nets (FP-N) (Looney, 1988)

A short discussion concerning these extensions of Petri nets and their uses follows.

Timed Petri nets. In Stotts and Cai (1988) a form of timed Petri nets, called binary timed Petri nets (BTP-Ns) is employed for the study of the lattice production line configuration of robots. BTP-Ns are formed using a combination of the binary Petri net model (Alayan and Newcomb, 1987) with the timing aspects of the hierarchical graph (HG) model of time-dependent concurrent systems (Stotts and Pratt, 1985). For BTP-Ns, an integer time is associated with each place in a binary Petri net, which represents the duration of the activity associated with the place (see also Huber et al., 1984).

Colored Petri nets. The use of CP-Ns was fully demonstrated and justified for manufacturing systems by Viswanadham and Narahari (1987) and Martinez et al. (1986). The CP-N is a compact version of the PN model. But of course this size reduction leads to the requirement of more complex analytic methods. CP-Ns are also useful for modeling fault detection/recovery processes in manufacturing systems.

The CP-N graph of the PN model shown in Fig. 6-5a has the form of Fig. 6-5b (Al-Jaar and Desrochers, 1988). The PN graph of Fig. 6-5a represents an

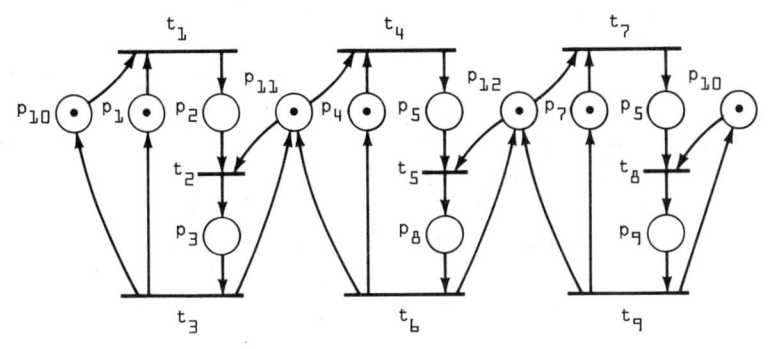

AI TECHNIQUES IN COMPUTER-AIDED MANUFACTURING SYSTEMS 189

p_1 C_1 requesting its left robot R_1 (p_{10}), t_1 C_1 acquires its left robot R_1
p_4 C_2 requesting its left robot R_2 (p_{11}), t_4 C_2 acquires its left robot R_2
p_7 C_3 requesting its left robot R_3 (p_{12}), t_7 C_3 acquires its left robot R_3

p_2 C_1 requesting its right robot R_2 (p_{11}), t_2 C_1 acquires its right robot R_2
p_5 C_2 requesting its right robot R_3 (p_{12}), t_5 C_2 acquires its right robot R_3
p_8 C_3 requesting its right robot R_1 (p_{10}), t_8 C_3 acquires its right robot R_1

p_3 C_1 and R_1 and R_2 are in use t_3 C_1 releases R_1 and R_2
p_6 C_2 and R_2 and R_3 are in use t_6 C_2 releases R_2 and R_3
p_9 C_3 and R_3 and R_1 are in use t_9 C_3 releases R_3 and R_1

(a)

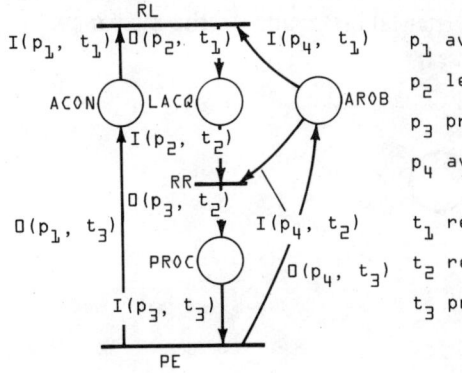

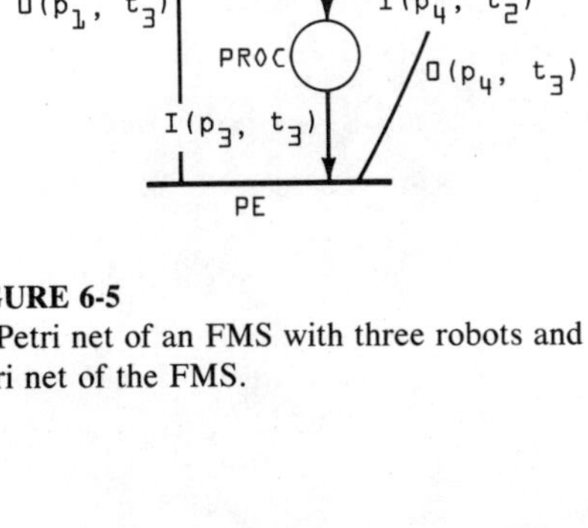

p_1 available conveyors, ACON
p_2 left robot acquired, LACQ
p_3 processing with both robots, PROC
p_4 available robots, AROB

t_1 request left robot, RL
t_2 request right robot, RR
t_3 process ends, PE

(b)

FIGURE 6-5
(a) Petri net of an FMS with three robots and three conveyors in triangular setup. (b) Colored Petri net of the FMS.

FMS consisting of three robots, R_1, R_2, R_3, and three conveyor belts, C_1, C_2, and C_3, in triangular configuration. Carrying out an assembly task requires any conveyor and its two neighboring robots. Each conveyor calls its left robot first, and when this robot is acquired the conveyor calls the right robot. The assembly operation is then started, and when assembly is complete the two robots are released by the conveyor.

The colored PN of Fig. 6-5b is obtained from the PN of Fig. 6-5a by folding the three symmetric subsystems of the FMS on top of each other and relabeling the places, transitions, and arcs to discriminate the different conveyors and robots.

Structured colored adaptive Petri nets. Structured adaptive Petri nets and structured colored adaptive Petri nets have been introduced in manufacturing system modeling and analysis by Gentina and his associates (Corbeel et al., 1985; Gentina and Corbeel, 1987; Bourey et al., 1987; Gentina et al., 1988). SP-Ns add the power of description and verification of the usual PNs to the strict nature of structured programming. A structured adaptive Petri net (SAP-N) is defined in the same way as an ordinary structured PN, as a bipartite multigraph having edges of the form shown in Fig. 6-6a.

When $q - 1$, the firing of the transition takes place as in the standard case. But q may also be the name of any place of the net. In this case the number of tokens moved from or to the place is equal to the actual number of tokens in the place named q only if this place q has at least one token. Thus an SAP-N has the ability to modify its own firing conditions and can be considered a structured Petri net for which dynamic change of the net structured is possible.

SCAP-Ns are obtained from SAP-Ns by associating color sets to tokens and introducing labels corresponding to net edges. The result is a simplification of the net structure through the transfer of information on the markings (colors) and on the transformations (net labels) made on the markings.

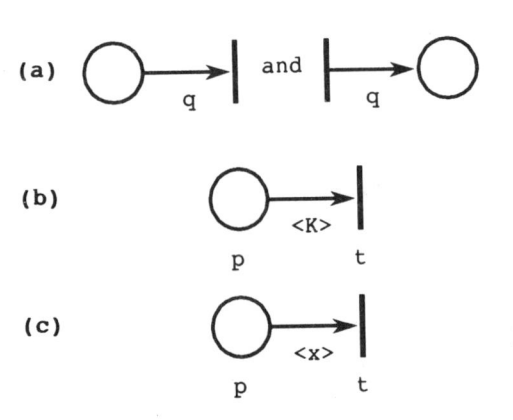

FIGURE 6-6
Basic elements of structured colored adaptive Petri nets.

Given a finite set $C = \{C_1, C_2, \ldots, C_n\}$ of colors, a marking M is a function

$$M(p):C(p) \to N, \quad p \in P$$

where $M(p)$ gives the number of tokens of each color in place p for the current marking.

The labels of the arcs are expressions that determine the use of the colored tokens. These expressions are $\langle K \rangle$, $\langle x \rangle$, and $\langle K, x \rangle$, where K is a subset of C and x is a free variable on a domain of colors. In $\langle K, x \rangle$ the domain of colors [dom(x)] and K are disjoint sets. All adaptive arcs between a place p and transition t have identical labels. The expression $\langle K \rangle$ associates with the firing of the transition t the presence of every color of K in the input place p (Fig. 6-6b). The expression $\langle x \rangle$ associates with the firing of the transition t the existence of one color of dom(x) in the input place p (Fig. 6-6c).

Modified Petri nets. Ordinary PNs have the following limitations:

Only one class of places is used to represent the system states.

Only one class of tokens is used to either represent an information item or control the flow through the system as the Petri net executes.

There is no indication of the exact flow pattern of tokens from input to output places through any transition possessing multiple inputs and multiple outputs.

The modified Petri nets of Jaswinder and Valavanis (1988) alleviate these limitations in two ways. First, the following types of place are defined: status place, action place, switch place, source place, sink place, and subnet. Second, it introduces multiple classes of tokens and multiple arcs associated with them.

Petrillo nets. The Petrillo nets (PR-N) introduced by Rillo (1988) possess the following features:

A token can be represented by a list of parameters, and a parameter can also be a list of parameters.

Arc labels can be either relations or functions of token parameters.

The firing of transitions is determined by markings, arc labels, and interpretations of transitions.

Time is an external variable. All nodes of the hierarchical manufacturing system "know" the absolute time, but it is also possible to work in relative time. All nodes have a program called "player," which performs in cycle the following sequence:

1. Determine enable transitions.
2. Read the input events.

3. Evaluate the functions associated to the enable transitions.
4. Fire the transitions that must be fired.
5. Determine the rules that must be applied.
6. Apply these rules.
7. Execute the actions and procedures associated to places with tokens and the consequent part of applied rules.

The overall system state is given by marking of nets, state of variables, and state of rule databases. The rules that have to be applied depend on the marking of the net and/or the status of the rule database. Some rules are always applicable. The rule part of the system is a controlled rule-based system.

Colored stochastic Petri nets. CSP-Ns are appropriate for modeling, representing, and validating systems in which several processes are of similar structure and have similar behavior both qualitatively and quantitatively (Zenie, 1987). Examples of such systems are distributed communication systems, distributed database management systems (DDMS), and CIM systems. A CSP-N is the association of the stochastic Petri net (SP-N) with a probability measure on the net. The CSP-N overcomes the inability of SP-Ns to characterize marks or to specify classes of marking or states. A full discussion of CSP-Ns is provided in Zenie (1985).

Fuzzy Petri nets. Our discussion on extended Petri nets is closed with the class of fuzzy Petri nets (FP-Ns) (Looney, 1988). The FP-N is an extension of the ordinary PN in which fuzzy values are allowed for rules and truths of conditions that appear in rules. In an FP-N, multiple copies, rather than the originals, of the fuzzy truth tokens are passed along all arrows that depart a node or transition bar where a truth token resides.

Reasoning with fuzzy values is an extension of reasoning with Boolean values. Fuzzy values are real numbers between 0 and 1 that express the degree of belief (or subjective certainty) in the truth statements. A fuzzy truth state component value $s(i)$ denotes the degree of belief in the truth of the corresponding condition $c(i)$. A fuzzy value in a rule matrix entry $R(i, j)$ designates the degree of belief that condition j implies condition i. The row-by-column dot product is similar to the Boolean (binary) case except that in place of the operations AND and OR we use the more general operations MIN (minimum) and MAX (maximum). Obviously, the MIN and MAX operations coincide with the AND and OR operations on Boolean values 0 and 1.

The FP-N model or PN model of fuzzy rule-based decision making develops as follows. The nodes $c(1), \ldots, c(K)$ are assumed to represent a set of K conditions of our rule-based system. The truths of the conditions (i.e., the tokens of the Petri net) are denoted by $\tau(1), \ldots, \tau(K)$, which make up a truth state **T** for the conditions. The truth tokens are allowed to take on fuzzy values. This generalizes the marking (state) of ordinary Petri nets, which use only 1 and 0 values. Also, each arrow departing a node is allowed to have associated with it a fuzzy value for fuzzy rules (multivalued logical implication rules). A threshold (decision) level $D(i)$ is also assigned to each transition i, if we don't want to fire at lower fuzzy values. We finally postulate that an activated node of the PN passes copies of its truth token along all arrows that depart that node. A PN with all of the above features (and with no cycles) is said to be an FP-N or FLN (fuzzy logic network). The transition bars behave like neurons, and so the truth state vector can be regarded as a neuron state vector **N**. With this interpretation the FP-N is seen to be a special type of neuron network. An FP-N executes when one or more transitions (neurons) fire. Given an FP-N N and a fuzzy truth token state **T**, the reachability set $\{N, \mathbf{T}\}$ is the set of all fuzzy truth token states $\{\mathbf{T}'\}$ that can be reached by a sequence of executions of N.

A simple example of an FP-N is shown in Fig. 6-7 (Looney, 1988). Suppose that conditions c1 and c2 have fuzzy truth token values $\tau 1 = 0.5$ and $\tau 2 = 0.6$, respectively. The neuron (transition) N1 will have a fuzzy value equal to N1 = MIN$\{0.5, 0.6\}$ = 0.5. Thus if the threshold value D1 is D1 = 0.4 (i.e., N1 > D1), the neuron will fire, and its token value will pass across it to node c4 (i.e., c4 = 0.5). Looney (1988) also developed a systematic procedure for implementing the FP-N model.

5.4 Merging Petri Nets with Knowledge-Based Techniques

Several results already exist in this area. Martinez et al. (1988) provide a set of concepts and tools that can be used for exerting real-time control of production systems. First they propose a general architecture of the hierarchical type (such as that described in Section 1) that involves four levels from bottom to top: local controllers (numerical control); a coordinator, to manage and super-

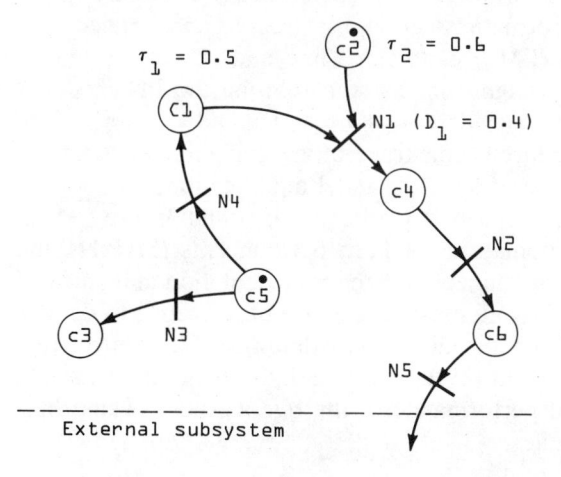

FIGURE 6-7
A simple fuzzy Petri net.

vise the operation of the local controllers; a real-time decision module (RTDM); and a planning and scheduling subsystem. The coordinator subsystem works on a CP-N model that is not completely deterministic. The RTDM is actually an intelligent interpreter of the current production schedule (provided by the next higher level). The planning and scheduling subsystem generates the schedule of operations for each period of production time. The conflict messages arriving at the RTDM are assigned priorities and loaded into the pending conflict message queue. All conflicts can be studied offline through quantitative analysis of the CP-N.

A simulation package based on the object-oriented programming methodology and on an extended form of PNs called PROT (process-translatable) Petri nets, has been developed (Bruno and Morisio, 1987; Bruno and Marchetto, 1986). Another system simulation environment package (SSE) for CIM systems using object-oriented programming and object Petri nets (OP-Ns) was presented by Hollinger and Bel (1987). This package runs on the LAMDA Lisp machine and is a good tool for building, analyzing, and simulating manufacturing systems using a set of predefined primitives. A similar description/modeling method for manufacturing systems using a type frame (object-oriented) language was presented by Castelain and Gentina, (1987).

We again mention here the work of Rillo (1988) where the rule-based methodology is merged with Petri nets of the Petrillo type. The resulting system combines the benefits of PNs at the lowest levels with the abilities of rule-based methods for the highest levels of a manufacturing system.

A useful approach to merging expert systems and Petri net models for the study of materials and information flow control in CIM systems is presented in Farah (1988). The concept of *information cell model* is introduced, which involves external entities such as the interface to a different information cell; the interface to a similar information cell; the human operator (supervisor) interface; a process for data evaluation, manipulation, and organization; and a local data store. Many cells that carry out similar or different operations may exist in a distributed way and are synchronized with each other if necessary. Then a PN representation of this information cell is constructed and applied to a flexible manufacturing system (FMS) example. Time and cost performance measures are discussed, and an algorithm for constructing the PN model is given. Finally the expert system considerations are added and an overall final intelligent FMS modeling procedure is constructed (involving model construction, model validation, model operation, and model modification).

The work described in Gentina and Corbeel (1987) and Bourey et al. (1987) also provides useful combinations of Petri net concepts (SAP-Ns and SCAP-Ns) with knowledge-based concepts for the representation and study of FMSs. The key idea consists of two issues: (1) the use of inference to deduce the procedural structure and then the global scheduling of the control that gives the first PN global model, and (2) the use of a hybrid simulator to validate the dynamic behavior and performance of the overall model using PNs and appropriate strategy metarules.

Finally, the work of Valette et al. (1984) combines PNs and production rules to link up the scheduling level and the monitoring and real-time control levels of FMSs. The scheduling is implemented using AI techniques, and a set of acceptable manufacturing plans is produced rather than a rigid unique plan. The PNs are used for local control and unambiguous representation of resource allocation mechanisms. The system has the ability to diagnose abnormal situations, analyze their consequences, and apply decision rules (metarules) to cope with them.

6 EXAMPLES OF CIM EXPERT SYSTEMS

In this section a few examples of CIM expert systems drawn from the open technical literature are described in some detail, in order to provide the reader with a more complete understanding of their structure and implementation issues.

6.1 Example 1. Operation Sequence Planning Expert System (OPEX)

OPEX (Sluga et al., 1988) is a generative CAPP system that covers some of the macrolevel planning activities. The purpose of OPEX is to produce all suitable machining operation sequences and choose the most promising ones on the basis of a given set of criteria. The final selection is made by the user.

The architecture of the system fits the general expert system architecture well, with the communication interface module at the base level (Fig. 6-8). The program involves two parts; the first part generates all sensible alternatives of operation sequences for all individual characteristics of the workpiece according to their attributes, and the second part, using the results of the first part,

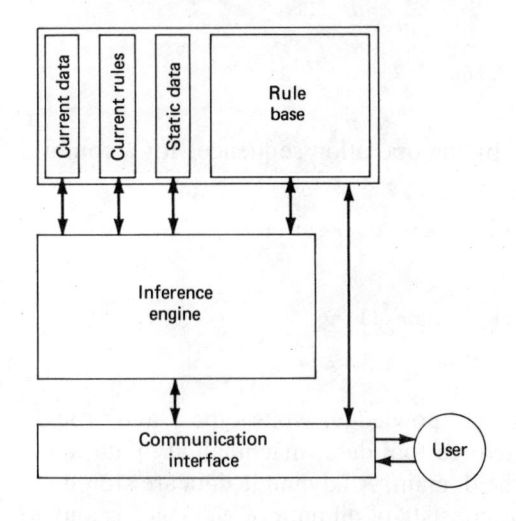

FIGURE 6-8
General structure of OPEX.

generates all sensible operation sequences for the entire workpiece, adds the number of cutting tools, and estimates the machining time for each alternative. Operation sequences are sorted according to the number of tools required, while operation sequences with the same number of tools are sorted according to the value of the performance function.

The inference engine is a Prolog program within which an interpreter performs and controls the execution of rules. Three types of rules are provided (Sluga et al., 1988); these are illustrated below.

Type 1 rules. These are used for applying basic machining operations.

> **Rule form** Operation Operation-name
> IF Condition
> THEN New-changes
> END.
>
> **Example**
> Operation drilling
> IF   gdb:fc is_a cylinder_in
>   gdb:dc included interval (3,40)
>   gdb:lc/max (gdb:dc) = 10
>   gdb:nc subset interval (11,12)
> THEN fc: = is_a blank
>   dc: = 0
>   nc: = undefined
> END.

Type 2 rules. These are used for defining various possibilities of linking machining operations within an individual feature.

> **Rule form** Form Operation 1 to Operation 2
> IF Condition END.
>
> **Example** From boring to drilling
> IF true END.

Type 3 rules. These are used for combining operation sequences for a combination of features.

> **Rule form** Combination Operation 1 and Operation 2
> IF Condition END.
>
> **Example** Combination drilling and drilling
> IF true-END.

Type 1 rules express technological knowledge, while type 2 and type 3 rules express planning logic. Facts involve tool data, machinability data, and other quantitative characteristics of the domain. All dynamic data are stored in a global database. The program input consists of all data of workpieces and a blank required for planning activities. The program output is a list of operation sequences. The generation of alternative operation sequences for individual features is done using backward planning and recursion (Matsushima et al., 1982). The program is written in Prolog for a VAX 11/750 in the Prolog programming environment.

> **Example (Sluga et al., 1988).** The task is to make a hole with three features, two internal cylinders and one face. A cylinder has three parameters (diameter, length, and surface quality). Arithmetic data can be numbers or intervals. The output consists of a list of sorted alternatives of machining sequences (PI = performance index, NT = number of tools). The input/output data and the trees of operation sequences for the two cylinders are shown in Fig. 6-9.

6.2 Example 2. Process Planning Expert System (PROPLAN)

PROPLAN was discussed in Sections 4.1 and 4.2. Here we shall briefly discuss the problem representation, the inference mechanism, and the flow of

Input data

```
cylinder_in (dc = 45, lc = 15, nc = 10),
face_in (nc = 10),
cylinder_in (dc = (18, 28.13), lc = 20, nc = 8).
```

Output data

```
Machining sequence                    P.I.   N.T.
1 drilling (), rough_turning (), . . .  211    2
. . . . . . . . .
3 drilling (), rough_turning (), . . .  370    3
. . . . . . . . .
```

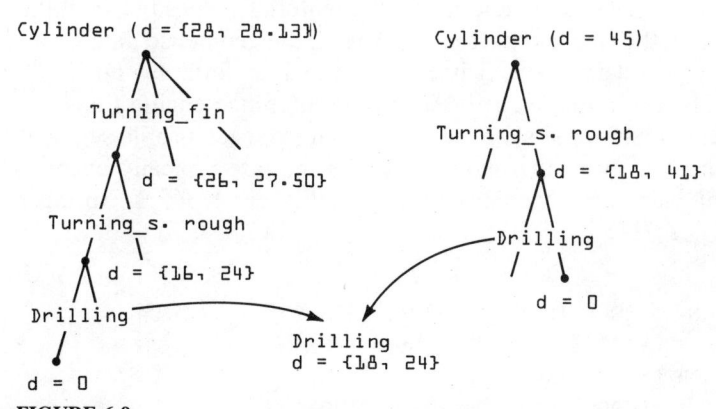

Cylinder (d = {28, 28.13})

Turning_fin
　　d = {26, 27.50}
Turning_s. rough
　　d = {16, 24}
Drilling
d = 0

Cylinder (d = 45)

Turning_s. rough
　　d = {18, 41}
Drilling
d = 0

Drilling
d = {18, 24}

FIGURE 6-9
Input/output data and trees of operation sequences for the two cylinders. Reprinted with permission from Sluga et al. (1988). © Pergamon Press PLC.

control to process part profiles with PROPLAN (Mouleeswaran and Fisher, 1986).

The graphic information and other part-related information supplied by the user during the design phase are interpreted and transformed into the following symbolic language {Mouleeswaran and Fisher, 1986, © Springer Verlag}:

```
(PART)                      ::  = [(VIEW)]*
(VIEW)                      ::  = [(EXTERNAL_PROFILE)(INTERNAL_PROFILE)
                                   (ADDITIONAL INFORMATION)]
(PROFILE)                   ::  = [(LINE)(ARC)]*
(LINE)                      ::  = [(X1 Y1)(X2 Y2)(SURFACE_FEATURE)
                                   (SURFACE_FINISH)(TOLERANCES)]
(ARC)                       ::  = [X1 Y1)(X2 Y2)(CX1 CX2)(ANGLE)(SURFACE_
                                   FEATURE)(SURFACE_FINISH)(TOLERANCES)]
(ADDITIONAL INFORMATION)  ::  = [(SLOT)]* [(KEYWAY)]* [(SPLINES)]*
                                   [(GEARTOOTH)]* [(HOLES)]* ...ETC.
```

An example of a part together with its symbolic representation is given in Fig. 6-10 (Mouleeswaran and Fisher, 1986).

Process planning in PROPLAN is actually a rule-based system that takes the initial state (raw material) to the final state (desired finished part profile). Operators that change the shape of the workpiece are the available machining operations. PROPLAN establishes the sequence of appropriate operations by focusing on the shape of the material between the raw form of the part and the finished part profile. The goal of the operations is to reduce the scrap portion to a state at which the part form is the same as the finished part profile, within acceptable tolerances, of course. The *means-end* analysis of artificial intelligence is applied for the process of successive refinement (comparison of intermediate goals with the final desired goal).

The system inference engine determines the material shapes between the workpiece profile and the finished part profile (using the geometric data about them), and if the segment is a line, it is characterized as horiz + , horiz − , vert + , vert − , slant + , and slant − . Then the inference engine finds, on the basis of the data at hand, the shape of material above each profile segment of the part. In symbolic form, the material shapes that are typically encountered in rotational parts are {Mouleeswaran and Fisher, 1986, © Springer Verlag}

```
REC   = (REC + / −   From_X To_X Height Y_Location)
AREC  = (AREC + / −  From_X To_X Height1 Height2
         Y_Location1 Y_Location2)
TREC  = (TREC + / −  From_X To_X Height1 Height2
         Y_Location1 Y_Location2)
```

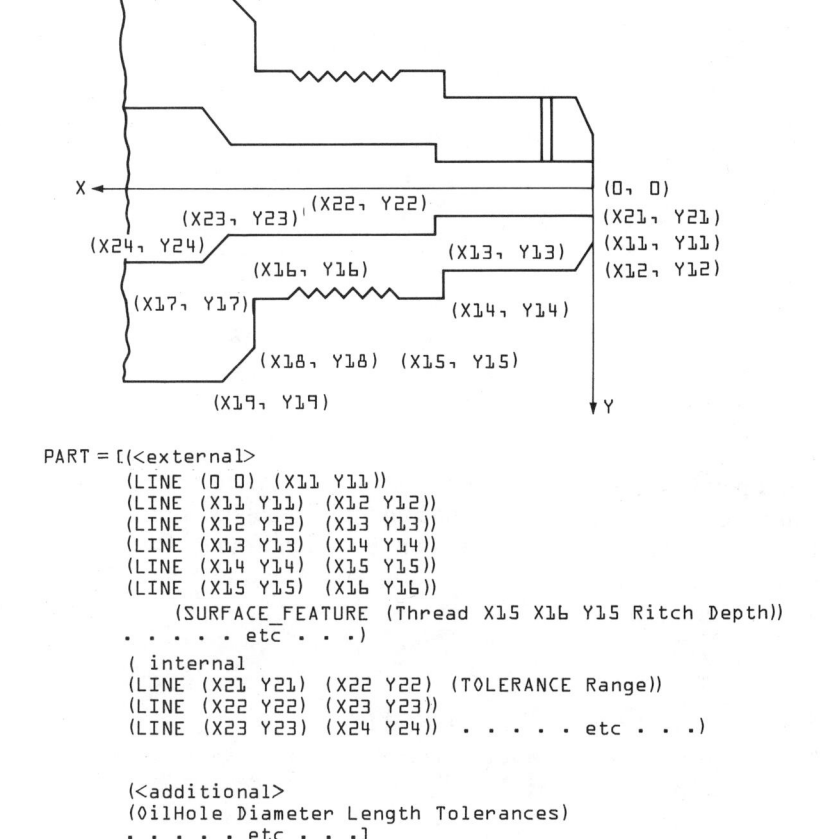

```
PART = [(<external>
        (LINE (0 0) (X11 Y11))
        (LINE (X11 Y11) (X12 Y12))
        (LINE (X12 Y12) (X13 Y13))
        (LINE (X13 Y13) (X14 Y14))
        (LINE (X14 Y14) (X15 Y15))
        (LINE (X15 Y15) (X16 Y16))
              (SURFACE_FEATURE (Thread X15 X16 Y15 Pitch Depth))
         . . . . . etc . . .)
        ( internal
        (LINE (X21 Y21) (X22 Y22) (TOLERANCE Range))
        (LINE (X22 Y22) (X23 Y23))
        (LINE (X23 Y23) (X24 Y24)) . . . . . etc . . .)

        (<additional>
        (OilHole Diameter Length Tolerances)
         . . . . . etc . . .]
```

FIGURE 6-10
Example of a part and its symbolic representation. Reprinted with permission from Mouleeswaran and Fisher (1986). © Springer-Verlag (Computational Mechanics Publications).

where REC + represents a rectangular portion of the workpiece material that can be accessed for a turning or grinding operation, REC − denotes a portion that can only be accessible using grooving tools or end box tools, AREC indicates a composite shape consisting of a sector and a rectangle, and TREC denotes a composite shape consisting of a triangular and rectangular region.

The machining operations that must be performed on the workpiece to modify its shape are determined by the shape of the materials involved between the workpiece profile and the finished part profile. The planning process is guided by a small set of heuristics. Thus, based on these heuristics, the system performs the first available operation that satisfies the need to remove a geometric shape on the workpiece form. The generation of optimal or near-optimal process plans is done with the aid of a heuristic graph search. Rule examples are {Mouleeswaran and Fisher, 1986, © Springer Verlag}:

```
IF   (Shape is REC + )
     (Height of REC +  is less than 0.002 Inch)
     (Surface Finish required is Extra Fine)
     (Profile is Internal)
THEN (Operation is Grinding)
           or
     (Operation is Honing)
IF   (Shape is AREC + )
     (Profile is External)
     (Height1 or Height2 of AREC +  = 0)
     (Difference between From_X & To_X of AREC +  is less
      than 0.25 Inch)
THEN (Operation is Fillet Cutting)
```

After the operation to be executed has been determined, the system's rule is consulted to fill the slots for the machining parameters. For each selected machine operation, the system saves an individual frame. The control structure of the system has the following form {Mouleeswaran and Fisher, 1986, © Springer Verlag}:

```
begin
part_profiles ← (external and internal profile of part)
raw_profile  ←  (profile after adding machine allowances to external
                  profile of part)
shape_list ←   (shapes of material between raw material profile and
                  part profile)
     while shape_list not empty do
              shape      ←   (choose a shape for processing from
                                shape list)
              shapeL     ←   (combine other shapes that can be
                                grouped for an operation)
              operation  ←   (determine operation using inference
                                tree)
         select machining parameters from knowledge base
         generate work instructions
         save frame
         update shape_list and raw_profile
         display workpiece
         end
end
```

Work is under way by PROPLAN's developers to remove its current limitations such as the lack of a realistic knowledge base, restricted domain of application, incomplete knowledge about a part, and absence of tolerance handling facility.

6.3 Example 3. Planning Expert System for Mechanical Assembly Using Robots

The system discussed here was mentioned in Section 4.3 (Chang and Wee, 1988). Two new features are proposed for improving planning efficiency, namely, problem analysis and goal-oriented hierarchical operation representation.

The analysis is based on domain heuristic rules that order subgoal sequences if their features can be distinguished, or suggest constraints in the case of ambiguous situations. Thus the analysis gives a sequence of ordered subgoals and constraints that can be met successively without any conflict. In the goal-oriented hierarchical operation representation, each operation of the system takes a name corresponding to the goal that it will satisfy. Operations are distinguished as *abstract* or *primitive*. Abstract operations can be refined into more detailed needs of various situations.

The system contains, as usual, a knowledge base, a control structure, and a blackboard. The knowledge base involves workpiece structures, assembly operators, and assembly principles. All these are domain-dependent, so changes in the environment cause changes in the knowledge base. The control structure involves two phases: structure analysis and plan generation. The structure analyzer employs assembly principles to analyze workpiece structures and generate an appropriate assembly sequence of components and constraints. The plan generator chooses operations that will assemble components in the assembly sequence and satisfy constraints for each component.

By introducing system heuristics into the system, it is possible to direct planning without fruitful search. Heuristic knowledge helps the system to identify the priorities of each subgoal and reveal the uncertain situations. Priorities help to eliminate conflicts implicitly by specifying which subgoal should be pursued first. The detection of uncertain situations helps the system to post constraints that must be satisfied in order to guarantee the smooth treatment of subsequent subgoals.

The system performance was tested in the case of a power supply assembly, and results were encouraging. We give here a little more information on this assembly problem. Full details can be found in Chang and Wee (1988).

The parts hierarchy of POWER SUPPLY (wiring does not affect planning and is not included) has two components, BASE and PANEL; BASE is a primitive component itself, whereas PANEL has six primitive components, TRANSFORMER, SWITCH, FUSE, BLACK-TERMINAL, RED-TERMINAL, and BOARD.

Each component of the system is represented by a frame consisting of a name and several property "slots." For example, the frame that represents PANEL is shown below (Chang and Wee, 1988; © 1984 IEEE).

```
(PANEL
  (ROLE       MAIN
   PARENT     POWER-SUPPLY
   SHAPE      RECTANGULAR
   MATERIAL   METAL
   MOUNTED-ON BASE
   TYPE       ATTACHED
   SURFACE    (ROUGH BOTH-SIDE)
   WEIGHT     3
   FIXTURE    (SCREW1 4)
   FIXED      (SCREW1 H1 H2 H3 H4)
   ALIGNMENT  ((H1 B1) (H2 B2) (H3 B3) (H4 B4))
   CONTENTS   (BOARD FUSE SWITCH TRANSFORMER RED-TERMINAL BLACK-
              TERMINAL)))
```

In this frame the slots ROLE, PARENT, and CONTENTS indicate that PANEL is the main structure of its parent, which is POWER SUPPLY, and has components listed in the slot CONTENTS. The slots SHAPE, MATERIAL, SURFACE, and WEIGHT are component properties slots. Finally, the information regarding the way in which components physically link to other structures is given here by the slot FIXED, which indicates that SCREW1s are used at holes H1, H2, H3, and H4, whereas the slot ALIGNMENT indicates that these holes should be aligned with the BASE holes B1, B2, B3, and B4, respectively. Each auxiliary component, for example, H1 and SCREW1, also needs a frame.

Scheduling principles for assembly component sequence are expressed in scheduling rules of the general type (Chang and Wee, 1988; © 1984 IEEE):

```
(SCHEDULING-RULE
  (SEQUENCE (ROLE POSITION TYPE)
   ROLE     (MAIN FOUNDATION)
   POSITION (BOTTOM CENTER SIDE TOP)
   TYPE     (REVERSE INSTALLED
             BOTTOM-INSTALLED
             TOP-INSTALLED)))
```

Constraint principles are similar to production rules: each contains a precondition and a constraint list. Examples are the following two constraints, one concerning EQUIPMENT and the other concerning ASSEMBLY.

```
((GRASPED-SURFACE SMOOTH)
   (4 EQUIPMENT GRIPPER RUBBER-GRIPPER))
((EXTENSION NON-STRAIGHT)
   (7 ASSEMBLY INSERT WITH CURVED MOTION))
```

Each constraint is assigned a *weight,* which is given as the list's first element (here the weights are 4 and 7, respectively).

Similarly, every operation in the system is represented by a frame, as shown by the ASSEMBLE-NEW-PART and PUTON operations (Chang and Wee, 1988; © 1984 IEEE):

```
(ASSEMBLE-NEW-PART
     (LEVEL ABSTRACT
      STAGE NIL
      TYPE SEQUENTIAL
      CONTENT (GETPART FASTEN-FIXTURE)))
(PUTON
     (LEVEL PRIMITIVE
      PURPOSE (PLACE $ PART ON $ RECEIVER)
      STAGE ASSEMBLY
      CONTENT PLACE-EFFECT))
```

The POWER-SUPPLY's final assembly sequence is

```
(THE ASSEMBLY SEQUENCE OF POWER-SUPPLY IS)
(PANEL BASE)
(THE ASSEMBLY SEQUENCE OF PANEL IS)
(BOARD TRANSFORMER SWITCH FUSE RED-TERMINAL BLACK-TERMINAL)
(BOARD IS A PRIMITIVE COMPONENT)
(TRANSFORMER IS A PRIMITIVE COMPONENT)
-------
-------
(BLACK-TERMINAL IS A PRIMITIVE COMPONENT)
(BASE IS A PRIMITIVE COMPONENT)
```

The final assembly plan contains 169 robot operation steps and needs 1.2 seconds to do the analysis and 2.8 seconds to do the plan generation on an AMDAHL 470 V/7A using the Standard Lisp interpreter. Full details are given in Chang (1986).

6.4 Example 4. Expert-System-Based Simulator of Petri Nets (ESPNET)

ESPNET (Duggan and Browne, 1988) is an expert system that provides a tool for quickly developing Petri net simulation models of the work flow through a manufacturing system. It accepts a Petri net as input and generates an OPS5 simulator as output. OPS5 is a rule-based language (production system) implemented in Lisp and has the following execution cycle:

1. *Matching:* Given the contents currently residing in the working memory, evaluate the left-hand side of the production to find which conditions are satisfied.
2. *Conflict resolution:* Choose one rule with a satisfied left-hand side. If no such rule exists, then halt the interpreter.

3. *Act:* Execute the rule; that is, do what is specified in its right-hand side.
4. Go to step 1.

The firing of transitions in a PN is similar to the recognize-act cycle of OPS5. Each transition of a PN can be regarded as a rule in which the left-hand side contains the conditions that must be satisfied for the transition to fire. As we know, a transition has two constraints (left-hand side conditions) that must be satisfied before it can fire: at least one token must reside in each of its inputs, and the transition must be scheduled for the current clock time.

In designing a timed OPS5 Petri net simulator, the following features must be provided:

- A transition calendar containing a list of all transitions to be fired as well as the time at which they have to be fired
- Additional left-hand side conditions in the transition rule to determine the time of transition firing
- Extra rules to take into account the nonavailability of resources (tokens) at the scheduled transition time
- A clock that will ensure that transitions will fire at their scheduled time

The OPS5 execution cycle is applied appropriately to the PN model by taking into account the corresponding matching, conflict resolution, and action features.

The data format of ESPNET is the following (Duggan and Browne, 1988; © IEE):

Transition	Preconditions	Postconditions	Following transition	Elapsed time
T_1	none	$C_1, \ldots, C_n$	T_n	n
T_n	$C_1, \ldots, C_n$	none	—	—

The first part of ESPNET accepts the initial conditions of the Petri net and uses them to write the OPS5 data file that stores the working memory elements. When the program is run, the user is requested to enter (1) the total number of conditions and (2) the number of tokens for each condition. Then the remaining initial states of the PN must be entered, that is, (3) the number of the starting transition and (4) the total number of jobs to be fed via the system. On the basis of this information, the OPS5 data file can be written.

The second part of ESPNET generates the rules from which the PN can be simulated. The input here is the tabular format of the PN, and the logic of this table is that captured by the generation of OPS5 rules. First, the type of transition should be entered (starting transition, decision transition, starting and decision transition, ordinary transition). ESPNET involves the following self-explanatory features: model net, compile net, simulate net, edit net, delete net, help, illustration, and exit. The OPS5 rule base simulates the logic of the

PN. A working knowledge of OPS5 is required for making basic modifications to the system using the Edit module.

The system was applied to a PN with the form of Table 6-1 (Duggan and Browne, 1988; © IEE). This table is entered into ESPNET, and the associated rules are written. For example, the rule that simulates transition nine (T_9) is (Duggan and Browne, 1988; © IEE)

```
(P Transition_9;;Operator F2 finishes order on M3
   (Condition   ^Number 12
                ^Tokens{(A1) > 0});;M3 is being operated by F2
   (Condition   ^Number 3
                ^Tokens (B1))
   (Condition   ^Number 6
                ^Tokens (B2))
   (Condition   ^Number 8
                ^Tokens (B3))
   (Clock       ^Time (Now))
   (Transition  ^Type Transition 9
                ^Time (Now);;Transition scheduled at
                ^Job (J));;current clock time
   →
   (write (crlf)|Transition_9 F2 Finishes M3 Job|(J))
   (Bind (Name)|F2 Finishes M3|)
   (Call Animate (J) (Now) 9 (Name) 1);;Call Interface
   (Modify 1^Tokens (Compute (A1) - 1));;Modify Conditions
   (Modify 2^Tokens (Compute (B1) + 1))
   (Modify 3^Tokens (Compute (B2) + 1))
   (Modify 4^Tokens (Compute (B3) + 1))
   (Make Transition^Type Transition_10
                   ^Time (Compute (Now) + 2)
                   ^Job (J);;Schedule Transition 10
   (Remove 6));; Remove Transition 9 from calendar
```

TABLE 6-1

Transition	Preconditions	Postconditions	Following transitions	Elapsed time
T_1	none	C_1	T_2, T_4	2, 2
T_2	C_1, C_7, C_4	C_9	T_3	7
T_3	C_9	C_7, C_4, C_2	T_6, T_8	2, 2
T_4	C_1, C_8, C_4	C_{10}	T_5	9
T_5	C_{10}	C_2, C_8, C_4	T_6, T_8	2
T_6	C_2, C_7, C_5	C_{11}	T_7	6
T_7	C_{11}	C_3, C_7, C_5	T_{10}	2
T_8	C_2, C_6, C_8,	C_{12}	T_9	7
T_9	C_{12}	C_3, C_6, C_8	T_{10}	2
T_{10}	C_3	none	none	—

The simulation model of the PN yields useful information about the performance of the corresponding manufacturing system (e.g., machine utilization, resource state, data about transitions). This information could be used for sizing and testing the capacity of a new system.

7 CONCLUSION

This chapter has provided an overview of the application of AI and expert system techniques to the important domain of CIM systems. First, an introduction to the primary CIM functions was given as a background, followed by a discussion of the AI and knowledge-based concepts and tools that are applicable to the manufacturing area. Then a survey of manufacturing expert systems, particularly for product CAD, CAPP, process scheduling, mechanical assembly, and equipment selection, was presented. Next the modeling of manufacturing systems using Petri nets was considered, and some existing results on the merging of Petri nets with knowledge engineering tools were outlined. Finally a set of expert systems examples drawn from the technical literature were discussed in some detail.

The field is very wide, and complete coverage of it is impossible in a single chapter. However, it is hoped that this chapter gives sufficient material, balanced between AI techniques and manufacturing concepts, accompanied by a rich list of references to enable the reader to appreciate the key issues, problems, tools, and methods available for treating CIM functions through AI and intelligent systems. The field is quite new and open, and further research and applied work are needed to develop more general and integrated tools for modeling, simulation, control, monitoring, and management of manufacturing systems both at the shop-floor and multiorganizational levels. My own work is presently concentrated on fault diagnosis problems and the merging of CIM models with knowledge engineering tools.

REFERENCES

Alayan, H., and Newcomb, R.W. (1987). Binary Petri-Net Relationships. *IEEE Trans. Circuits Syst.* **CAS-34**:565–568.

Alexander, S.M., and Jagannathan, V. (1983). Computer-Aided Process Planning Systems: Current and Future Directions, Proc. IEEE Int. Conf. on Systems, Man and Cybernetics, New York.

Al-Jaar, R.Y., and Desrochers, A.A. (1988). A Survey of Petri Nets in Automated Manufacturing Systems. Proc. 12th IMACS World Congress, Paris, July, Vol. 3, pp.503–510.

Ambler, A.P., Barrow, H.G., Brown C.M., Burstall, R.M., and Popplestone, R.J. (1975). A Versatile System for Computer-Controlled Assembly. *AI* **6**:129–156.

Andreasen, M.M., Kahler, S., and Lund, T. (1982). *Design for Assembly*. IFS Publications Ltd., Bedford, U.K.

Anonymous (1982). N.N.: DIN-ISO 7942. Graphic Kernel System—A Functional Description.

Appleton, D.S. (1984). The State of CIM. *Datamation* **15** (December): 66–72.

Barr, A., Feigenbaum, A., and Cohen, P.R. Eds. (1981). *The Handbook of Artificial Intelligence*. William Kaufmann, Los Altos, Calif.

Beck, C.L., and Krogh, B.H. (1987). Models for Simulation and Discrete Control of Manufacturing Systems. Proc. IEEE Int. Conf. on Robotics and Automation, Raleigh, N.C., pp. 1005–1011.
Berenji, H.R., and Khoshnevis, B. (1986). Use of Artificial Intelligence in Automated Process Planning. *Comput. Mech. Eng.*, 47–55.
Boothroyd, G., and Dewhurst, P. (1983). Computer Aided Design for Assembly. *Assembly Eng.* 26(2):18–22.
Boothroyd, G., and Dewhurst, P. (1984). *Design for Assembly—A Designers Handbook*. University of Massachusetts, Amherst, Mass.
Bourey, J.P., Corbeel, D., Craye, E., and Gentina, J.C. (1987). Adaptive and Colored Structured Petri Nets for Description, Analysis and Synthesis of Hierarchical Control and Reliability of Flexible Cells in Manufacturing. In: *System Fault Diagnostics, Reliability and Related Knowledge-Based Approaches* (S. Tzafestas, M. Singh, and G. Schmidt, Eds.), D. Reidel, Dordrecht and Boston. Vol. 1, pp. 281–295.
Bourne, D.A., and Fox, M.S. (1984). Autonomous Manufacturing: Automating the Job-Shop. *Computer* 17(9):76–86.
Bratko, I. (1982). Knowledge-Based Problem Solving in AL3. In: *Machine Intelligence* (J. Hayes, D. Michie, and J.H. Pao, Eds.). Harwood, Chichester, U.K., pp. 73–100.
Bratko, I. (1988). AI Tools and Techniques for Manufacturing Systems. *Robotics Comput. Integrated Manuf.* 4(1/2):27–31.
Bratko, I., Mozetik, I., and Lavrac, N. (1988). Automatic Synthesis and Compression of Cardiological Knowledge. *Machine Intelligence*, Vol. 11. Oxford University Press, Oxford, England.
Brown, D.C., and Chandrasekaran, B. (1983). An Approach to Expert Systems for Mechanical Design. Proc. Trends and Applications, Gaithersburg, Md., pp. 173–180.
Brown, D.C., and Chandrasekaran, B. (1986). Knowledge and Control for a Mechanical Design Expert System. *Computer* 19:92–100.
Bruno, G., and Marchetto, G. (1986). Process-Translatable Petri Nets for the Rapid Prototyping of Process Control Systems. *IEEE Trans. Software Eng.* SE-12(2).
Bruno, G., and Morisio, M. (1987). Petri Net Based Simulation of Manufacturing Cells. Proc. IEEE Int. Conf. Robotics and Automation, Raleigh, N.C. March, pp. 1174–1179.
Bruno, G., Elia, A., and Laface, P. (1986). A Rule-Based System to Scheduling Production. *Computer* 19:32–39.
Bürle, G. (1987). The Role of Qualitative Reasoning on Modelling. Proc. IMACS Symp. on AI, Expert Systems and Languages in Modelling and Simulation, Barcelona, pp. 117–122.
Bundy, A. (1984). What Has Learning Got To Do with Expert Systems? Paper No. 214, Dept. of Artificial Intelligence, Univ. of Edinburgh.
Carringer, R. (1986). Product Definition Data Interface (PPDI). Proc. CIMTECH Conf., SME Computing and Automated Systems Association, Dearborn, Mich.
Castelain, E., and Gentina, J.C. (1987). Description of Manufacturing Process by Means of a Type Frame Language. *Preprints,* IMACS Symp. on AI Expert Systems and Languages in Modelling and Simulation, Barcelona, pp. 179–183.
Chang, K.H. (1986). A Planning Model with Problem Analysis and Operator Hierarchy. Ph.D. Dissertation, Dept. Electr. and Computer Eng., Univ. of Cincinnati, Ohio.
Chang, K.H., and Wee, W.G. (1988). A Knowledge-Based Planning System for Mechanical Assembly Using Robots. *IEEE Expert* Spring, 18–30.
Chang, T.C., and Wysk, R.A. (1985). *An Introduction to Automated Process Planning Systems*. Prentice-Hall, Englewood Cliffs, N.J.
Chiu, M.-Y., and Niedermayr, E. (1985). Knowledge-Based Diagnosis of Manufacturing Cells. *Siemens Forsch.-u. Entwick.-Ber.* 14(5):230–237.
Choi, B.K., Barash, M.M., and Anderson, D.C. (1984). Automatic Recognition of Machined Surfaces from a 3D Solid Model. *Computer-Aided Design* 16(2):81–86.
Connor, D.E. (1984). Using Expert Systems to Manage and Change Complexity in Manufacturing. In: *Artificial Intelligence Applications for Business* (W. Reitman, Ed.). Ablex, pp. 149–158.

Conterno, R. (1987). Hierarchical and Decentralized Control for Batch and Repetitive Manufacturing. Proc. 1987 IEEE Int. Conf. Robotics and Automation, Raleigh, N.C., March 30–April 3.

Coolahan, J., and Roussopoulos, N. (1983). Timing Requirements for Time Driven Systems Using Augmented Petri Nets. IEEE Trans. Software Eng. SE-9(5).

Corbeel, D., Gentina, J.C., and Vercauter, C. (1985). Application of an Extension of Petri Nets to Modelization of Control and Production Processes. Proc. 6th European Workshop on Applications and Theory of Petri Nets, Espoo, Finland, June, pp. 53–74.

Daniel, L. (1984). *Artificial Intelligence: Tools, Techniques and Applications.* Harper & Row, New York.

Darbyshire, I., and Davies, E.J. (1984). EXCAP—An Expert System Approach to Recursive Process Planning. Proc. 16th CIRP Int. Seminar on Manufacturing Systems, Tokyo.

Dechter, R., and Michie, D. (1984). *Structured Induction on Plans and Programs.* IBM, Los Angeles, Calif.

Descotte, Y., and Latombe, J.C. (1984). GARI: An Expert System for Process Planning. *Solid Modelling by Computers: From Theory to Applications.* New York.

De Winter, D., and Van Brussel, H. (1985). An Expert System for Flexible Assembly System Design. Proc. 8th Annual British Robot Association Conf., Birmingham, U.K., pp. 133–142.

Dillmann, R. (1986). Computing Aids to Plan and Control Manufacturing. *Computer-Aided Design and Manufacturing: Methods and Tools* (U. Rembold and R. Dillmann, Eds.). Springer-Verlag, New York, Chapter 6.

Dixon, J.R., and Dym, C.L. (1986). Artificial Intelligence and Geometric Reasoning in Manufacturing Technology. *Appl. Mech. Rev.* **39**(9):1325–1330.

Dixon, J.R., and Simmons, M.K. (1985). Expert Systems for Design: A Program of Research. ASME Conf. on Design Engineering, Cincinnati, Ohio, Paper No. 85-DET-78.

Dixon, J.R., Libardi, E.C., Luby, S.C., Vaghul, M.V., and Simmons, M.K. (1985). Expert Systems for Mechanical Design: Examples of Symbolic Representations of Design Geometries. In: *Applications of Knowledge-Based Systems to Engineering Analysis and Design* (C.L. Dym, Ed.). ASME AD-10. ASME, New York.

Dixon, J.R., Howe, A., Cohen, P.R., and Simmons, M.K. (1987). DOMINIC I: Progress Towards Domain Independence in Design by Iterative Redesign. *Eng. Comput.* **2**:137–145.

Doll, T.J. (1988). An Expert System for Selecting Sensors and Grippers for Robot Applications. Proc. 12th IMACS World Congress, Paris, pp. 412–414.

Dufay, B., and Latcombe, J.-C. (1987). An Approach to Automatic Robot Programming Based on Inductive Learning. *Int. J. Robotics Res.* **3**:3–20.

Duggan, J., and Browne, J. (1988). ESPNET: Expert-System-Based Simulator of Petri Nets. *IEE Proc.* **135**(Pt. D)(4):239–247.

Dungern, O.V., and Schmidt, G.K. (1987). Fault Detection Mechanisms and Approaches to Autonomous Operation of Flexible Assembly Cells. In: *Fault Detection and Reliability: Knowledge Based and Other Approaches* (M. Singh, K. Hindi, G. Schmidt, and S. Tzafestas, Eds.). Pergamon, New York, pp. 165–172.

Dunn, M.S., and Mann, S. (1978). Computerised Production Process Planning. Proc. 15th Numerical Control Society Annual Meeting and Tech. Conf., Chicago, Ill.

Ernst, G.W., and Newell, A. (1969). *GPS: A Case Study in Generality and Problem Solving.* Academic Press, New York.

Eversheim, W., Fuchs, H., and Zons, K.H. (1980). Anwendung des Systems AUTAP zur Arbeitsplanerstellung. *Ind. Anz.* **H.55**:29–33.

Farah, B. (1988). Expert Systems: An Application in Flexible Manufacturing. *J. Intell. Robotic Syst.* **1**(1):73–88.

Farber, H.B., and Fisher, E.L. (1985). MATHES: Material Handling Equipment Selection Expert System. NCSU-IE Tech. Report 85-16. North Carolina State Univ., Raleigh, N.C.

Feder, A., and Victor, K. (1980). Computer Graphics Benefits for Manufacturing Tasks That Rely Directly on the Engineering Design Data Base. *CAD/CAM: Meeting Today's Productivity Challenge.* SME Computing and Automated Systems Association, Dearborn, Michigan.

Fellenstein, C., Green C.O., Palmer, L.M., Walker, A., and Wyler, D.J. (1985). A Prototype Manufacturing Knowledge Base in Syllog. *IBM Res. Develop.* **29**(4):413–421.

Ferreira, P.M., Kochar, B., Liu, C.R., and Chandru, V. (1985). AIFIX: An Expert System Approach for Fixture Design. In: *Computer-Aided/Intelligent Process Planning* (C.R. Liu, T.C. Chang, and R. Komanduri, Eds.). ASME, New York, pp. 73–82.

Fikes, R.E., and Nillson, N.J. (1971). STRIPS: A New Approach to the Application of Theorem Proving to Problem Solving. *AI* **2**:189–208.

Fikes, R., Hart, P., and Nillson, N. (1973). Learning and Executing Generalized Robot Plans. *AI* **3**:251–288.

Fisher, E.L. (1985). Expert Systems Can Lay Groundwork for Intelligent CIM Decision Making. *Ind. Eng.* **17**(3):78–83.

Fisher, E.L., and Maimon, O.Z. (1987). Integer and Rule Programming Models for the Specification and Selection of Robots. In: *Artificial Intelligence: Computer Integrated Manufacturing* (A. Kusiak, Ed.). IFS, Kempston, Bedford, U.K.

Forsyth, R. (1984). *Expert Systems: Principles and Case Studies*. Chapman and Hall, New York.

Fox, M.S., and Smith, S.F. (1984). ISIS: A Knowledge-Based System for Factory Scheduling. *Expert Syst.* **1**:25–49.

Gairola, A. (1985). Design for Automatic Assembly. In: *Factory of the Future* (H.J. Warnecke and H.J. Burlinger, Eds.). Springer-Verlag, New York.

Gairola, A. (1986). Design for Assembly: A Challenge for Expert Systems. *Robotics* **2**:249–257.

Gentina, J.C., and Corbeel, D. (1987). Colored Adaptive Structured Petri Net: A Tool for the Automatic Synthesis of Hierarchical Control of Flexible Manufacturing Systems. Proc. IEEE Int. Conf. Robotics and Automation, Raleigh, N.C,. pp. 1166–1173.

Gentina, J.C., Bourey, J.P., and Kapusta, M. (1988). Colored Adaptive Structured Petri Net. *Computer-Integrated Manuf. Syst.* **1**:39–47.

Gerencser, M., and Smetek, R. (1985). Artificial Intelligence Technology and Applications. *Militech. Technol.* **6**:67.

Gidwani, K.K. (1986). The Role of AI in Process Control. Proc. ACC, pp. 881–884.

Gliviak, F., Kubis, J., Mikovsky, A., and Karabinosova, E. (1984). A Manufacturing Cell Management System: CEMAS. In: *Artificial Intelligence and Information: Control Systems of Robots* (I. Plander, Ed.). North-Holland, Amsterdam, pp. 153–156.

Hayes-Roth, F., Waterman, D., and Lenat, D. (1983). *Building Expert Systems*. Academic Press, New York.

Henderson, M.R., and Anderson, D.C. (1984). Computer Recognition and Extraction of Form Features—A CAD/CAM Link. *Comput. Ind.* **5**(4):329–339.

Heragu, S.S., and Kusiak, A. (1987). Analysis of Expert Systems in Manufacturing Design. *IEEE Trans. Syst. Man Cybern* **SMC-17**(6):898–912.

Hollinger, D., and Bel, G. (1987). An Object-Oriented Approach to CIM Systems Specification and Simulation. In: *Computer Applications in Production Engineering* (K. Bo, L. Estensen, P. Falster, and E.A. Warman, Eds.). IFIP-Elsevier, New York.

Huber, P., Jensen, A.M., Jepsen, L.O. and Jensen, K. (1984). Towards Reachability Trees for High-Level Petri Nets. Proc. 5th European Workshop on Applications and Theory of Petri Nets, Aarhus, pp. 86–104.

Jaswinder, S.A., and Valavanis, K.P. (1988). Modified Petri Nets for Comprehensive Modelling of Flexible Manufacturing Systems. Proc. 12th IMACS World Congress, pp. 532–534.

Jozefowicz, W., and Urbanski, A. (1984). Expert Systems and Automatic Component Assembling in CAD. Proc. Int. Conf. on Computer-Aided Engineering. IEE, London, U.K.

Kaemmerer, W.F., and Christopherson, P.D. (1986). Using Process Models with Expert Systems to Aid Process Control Operators. Proc. ACC, pp. 892–897.

Kak, A.C., Boyer, K.L., Chen, C.H., Safranek, R.J., and Yang, H.S. (1986). A Knowledge-Based Robotic Assembly Cell. *IEEE Expert* 64–83.

Kamath, M., and Viswanadham, N. (1986). Applications of Petri Net Based Models in the Modelling and Analysis of Flexible Manufacturing Systems. Proc. IEEE Int. Conf. Robotics and Automation, San Francisco, pp. 312–317.

King, M.S., Brooks, S.L. and Schaefer, R.M. (1985). Knowledge-Based Systems—How Will They Affect Manufacturing in the 80's? Proc. 1985 ASME Int. Computers in Engineering Conf., Boston, Mass., Vol. 2, pp. 383–390.

Koren, Y. (1984). *Robotics for Engineers*. McGraw-Hill, New York, Chapter 10.
Kusiak, A. (Ed.). (1987a) *Artificial Intelligence: Computer Integrated Manufacture*. IFS, Kempston, Bedford, U.K.
Kusiak, A. (1987b). The Production Equipment Requirements Problem. *Int. J. Production Res.* **25**:319–325.
Kusiak, A., and Heragu, S.S. (1987). The Facility Layout Problem. *Eur. J. Oper. Res.* **29**:229–251.
Lee, K., and Gossard, D.C. (1985). A Hierarchical Data Structure for Representing Assemblies: Part I, *Comput. Aided Design*, **17**(1):15–24.
Link, C.H. (1976). CAM-I, Automated Process Planning System (CAPP). Tech. Paper. Dearborn, Mich.
Litt, M., Chung, J.C.H., Bond, D.C., and Keininger, G.G. (1988). A Scheduling and Planning Expert System for Multiple Furnaces. *Eng. Appl AI* **1** (March): 16–21.
Looney, C.G. (1988). Fuzzy Petri Nets for Rule-Based Decision Making. *IEEE Trans. Syst. Man Cybern.* **SMC-18:**(1):178–183.
McGlennon, J.M., Cassidy, G., and Browne, J. (1987). ROBOSPEC: A Prototype Expert System for Robot Selection. In: *Artificial Intelligence: Computer Integrated Manufacturing* (A. Kusiak, Ed.). IFS, Kempston, Bedford, U.K.
Malmborg, C.J., Agee, M.H., Simons, G.R., and Choudhry, J.V. (1987). Selection of Material Handling Equipment Alternatives for CIM Systems Using AI. *Ind. Eng.* **19** (May): 58–64.
Martinez, J., Alla, H., and Silva, M. (1986). Petri Nets for the Specification of FMSs. In: *Modelling and Design of Flexible Manufacturing Systems* (A. Kusiak, Ed.). Elsevier, New York, pp. 389–406.
Martinez, J., Muro, P.R., Silva, M., Smith, S.F., and Villaroel, J.L. (1988). Merging Artificial Intelligence Techniques and Petri Nets for Real Time Scheduling and Control of Production Systems. Proc. 12th IMACS World Congress, Vol. 3, pp. 528–531.
Matsushima, K., Okada, N., and Sata, T. (1982). The Integration of CAD and CIM by Application of Artificial Intelligence Techniques. In: *Manufacturing Technology*. Techn. Rundschan, Berne, Switzerland.
Meister, A. (1985). The Problems of Using CAD-Generated Data for CAM. *CAD/CAM: Integration and Innovation*. SME Computing and Automated Systems Association, Dearborn, Mich.
Meyer, R.J. (1987). AI and Expert Systems: In Pursuit of CIM. *Manuf. Eng.* Feb.: CT15–CT18.
Michalski, R.S., Carbonell, J.G., and Mitchell, T. (1983). *Machine Learning*. Tioga, Palo Alto, Calif.
Milačič, V.R., and Urosevič, M. (1988). SAPT—Knowledge-Based CAPP System. *Robotics Comput.-Integrated Manuf.* **4**(1/2):69–76.
Mill, F.G., and Spraggett, S. (1984). An Artificial Intelligence Approach to Process Planning and Scheduling for Flexible Manufacturing Systems. Proc. Int. Conf. Computer-Aided Engineering. IEE, London.
Miller, D.M., and Davis, R.P. (1977). The Machine Requirements Problem. *Int. J. Prod. Res.* **15**:219–231.
Minsky, M. (1986). *Semantics Information Processing*. MIT Press, Cambridge, Mass.
Mittal, S., Dym, C.L., and Morjaria, M. (1985). PRIDE: An Expert System for the Design of Paper Handling Systems. In: *Applications of Knowledge-Based Systems to Engineering Analysis and Design* (C.L. Dym, Ed.). ASME AD-10, ASME, New York.
Moore, R.L., Hawkinson, L.B., Knickerbocker, C.G., and Churchman, L. (1984). A Real-Time Expert System for Process Control. Proc. 1st Conf. on AI Applications, Denver, pp. 569–576.
Mouleeswaran, C.B. (1984). PROPLAN: A Knowledge-Based Expert System for Process Planning, MS Thesis, Univ. of Illinois, Chicago, Ill.
Mouleeswaran, C.B., and Fisher, H.G. (1986). A Knowledge-Based Environment for Process Planning. In: *Applications of Artificial Intelligence in Engineering Problems*, Vol. 2 (D. Sriram and R. Adey, Eds.). Springer-Verlag, New York, pp. 1013–1027.
Murphy, T. (1985). Setting Up an Expert System. *Ind. Process Control Mag.* March: 54–60
Nau, D.S., and Chang, T.C. (1985). A Knowledge-Based Approach to Generative Process Plan-

ning. In: *Computer-Aided/Intelligent Process Planning* (C.R. Liu, T.C. Chang, and R. Komanduri, Eds.). ASME, New York, pp. 65–71.
Nevins, J.L., Whitney, D.E., and Endsall, A.C. (1987). Intelligent Systems in Manufacturing. Preprints of 10th IFAC World Congress on Automatic Control, Munich, Vol. 4, pp. 130–139.
O'Keefe, R. (1986). Simulation and Expert Systems. A Taxonomy and Examples. *Simulation* **46**(1):10–16.
Peterson, J.L. (1981). *Petri Net Theory and the Modelling of Systems.* Prentice-Hall, Englewood Cliffs, N.J.
Petri, C.A. (1962). Kommunikation mit Automaten. Doctoral Dissertation, Univ. of Bonn, Bonn, FRG.
Preiss, K., and Kaplanski, E. (1983). Solving CAD/CAM Problems by Heuristic Programming. *Comput. Mech. Eng.* **2**(2):56–60.
Quinlan, J.R. (1981). Discovering Rules by Induction from Collections of Examples. In: *Expert Systems in the Microelectronic Age* (D. Michie, Ed.). Edinburgh Univ. Press, Edinburgh, pp. 168–202.
Ranky, P. (1983). *The Design and Operation of FMS.* JFS (Publications) Ltd. and North-Holland, Amsterdam.
Ranky, P. (1986a). Dynamic Simulation of Flexible Manufacturing Systems. *Appl. Mech. Rev.* **39**(9):1339–1344.
Ranky, P. (1986b). *Computer-Integrated Manufacturing.* Prentice-Hall, Englewood Cliffs, N.J.
Rayson, P.T. (1985). A Review of Expert Systems Principles and Their Role in Manufacturing Systems. *Robotica* **3**(4):279–287.
Rembold, U., and Dillmann, R. (Eds.) (1986). *Computer-Aided Design and Manufacturing: Methods and Tools.* Springer-Verlag, New York.
Rich, E. (1983). *Artificial Intelligence,* McGraw-Hill, New ;York.
Rillo, M. (1988). Using Petri Nets and Rule-Based System in Manufacturing Systems. Proc. 12th IMACS World Congress, pp. 535–537.
Rolstadås, A. (1977). Scheduling Batch Production by Means of an Online Minicomputer. SINTEF Report STF17 A77064 (November).
Sacerdoti, E.D. (1977). *A Structure for Plans and Behavior.* Elsevier, New York.
Schaffer, G. (1980). GT via Automated Process Planning. *Amer. Machinist* May: 119–122.
Schmidt-Streier, U., and Altenhein, A. (1985). Computer-Aided Procedure for the Application Planning of Industrial Robots. IPA Report, Stuttgart.
Schneider, J.-J. (1987). Systems of the 5th Generation and Their Impact on the Qualification, Training, and Retraining of Management. In: *Artificial Intelligence in Manufacturing* (T. Bernold, Ed.). Elsevier/North-Holland, New York, pp. 85–96.
Shah, J.J. (1985). Development of a Knowledge Base for an Expert System for Design of Structural Parts. Proc. 1985 ASME Int. Computers in Engineering Conf. and Exhibition, Boston, Mass.
Shepherd, B.A. (1983). An Appraisal of a Decision Tree Approach to Image Classification. Proc. 8th Int. Joint Conf. on Artificial Intelligence (IJCAI'83), Vol. 1, pp. 473–475.
Singh, M., Hindi, K.S., Schmidt, G. and Tzafestas, S. (1987). *Fault Detection and Reliability: Knowledge-Based and Other Approaches.* Pergamon, New York.
Sluga, A., Butala, P., Lavrac, N., and Gams, M. (1988). An Attempt to Implement Expert Systems Techniques in CAPP. *Robotics Integrated Manuf.* **4**(1/2):77–82.
Smith, B.M., and Wellington, J. (1985). IGES—A Key Interface Specification for CAD/CAM System Integration. In: *CAD/CAM Integration and Innovation.* SME Computing and Automated Systems Association, Dearborn, Mich.
Snyder, R.A. (1984). Artificial Intelligence in the Future Factory—Test Program. *Test Measure World* **4**(12):97–109.
Spur, G., and Hein, E. (1981). Ergebnisse zur recherunterstrützten Prüfplannung. *Endbericht* P6.4/28; B-PRi/2, KfK-BMFT.
Spur, G., and Krause, F.-L. (1986). Technological Planning for Manufacturing—Methodology of Process Planning. In: *Computer-Aided Design and Manufacturing: Methods and Tools* (U. Rembold and R. Dillmann, Eds.). Springer-Verlag, New York, Chapter 3.

Stoll, H.W. (1986). Design for Manufacturing—An Overview. *Appl. Mech. Rev.* **39**(9):1356–1364.

Stotts, P.D., and Ning Cai, Z. (1988). Modelling Temporal Behavior of Robot Lattices with Binary Timed Petri Nets. University of Maryland, College Park, Md.

Stotts, P.D., Jr., and Pratt, T.W. (1985). Hierarchical Modeling of Software Systems with Timed Petri Nets. Proc. Int. Workshop on Timed Petri Nets, pp. 32–39.

Szenes, K. (1982). An Application of a Parallel Systems Planning Language in Decision Support-Production Scheduling. In: *Advances in Production Management: Production Management Systems in the Eighties*. Proc. IFIP WG 5.7 Working Conf., Bordeaux, France. pp. 241–249.

Tulkoff, J. (1981). Lockheed's GENPLAN. Proc. 18th Numerical Control Society Annual Meeting and Tech. Conf., Dallas, Texas.

Tzafestas, S.G. (1986). Knowledge Engineering Approach to System Modelling, Diagnosis, Supervision and Control. *Preprints,* IFAC Int. Symp. on Simulation of Control Systems, Vienna, pp. 17–31.

Tzafestas, S. (1988a). AI Techniques in Control: An Overview. In: *AI, Expert Systems and Languages in Modelling and Simulation* (IMACS Proc. 1987) (C. Kulikowski and G. Ferrate, Eds.). North-Holland, Amsterdam.

Tzafestas, S.G. (1988b). Expert systems in CIM Operations: Key to Productivity and Quality. Proc. 3rd Int. Symp. in Systems Analysis and Simulation, Berlin, GDR.

Tzafestas, S.G. (1988c). System Fault Diagnosis Using the Knowledge-Based Methodology. In: *Fault Diagnosis in Dynamic Systems: Theory and Applications* (R. Patton, P. Frank, and R. Clark, Eds.). Prentice-Hall Intl. (UK) Ltd., London, Chapter 15.

Tzafestas, S. (1988d). *Knowledge-Based System Diagnosis, Supervision and Control*. Plenum, New York.

Tzafestas, S.G., and Tsihrintzis, G. (1988). ROBBAS: An Expert System for Choice of Robots. In: *Managerial Decision Support Systems and Knowledge-Based Systems* (M. Singh and D. Salassa, Eds.). Elsevier/North-Holland, Amsterdam.

Tzafestas, S.G., Singh, M., and Schmidt, G. (1987). *System Fault Diagnostics, Reliability and Related Knowledge-Based Approaches*, Vol. 2, D. Reidel, Dordrecht and Boston.

Valette, R., Cardoso, J., Aatabakhche, H., Courvoisier, M., and Lemaire, T. (1984). Petri Nets and Production Rules for Decision Levels in FMS Control. Proc. 12th IMACS World Congress, Paris, Vol. 3, pp. 522–524.

Vancza, J. (1988). Organizing Classificatory Knowledge by Induction: A Case Study in Manufacturing Process Planning. Proc. 12th IMACS World Congress, Vol. 4, pp. 258–260.

Viswanadham, N., and Narahari, Y. (1987). Colored Petri Net Models for Automated Manufacturing Systems. Proc. IEEE Int. Conf. Robotics and Automation, Raleigh, N.C., pp. 1935–1990.

Walker, A. (1985). Syllog: An Approach to Prolog for Nonprogrammers. In: *Logic Programming and Its Applications* (M. van Caneghem and D.H.D. Warren, Eds.). Ablex, Norwood, N.J.

Warman, E. (1985). AI in Manufacturing: An Organic Approach to Manufacturing Cells. *Data Proc.* **27**(4):31–34.

Warren, D.H.D. (1974). WARPLAN: A System for Generating Plans. DCL Memo 76, Dept. of AI, Edinburgh Univ.

Weill, E., Spur, G., and Eversheim, W. (1982). Survey of Computer-Aided Process Planning Systems. *Ann. CIRP* **31**(2).

Wilkins, D.E. (1985). Recovering from Execution Error in SIPE. *Comput. Intell. J.* **1**.

Williams, T.J. (1983). Developments in Hierarchical Computer Control Systems. Proc. CAPE'83, Amsterdam.

Woo, T.C. (1982). Feature Extraction by Volume Decomposition. Proc. Conf. CAD/CAM Technology in Mechanical Engineering, Cambridge, Mass., pp. 76–94.

Zenie, A. (1985). Colored Stochastic Petri Nets. Proc. Int. Workshop on Timed Petri Nets, pp. 262–271.

Zenie, A. (1987). Qualitative and Quantitative Validation of a DDMS Model Using a CSPN. In: *Applied Modelling and Simulation of Technological Systems* (P. Borne and S. Tzafestas, Eds.). Elsevier/North-Holland, New York, pp. 537–545.

CHAPTER 7

AI TECHNIQUES IN SOFTWARE ENGINEERING

GAIL E. KAISER

1 INTRODUCTION

The idea of using artificial intelligence techniques to support programming has been around for a long time. The earliest notion was to avoid programming entirely. The human user would just tell the computer what to do, without saying how to do it, and the computer would do the right thing. Even if this were feasible, however, it would be much too tedious, since each time the user would have to repeat the details of what he wanted done. So the goal of programming was to explain things to the computer only once, and then later on be able to tell the computer to do the same thing again in some short form, such as the name of the "program." Thus the idea evolved that a user would somehow tell the computer what program was desired, and the computer would write down the program in some internal form so that it could be remembered and repeated later. The assumption was that the resulting program would be correct, complete, efficient, easy to use, and so forth. It would also be exactly what the human user wanted.

Several problems would have to be solved to achieve this goal. The first is determining exactly what the human really wants. This is a notorious problem in software engineering; the customer states extensive requirements, the company develops software that seems to them to meet all requirements to the fullest extent, but then the software is next to useless for the customer because what he said he wanted was not really what he needed. It may have been a computerized version of manual procedures that were themselves idiosyncratic, or there may be a better way to do things once computers are introduced, or the customer's employees just might not be ready to accept computerization. Today there is often no explicit customer, but a perceived marketplace for which software is developed. Understanding and predicting the marketplace is more of a black art than a science.

When there is a specific customer, or an internal marketing group simulating the potential customers, some of these problems can be solved by *rapid prototyping*. Rapid prototyping generally involves a "quick and dirty" version of the program, often in an interpretive language such as Lisp or Smalltalk. This version usually does only a tiny fraction of the things needed and most likely does them extremely slowly. The point is that it is relatively fast and inexpensive to build a prototype, and then the customer can get the feel of the eventual program by playing with this prototype. In theory, any problems with the requirements are discovered during this phase, when only a small amount of time and energy have been expended. Some programs go through multiple prototypes before the customer finally agrees that this was what he was looking for. Then development of production quality software begins.

The second problem with our scenario of the user telling the computer what is desired and the computer then writing the program is, How does the user tell the computer what he wants? Once upon a time, it was assumed that natural language would do the trick. But research on natural language understanding has not advanced to the point where this scenario is feasible and possibly never will. One problem is that natural language is inherently imprecise, and it may be impossible for the human to express *exactly* what he wants in natural language. Another problem is that conversation among humans presumes a large amount of shared context, based on similar education, social and corporate culture, working together toward a common goal or on a shared task, and generally being in the same place at the same time. Popular psychology dwells on how people do not always understand each other, even when they speak the same language and have very similar backgrounds, except for the very simplest of communication scenarios. The knowledge acquisition task is formidable for humans, perhaps impossible for computers (at least until someone invents the "mind reading" module).

Once natural language was abandoned (or perhaps just put on the shelf for a while), researchers turned to more precise notations for describing what is desired. Formal and informal specification languages have been developed for expressing the requirements for computer programs. Formal specifications are typically based on mathematics and logic, and the concerns include making sure a particular specification is complete, consistent, and correct. An often neglected issue is whether the specification defines what the program should not do as well as what it should do. An informal specification, by definition, cannot be entirely complete, consistent, and correct. Some means must be provided for user feedback, for example, "No, that's not quite right—I really meant such-and-such." The obvious preference is for an interactive, incremental style of debugging the specification, where the user can quickly try out small changes to each part and immediately determine at least the gist of the resulting change in the final program.

Given that the computer understands what the human wants, the third problem is producing the software. It must run on the available hardware and devices, most likely using the available operating system and utilities rather than the bare machine. Resource usage must be reasonable—there are many slow, wasteful ways to do things, but these are not usually acceptable. However, some resource-related desires may not be feasible to achieve in a given operating environment, while others involve trade-offs—for example, the usual time–space trade-off. Some requirements are just plain impossible with current technology, or with any technology; for instance, there are physical limits to how fast a single-processor computer can execute instructions.

There have been a number of research efforts toward this goal of *automatic programming* based on both formal and informal notations. One caveat is in order: Program generation is not the same thing as automatic programming. As with automatic programming, the user provides a formal specification as input and the system generates the desired program. However, automatic programming systems are general-purpose, while program generation systems support an extremely limited but very well understood domain (for example, window systems, parsers, database reports, syntax-directed editors). In the following section, we briefly sketch two of the best-known and longest-term automatic programming efforts, and provide references to the literature for these and a few other projects.

A perhaps more realistic approach to applying artificial intelligence to software development is to automatically perform certain menial tasks rather than attempt to take over the creative activities such as programming. The term "menial" is not intended to be pejorative. Menial tasks have to be done but do not involve the same levels of analysis and synthesis as does programming. Most bookkeeping tasks are relatively menial, for example, keeping track of the status of bug reports, major and minor releases, documentation updates, test data used for regression test suites, and so on. Invocation of many tools, particularly batch (noninteractive) tools, is also menial; it is necessary for someone (or something) to know what processing tools to invoke in what order with which switches and arguments and where to store away their results.

Here again we run into the problem of how to describe the menial tasks that need to be done and, more significantly, exactly under what circumstances they should be done. In most cases, it is not appropriate for the human user to remember that the task has to be done, recognize that now is the best time to do it, and then tell the computer "do such and such task right now," because this is likely to take more effort on the part of the human than just doing the task herself. Therefore, the system must continuously monitor the user's activities in order to keep track of what is going on and what is the right thing to do next.

The bulk of this chapter is concerned with *intelligent assistance* as a practical alternative to automatic programming. Intelligent assistance is loosely defined as any knowledge-based technology that assists human users in carrying out their activities in a manner that does not require any creativity on the part of the assistant. Intelligent assistance is feasible as an extension of existing software development environments and tools and needs relatively little additional effort to become commercially viable.

2 AUTOMATIC PROGRAMMING

Refine is a commercial product marketed by Reasoning Systems, Inc. It is based on many years of research on automatic programming and intelligent assistance at Kestrel Institute (Goldberg, 1986; Kedzierski, 1984; Smith et al., 1985). Refine is essentially a programming environment for a wide-spectrum programming language called the Refine language. A wide-spectrum language is one that includes a range of facilities from very high-level constructs that are not directly executable (except perhaps by *extremely* slow interpretation) to relatively low-level (and efficient) constructs in a conventional programming language. Refine in particular integrates programming language constructs from set theory, logic, conventional procedural programming, and transformation rules. The rules are used to semiautomatically transform a Refine program—basically a formal specification of the desired software system—into a conventional Lisp program. The user interacts with the transformation process when Refine gets stuck or has multiple choices. Refine may be considered an automatic programming system, since it generates a software system from its specification, but it cannot operate without a lot of help from a human user. Very large programs have been successfully developed using Refine, including the Refine system itself. However, since Refine generates Lisp, which is itself a prototyping language, even the final output of the Refine system is really only a prototype.

A number of other research projects have investigated program transformation systems, with two basic orientations. The first, which appears for example in CIP (Broy and Pepper, 1981), is based on a small set of mathematical formalisms. The system automatically replaces components of the specification by applying correctness-preserving transformations. In contrast, Draco (Freeman, 1987), FSD (Balzer, 1985), PDS (Cheatham et al., 1979), and similar systems allow transformations to be selected by the programmer to reflect design decisions. This kind of system can deal with incomplete specifications and a growing catalog of transformations, as the programmer works together with the system to produce a complete program.

The Programmer's Apprentice (Rich and Waters, 1988a; Waters, 1986) is a long-term research project at the MIT AI Laboratory. Several automatic programming systems have been developed as part of this project. The best known is KBEmacs, for Knowledge-Based Emacs, which extends the well-known Emacs word processing system (Stallman, 1981) with facilities for understanding a very restricted natural language description of the desired program and interactively producing a program in any one of several languages (e.g., Lisp, Ada). The description is in terms of a library of programming clichés, which consists of abstract program fragments ranging from very simple abstract data types such as lists to abstract notions such as synchronization and complex subsystems such as peripheral device drivers. The apprentice interacts with the human user, who is thus able to make corrections and rearrange parts of the program. At any time the human can completely take over the programming task, interact directly with Emacs and other programming tools, and then return control to the apprentice. Only very small programs have been produced to far, in large part due to underestimating the inherent difficulties of this approach (Rich and Waters, 1988b). Another aspect of the Programmer's Apprentice project has been to "reverse engineer" existing programs by recognizing the clichés. This technology is still in its infancy but has great potential for solving at least part of the "corporate memory" (or lack thereof) part of the maintenance problem, since it may become possible to extract (and presumably go on to change) previous design decisions.

3 INTELLIGENT ASSISTANCE

Genie and Marvel are two representative examples of intelligent assistants. Both take over some of the programmer's more menial burdens. Genie is passive, essentially an intelligent help system component of a programming environment, and responds only to questions from the programmer. Genie figures out and tells the programmer what sequence of commands (i.e., bookkeeping operations and tool invocations) should be used to accomplish some goal selected by the programmer. Marvel is an active knowledge-based programming environment and continuously monitors the programmer's activities. Marvel participates when appropriate by automatically carrying out sequences of commands (again, bookkeeping operations and tool invocations) according to goals set in advance by the programmer or project management. For simplicity in the rest of this chapter, we will refer to commands, functions, operations, tools, and so on, as "commands."

3.1 Genie

Programming environments provide resources and facilities intended to support and assist programmers. A conflict arises between creating an environment simple enough for a new user of the environment yet sophisticated enough to accommodate an expert. Note that a new user may be an expert programmer, while an expert user of the environment need not be a programmer at all, as most large software development teams involve some nonprogrammers; to reduce confusion, we will refer to "users" rather than "programmers." A common solution to this conflict is to expose beginners to a set of starter commands but also provide more comprehensive features they can learn later. However, many beginners get trapped in the starter set, since they are not encouraged to progress to more powerful commands. One solution to this problem would be an *automated consultant* that answers a user's questions about the environment in a manner designed to provide this encouragement, enhancing rather than detracting from the user's productivity.

All programming environments can be characterized as consisting of a set of commands with which a user can accomplish tasks or goals specific to software development in that environment. The means of access to the environment might include command languages, menus with keystroke or pointing devices, or even more sophisticated interfaces such as speech. At the core, however, a set of commands must be executed as a *plan* (i.e., sequence of steps) to carry out some task for the user.

An intelligent assistant that can behave as an automated consultant, giving appropriate help for the task at hand, can increase user productivity and the quality of the software product. The problem is then how to provide the appropriate information that neither swamps the novice with too much complex information nor insults the expert by providing an overly pedantic tutorial. The problem lends itself well to a solution using expert system techniques, namely, how to choose and articulate appropriate information from a vast and complex knowledge base.

Genie (Wolz, 1988; Wolz and Kaiser, 1988) is an intelligent assistant that behaves as an automated consultant. It generates text based both on what the user is trying to do and what the user already knows how to do. Genie takes a task-centered approach in which the help given is a direct function of a user's needs within the current context. In particular, the focus is on the content of the answer provided to a user, in order to be immediately useful without wasting time or attention span.

The first component of the approach is a small rule base that defines the assistant's behavior and a large hierarchical knowledge representation that provides the assistant's domain knowledge. The domain knowledge includes explicit information about the relationships between the tasks that can be performed within the environment, the plans used in accomplishing them, and the commands that make up the plans. The rule base allows Genie to reason about the actions associated with commands but also allows it to analyze whether plans can satisfy goals and which of many equally good plans is most appropriate in a given state of software development. In a modification request (MR) environment, for example, a task might be to read a set of MRs submitted by customers and forward the subset concerned with a particular subsystem to the manager responsible for that subsystem. The plan for executing that task will depend upon the particular commands available within the MR environment.

The second component follows from the beliefs that classifying commands, plans, and goals according to the level of expertise is inappropriate and that global categorization of users as "novice," "intermediate," or "expert" is inadequate. Instead, information on an individual's exposure to goals, plans, and commands influences what specific information the intelligent assistant presents following a user's query. Expectations about what the user knows and should be told is based on the tasks that the user has completed in the past rather than on broad ad hoc classifications of commands and plans as "easy" or "hard." A task-centered representation is used as a user model in order to exploit the structure of the knowledge base. Decisions about how to answer a user's questions are based on an analysis of the match between the knowledge base and the user model. Taking another example from an MR environment, a user may have extensive experience with forwarding MRs to other users and almost none with annotating completed MRs—to refer to the corresponding source code changes—and installing them in the permanent database. Such a user will not fall nicely into a categorization of expertise. A question relating to sending simple messages will require introducing very little new information into the discussion, while a question about modifying and installing MRs may require an extensive introduction to database facilities.

3.1.1 CONSULTING IN PROGRAMMING ENVIRONMENTS. In order to use an environment effectively, a user must know its capabilities and how to make best use of them. This requires access to information that describes the specific features of the programming environment, that is, the commands available. It also requires access to methods or plans for best accomplishing goals.

There is a large middle ground between a novice who knows only the rudiments of an environment and an expert who has gained complete mastery over it. The continuum in between is one in which user expertise may not be optimal for a given task. When the user must take time to find the appropriate command or develop an efficient technique, productivity decreases. Furthermore, in some environments in which the tasks are perceived as primarily bureaucratic (e.g., writing documentation), users may rely on inefficient methods that are well known rather than taking time to develop more sophisticated expertise. A primary reason for the inefficiency of learning new skills within a programming environment is that users bear the burden of locating the appropriate information. This is typically done by searching through manuals, asking help of others, or simply experimenting with the environment. Expert system techniques should be able to provide mechanisms that can relieve some of this burden. The objective of the Genie research effort is to address these issues and offer a theory of how to build an intelligent assistant that aids users in extending their expertise with the programming environment.

There is rarely a direct correspondence between a precise statement of a user's task and a plan to satisfy it. It is more often the case that the user's goal is poorly defined. Furthermore, a goal may be satisfied by more than one plan. The problem presents itself as requiring a mapping of many user queries to many possible answers. In order to constrain the potential mappings, user queries can be categorized at least partially as relating goals to plans as summarized in Fig. 7-1.

There is a distinction between information that is definitional and information that is instructional. Figure 7-2 further refines this distinction. *Definitional information* is more appropriate for reminding someone about some-

> 1. Command specification: What does command C do?
> 2. Goal satisfaction:
>   a. What do I do to accomplish goal G?
>   b. Plan P accomplishes goal G, but is there a better way?
> 3. Analyze or debug a plan:
>   a. What does plan P do?
>   b. Why doesn't plan P accomplish goal G?

FIGURE 7-1
Typical questions users ask.

thing they have previously used, while *instructional information* is more appropriate for introducing new commands. These types differ not only in their format and level of detail, but also in their emphasis and the degree to which related information is included. Clarifying and elucidating require a careful mixture of reminding and introducing. Genie addresses only the first four types of answers. Marvel, described in the next section, automatically generates and executes plans for the user.

Although the categorization in Fig. 7-1 constrains the question, while the taxonomy in Fig. 7-2 constrains the answer provided, the requisite knowledge and the processes needed to search that knowledge are still complex. The processes include the abilities to estimate the user's goal, to understand the user's plan, to evaluate the current situation in order to formulate an answer that does not digress from the current task, to analyze the user's plan in terms of the estimate of the goal and within the current situation, and to choose an appropriate answer and explanation depending on the user's current knowledge of the environment. This requires knowledge of the commands provided, the possible tasks that can be accomplished, the plans that may accomplish those goals, the things that typically go wrong (bugs), and what the user currently does and does not know about the commands, goals, plans, and bugs.

Introduce:	Present commands and plans that the user has not encountered before.
Remind:	Briefly describe commands and plans that the user has been exposed to but may have forgotten.
Clarify:	Explain details and options about commands and plans to which the user has been exposed.
Elucidate:	Clear up misunderstandings that have developed about commands and plans to which the user has been exposed.
Execute:	Perform commands and plans directly for the user.

FIGURE 7-2
Types of responses a consultant might provide.

Much of this cannot be completely known. For example, it seems unlikely that all possible goals achievable within a given programming environment will be known before the environment is used extensively. It also does not seem possible to predict with certainty what the user's task is and what the user knows. Thus not only must the processes described above operate with incomplete information, but also they ought to be able to do so effectively. Innovative techniques or novel applications ought to be easily and reliably incorporated into the knowledge base.

From an AI perspective, these issues can be encapsulated in two fundamental problems:

1. How can the search through a vast and complex knowledge base be restricted in order to glean the appropriate information for the immediate needs of the user?
2. What decisions must be made in order to choose the appropriate form in which to present that information?

Genie solves both of these problems.

3.1.2 AN INTELLIGENT ASSISTANT FOR CONSULTING. Consulting can be characterized as a three-stage process of question understanding, problem analysis, and answer generation. Genie's understanding component is currently a simple menu-based front end, sidestepping the natural language understanding problem, since it concentrates on the latter two stages: analysis, through a rule base called the Plan Analyst, and generation, through a rule base called the Explainer. The organization of Genie is depicted in Fig. 7-3. Genie attempts to answer a question by doing a two-phase search of the knowledge bases. In the first, the Plan Analyst constructs a relationship between the user's question, his user model, and the capabilities of the environment in an attempt to find the most appropriate information. Based on the Plan Analyst's output, the Explainer constructs a coherent textual explanation that takes into account what the user already knows. Both rule bases will be discussed extensively in the examples later in this section. The structure of the knowledge representation and details of the understanding and generation components that are not obvious from the examples follows below.

Genie's "understanding" component is a simple menu-based interface. Figure 7-4 shows the top-level menu, which is a reformulation of the questions of Fig. 7-1. The user can select a task or a command by typing the proper word or phrase at a command prompt or by browsing a menu of goals or commands. The menus can be arranged alphabetically, or the order of presentation can be based on links between related goals in the expert knowledge base. Plans that can be identified by name from the knowledge base can be entered from the command prompt. Otherwise, the user must construct a plan by selecting an ordered list of commands and goals.

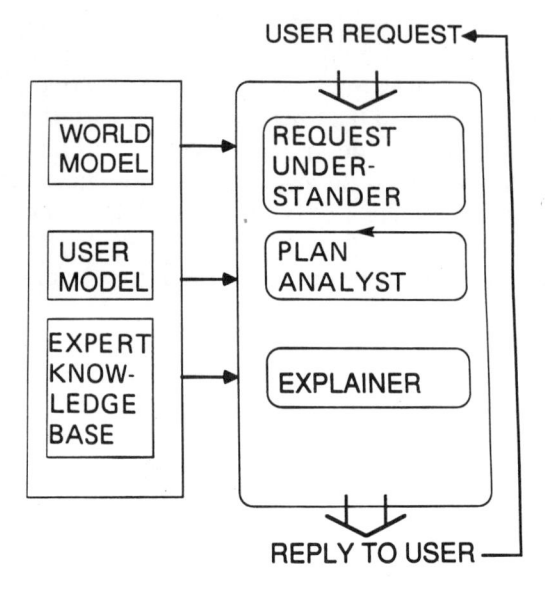

FIGURE 7-3
Genie organization. Please select a question:

When Genie is invoked within a programming environment, both the expert knowledge base and user model are loaded. The world model is constructed on the basis of the user's current status within the software development project. Depending on the question type selected, the user is prompted to provide a command C or a goal G, or to construct a plan P.

The expert knowledge base is a hierarchy of the goals that can be satisfied in the target environment. Goals contain links to alternative plans for satisfying the goal. A plan can be linked to a subgoal or an ordered sequence of subgoals that describe how it can be executed, or to a command that executes it directly. Encoded within a goal are links that describe the relationship between plans.

Commands describe the operators, functions, tools, and so on, of the environment. Their representation includes information about the correct syntax of the command, its precondition and postcondition, and the actions associated with switches and parameters. The precondition defines a state that must

---

1. What does *(select command)* do?
2. What do I do to accomplish *(select goal)*?
3. I use *(construct plan)* to *(select goal)*, but is there a better way?
4. What does *(construct plan)* do?
5. Why doesn't *(construct plan)* accomplish *(select goal)*?

FIGURE 7-4.
Top Level Menu for Question Selection

be true before a command can be correctly executed. It may also contain a link to a goal that could satisfy it. The postcondition encodes the actions of commands when they are applied to the world model. Currently the world model is represented as a simple add/delete list that describes possible states in the environment. Therefore postconditions are encoded as directives to add or delete a state from the world model. (It would probably be better to maintain the world model as an objectbase, as is done for Marvel.)

The user model has exactly the same representation as the expert knowledge base. It contains a history of what the user has done in the past in terms of what tasks have been completed and what plans and commands were used. It is currently coded and updated by hand, but a monitoring system like Marvel could update the user model automatically.

Most of Genie's responses are stereotypical. At the same time, the content of a response must be customized to the user's needs and expertise. Therefore, a rule-based system that ultimately leads to "canned" text is inappropriate, since the text is fixed in advance. Similarly, since Genie's range of discourse is limited, a completely open-ended natural language generation facility seems equally inappropriate. Template filling is a technique that allows both customization and stereotyped responses. To generate an answer, the Explainer selects an appropriate set of *response agenda* based on the output of the Plan Analyst. The response agenda comprises directives for filling textual templates. Representative templates are presented in Fig. 7-5.

3.1.3 MAIL SYSTEM EXAMPLE. The feasibility of this approach is explored through a relatively simple example environment. In particular, Genie has been applied to the real-world problem of the Berkeley Unix mail system, notorious for the great power it provides experts and the great confusion it creates for novices and even long-term nonexpert users. While electronic mail systems are not programming environments, they are mandatory components or adjuncts of programming environments and provide a smaller-scale laboratory for experimenting with intelligent assistance. It is important to keep in mind that Genie is not intended to replace this mail system but to augment it with intelligent behavior that makes its capabilities accessible to casual users.

We now consider two example queries based on the question types in Fig. 7-1 to demonstrate Genie' capabilities. The examples describe the rules used by the Plan Analyst to select the appropriate information. They also show typical scenarios of how the content of the user model and the user's question affect the output of both the Plan Analyst and the Explainer.

The first question is: What does type do? This is an instantiation of the "What does C do?" category of Fig. 7-1. In order to ask this question, the user selects question 1 in the menu of Fig. 7-4. A second menu allows the user to enter a command name, or to search commands alphabetically or by traversing

COMMAND_INTRODUCE(c)
> {c->name} is used to {c->satisfies->description}. It has the form {c->form}, where FOR_EACH (x,f->parameters, "{x} refers to {px->description}"). {c->name} requires that EXPAND_PRECOND(c->precond). It causes EXPAND_POSTCOND(c->postcond). For example, EXAMPLE(c->form,WM).

COMMAND_REMIND(c)
> {c->name}: {c->form}. It is used to {c->satisfies->description}. For example, EXAMPLE {c->form,WM}.

GOAL_REMIND_SIMPLE(g)
> You can {g->description} by using the command {g->command}. For example, EXAMPLE(c->form,WM) would EXPAND_POSTCOND(c->postcond).

GOAL_INTRODUCE_SIMPLE(g)
> GOAL_REMIND_SIMPLE(g). You must make sure EXPAND_PRECOND(g->command->preconds).

GOAL_ INTRODUCE_COMPLEX(g,fault)
> In order to {g->description}, you must FOR_EACH(gx,g->subgoals,"GOAL_INTRODUCE_COMPLEX(gx)"). IF fault DESCRIBE_FAULT(fault->plan). The commands to {g->description} are
> FORMAT_PLAN_INSTANTIATION(gx,g->subgoals,gx->command,WM).
> SHOW_MAPPING(gx,g->subgoals,gx->description,gx->command).

GOAL_REMIND_COMPLEX(g)
> In order to {g->description}, use
> FORMAT_PLAN_INSTANTIATION(gx,g->subgoals,gx->command,WM).
> SHOW_MAPPING(gx,g->subgoals,gx->description,gx->command).

/* Operations appear in capital letters. Variables are surrounded by braces. WM = World Model. Simple goals are satisfied directly by commands. Complex goals are satisfied by a plan that maps to subgoals. */

FIGURE 7-5
Representative response agenda.

links between goals. Using one of these methods the user indicates that the desired command is type.

Figure 7-6 shows the portion of the expert knowledge base required to answer this question. The Plan Analyst uses the following rules to determine what information is relevant to the Explainer:

1. If the user model contains command C, then report knowledge of C, else report no knowledge of C.
2. If there exists a command that is directly satisfied by some goal H, which has the least complex link to the goal G that satisfies command C, then D = that command.
3. If D exists in the expert knowledge base and the user model contains C, then report knowledge of D.

In the example, the Plan Analyst would determine whether the user already knows about type, and in this case, since there is a link to print, whether the user knows about print. The outcome of this analysis is passed to the Explainer.

Four analyses are possible based on the existence of C and D in the user model. These are illustrated in Fig. 7-7 along with the corresponding Explainer output. If the user knows nothing about either `type` or `print`, Genie generates the standard introductory template for `type` and does not overwhelm the user with the fact that `print` is a synonym. Figure 7-8 shows how the response agenda for `COMMAND_INTRODUCE(type)` is filled from the expert knowledge base. If the user knows about `print`, Genie states the fact that `type` is a synonym, reminds the user about `print`, and then introduces `type`. If the user knows about `type` but not `print`, Genie reminds the user about `type` and makes an aside that there is a synonym for `type` called `print`. Finally, in the last case, if the user knows about both, Genie just reminds him about `type`.

The second question is: How can I reply to a message? This is an instantiation of the "How can I satisfy G?" category of Fig. 7-1. To ask this question, the user selects question 2 in the menu of Fig. 7-4. In a second menu, the user selects the desired goal. Let us assume the user chose "`reply.to.message`." In this case it might be easier to locate the goal by

```
Goal type.goal,
        G_type:   Direct /* Satisfied directly by command */
        Satisfied by:    Command type;
        Related goals:   RL1
Goal print.goal,
        G_type:   Direct
        Satisfied by:    Command print;
        Related goals:   RL1
Goal display.list.of.messages,
        Description:  display each message in the sequence specified
        G_type:   Subgoals /* Satisfied through subgoals */
        Satisfied by:    Goal type.goal; Goal print.goal;

Command print,  Form: print {message_list}
        Precondition:  PR1 and PR2 and PR3,
        Postcondition: PO1,
        Satisfies:  print.goal
        Parameters: message-list
Command type,   Form: type {message_list}
        Precondition:  PR1 and PR2 and PR3,
        Postcondition: PO1,
        Satisfies:  type.goal
        Parameters: message-list

Plan P1,  state: (exists contents_of {message_list})
          use: list.message
Plan P2,  state: (at read-level)
          use: get.to.read.level
Plan P3,  state: (size {message-list} > screen-size)
          use: set.window.scroll

Rule RL1, type.goal, print.goal
          Relation: synonyms
```

FIGURE 7-6
Expert knowledge for question 1.

226   KNOWLEDGE ENGINEERING: APPLICATIONS

```
/* user model does not contain either type or print */
Plan Analyst output:   command: type      no_knowledge
Explainer output:      COMMAND_INTRODUCE(type)

/* user model contains print, but not type */
Plan Analyst output:   command: type no_knowledge
                       command: print knowledge
Explainer output:      DESCRIBE_LINK(type,print)
                       COMMAND_REMIND(print)
                       COMMAND_INTRODUCE(type)

/* user model contains type, but not print */
Plan Analyst output:   command: type knowledge
                       command: print no_knowledge
Explainer output:      COMMAND_REMIND(type)
                       MAKE_SIDE_COMMENT(DESCRIBE_LINK(type,print))

/* user model contains both type and print */
Plan Analyst output:   command: type knowledge
Explainer output:      COMMAND_REMIND(type)
```

FIGURE 7-7
Responses to question 1.

searching a goal-based menu rather than an alphabetized one. Let us further assume that the world model contains a message that was sent only to that user and not to other group members. The Plan Analyst constructs a trace through the goal hierarchy and passes it to the Explainer. The Plan Analyst uses the following rules:

1. If the user model contains a plan P for G, then report user_plan = P and user's knowledge of relevant commands.
2. If the expert knowledge base contains a most efficient plan Q for G, then report best_plan = Q and user's knowledge of any relevant commands.
3. If the expert knowledge base does not contain P (the user's plan), then report plan_not_known = P.

```
type is used to type a sequence of messages on the terminal. It has
the form:

      type {message_list}

where {message_list} refers to a sequence of messages. type requires
that the contents of the message_list exist, that the user is at read
level and that the messages fit on the screen. It causes the text of
each message in the message list to be displayed on the screen. For
example:

      type 1:3

      displays messages 1 through 3.
```

FIGURE 7-8
Text generated to introduce the command type.

4. If `P = Q`, then report `best_plan = user_plan`.
5. If `plan_not_known` is a valid plan, report `plan_not_known`, else report `fault = plan_not_known`.

Three possible responses are illustrated in Fig. 7-9. If the user does not know anything about how to reply to a message, Genie selects a "best" plan based on the context and metaknowledge of links. In this case, the context indicates that the response should be to reply only to the sender, and the metaknowledge indicates that a task should be done now rather than later. Since the user knows about "`compose.message`," the only relevant command is `Reply`.

Figure 7-10 shows how the response agenda for this case is expanded to produce text. If the user has replied to messages in the past and does it efficiently, then Genie simply reminds the user about the command `Reply`. However, if the user seems to know how to reply to messages but does it awkwardly, then Genie introduces a better way. Genie explains why it is better by providing the links between goals of the user's plan and the better plan. Genie considers a plan to be awkward when the user's plan does not match Genie's plan or when the user's plan is not even in the expert knowledge base. The latter case is the last case shown in Fig. 7-9. Here the plan works and is classified as not known, rather than as faulty. Ideally plans that happen to work but are not already in the expert knowledge base would be added automatically.

```
/* user model contains send.mail compose.message */
Plan Analyst output:   user_plan: nil
                       best_plan :reply.to.message -> reply.now ->
                         reply.only.to.sender
                       command: Reply no_knowledge
Explainer output:      SUMMARIZE.PLAN(best_plan)
                       GOAL_INTRODUCE_SIMPLE(reply.to.message)

/* user model contains reply.to.message
   -> reply.now -> reply.only.to.sender */
Plan Analyst output:   best_plan = user_plan
                       best_plan: reply.only.to.sender
                       command: Reply knowledge
Explainer output:      GOAL_REMIND_SIMPLE(reply.only.to.sender)

/* user model contains reply.to.message -> save.message
   -> leave.read.level -> send.message */
Plan Analyst output:   best_plan: reply.now -> reply.only.to.sender
                       plan_not_known: plan -> reply.now
                              ->save.message ->
                              leave.read.level -> send.message
                       command: Reply no_knowledge

Explainer output:
    GOAL_INTRODUCE_COMPLEX(reply.only.to.sender,fault->plan)
```

FIGURE 7-9
Genie's responses to question 2a.

```
In order to reply to a message it is assumed you want to reply right
away and reply only to the sender. To do this, you must indicate you
wish to reply and compose a message. You can indicate you wish to
reply by using the command 'Reply'. For example,

      Reply

would put you in write mode, the receiver of your message would be
identical to the writer of the message you just received.
```

FIGURE 7-10
Text generated to introduce the goal "reply to a message."

A refinement of the second question is: To reply to a group of users, I reply to each individually—is there a better way? This is an instance of the "Given P, is there a better plan for G?" category of Fig. 7-1. In this case the user must identify the question type and select a goal and plan. Let us assume the user selected the goal "reply.to.all" and the plan

```
FOR_EACH (x in group)
send.mail.to.individual
```

In the first case in Fig. 7-9, the world model contains a message that was sent to the user and others. In the second case, it contains a message that was sent only to the user. In the third case, the world model does not contain any message.

This question is analyzed using rules 2–5 of the last example. Rule 1 is unnecessary since plan P chosen by the user should be in the user model.

Three possible responses are illustrated in Fig. 7-11. In the first, the message to which the user wishes to reply was addressed to a group of users. Genie chooses to tell the user about the reply command since a group exists in the world model. In the second case, the message was addressed only to the user. Genie chooses a plan that requires the user to identify a group of users. In both cases, since the user knows how to send mail, Genie simply reminds the user about how to send mail and describes the links between the suggested plan and the user's. In the third case, the context does not allow a choice between these plans. Genie presents both options. Both plans are preferred to the user's plan because they require less work on the user's part. In the event that the user's plan is equivalent to the suggested solution, Genie would inform the user of this and follow links to justify why the user's plan is best.

In summary, Genie is an intelligent assistant for automated consulting within programming environments. The research focuses on answer generation. Genie's knowledge is separated into two components, a rule base that captures knowledge of how to consult, and a frame-based hierarchical knowledge representation that encodes knowledge of the domain about which to consult—the programming environment (the Berkeley Unix mail system in the example). Users are not categorized along a spectrum of expertise, nor commands along a spectrum of level of difficulty. Instead Genie reflects a task-centered approach where an answer to a question about the environment is based on knowledge of what the user has done in the past and is trying to, accomplish now. There are several other research efforts similar to Genie, where the intelligent assistant is essentially passive and answers user questions. Rather than preencode expected plans, however, Grapple (Huff and Lesser, 1988) and Agora (Bisiani et al., 1988) perform planning as needed with respect to the commands provided by the programming environment.

3.2 Marvel

Software systems are getting larger and more complex all the time. Typically, many programmers work together on developing and maintaining a system composed of numerous parts. Each part often has several variants, for instance because of revisions to repair errors or to run on different kinds of computers, which are combined into configurations that select the appropriate

```
/* the world model contains message that was sent to user and others */
Plan Analyst output:
user_plan: reply.to.each.in.group
best_plan: reply.to.all -> reply.group.known
command: reply no_knowledge

Explainer output:
GOAL_REMIND_SIMPLE(reply.to.each.in.group)
GOAL_INTRODUCE_COMPLEX(reply.group.known)
DESCRIBE_LINK(reply.to.each.in.group, reply.group.known)

/* the world model contains message that was just sent to user */
Plan Analyst output:
user_plan: reply.to.each.in.group
best_plan: reply.to.all -> reply.group.create.alias
command: alias no_knowledge

Explainer output:
GOAL_REMIND_SIMPLE(reply.to.each.in.group)
GOAL_INTRODUCE_COMPLEX(reply.group.create.alias)
DESCRIBE_LINK(reply.to.each.in.group, reply.group.create.alias)

/* the world model does not contain explicit reference to a message */
Plan Analyst output:
user_plan: reply.to.each.in.group
best_plan:reply.to.all -> reply.group.create.alias
command: reply no_knowledge
command: alias no_knowledge

Explainer output:
GOAL_REMIND_SIMPLE(reply.to.each.in.group)
GOAL_INTRODUCE_COMPLEX(reply.group.create.alias)
DESCRIBE_LINK(reply.to.each.in.group, reply.group.create.alias)
GOAL_INTRODUCE_COMPLEX(reply.group.known)
DESCRIBE_LINK(reply.to.each.in.group, reply.group.known)
```

FIGURE 7-11
Response to question 2b.

variants of each part of the system. Programmers working on a large-scale system spend a considerable portion of their time coordinating their activities, locating the right system components, and building tools to help them in their efforts. These facts point to the importance of programming environments that manage and automate the "menial" jobs programmers would otherwise do manually.

It is not sufficient to create a single, very powerful programming environment to take care of all these menial tasks. Each software project has its own characteristics: its own organization, its own development method, and its own relations among its components. It is thus necessary for the programming environment to understand these characteristics and behave differently for different characteristics. In other words, a knowledge-based programming environment can provide better assistance than a "moronic" programming environment that treats every development project in the same way.

Many programming environments are tailored to a chosen programming language, support some particular development methodology, and incorporate a selected set of tools. A knowledge-based programming environment, on the other hand, is fairly easy to retarget to another language, another methodology, or new tools by modifying the knowledge base. Marvel (Kaiser et al., 1988a; 1988b) is a knowledge-based programming environment in the sense that its behavior is dictated by the policies set by the manager of each distinct project. Marvel actively participates in the development of a system by automating many of the tasks peculiar to that project as well as those common to a wide range of projects. In order to do this, Marvel needs to know the following:

- The organization of the project including the *classes* or types of software objects, such as source code in the programming language, binary machine code, and text documentation, and the valid operations on these objects, such as compilers, loaders, and word processors.
- The relations among the various objects input and produced by the project—for example, one object is a variant of another and uses a third.
- The rules specific to the chosen development process, as determined partially by management and partially by the requirements of the software development tools available. Marvel rules are based on the rules of production systems.

All three factors may change over the project's lifetime, so Marvel must be able to adjust dynamically.

Marvel uses this knowledge to tailor itself to the specific needs of each individual project. For example, the team of programmers working on project A might need a set of commands C(A) while another team working on project B might need another set of commands C(B). If Marvel knows how the commands in each set interact among themselves and how they manipulate the different components of systems A and B, respectively, it can participate in the development of A and B in different ways. Marvel would automatically invoke commands from the set C(A) only with project A, and only in accordance with the rules that define A's development process. It can do the same for B.

3.2.1 ORGANIZATION OF PROGRAMMING ENVIRONMENTS. A Marvel programming environment is created by tailoring a standard kernel to the policies desired for the system being developed or maintained. This is done in two phases, as illustrated in Fig. 7-12. First, a skilled user called the *superuser* writes a description of the project using a special notation called the Marvel Strategy Language (MSL). This description specifies the organization of the software project (e.g., a program is made up of modules and procedures) and models the process of development of that particular project (e.g., a procedure can be printed only after it has been formatted). Any user can then load this description into Marvel and start using this instantiated Marvel to work on the project. Marvel actively participates in the development of the project by using the description it was fed, organizing the components of the project in the way requested, and automatically invoking the appropriate commands at the right times.

For example, a superuser might write a description for an arbitrary C system, stating that any such project would include a number of module (source file) objects, whose attributes (subparts) include macros, types, variables, and procedures. The description might also state how to invoke commands on the corresponding objects to do C-specific type checking, compilation, and so on. It could further state that this project requires programmers to sign off all program modifications with their respective managers, and the environment should automate this communication task by sending electronic mail after a programmer completes each modification task.

The organization of a project is the way that the various software artifacts are set up in relation to each other. Marvel uses an *objectbase* to main-

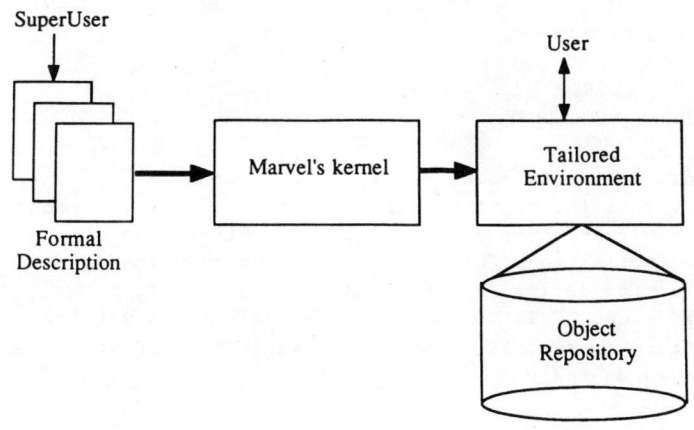

FIGURE 7-12
Marvel organization.

tain all the software artifacts that are components of the software system itself or are used in its development, including mechanisms for invoking external tools such as the editors, compilers, and mail systems represented by commands. Each object in the objectbase is an instance of a class (that is, the class defines the type of the object). The organization of the project includes all the classes and the *syntactic relations* among the various classes. Figure 7-13 shows three classes of objects, PROJECT, MODULE, and PROCEDURE. From this declaration, Marvel deduces that instances of the MODULE class are enclosed in PROJECT objects.

```
objectbase:
    PROJECT:: = superclasses: ENTITY:
        printname : string ;
        status : (Linked, NotLinked) = ''NotLinked'';
        timestamp : real = ''0.0''
        mods : set_of MODULE ;
        executable : binary ;
    END

    MODULE:: = superclasses: ENTITY:
        status : (ModIsComp,ModInComp,ModNoComp) =
                ''ModNoComp'';
        Procs : set_of PROCEDURE;
    END

    PROCEDURE:: = superclasses: ENTITY:
        analyzed : (Analyzed,InAnalysis,NotAnalyzed) =
                ''NotAnalyzed'';
        edited : (Edited,NotEdited) = ''NotEdited'';
        state : (Changed,NotChanged) = ''NotChanged'';
    END
Relations:

    inproject: PROJECT MODULE
    exp: MODULE PROCEDURE
    imp: MODULE PROCEDURE
    contains: MODULE PROCEDURE

/* Each class consists of its name, a list of zero or more
superclasses (ENTITY is the built-in root class), and a list of zero
or more attributes. Class names are in UPPERCASE. Attributes are
typed, and may be initialized. The type is either a class name, a
built-in type given in italics, a constructor (none shown), or an
enumerated set of values. Relations consist of their names and the
names of two classes, since only binary relations are supported
currently. MSL keywords are only underlined.*/
```

FIGURE 7-13
Classes and relations.

Besides syntactic relations among classes of objects, components of a software project can be related by *external* relations. Unlike syntactic relations, these do not imply any particular organization on the participating components. The relations are simply stored in the objectbase to maintain information that cannot be deduced from the hierarchical structure. Using the example in Fig. 7-13, a relation named `contains` maps the MODULE class to the PROCEDURE class. An instance of this relation, `contains(m,p)`, would be stored in the objectbase.

The syntactic and external relations define how the project is set up. However, Marvel must also understand the model of development and/or maintenance desired for the system. Marvel needs to know the capabilities of each object, that is, the operations that can be performed on the object, including the activities that affect more than one object.

3.2.2 OPPORTUNISTIC PROCESSING IN PROGRAMMING ENVIRONMENTS. One aspect of intelligent behavior by a programming environment is understanding the process of software development and maintenance. This requires understanding the activities that can be performed to transform the system from one stage in its life cycle to another. For example, Marvel needs to know how to add a new object to the project. If the team is developing a C program, Marvel needs to know how to add a new procedure definition in terms of how the procedure relates to all the existing objects, including how to place it in the source file representing its module, what other modules (files) to recompile, and so on. The *rules* part of strategies instantiates Marvel with the model of the development process. Rules formalize the application of one object (a command) to another (a software artifact) and define Marvel's automatic behavior.

Marvel rules are based on those of expert systems but differ from most others by having three parts instead of the conventional condition–action pair. Marvel rules have preconditions, an activity, and a set of postconditions, where preconditions are more or less the same as the traditional condition and the activity together with the postconditions roughly correspond to the action. As in expert systems, preconditions and postconditions are written in the first-order predicate calculus.

One big difference is that expert system rules have a single action, deterministically selected by the condition. Marvel rules, on the other hand, must have multiple postconditions, since it is impossible for the condition to uniquely determine the result. A programming activity might have a set of postconditions, exactly one of which is true after the activity terminates. The processing performed by the command (tool) invoked in the activity determines which of the postconditions is true. For example, a compiler might produce either error messages or object code, but which one cannot be determined except by running the compiler. This notion of multiple postconditions distinguishes Marvel's rule base from most other rule-based systems. Through chaining the preconditions and postconditions of several rules, Marvel performs what is called *opportunistic processing,* because Marvel carries out chores as the opportunity arises. Marvel uses both *forward chaining* and *backward chaining* to invoke commands automatically, switching from one to the other as explained below.

The typical operation of opportunistic processing is as follows. The user requests some command. Marvel checks whether the precondition of the command is already satisfied (i.e., it evaluates to "true"). If so, Marvel invokes the command. If not, Marvel attempts to do whatever is necessary to satisfy the precondition. This involves finding one or more other rules whose postconditions may change the state of the project in such a way as to make the precondition true. So Marvel tries to invoke the command in the activity part of these rules. But before it can do that, the preconditions of these rules must be true. So Marvel applies another round of backward chaining. Eventually, Marvel will either satisfy the original precondition and invoke the command originally requested by the user, or it will explain to the user why it is impossible to do so given the rules and what the user has to do to fix things.

After Marvel has invoked a command, the correct one of its several postconditions is asserted, changing the state of the project—usually in some small way, just new values for a few attributes. But the postcondition may cause the preconditions of one or more other rules to now be satisfied, so Marvel can go ahead and automatically carry out the corresponding activity (that is, invoke its command), under the assumption that the user will soon want its results. These commands have their own postconditions that may make true the preconditions of other commands, so forward chaining repeats until Marvel runs out of things to do—all preconditions in the entire rule base are now unsatisfied (false).

For example, the compile rule in Fig. 7-14 states that the compiler can be applied to a MODULE object only after checking that there exists a PROCEDURE object that is a component of this module and that has been edited and analyzed successfully since the last time the module was compiled. The result of applying the compile command could be either errors or successful compilation into machine code.

3.2.3 STRATEGIES. *Strategies* are metadescriptions of a project or a family of similar projects. A strategy encapsulates information about classes of objects, their capabilities, the external relations among them, and the rules guiding their manipulation as part of software development activities. Each strategy consists of four parts. The first describes the interface between this and other strategies by means of imports and exports. The second part describes a view of the objectbase by specifying classes of objects with their operations and syntactic relations. The third part defines the external relations among instances of these classes by declaring the name of each relation and the domain and range classes. The last part of a strategy is the rules that model the software development process.

Rules:

    edit[?p:PROCEDURE]:

        { EDITOR edit ?p }

        (?p.edited = Edited)

    analyze[?p:PROCEDURE]:
        <u>IF</u> (?p.edited = Edited)

        { ANALYZER analyze ?p }

            (?p.analyzed = Analyzed) <u>AND</u>
            (?p.state = Changed) <u>AND</u>
            (?p.edited = NotEdited)
        <u>OR</u>
            (?p.analyzed = NotAnalyzed) <u>AND</u>
            (?p.edited = NotEdited)

    compile[?m:MODULE]:
        (<u>forall</u> PROCEDURE ?p) <u>such that</u>
            (<u>member</u> (?m.procs ?p))
        :
        (?p.analyzed = Analyzed) <u>AND</u>
        (?m.status = ModNoComp)

        { COMPILER compile ?m }

        (?m.status = ModIsComp)
        <u>OR</u>
        (?m.status = ModNoComp)

    profile[?proj:PROJECT]:

        { PROFILER type_info ?p }

    build[?proj:PROJECT]:
        (<u>forall</u> MODULE ?m) <u>such that</u>
            (<u>member</u> (?proj.mods ?m))
        :
        (?m.status = ModIsComp)

        { BUILDER build ?proj }

        (?proj.status = Linked)
        <u>OR</u>
        (?proj.status = NotLinked)

/* A rule consists of its name, formal parameters with their types, and then its body. The body consists of a precondition indicated in a variant of first order predicate logic, an activity, and one or more postconditions separated by "OR". The activity consists of the name of the tool, the particular operation to be carried out by the tool, and its arguments. "=" and similar operators are provided by MSL. */

FIGURE 7-14
Rules.

Strategies combine three major concepts:

1. Classes of objects and multiple inheritance similar to object-oriented languages
2. Rules that are similar but not identical to rules in production systems
3. Modularization and information hiding

A single strategy might provide only a partial view of the project. Then the complete description of the project is captured in a collection of interacting strategies in a way similar to modules or packages in a conventional programming language. Modularization has become a standard concept in large-scale programming, the basic idea being that programmers work on one piece at a time and then put together all the pieces. The same concept was followed in designing strategies. Different superusers, or the same superuser at different times, develop a set of strategies where each strategy encapsulates a single role of a class of team member, part of the development process, or subpart of the software system.

Each strategy requires other strategies and uses their exported *facilities*. These facilities include both class definitions and specific objects—commands—such as a performance profiler object. Consider a set of two strategies: a programming language strategy and a programming environment strategy. The Clanguage strategy defines the syntax and semantics of an extension of C, as depicted in Fig. 7-15. A C module consists of a set of procedures. Each procedure has a source code segment and an object code segment. Statements, expressions, and such are ignored for simplicity.

The Cenvironment strategy of Fig. 7-16 combines the MODULE class imported from the Clanguage strategy with the separate MODULE class defined locally. The result is the internal representation of a single MODULE class defined according to the *union* of the Cenvironment and Clanguage definitions of MODULE. Objects in the combined class may appear as elements of the mods attribute of PROJECT objects and any other places in the objectbase where instances of the MODULE class are expected. Both EDITOR and COMPILER specialize the TOOL class by giving a command string for invoking themselves. Note that both EDITOR and COMPILER are specific objects rather than classes of objects.

Strategies can be reused by other strategies, due to the information hiding and strict interfaces. The ease of reusability is enhanced by building a library of strategies, where each strategy is categorized according to the task(s) it performs. For example, strategies that define programming languages are all grouped together while those describing memory management techniques are also grouped together, leading to a lattice of strategies. The interface to the library includes methods for depositing a new strategy, retrieving an existing strategy, and searching for strategies that perform a specific task.

```
STRATEGY: Clanguage;

Interface:
    Imports: none;
    Exports: all;

Objectbase:

    MODULE::= superclasses: ENTITY:
        printname : string ;
        procs : set_of PROCEDURE ;
        exportlist : set_of EXPITEM ;
        importlist : set_of IMPITEM ;
    END

    PROCEDURE::= superclasses: ENTITY:
        printname : string ;
        code_c : text ;
        code_o : binary ;
    END

    EXPITEM::= superclasses: ENTITY:
        expelem : PROCEDURE ;
    END

    IMPITEM::= superclasses: ENTITY:
        impelem : PROCEDURE ;
        module : MODULE ;
    END

END Clanguage

    /* None and all have the obvious meaning.  In the general case, Imports
    lists the names of imported strategies while Exports lists the names of
    exported classes, relations, tools and rules. */
```

FIGURE 7-15
Strategy.

3.2.4 MERGING STRATEGIES. When two or more strategies are loaded into Marvel, they are merged into a single internal representation that is treated as if it were based on a single strategy. As mentioned earlier, a strategy provides a view of the objectbase. When several strategies are active (i.e., loaded), there are several views of the same objectbase. These views have to be merged into one unified, composite view. Merging of strategies implies merging of classes of objects, merging of relations, and merging of rules. If the strategies being merged do not overlap, their merger is simply the aggregate of all parts of all strategies. Two strategies are said to be overlapping if they contain

- Classes with the same name
- Relations with the same name
- Rules with the same name, same preconditions, or same activity

Merging overlapping strategies involves checking the consistency of overlapping class definitions, overlapping relation definitions, and potentially

STRATEGY: CEnvironment;

<u>Interface</u>:
    <u>Imports</u>: Clanguage;
    <u>Exports</u>: <u>all</u>;

Objectbase:

    PROJECT::= <u>superclasses</u>: *ENTITY*:
        printname : *string* ;
        status : (Linked, NotLinked) = "NotLinked";
        timestamp : *real* = "0.0";
        mods : *set_of* MODULE ;
        executable : *binary* ;
    <u>END</u>

    MODULE::= <u>superclasses</u>: *ENTITY*:
        status : (ModIsComp, ModInComp, ModNoComp) =
                "ModNoComp";
    <u>END</u>

    PROCEDURE::= <u>superclasses</u>: *ENTITY*:
        analyzed : (Analyzed, InAnalysis, NotAnalyzed) =
                "NotAnalyzed";
        edited : (Edited, NotEdited) = "NotEdited";
        state : (Changed, NotChanged) = "NotChanged";
    <u>END</u>

<u>Relations</u>:

    inproject: PROJECT MODULE
    exp: MODULE PROCEDURE
    imp: MODULE MODULE
    contains: MODULE PROCEDURE

    COMPILER:: <u>superclasses</u>: *TOOL*:
        <u>operations</u>:
            compile : *string* = "compile";
    <u>END</u>

    ANALYZER:: <u>superclasses</u>: *TOOL*:
        <u>operations</u>:
            analyze : *string* = "analyze";
    <u>END</u>

    BUILDER:: <u>superclasses</u>: *TOOL*:
        <u>operations</u>:
            build : *string* = "build";
    <u>END</u>

    EDITOR:: <u>superclasses</u>: *TOOL*:
        <u>operations</u>:
            edit : *string* = "runeditor";
    <u>END</u>

    PROFILER:: <u>superclasses</u>: *TOOL*:
        <u>operations</u>:

FIGURE 7-16
Another strategy.

```
                    type_info : string = "profiler";
    END

Rules:

    edit[?p:PROCEDURE]:

            { EDITOR edit ?p }

            (?p.edited = Edited)

    analyze[?p:PROCEDURE]:
            IF (?p.edited = Edited)

            { ANALYZER analyze ?p }

                (?p.analyzed = Analyzed) AND
                (?p.state = Changed) AND
                (?p.edited = NotEdited)
            OR
                (?p.analyzed = NotAnalyzed) AND
                (?p.edited = NotEdited)


    compile[?m:MODULE]:
            (forall PROCEDURE ?p) such that
                (member (?m.procs ?p))
            :
            (?p.analyzed = Analyzed) AND
            (?m.status = ModNoComp)

            { COMPILER compile ?m }

            (?m.status = ModIsComp)
            OR
            (?m.status = ModNoComp)

    profile[?proj:PROJECT]:

            {. PROFILER type_info ?p }

    build[?proj:PROJECT]:
            (forall MODULE ?m) such that
                (member (?proj.mods ?m))
            :
            (?m.status = ModIsComp)

            { BUILDER build ?proj }

            (?proj.status = Linked)
            OR
            (?proj.status = NotLinked)

END Cenvironment
```

/* TOOL is a built-in class. Each tool lists its operations (only one each shown here), each with an indication of what the user has to do to invoke the operation. */

FIGURE 7-16 (cont.)

contradictory rules. Unloading of strategies, on the other hand, may cause portions of the objectbase to become inaccessible. If a strategy was loaded in the first place only because it was imported by the strategy now being unloaded, it will be unloaded also.

When two overlapping strategies are merged, a consistency checker verifies that the overlapping items can be unified. If two object classes in two strategies have the same name, they can be unified if their sets of attributes are disjoint or if attributes having the same name are identical. Two attributes are identical if they have the same name and the same type. Similarly, two relations are identical if they have identical domain and range classes. Checking the consistency of rules is much harder, since multiple rules with the same activity but different preconditions and postconditions are not necessarily conflicting. In particular, Marvel checks only that their preconditions and postconditions, respectively, are not obviously contradictory.

For example, consider three strategies A, B, and C. B imports some facilities from C, and both A and B define a class called X. A defines X as having two attributes *att1* and *att2*, while B defines X as having only one attribute, *att3*. If the user loads only strategy A, any instance of class X will have only two attributes, *att1* and *att2*. However, if she later loads strategy B, all instances of X are updated to have a third attribute *att3*. Also, strategy C is loaded automatically because it is used by B. The rules available at this point on instances of X assume that X has three attributes. However, rules that were defined in strategy A operate only on *att1* and *att2*, while rules defined in B assume only the existence of *att3*. Now if strategy B is unloaded, C is also. Furthermore, *att3* will no longer be accessible. This does not mean that *att3* is deleted from all instances of class X, but rather that the current rules (i.e., those defined in strategy A) cannot access *att3*. Thus, *att3* will be "unused" until B is reloaded; *att3* retains its previous value.

Merging rules from different strategies is more complicated. There are several issues. First, if two or more rules invoke the same activity, how does one combine their preconditions and their postconditions? Second, if several rules invoke distinct activities but they have the same preconditions, which of them is invoked if the precondition becomes true? Third, if several rules have the same postcondition but invoke distinct activities, which does one invoke during backward chaining?

The first problem has two solutions: Marvel can either AND all the preconditions or it can OR them. The example in Fig. 7-17 depicts two rules in two strategies. Both rules have the same activity (build system). When Marvel merges these two rules, it can build the system either when all the procedures are compiled AND analyzed or when all the procedures are either compiled OR analyzed. Since the former is probably what is intended, the default interpretation ANDs all the preconditions for the same activity; Marvel allows the user to change the interpretation to OR.

In summary, Marvel defines a methodology for acquiring the knowledge required by knowledge-based programming environments. The methodology

```
STRATEGY: A;
   ...

   Rules:

   build[?proj:PROJECT]:
           (forall MODULE ?m) such that
               (member (?proj.mods ?m))
           :
           (?m.status = ModIsComp)

           { BUILDER build ?proj }

           (?proj.status = Linked)
           OR
           (?proj.status = NotLinked)

END A


STRATEGY: B;
   ...

   Rules:

   build[?proj:PROJECT]:
           IF (?proj = ?current_focus)

           { BUILDER build ?proj }

           (?proj.status = Linked)
           OR
           (?proj.status = NotLinked)

END B
```

FIGURE 7-17
Overlapping rules in two strategies.

consists of a notation for describing families of software projects and a kernel that is instantiated by the description. The modular units of the language is strategies, which describe the classes of objects making up the objectbase, the relations among these objects, and the rules for manipulating objects and applying commands to them in the process of developing and maintaining the system. The kernel tailors its behavior according to the description and thus provides the user with a specialized environment that provides more intelligent assistance than previous programming environments.

Strategies are merged to give a complete description of the objectbase and the development process at any time. Marvel adjusts dynamically to the loading and unloading of strategies, which may cause the perceived state of the objects to change according to the role of the user or the phase in the project's life cycle. Changes may be made to capabilities of objects, types of attributes of objects, and interactions among objects (most notably, automated application of command objects to other objects). Changes are propagated throughout the objectbase to ensure that all the objects possess a consistent view of the objectbase. In particular, only those parts of a class definition that are defined in the currently loaded strategies are visible.

The approach is novel in that Marvel handles the incorporation of new commands without modifying the kernel or the tool executed by the command and without physically moving the tool into the objectbase. A strategy simply describes how to locate the tool externally and how it interacts with existing objects before incorporating it in the objectbase.

Smile (Kaiser and Feiler, 1987) and the Common Lisp Framework (CLF) (Balzer, 1987) are the immediate ancestors of Marvel. Smile is a hand-coded programming environment for C that behaves as an intelligent assistant, actively participating in the development process, but it cannot be modified without recoding. CLF is a rule-based programming environment for Common Lisp that supports forward chaining but not (directly) backward chaining. The rules are written in AP5 (Cohen, 1986), a logical specification notation that can be efficiently compiled into Lisp. It is possible to simulate Marvel-like behavior in CLF, but CLF is limited by its Lisp orientation and implementation and cannot integrate external tools.

Darwin (Minsky, 1985) is another rule-based programming environment that supports backward chaining. Darwin does not actively participate in software development in the sense of automatically carrying out activities on behalf of the user, but instead it monitors the user's activities and will not permit him to do anything against the policies dictated by the project manager and encoded in the rules. This kind of behavior can be simulated in Marvel using restrictive preconditions as constraints but is outside its normal scope of behavior. It would be interesting to combine Darwin and Marvel capabilities in a more general intelligent assistant.

Finally, Inscape (Perry, 1989) is a programming environment that combines a form of automatic programming with a form of intelligent assistance. Inscape supports the creative labors of its users—programming—but uses facilities more in line with intelligent assistance rather than automatic programming. It operates in a monitoring mode similar to Marvel, always looking over the programmer's shoulder and joining in when appropriate.

Inscape provides a special notation for specifying, for each subroutine, its preconditions (things that must be true before executing the subroutine), postconditions (things that become true by virtue of executing the subroutine), and obligations (things that must be done later on because the subroutine has been executed). As a program is written and modified, Inscape checks whether all preconditions and obligations have been satisfied by previous and subsequent postconditions, respectively. This is done using a relaxed form of theorem proving. This checking is similar to but much more significant than the symbol resolution, type checking, anomaly detection, and so on of typical language-based editors such as the Cornell Program Synthesizer (Teitelbaum and Reps, 1981), since semantic as well as syntactic errors can be detected. Inscape has been implemented for the C programming language, but the ideas could be applied to any procedural language.

4 CONCLUSIONS

As discussed in the introduction, applications of artificial intelligence to software engineering have tended in two directions, automatic programming and intelligent assistance. Automatic programming in its full glory is a very long term goal, although at least one commercial product is already available. Much additional work is needed in this field, and the notion of reverse engineering of existing programs seems particularly important.

Intelligent assistance is a more immediately practical approach for improving the productivity of individual programmers as well as the quality of their programs. The next major research problem is to apply intelligent assistance to coordinating a full software development team rather than interacting with just one user at a time. In the meantime, commercial exploitation of intelligent assistance seems imminent for single-user programming environments.

There is one catch, however: user acceptance of intelligent assistance. Many programmers consider themselves pioneers fighting a rugged frontier, making the computer do what they want it to do. The notion of the computer telling the programmers what to do, as in Genie, or the computer just going ahead and doing things for them, as in Marvel, is likely to meet with initial resistance. Marketers of intelligent assistance products must be highly concerned with human–computer interaction, and managers of software engineers must be extremely careful in the introduction of intelligent assistance tools into their workplace. A technology that is not used will never achieve its promise for higher programmer productivity and higher program quality.

ACKNOWLEDGMENTS

The Genie examples were developed by Ursula Wolz and the Marvel examples by Nasser Barghouti and Mike Sokolsky. Professor Kaiser's Programming Systems group is supported by National Science Foundation grants CCR-8858029 and CCR-8802741, by grants from AT&T, DEC, IBM, Siemens, Sun, and Xerox, by the Center for Advanced Technology, and by the Center for Telecommunications Research.

REFERENCES

Balzer, R. (1985). A 15 Year Perspective on Automatic Programming. *IEEE Trans. Software Eng.* **SE-11**(11):1257–1268.

Balzer, R. M. (1987). Living in the Next Generation Operating System. *IEEE Software,* November, pp. 77–85.

Bisiani, R., Lecouat, F., and Ambriola, V. (1988). A Planner for the Automation of Programming Environment Tasks. In: 21st Annual Hawaii Int. Conf. on System Sciences (Bruce D. Shriver, Ed.), pp. 64–72.

Broy, M., and Pepper, P. (1981). Program Development as a Formal Activity. *IEEE Trans. Software Eng.* **SE-7**(1):14–22.

Cheatham, T., Townley, J., and Holloway, G. (1979). A System for Program Refinement. 4th Int. Conf. on Software Engineering, pp. 53–62.

Cohen, D. (1986). Automatic Compilation of Logical Specifications into Efficient Programs. 5th Nat. Conf. on Artificial Intelligence, pp. 20–25.

Freeman, P. (1987). A Conceptual Analysis of the Draco Approach to Constructing Software Systems. *IEEE Trans. Software Eng.* **SE-13**(7):830–844.

Goldberg, A. T. (1986). Knowledge-Based Programming: A Survey of Program Design and Construction Techniques. *IEEE Trans. Software Eng.* **SE-12**(7):752–768.

Huff, K. E., and Lesser, V. R. (1988). A Plan-Based Intelligent Assistant That Supports the Software Development Process. In: ACM SIGSoft/SIGPlan Software Engineering Symposium on Practical Software Development Environments (Peter Henderson, Ed.), pp. 97–106.

Kaiser, G. E., and Feiler, P. H. (1987). Intelligent Assistance Without Artificial Intelligence. 32nd IEEE Computer Society Int. Conf., pp. 236–241.

Kaiser, G. E., Barghouti, N. S., Feiler, P. H., and Schwanke, R. W. (1988a). Database Support for Knowledge-Based Engineering Environments. *IEEE Expert* **3**(2):18–32.

Kaiser, G. E., Feiler, P. H., and Popovich, S. S. (1988b). Intelligent Assistance for Software Development and Maintenance. *IEEE Software,* May, pp. 40–49.

Kedzierski, B. L. (1984). Knowledge-Based Project Management and Communication Support in a System Development Environment. 4th Jerusalem Conf. on Information Technology.

Minsky, N. H. (1985). Controlling the Evolution of Large Scale Software Systems. Conf. on Software Maintenance—1985, pp. 50–58.

Perry, D. E. (1989). The Inscape Environment. 11th Int. Conf. on Software Engineering, pp. 2–9.

Rich, C., and Waters, R. C. (1988a). The Programmer's Apprentice: A Research Overview. *Computer* **21**(11):10–25.

Rich, C., and Waters, R. C. (1988b). Automatic Programming: Myths and Prospects. *Computer* **21**(8):40–51.

Smith, D. R., Kotik, G. B., and Westfold, S. J. (1985). Research on Knowledge-Based Software Environments at Kestrel Institute. *IEEE Trans. Software Eng.* **SE-11**(11):1278–1295.

Stallman, R. M. (1981). Emacs—The Extensible, Customizable, Self-Documenting Display Editor. SIGPlan SIGOA Symp. on Text Manipulation, pp. 147–156.

Teitelbaum, T., and Reps, T. (1981). The Cornell Program Synthesizer: A Syntax-Directed Programming Environment. *Commun. ACM* **24**(9):563–573.

Waters, R. C. (1986). KBEmacs: Where's the AI? *AI Mag.* **VII**(1):47–56.

Wolz, U. (1988). Automated Consulting for Extending User Expertise in Interactive Environments: A Task Centered Approach. Columbia Univ. Department of Computer Science, Tech. Rep. CUCS-393-88.

Wolz, U., and Kaiser, G. E. (1988). A Discourse-Based Consultant for Interactive Environments. 4th IEEE Conf. on Artificial Intelligence Applications, pp. 28–33.

CHAPTER 8

KNOWLEDGE-BASED VISION SYSTEMS

M. G. RODD

1 INTRODUCTION

Computer vision systems set out to replicate, to some extent, our powerful human ability to recognize and classify visually acquired images, or scenes. Inherently they form a major component in the general category of scientific endeavor referred to as artificial intelligence. Also, inherently, one accepts them to be knowledge-based—although it has been argued that early computer vision systems, like classic, sequentially programmed computers, only made use of implicit knowledge, essentially that of the designer! This chapter takes a pragmatic, user-oriented view of so-called knowledge-based computer vision systems—a viewpoint highly biased toward the practical applications of the technology as a component in a manufacturing, or process-plant, control system. It investigates the characteristics of this area of application and defines the potential role of vision-based systems. On the basis of this, it reviews current progress in fulfilling these roles. It highlights critical areas, especially the need to recognize that the industrial environment requires solutions that can coexist in those very environments and can react at speeds that are acceptable in the closed-loop control situation of which they form a part. It is argued strongly that simply gluing together well-understood low-level processing systems and currently available expert-systems-based high-level processing is bound to end in disaster! In practice, a total systems approach must be made, recognizing the realities of the application, including the still-unresolved problems relating to knowledge acquisition. Low- and high-level processing are integrated into highly flexible, explicit knowledge-based solutions: industrially acceptable solutions that are capable of fast and totally deterministic performance.

Despite many claims to the contrary, computer vision has yet to make its mark in industry, particularly in terms of applications in online process control or in direct manufacturing control. While it is undeniable that certain specific problems can be solved using the various commercially available vision systems and that in many cases these are, indeed, very successful, it also cannot be denied that there is still a whole range of industrial problems looking for solutions. According to Rao and Jain (1988), computer vision research seeks to "understand complex visual processes and to construct effective computer-based visual systems." However, what is so often forgotten by researchers in this subject is the *real world* in which the results of their research are to be applied.

On the one side of the application/research divide, in searching for higher levels of automation the process engineer is constantly running up against the problem of measuring process variables for which no commercially viable solution exists (Rodd and Deravi, 1987). While strides have been made in instrumentation over the years, its applied nature keeps it a Cinderella discipline, and there are many variables to be measured that are still beyond the capability of current techniques. Therefore the process engineer has to attempt to close many loops based on inaccurate or insufficient information or on measurement techniques that are highly suspect. In many cases proposed control algorithms are shown to be theoretically highly effective but to suffer in practice from a lack of access to fundamental process measurements.

When considering many of these industrial measurement problems, one is continually struck by a common characteristic: in many cases the parameters that are required to be measured *are available* to the *human eye*—albeit under special or difficult circumstances. Thus, for example, one can stop a conveyor belt feeding rock into a crushing mill and clearly see the rocks (Rodd and Deravi, 1987). One can then use suitable measuring tools to determine their size. Likewise, flaws on metal emerging from a rolling mill can be detected by the human eye, and an intelligent or, more specifically, *well-trained* observer can make deductions as to where the flaw originated and whether the metal should be rejected. Similarly, an operator of a numerically controlled tool can see the result of the processes performed on, say, a piece of metal and quickly decide whether the tool has obeyed the instructions given to it or whether it has malfunctioned. Likewise, a human operator can observe articles coming out of an oven in the food industry and decide whether the articles are overcooked, are the correct size, are broken, and so on (Wu, 1989).

The point is that in each case the human operators can *visually* observe the result of some process and make an informed decision as to whether it has occurred correctly. Whether they can do it reliably, accurately, fast enough, or at an acceptable cost are the prime issues involved in seeking alternative solutions.

The *visual observability* of such parameters must provide much food for thought for the instrument design engineer, as they have for me. Analogous to this visual information, of course, is the way in which operators of large plants use other senses; touch, hearing, and even the sense of smell are used to monitor many processes. Mill operators, for example, often listen to the mill running and can somehow infer from this sensory input something about the performance of the system. Although difficult to quantify, it is clear that they are using some of their *human senses* to *measure* various parameters, and then their *intelligence* to determine suitable, *learned,* control strategies. It follows, therefore, that faced with the need to measure physically observable parameters and driven by the desire to improve consistency of control, researchers are continually attracted to the intriguing possibilities of replicating the senses by some form of artificial intelligence. (In fact, in the area of acoustical measurements, for example, such approaches have proved to be successful. For example, in the control of furnaces, algorithms have been developed that are based on information extracted from the acoustic emissions from a given process.)

Moving on to the other side of the application/research divide, machine vision (or computer vision) is by no means a new technology and has been the subject of much effort for many years. It has become a relatively well established technology; an indication of this is the maturity of some of the texts that have emerged, such as the definitive text by one of the giants of the subject, Berthold Horn (1986). However, as a control engineer, I must rush to point out that much of the claimed success, particularly as illustrated in the journals, has been in highly theoretical laboratory environments involving problems that, although tough, are simply not true representations of the industrial environment. Huge gulfs still exist in many areas of application. This chapter investigates some of these and tries to highlight some of the real, practical problems and point the way ahead for future research. It is a totally biased approach, written from the point of view of the engineer who is not really fascinated by the mathematics of the technology, or by the wonder of a new science, but rather has to solve real day-to-day control problems for an industry that must strive to produce products with improved quality, at lower costs, and with higher reliability and more uniform characteristics.

In the context of this book there can be no doubt that the vision systems that are required in these applications are all inherently knowledge-based. One could, indeed, claim that *any* software system that solves problems is knowledge-based; however, in these next-generation control and instrumentation systems, we are clearly using *explicit* knowledge (in some form) to assist us in making a decision. We have to analyze a scene, representing some part of our process, which is captured by some form of sensing device, and analyze that information *in its engineering context*. As with the equivalent human observer, we have to call on an extensive amount of a priori information about the measurement that we are trying to make. Having used that knowledge to identify the object of our observations, we then have to go to the next level of solution and actually make process measurements—size, color, shape, and so on—and in addition these measurements must be made with an accuracy appropriate to the devices or controllers that are using the information for some subsequent control function.

Underlying many of the problems of utilizing vision systems is that very few commercially available systems can operate in real time. For many decades the computer boffin has run amok in the industrial world with wonderful solutions—ranging from complex computing systems to sophisticated process algorithms, all the way through to advanced communications systems, which in themselves are magnificent achievements. However, when one looks at the reality of applying many of these techniques, one sees relatively little progress being made. (Consider the wonderful world of MAP—the General-Motors-inspired initiative in common communications—a wonderful solution, but very few takers!) In most cases the answer to the nonacceptance of many solutions lies not only in their inherently high costs, but even more in the *real-time* nature of the very processes that we are required to control.

The point is that any real-world process system, to be controlled, must have its control system designed to the needs of the process. Thus, for example, in a chemical process it doesn't matter how wonderful the algorithms might be; unless they can deliver controlling instructions to the process under control *in time to affect that process,* there is very little point in doing the calculations. In a similar vein, therefore, unless a computer vision system produces its outputs quickly enough to be fed back to the process that is producing the articles being observed, in time to affect that process, there is little point in making the measurement. A computer vision system, for example, undertaking the measurement of the size of the rocks is of no value if it cannot produce measured variables fast enough to provide useful information to the control system. In the case of a vision system looking at the result of a numerically controlled metal-forming operation, it must react quickly enough to detect, say, that a tool is broken before the next operation occurs.

We therefore, have, in certain potentially critical arenas, a mismatch between current computer vision products and their application requirements. Current vision products simply cannot match the speed or the complexity required in many industrial applications. The answer must lie in developing a new breed of highly flexible, reconfigurable, high-speed (but low-cost) vision systems—which clearly calls for the use of explicit knowledge.

2 AN OVERVIEW OF COMPUTER VISION

Computer vision is a multidisciplinary research field that involves the vision algorithms together with an understanding of the physical nature of both the senses and the process being observed (Sanz, 1988). It involves a wide range of mathematics, computer science, practical engineering, and, most important from the industrialist's point of view, control theory. As with many other aspects of artificial intelligence and knowledge engineering, it is the meeting point of a variety of technologies and sciences. It blends optical processing and sensing, computer architecture, mechanics, and a deep knowledge of process control. Despite some successes, in many fields of application it really is still in its infancy.

Essentially, computer vision involves the manipulation of images by a computer or a computerlike structure. It is bound by the fact that with the current state of computing technology, only *digital images* can be processed by our machines, and such images are essentially mere representations of the objects they represent. Of course, there is a host of critical work still to be done in alternative processing structures, and optical processing is naturally critical to future progress in this and related fields. However, because in our current image-processing systems a correspondence has to be established between a physical object and the internal data fields (or image) that represent it, and because our computers currently work with numerical rather than pictorial data, an image must be converted into *numerical form* before processing. This image is normally sensed by an electronic camera system, which produces an analog electrical signal that is converted into digital form, typically by a process referred to as digitization.

The image itself is divided into small regions called picture elements, or *pixels* for short. The most common subdivision scheme is a rectangular grid with the image divided into horizontal lines made up of adjacent pixels. At each pixel location, the image's brightness has to be sampled and quantized—in other words expressed in digital form—typically as an integer. Each pixel has a unique data location (or address) and has an integer value, normally referred to as its *grey-scale value*. For example, black might be represented by 0 and white by, say, 255 for a system in which there are eight information bits available. Between these two extremes, the *grey value* is represented by an integer between 0 and 255. Of course, it is also possible to obtain color information, typically implemented by extraction of the three primary colors and expressing the equivalent grey scale of each of these three colors. While clearly color is critical to aiding the visual process, we still have little insight into its very fundamental nature, and it will not be discussed here.

It must be noted that the size of the array naturally establishes the inherent *resolution* that the computer vision system is able to provide. The more detail required, the higher the resolution, and therefore the larger the number of pixels that must be available. Current commercial systems normally offer resolutions of between 256 and 512 points in each dimension of the array; this means that for an image covering a 1-meter object the best possible resolution is no better than 2 millimeters!

The image that has been acquired is then made available to a digital processor. This processor has typically been a general-purpose digital computer, but because of the problems that will be discussed later in this chapter, there is a trend toward custom-built systems—which are more suited to processing the types of arrays met with in computer vision processing. The processor analyzes the pixel data and is programmed to make the appropriate decision or deductions. In most industrial situations, the processor would also have some direct control over the sensing element, or even over the environment. For example, it might be necessary to focus the camera, or adjust the gain, or possibly change the level of illumination. This *feedback effect* will be referred to later.

In terms of the actual processing, it is now customary to divide the processing into two phases: low-level and high-level. Low-level processing essentially attempts to extract features describing the acquired data in a more abstract, compact, and hopefully more symbolic fashion, whereas high-level processing attempts to assess these features and provide outputs that are of value to the user—be it a human observer or some further processing system such as a process controller.

2.1 Low-Level Processing

One of the first tasks to be tackled attempts to distinguish features from the surrounding environment. Two relatively simplistic approaches are commonly adopted at this stage: thresholding and edge detection. In the case of thresholding, the basic assumption is that in many practical situations the objects we are looking for are much darker (or possibly much lighter) than the background. This might be either an inherent feature or one that we could contrive by controlling the lighting conditions. For example, we could place the object on a lighted table, hence creating shadows. Likewise, we might shine light onto the object, at specific angles, also to create shadows.

The simplest method of distinguishing dark pixels from light ones is to establish a *threshold value*. Any pixel that has a darkness beyond this level is regarded as being black, and one with less than the chosen level, as white. This process is thus often referred to as *binarization* of the image. Determining the actual value at which the threshold is set is itself not a simple task and might have to be tackled dynamically or with a degree of explicit knowledge. In most commercially available computer vision packages, routines are available to extract, say, the histogram of the total range of pixel grey values, which can be used as a basis for threshold determination.

The other process that is often used at this stage is known as *edge detection*. This process sets out to determine the boundaries between various areas of different light intensities, which typically indicate the edges of objects. So we analyze the rate of change of grey levels; clearly, a high rate of change will identify borders. A wide range of edge-detection algorithms have been produced, and these will be discussed briefly in a subsequent section of this chapter. The right choice will normally be primarily dependent on the application.

In all cases of low-level processing, however, a general problem that normally occurs relates to the fact that most pictures we acquire are inherently imperfect. This means, for example, that even to the human eye the actual boundary between the objects is seldom obvious. Many objects, for example, have rounded edges rather than square ones, and with normal illumination we get a gradual shift from one shade of grey to another. In other cases, if the illumination is not orthogonal to the object being viewed, one edge will have a greater degree of shadow than the other. In addition, every stage of the image-acquisition process is subject to the introduction of noise, or unwanted signals. These can be electronically generated, optically introduced (flicker, lamp fluctuations), the result of physical contamination (dust or metal particles), and so on. These problems, among many others, make the extraction of absolute edges of an object extremely difficult. Clearly, then, the idea of *filtering* an image, using the host of signal-processing techniques available, is extremely important. The nature of the noise is, once again, application-dependent and will in turn determine the appropriate filtering strategy. It is also important to realize that the noise will change with surrounding environmental conditions.

Following these relatively well researched and well understood procedures, low-level vision also seeks to present to the subsequent processing stages features describing the image in an abstract fashion. This normally consists of fragmenting (more frequently referred to as *segmenting*) images by labeling different distinguishable regions according to the satisfaction of specified conditions or features. Again, while this aspect will be dealt with in greater detail later, the essential objective is to attempt to divide an image into regions that correspond to attributes of the physical object being observed.

In summary, low-level image processing attempts to provide the higher levels of processing with an abstract and symbolic version of an extremely complex numeric data array. The complexity is naturally a function of the original scene being observed and also of whether we are working in two or three dimensions.

2.2 High-Level Image Processing

The objective of high-level computer vision is to make "sense" of the images being received. From low-level processing we hope to receive a collection of rudimentary information, now no longer simply expressed as a data array but with some form of structure to it in the way of possible edges, connected edges, regions of similarity, and so on. In addition, the image data might now be in a simple binary form. The object of high-level processing is to use appropriate techniques to deduce useful information about the original observed image. It is extremely critical at this point to remember that the context of the work in this particular chapter is focused on industrial image scenes. This means that the high-level processing has to result in *useful information* for forwarding to a *control system*. This might be in the form of measurements relating, say, to hole sizes, the average size of particles, or the number and position of the objects. It also might require quantitative information, such as the condition of surface finishes, or the presence of defects. The whole point is that high-level processing is heavily context-dependent, and no generic, inflexible, implicit knowledge-based solutions will ever be possible, although the tools used might, themselves, be generic.

In summary, it is important to recognize that to apply vision, a total system is required. Figure 8-1 indicates the various aspects of such an industrial computer vision system, whose functions will include the following.

1. *Sensing:* Here the visual image (not necessarily visible only to the human eye—it could be an infrared, ultrasound, or X-ray image) is captured by a "camera" and held in store, typically referred to as a *frame store*. This information is then made available to:
2. *Preprocessing:* Here we attempt to improve the signal, typically by removing irrelevant noise by such means as filtering, edge detection, or thresholding. This set of improved (or enhanced) data is then provided to:
3. *Feature extraction:* Here we attempt to extract object features that *might* correspond to geometric or critical features of the object being viewed: moments, perimeters, Fourier descriptors, and so on. Essentially, we are compacting the data before sending it to the next stage of vision processing:
4. *Feature interpretation:* Here we essentially attempt to take the data and *map* it back to the *real objects* that we, with our human visual systems, would recognize. The output here is in some form of symbolic representation, which we would subsequently pass on to:
5. *Postprocessing:* This section is used to feed information back to system users or, increasingly, to the overall control system.

It is important to realize that these steps are all closely interrelated, and (as will be highlighted throughout this chapter) it is often necessary to feed back

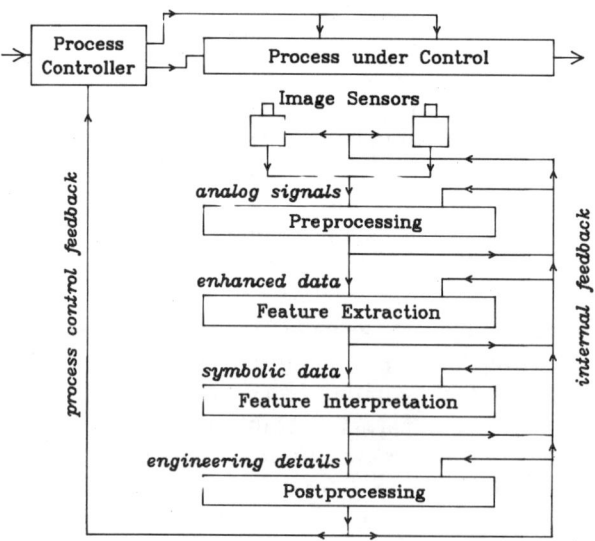

FIGURE 8-1
Computer vision as part of the control loop.

information, in a normal control-loop fashion, to assist in any of the preceding processes.

Computer vision has naturally become a major aspect of artificial intelligence research, calling as it does on knowledge of the environment, of the specific nature of the object being observed, and of the required parameters to be assessed. Although extensive work has been carried out in this area and in some specific cases has proved to be most successful, in general very few useful, commercially acceptable solutions have emerged for the industrial user. It must be acknowledged that the problem is extremely difficult, particularly as the actual objectives of computer vision in such environments are often poorly understood by those researchers required to produce the solutions.

3 FUNDAMENTALS OF SCENE RECOGNITION

The critical and most fundamental problem that faces computer vision researchers is the manner in which we represent, and which we subsequently use to recognize, scenes or components thereof. If we are to recognize anything from our acquired images, we must be able to partition a scene, assess its components, and then reconstruct it in a symbolic and meaningful fashion. This is a meeting point for the knowledge engineer and the psychologist/physiologist. Although relatively unacknowledged in the literature, the paper by Fischler and Bolles (1986) seems to offer some intuitively valuable guidelines. They recognize that a basic attribute of the human visual system seems to be its ability to group relatively primitive elements of a scene into meaningful or coherent clusters. In addition, the human system seems to impart structure, and often semantic interpretation, to the data. While we cannot really strive to reproduce the human capacity for interpretation, it is clear that some clues that we might get from studying the human system (or at least from how we interpret the human system) would be useful in aiding scene recognition. Experiments on recognition, such as those described by Fischler and Bolles, are useful. Even if they do not truly reveal the manner in which our human system actually operates, they do give us a way of interpreting its functions. One can postulate, for example, that humans have the ability to store hundreds of thousands of iconic primitives in their visual range, in the same way as they might store thousands of words or parts of words. There is, of course, evidence to indicate that the visual recognition component of our brain is at least as good as its speech recognition counterpart, and it is reasonable to postulate that a very similar mechanism is at work—indeed probably the same one.

Essentially, the work described by Fischler and Bolles is based on evidence that, given a specific object, most humans will interpret it as a structure made up of iconic, or possibly even simpler, geometric primitives. When posing the problem of recognizing an unknown shape to relatively unsophisticated observers such as eight- or nine-year-old children, one finds that most describe the object as being some basic shape "like a box" with, say, "a corner missing" and "a wiggle" in the middle. As the person's learning power and their experience expands, they might describe one of the shapes as "a triangle" or as "part of a sine wave," for example.

This work gives us some clue as to possible ways we can use to construct, or conversely to partition, a two-dimensional object. We can begin by highlighting critical or outstanding points, such as major changes in curvature or corner points, and then describe the planar components (or *primitives*) that exist between these important points, in terms of, say, some mathematical formulation. We could then describe a complete object by a set of coordinates, followed by a particular planar geometrical structure that ends at a specific set of coordinates, followed by another geometric construction, and so on. Having described simple objects in this way, we could then proceed to describe a complex scene as sets of such objects. Fischler and Bolles (1986) provide some useful evidence as to the value of this approach.

We can move on to describing other objects by a far more complex set of primitives chosen according to the needs. Naturally, if we move into the three-dimensional world, then we have to use primitives such as cones and spheres, but the same principle applies.

If we then accept that we can describe objects by selecting an appropriate collection of primitives (restricting ourselves here to two-dimensional scenes), representing and detecting planar curves becomes a critical issue in computer vision. We need to represent curves internally in a manner that is unambiguous and relatively simple to handle. These become essential components of the knowledge-base of our system. Having received an image, we need to transform it rapidly into a form from which we can deduce its curvature characteristics so as to compare these to the set of recognized components.

It is important to note that if we select an appropriate, but limited, set of primitives, they can all be represented as a single line with a starting point and a specified curvature. At first sight it then appears to be just a problem of representing a curve by an equation! Of course, the problem lies in turning this statement around and, given a particular primitive curve, get it back into a mathematical formulation for comparison with that which is being sought.

It is in this area that there is much merit in the scale-space approach, originally discussed by Witkin (1983), and extended and explored by many authors, among whose results one of the most important is that of Asada and Brady (1986). These authors extended the scale-space approach to a set of relatively complex primitives and showed that it provides a relatively compact way to express complex primitive shapes. Their work is further extended by the work of Mokhtarian and Mackworth (1986), in which it is shown that a complex curve can be represented in scale-space and also with various degrees of accuracy. It is then possible to do a coarse-to-fine recognition process—which allows a rapid, cursory look to be taken—and if one is relatively certain that one is focusing in on an appropriate candidate, only then do accurate calculations have to be made. It must also be pointed out that the scale-space approach is important in that it can be used in general to detect two-dimensional curves under conditions that are *invariant to rotation, scaling, and translation* of the curve; that is, the curve can be located anywhere in the picture and at any angle or scaling. It is purely the *changes of curvature* that are stored and subsequently recognized.

Despite the important work that has been done on representing and detecting fairly complex primitives, recent work reported by Wu et al. (1988a) shows that much advantage can be gained by finding initially (using a new set of algorithms developed by Wu et al.) major points of discontinuity. Then we handle the sections of the curve between those points, by, say, scale-space methods. This approach permits a compact representation and leads to high-speed computations.

4 REQUIREMENTS OF INDUSTRIAL VISION SYSTEMS

There are at least two, very different, categories of application-oriented problems that vision systems will face in industrial control. In the first, there are a range of *unstructured* images that occur in applications such as particle size analysis and surface inspection. The differing aspects of these problems are dealt with by Berger (1985). Although some of the ideas that are expressed throughout the rest of this chapter are applicable, this area will receive relatively little further attention here. It must be pointed out that this is not an inadvertent omission but an acknowledgment that there is extensive and important work taking place in this area—relating more specifically to medical and topographical imaging. Particularly important work, and a useful illustration of the success that has been achieved using intelligent systems applied to unstructured images, is covered in the paper by Lin et al. (1988).

The other common type of industrial application occurs where the images are, to a high degree, well structured. Much attention was paid in the early days of vision to certain aspects of this, and some successful work will be highlighted later, but many applications are still unfulfilled. We refer here generally to areas in which the objects are relatively regular and are typically formed with well-understood and well-defined geometric features. In many cases, indeed, one of the prime objectives of introducing computer vision systems into these environments is to distinguish *variations* from the idealized geometric properties.

An important fact that is now being increasingly recognized is that in many cases the objects are themselves not only built with regular geometric features, but have also been developed on computer-aided design (CAD) systems in which they have to be based on relatively simple mathematical formulations! For example, in the sheet-metal handling industry, punching and nibbling numerically controlled machines are used to produce panels, boxes, and so on. These machines are programmed from data originally captured from designs produced using CAD systems. This is an extremely important fact, as it means that a significant amount of knowledge is available in a database right from the start. This naturally alleviates many of the problems that occur in capturing knowledge about specific objects (see the later discussions on knowledge acquisition).

It is critical, therefore, in reviewing the problems of applying computer vision systems in the industrial environment, to discuss some of the properties of the objects being observed and the environment in which we will have to operate.

Geometric features: Here absolute or relative position, orientation, position and condition of edges and corners, width, surface volume, roughness, shape, and proximity may have to be considered. We might have not only to recognize any or all of these geometric properties, but also to *measure* their absolute parameters. It is simply insufficient in an inspection task to say where the center of a hole is; we must also know its radius, as well as the condition of its boundary.

Optical features: Again, this is where the laboratory departs from the factory! In an industrial environment it is extremely difficult to control specific lighting levels and conditions. In order to make sense of any acquired images, aspects such as reflectance, chromatic characteristics, color, and texture might have to be observed and defined. Indeed, some of these characteristics might well be used to the advantage of the inspecting system! For example, useful information about the heating of components (say, electronic components) can be found by observing infrared radiation rather than just looking at normal white-light conditions. Also, as has been reported recently, the reflectance characteristics of various materials under varying light conditions can provide useful information.

Mechanical characteristics: Many an industrial inspection system fails because the general mechanical or inherent material characteristics of the objects being observed have not been considered. A simple illustration is a situation in which the heat from the illumination system can result in objects being distorted. Aspects such as acoustic performance, hardness, and temperature characteristics of objects being observed must be taken into consideration.

Environment: A nasty shock is in store for laboratory-based vision experts when they venture onto the shop floor! The environment can be dusty, polluted by sizable particles, smoky, full of electromagnetic interference, oily, dirty, and so on. Maintenance is normally done by unskilled or unmotivated technicians—100-watt bulbs are replaced by 60-watt (if at all), and cameras are adjusted with a large, dirty hammer! Electrical supplies are full of spikes, and power failures occur at regular intervals.

It is also critical to consider the *actual, stated needs* of the potential user of a computer vision system. While to an engineer this is an obvious statement, so often to those involved in high-technology research it is the most-often-forgotten parameter! It is difficult to generalize this need, but it can be confidently stated that the fundamental need in the industrial environment is for inspection, manipulation, and process control. The fundamental requirement is for a system that works under plant conditions and matches the rest of the system and the operational needs.

In terms of *inspection,* the need is normally to determine whether an article has been correctly manufactured and meets the required tolerances. It is unreasonable to require objects to be well-oriented, so a relatively free environment is inherent. Thus, although one could constrain an object to, say, a conveyor belt, one cannot precisely predict where it will be or which way around it will arrive! (Currently, of course, many of the installed systems require this rigid part location, and, by means of mechanical devices, a certain degree of alignment can take place. However, it can be argued that the cost of this will, in most cases, outweigh the real benefit of having the vision system in the first place.)

In this environment, therefore, it is essential first to *find,* via the vision system, the objects being inspected, and then to undertake the tasks necessary to ensure that all the design parameters have been met. This will require not only recognition of the object, and also of any subobjects within that object, but actual undertaking of precise measurements relating to size, position, curvature, and so on. To be of value, these calculations must be undertaken to an accuracy that is appropriate to the application. It is critical to repeat that not only must a hole be found, but also we must be able to calculate its precise position and radius and also how good the edges are. In this case, such information can be used to determine if the correct drill has been used, if the hole is in the correct position, and, finally, whether the drill is sharp or is broken or worn.

In the second case, that of *manipulation,* it is important to recognize the object, but also to know *precisely* its orientation and position. Since such processes will subsequently be used for manipulating the article—say, by a robot—it is critical to match the accuracy of measurement to that of the manipulator.

Here we must return to an underlying aspect of industrial applications and restate that the failure of current vision systems is not only that they cannot meet a large number of the above criteria, but that also, almost without fail, they do not meet the application requirements in terms of the speed of operation. The biscuit maker, for example, requiring automatic inspection (critical in the competitive world) cannot afford simply to stop the production line in order to allow the inspection to take place. Also, he cannot just examine on a sampling basis. It does not matter how sophisticated the algorithms are or how efficiently they have been coded, if the real-time response is inappropriate, the solution is irrelevant. It is critical, also, that a measurement of the *average* response is not good enough; the *absolute* processing time must be well defined. This imposes particularly important conditions on the higher levels of processing, where knowledge-based systems appear to hold many answers to the complex recognition problems posed. While one can handle the lower levels in a deterministic fashion, it is extremely difficult, with the current state of technology, to handle the recognition side in a totally deterministic fashion.

In all time-critical processes the actual definition of real time is a function of the process being controlled. Again this takes us back to defining the real needs of the user. If, say, the conveyor belt on which objects are being inspected runs at 2 meters per second, and we capture an image covering a 0.1 meter length of belt, then we simply have to accept that we must process 20 images per second *and provide outputs in time to halt production if necessary, or alternatively to reject articles from the belt, without stopping it!*

This raises one final aspect that must be considered by the designer. Whatever the output from the system, it must be in a form that suits the control application. This might be feedback information to the operator, a control signal to a control loop, or impulses to a series of actuators moving faulty articles off the inspection site. It is always a case of *completing the control loop—we measure only in order to control!*

5 A FIRST LOOK AT KNOWLEDGE-BASED COMPUTER VISION SYSTEMS

While we can say that all software systems that solve problems are essentially knowledge-based, it is important to understand whether we are making use of *explicit* or *implicit* knowledge. The system that uses explicit knowledge has the advantage that the user can enhance the system itself, improve the system's performance, or indeed change its whole application by improving the quality, extent, or nature of the knowledge available. Essentially we aim in explicit knowledge-based systems to separate the *knowledge-source* from the *processing* of the knowledge. Systems based on implicit knowledge, however—and this is true of most (conventional) sequentially programmed systems—require extensive system modifications to improve or modify their application or performance. Therefore, implicit knowledge systems are inflexible and will have to be reprogrammed as the problem they solve changes. However, they do not require the apparently extensive amount of knowledge management of an explicit system. A serious issue is that the more flexible we make a system, the more the system is in control of parameters, such as total run time. Therefore, we have a dilemma: The more flexible we make a system, the more nondeterministic it seems to become and the less control we have over its performance.

So, it terms of explicit knowledge vision systems, it is essential to embed the description of the objects we are seeking to recognize as efficiently as possible into the system. This should mean that our final system can be faced with a large number of different objects to handle without reconfiguration, *but* we must also strictly control the processing so as to meet the application demands in terms of processing throughput.

The best-known form of knowledge-based system is, of course, the ubiquitous *expert system*. However, as has been pointed out in the past, it is not strictly correct to call current vision systems, which analyze scenes, expert systems, knowledge-based and rule-driven though they may be; the tasks normally performed do not require access to expertise. This is by no means a mere semantic quibble; expertise in vision is not easy to describe, and the problem is not one of simply determining the right rules for an expert system kernel. Expert systems typically solve expert-type problems: complex problems requiring highly specific knowledge that is used in a specific way. We require our vision systems, however, to use relatively poor knowledge, in a poorly defined field, in whichever way they choose, to solve a problem that is not well understood by human experts!

Typically, an expert system can be described as having two major components: a knowledge base and an inference engine or knowledge processor. The knowledge base typically holds only information that is used to solve problems presented to the system. The inference engine uses this knowledge to solve these specific problems. There are obvious disadvantages to this structure, for example, in complex areas in which the available knowledge is limited. Thus, in the case of vision systems the system cannot itself determine a strategy to solve a problem—necessary when the knowledge is so ill defined. With current expert systems, therefore, the problem-solving strategy adopted will be that of the system's architect.

The expertise available to an expert is naturally limited by the current problems related to gathering together, and subsequently handling, large quantities of knowledge. Current systems are also normally restricted in having in their knowledge bases only the initial knowledge available to the system's designer (no deduced information, etc.). The knowledge base can so easily be considered purely as a *rule base*—which can cause the system to restrict the power of the available knowledge. We should clearly strive toward knowledge bases that contain *knowledge sources*—in which each knowledge source is of similar format to, and has the same function as, a rule in a conventional expert system. We require, however, a knowledge-based system that is able to reason about how it should manage knowledge; it should be able to choose, say, between possibly contradictory knowledge sources on the grounds of other evidence. This brief review of the problem of fixed knowledge bases presents one argument for not using conventional expert systems in solving computer vision problems! Other, more technical reasons will be discussed later.

Despite some of the expressed reservations, knowledge-based systems are penetrating the image-processing arena, and there is much evidence of useful work being carried out. Nazif and Levine (1984) present an application of expert systems techniques to low-level image segmentation, which, according to the paper, gives good results. In a similar way Lin et al. (1988) show how an expert system can integrate image segmentation and recognition. Niemann et al. (1985) describe another system that uses knowledge to interpret results from a segmented picture. This work appears, however, to use implicit knowledge to segment the picture and subsequently to extract the information needed for its analysis. Wu (1989) shows how an integrated approach to the use of knowledge-based systems in computer vision can be used with much success for handling real industrial objects.

We cannot leave this introductory section without referring to the work done in the early days of computer vision, when researchers promoted the idea of using model knowledge. In this they attempted to match image features against features predicted by models. This approach had its origins in simple template matching. While it cannot be denied that template matching, and variations thereof, have met with some success, the approach suffers from rigidity and inflexibility and, in many cases, poor speed of processing. A general approach to this area has been referred to as image feature access (Rao and Jain, 1988), which includes the introduction of knowledge of the objects at an early stage to guide interpretation. As discussed in Rao and Jain (1988), the approach leads to a classic chicken-and-egg problem: How can we interpret before we segment, and vice versa! It is not clearly recognized that image recognition is a cyclic rather than a linear process. This point will be referred to later, since it is part of the feedback necessary in applying intelligent control over each stage in the image-processing chain.

6 KNOWLEDGE-BASED EDGE DETECTION AND SEGMENTATION

As was suggested in the diagram indicating the various stages necessary in computer vision (Fig. 8-1), the practical realities of applying the techniques indicate that no single optimal solution exists. In this section we look first at the edge-detection level, where we can get a glimpse of the role that knowledge can play in enhancing a seemingly well-defined operation. For example, if one can deduce the information relating to the characteristics of, say, the noise present, then one can estimate the most appropriate edge-detection algorithm to use, or determine the value of parameters such as the Gaussian deviation. Likewise, if one deduces that the edges are extremely *fuzzy*, this information can well be fed back to the illumination, or the camera system, in an attempt to sharpen up the acquired image. Finally, it is clear that if one has a priori knowledge about the *types* of edges that have to be searched for, then one can try to fit these characteristics to the observed edges.

However, as we shall see, such operations are best considered as aspects of the segmentation procedures. Having reviewed segmentation, I feel it is evident that it is highly questionable whether edge detection should ever be separated from segmentation.

Further, as a final point, it is becoming increasingly clear that *all* low-level processes are highly knowledge-based and relate directly to the total knowledge we have about any given class of scene. Therefore, we may conclude that in a true knowledge-based computer vision system, *no* rigid boundaries should be drawn between phases of processing.

6.1 Edge Detection

Physical edges are one of the most important properties of scenes, since they correspond to object boundaries or to changes in surface orientation, material properties, and so on (Torre and Poggio, 1986). Fast and reliable edge detection appears to be essential in most industrial image-processing tasks. However, at the same time it must be acknowledged that the existence of noise, reflection, shadows, nonuniform illumination, and so on, in acquired scenes make the selection, and subsequent design, of fast and effective boundary extraction systems extremely difficult. Despite the vast amount of literature dedicated to the question of edge detection [well reviewed in the paper by Torre and Poggio (1986)], it is clear that the computer vision community is still searching for effective, and more important, computationally efficient, methods for the extraction of edges of images in a manner that is reliable and robust.

As discussed in Section 3, it is clear that psychologists have suggested that boundary information plays a dominant role in our human visual systems and that it is highly likely that edges are used to form the basic primitives upon which we base our initial decisions regarding the objects we are observing. (It is only with more detailed investigation that we can confirm or retract our immediate reaction.)

One can also look at edge detection from another point of view. It has been suggested that edge detection is really an *information compression technique* whereby we map a vast amount of data (which we acquire when fully visualizing a scene) into a series of reduced symbols or equations representing the scene.

It is therefore not surprising that a large amount of material has been produced on edge detection. It is evident that much is either very complex mathematically or extremely difficult to implement in practical industrial environments. This is not denying that much success has been achieved, but in general it is necessary to choose and then *tune* the detection algorithms to the specific task at hand. Little guidance is given to the user as to which extraction techniques should be considered for a particular application.

Indeed the exact definition of edge detection itself is rather unclear. Not all of the so-called "edge-detection algorithms" perform the same function; some merely enhance the edges of an image, and the output "edges" require further thinning and possibly linking together before boundaries are obtained. More sophisticated and complex detection schemes take on the task of filtering, detection, thinning, and linking and result in a definitive well-defined set of (typically binarized) points that fully define the edge pattern. In reality most detectors fit somewhere between the two.

The ultimate goal should be the characterization of intensity changes occurring in the image in terms of the physical processes that produce those changes. Typically, then, the first stage in any edge-detection scheme requires the determination of image intensity derivatives, that is, looking for intensity changes and finding actual derivatives of those changes. Thus it appears that this is a problem of numerical differentiation, and it tends to be a localized problem. Once we have undertaken this, the second component of edge detection includes tasks such as boundary tracking, segmentation, and grouping together of the local edges in order to reconstruct a complete picture in terms of the edges.

Torre and Poggio (1986) make the point that in attempting to compute the derivatives of image intensity changes, we are dealing with a problem that is inherently ill-posed. As engineers we know from experience that numerical differentiation is not robust against noise, and in image processing we are inherently dealing with noisy processes. Even a small degree of noise might disrupt the differentiation process. These authors propose, therefore, that the first step in edge detection has to be the transformation of ill-posed problems into well-posed problems, and suggest that filtering of the initial image can regularize the ill-posed problem and should always be performed before the differentiation operation. They suggest, and this is borne out in practice, that Gaussian filtering has advantages over other possible filtering functions.

Work along these lines was pioneered by Marr and Hildreth (1980) and led to the introduction of a whole class of edge detectors. In the Marr-Hildreth approach, the operation is initiated by first filtering the image with a Gaussian filter and then using a Laplacian operator to find the second-order derivative. The centers of the edges in the original image are represented by zero-crossings in the output. This so-called Laplacian-of-Gaussian masks approach has several advantages, among which is the fact that scale-space techniques can be used immediately (Witkin, 1983). An additional advantage shown by Powrie (1989) is that the implementation of the approach can be made extremely efficient from a computational point of view.

For completeness it should be pointed out that several widely used edge-detection systems are based on variations of the original Marr-Hildreth work. These include Haralick's detector (Haralick, 1984) and those of Canny (1986), Torre and Poggio (1986), and Nalwa and Binford (1986).

6.2 Segmentation

Edge detection aims to extract possible lines of discontinuity within the image being observed. The object of image segmentation is, however, to partition the image into defined regions that can subsequently be analyzed by the higher levels of processing. As with edge detection, segmentation techniques have been the subject of much research, and once again it has been found that no particular algorithm will work for more than a narrow range of images. Possibly the problem is that we do not have any general formulation of the problem or, perhaps more likely, that we are putting an artificial boundary between low-level and high-level processes, whereas they are, in fact, one and the same.

One can distinguish at least three different approaches to segmentation, and it is important to note that in all cases a degree of knowledge has to be introduced at some point—either implicitly or explicitly. These three approaches are:

1. Extension of simple edge-detection systems
2. Feature thresholding
3. Region extraction

In practice we tend, as always, to see combinations being used—often to great effect but with poor computational efficiency.

EDGE DETECTION EXTENSION ALGORITHMS. Essentially, in this category one attempts to take the edges extracted by one of the previously mentioned techniques and to join together the *localized* edge elements into complete *boundaries*. At the same time, attempts are made to eliminate possible false elements generated, possibly, by noise. The approach has been widely exploited, and some elaborate techniques have been suggested. Among the more interesting mathematical approaches is that of Montanari (1971), who suggested the use of dynamic programming techniques. Essential to this group of approaches is the concept of heuristic searching. Every possible contour is examined, and the best one is chosen according to some predefined criteria or cost function. The objective is to search for an optimal boundary path. While mathematically these techniques can be extremely elegant, the computational complexity is a major restriction on their wide use.

Departing from the dynamic programming approach, work has gone into heuristic searching techniques involving boundary tracking. An example of this is Liu's algorithm (Liu, 1977). In this a suitable starting point is determined, and a search is undertaken by repeatedly determining the next pixel on the boundary that is both adjacent to the current pixel and has the highest associated gradient out of all the candidates. If, at any stage, the gradient calculated is less than a certain preselected minimum, then a backtracking routine is activated. It is claimed that the algorithm gives robustness and is relatively effective in the presence of noise. Such approaches have been extended and have proved to be useful; among these is that of Chen and Siy (1987), which employs both forward and reverse contour tracing and demand-driven filtering.

Template matching is a closely related approach in which we attempt to fit a previously well-defined object (in terms of its edges) to a set of possible localized edges. This approach has been shown to work extremely well, but it fails to meet the processing-time criteria, especially when a great variety of patterns are to be matched or where one cannot detect relatively well-defined local edges. It is, naturally, a knowledge-based approach—and indeed when the template is defined in, say, a structured, symbolic format it forms the basis of many so-called knowledge-based detection algorithms. Away from the contour tracing work is the approach suggested by Rosenfeld (1977), which introduces relaxation techniques to connect the localized edge elements. The approach is iterative, in that the probability of a candidate edge element being a true edge element is reestimated at each iteration.

One of the most common approaches involves the fitting of various lines and curves to the primitive edge elements. If one knows the shape of a curve or line that one is searching for, then it becomes a relatively simple task to fit this to the observed candidate local edges. In this latter class one should include the well-known Hough transforms, which were originally used to detect lines by transforming the initial image into a feature space: peaks in this feature space correspond to strong lines in the image. The work has been extended to cover circular images and, more recently, important work has revealed that the approach can be generalized for any regular geometric feature (Ballard, 1981). Also the so-called adaptive Hough transform technique has been shown to be most useful in detecting multiple simple geometric images, as illustrated by the work of Cao et al. (1988).

THRESHOLDING. Thresholding essentially involves choosing a specific grey level for a given scene, such that all grey levels that exceed the chosen value are mapped into a single logical state (say, logic 1) and all others are mapped into the alternative state (say, logic 0). In many ways thresholding is a simple technique that *binarizes* an image and is successfully used in many practical applications. It should be noted that it has been shown that thresholding at *multiple levels* can be extremely beneficial and also that it can be regarded as a form of filtering. The work by, for example, Berger (1985) shows that when viewing a particular industrial scene—in this case a particle analyzer viewing rocks on a feed-conveyor belt—it is appropriate to divide the image into five levels of thresholding. At first sight, one can regard such approaches as grouping together bands of approximately similar grey-level values—essentially cutting down the amount of data being handled (i.e., the number of bits per pixel). As the following comments point out, though, one must be aware of exactly what the process of thresholding does to the information content of the image.

In general, thresholding methods can be divided into two broad classes. *Global thresholding* assumes that a single threshold value is adopted throughout the image. Typically one can determine the appropriate threshold value by obtaining complete histograms of the grey-level values in a picture. Experience has shown that in many cases, especially those with well-defined environmental lighting conditions, these group around two hills, and the valley point between them is an appropriate thresholding point. Such thresholding routines are available in most commercial vision software packages (e.g., the Spider Manual of the Joint Systems Development Corporation, Tokyo). Other global thresholding mechanisms, not based on histograms, have been developed, and the work by Deravi and Pal (1983), using statistical techniques, is particularly significant.

Alternatively, *variable thresholding* can be used, in which the thresholding scheme is localized and different threshold values are adopted at various points of the image. It must be pointed out, however, that any thresholding scheme could introduce *artificial edges* as a direct result of the thresholding. This is simply because one is putting a rigid break point, determined by some statistical calculation, into regions that in fact might have relatively slowly changing intensities. This is especially the case when a single global threshold value is selected.

In summary, however one thresholds, in the end, regions of the picture are grouped together into two (or more) categories, and thresholding is therefore an approach to segmentation. However, it should be emphasized again that one could well be guilty of introducing false edges in carrying out the thresholding process. It does, however, imply that one obtains closed boundaries for the objects in the images that are grouped together, and it does inherently smooth out any noise present. The nature of the noise does affect the thresholding, but that topic is not covered here.

REGION EXTRACTION. This area covers a wide range of interests but includes all those approaches in which the image is divided into regions of similar properties. It is naturally a grouping that really also includes thresholding, as these groupings are often formed on the basis of grey-scale intensity. However, this simple approach is extended in the case of images in which some *texture* is present—represented by some constant, or semiconstant, *variation* in intensity levels. In many practical situations, use is first made of edge-tracking algorithms to attempt initially to give some idea of the rough positions of edges, particularly those that enclose surfaces. Then information within these regions is observed, and areas having similar characteristics are searched for in order to determine whether the closed contour is in fact the real edge of the area being observed.

It is here that one starts to get some idea of where explicit knowledge becomes essential in the image-processing arena. Segmentation without knowledge of the characteristics being sought is virtually impossible. Indeed, no segmentation can really work without appropriate access to knowledge of the problem, and the knowledge base must include dynamic features, since many of the characteristics of real images change with environmental conditions, product variations, changing materials, and so on.

Turning to the current literature on knowledge-based segmentation, there is an extremely interesting introduction to the application of knowledge-based segmentation in the work by Lin et al. (1988). This paper also highlights the pioneering work by Tenenbaum and Barrow (1977), who used standard office scenes as models to label areas in an unknown scene, but with the assumption that they were in an office environment. The conditions used included (1) the highest region in the image is the ceiling and (2) the wall is adjacent to the floor and ceiling. These serve as constraints in the segmentation and in the subsequent labeling process. In a similar way, Ohta (1985) created a system that labels regions in outdoor scenes according to color images. In this approach an overall rough plan is generated by initial edge-detection and regional segmentation processes. Using a knowledge-based system, a symbolic description of the scenes is obtained using an image model. This model contains relations such as "the sky touches the upper edge of the picture," "a road touches the lower edge of the picture," and "trees are in the middle somewhere." The feature classifications used in this intriguing contextual system include colors, texture, and geometric properties.

Lin et al. (1988) propose a prototype rule-based system that integrates segmentation and recognition processes to analyze and classify objects in an image. They further show how this approach might be applied both to relatively well structured environments (in which they inspect automobile components) and to unstructured environments (in which they look into medical applications). Of importance is the fundamental idea, backed up by the work of other researchers, that one should not attempt to isolate the edge-detection or segmentation of components from the recognition environment. This is our experience—as discussed in Wu et al. (1988b)—in which the edge-finding algorithms and the recognition algorithms are knowledge-based from the first instant. It is, however, often time-saving to precede these by appropriately selected simple edge-detection algorithms—primarily to reduce the amount of data handling (i.e., using the low-level stages only as image compactors).

In summary, segmenting and labeling (the process of giving a symbol to one or a group of specific regions) is inherently knowledge-driven. The process is highly dependent on the detection of edges; however, the converse is equally true. There does appear to be a strong argument for undertaking, preferably in dedicated hardware, an initial stage of relatively blind edge detection, but after this there must be a unified approach, and the traditional divisions between low- and high-level processing are inappropriate.

7 KNOWLEDGE REPRESENTATION AND ACQUISITION FOR COMPUTER VISION

Essential to any knowledge-based system is the acquisition of the knowledge and the way it is internally represented. In this chapter we will not be tackling these aspects in great depth, and more-detailed information can be gathered from other parts of this book, but it is appropriate to look briefly at them in the context of vision systems, particularly where they have extensive impacts on the computational facilities required for applying the ideas to industrial systems.

Turning first to the question of knowledge representation, and using the pioneering survey by Brachman and Smith (1980), we build on definitions including these:

- *Knowledge* is a collection of descriptions, simulations, assimilation procedures, and problem-solving methods.
- A *representation* of knowledge combines data structures and interpretation procedures that, if used correctly, will lead to knowledgeable behavior.

Artificial intelligence researchers have produced many candidate data-structure classes for holding information and several procedures that enable suitable manipulation of these data structures to draw required inferences.

As has been pointed out previously in this book, knowledge-based systems require good representations of knowledge to assist us in striving toward good solutions. Unfortunately the choice of representation is not normally free but is constrained by the problem at hand. For this reason, knowledge-representation structures that can be used in certain applications are not always appropriate in, say, computer vision work. It is also obvious that we have to include various types of knowledge for image understanding. We must, for example, represent knowledge relating to object edges as well as to an object's total structure. It is also important ultimately to be able to *measure* accurately aspects of the object. We will also have to define certain performance parameters so that we have some idea of how *efficiently* our analysis is proceeding, to give a quality of measurement or recognition factor. Also, we must have knowledge about the environment—such as how fuzzy our images are likely to be—so as to adjust filtering factors and so on.

As has been reviewed in the paper by Rao and Jain (1988), at least four knowledge-representation techniques are currently in vogue: semantic networks, frames, rules, and first-order logic. One suspects that most work in the field is still relatively ad hoc and that decisions as to representation structures are made on an arbitrary basis! It is interesting to note that most application papers propose knowledge representations that have constituents of two or more of the above approaches. Maybe this is appropriate anyway. Thinking of a piece of knowledge, say, as a rule, and thinking of it solely in those terms, does seem to restrict our perception of the potential of knowledge, since it is far too easy to get distracted by the strict implications of the "if-then" construct (particularly when we are still trying to define an ill-defined problem!).

Inherently, the use of semantic networks appears to be a good starting point, as they represent structures in which knowledge is represented by links of different types between nodes. Nodes themselves usually represent objects, and the links describe the relationships that exist between them. Thus, as in the well-documented cases of inspection of printed circuit boards, one could start with the fact that the board consists of chips, resistors, capacitors, and tracks. In turn, each of these consists of subcomponents; for example, a chip consists of an object that is essentially a rectangle surrounded by 16 tiny rectangles. Each of the rectangles is in turn made up of lines. So one represents the board by a semantic network that has at the lowest levels some well-defined primitive shapes. Indeed, as we have seen before, the whole concept of primitives is extremely important to consider in the visual field and could well be the key to recognition and hence a major consideration in representation.

Turning to the widely used production-system architecture approach, we find that this knowledge-representation method has become popular in expert-system-based visual systems. This is not unexpected, as indeed it has been proposed by several authors that this is a model of the basic human reasoning process. The concept is simply that a piece of knowledge is expressed in an "*if* (conditions) *then* (actions)" form. Clearly, one can also use such structures to represent a form of semantic network.

The implementation of production-system architectures consists, essentially, of a rule-based system that contains antecedent–consequence pairs: The antecedents usually examine data, and the consequences of the rules result in data modification. Normally such production systems have three components: a database, a set of rules, and an interpreter or inference engine. The problem, of course, is to derive the rules for a particular application, and this gets us to the problem of knowledge acquisition.

It must be said at this stage that little is coming out of the research world to give us any solid guidelines for knowledge acquisition. It is important to note that in many industrial inspection systems it is possible to use some information directly from the CAD system used to produce the original parts. Indeed, one can also go as far as scanning original diagrams of mechanical components in order to acquire their characteristics. An alternative is to acquire the knowledge from a vision system that looks at an idealized picture of the objects to be inspected. Such techniques have been widely explored with some success in application areas such as printed-circuit-board inspection, but little has been reported in applications to mechanical components (possibly because it is extremely difficult to get a "very good" original image).

Naturally, any information gathered as suggested above represents only part of the story, as it ignores environmental factors, changing conditions, materials, and so on. It also provides only an ideal version of the object and ignores any optical effects.

It is important to point out that most successful applications of knowledge-based expert systems to computer vision appear to acquire data by observing the human operator at work—not surprising, since this is the stated objective of an expert system! As has been illustrated by Bartlett et al. (1988), the very first question to be asked in designing an expert system for, in this case, solder joint inspection is simple: "What visual cues are used by inspectors to classify the solder joints if checking via a camera image?" Essentially, what one is doing is to find out what the human inspector is observing, and try to match that knowledge by a set of rules. All very obvious, but in practice the task is by no means simple when it is realized that in any particular inspection task a multiplicity of indications have to be individually weighed to come up with some reasonable guess. Thus, when inspecting a particular mechanical component—say, an automobile disc brake—much time has to be spent in the actual factory looking at how current inspection is undertaken. In an actual example this required many weeks of work, as it was found that at least 200 different characteristics could exist and might be used as clues by inspectors to determine whether the surface was acceptable—and this was outside of mere mechanical measurements of flatness and so on. Slight color variations, observed at different angles of incident light, gave clues as to unacceptable heat treatment, slight mismachining, and other flaws. Likewise, very slight shadows could indicate either minute pits or slight burn marks.

In a similar way, in developing a knowledge-base to assist in the inspection of biscuits (a common task in the food industry), as discussed in Section 9, it was a question, in the first place, of asking the manufacturers what the ultimate, acceptable parameters were in terms of size, breakage, and so on. It was also essential to find out from the human inspectors (who are, anyway, reluctant to impart their know-how) what conditions they would accept in terms of overcooking, burning, and other possible problems. All this information has to be fed into the sets of rules that are created for a particular application. (Of course, the knowledge should not be in the rules, but handled as a knowledge source.)

The problem is that the whole problem is starting to look highly application-specific, and indeed the current state of the art illustrates this. One immediately jumps to the conclusion that it is appropriate to use available expert system shells to implement the higher levels of processing required for computer vision. This temptation, however, must be resisted! As has been pointed out in the past by one of the "godfathers" of expert systems, Yoh-Han Pao (1986), important as expert system shells are, they are inherently very generalized structures and tend to be relatively inefficient. (Of course, from a realistic economic point of view one can expect this when it is understood where most shells have come from. Typically, they are derived from special-purpose systems that have been produced for well-defined applications. When it was found that the investment could not be recovered in the application area for which they were designed, they were then stripped of application-specific knowledge and marketed as shells!)

We cannot leave the subject of expert systems without referring to the questions of data and real-time compatibility. In attempting to match the low-level image-processing tasks to the upper-end knowledge-based processing area, the question of data compatibility becomes a major consideration. Typically, at the lower end one is working with integers, and at the top end, with symbolic manipulation—and never the twain shall meet! This is particularly the case where one is trying to graft an expert system shell on top of a low-level processing system. It is a common experience (Wu, 1989) that the only real solution lies in developing special-purpose, "expert-system-like" structures—otherwise, extensive data manipulation routines are required, with very alarming and time-consuming overheads.

In summary, much current research is being undertaken in knowledge acquisition for subsequent scene analysis. The danger is that much of this work is built on existing tools and tool sets used in the more general knowledge-engineering world. The difficulty is that for most industrial scenes these tools are simply inappropriate. However, the methodologies that are being employed are supplying useful keys to the way ahead. The paper by Tranowski (1988), for example, provides a useful description of a knowledge-acquisition environment that has been developed to aid in the capture of expertise from experts involved in analyzing scenes from the aerial imagery world. The work is based on the use of an integrated knowledge-acquisition environment. Its goal is to integrate the various inputs, to translate that acquired knowledge into internal representations, and to provide actual execution of the knowledge, with subsequent feedback to the user. The environment used contains a collection of tools facilitating the viewing and editing of knowledge, in both textual and graphic formats, and supporting testing of the knowledge base; it also provides a degree of performance analysis. However, it does not provide any indication of how one captures the knowledge stored in the heads of the inspectors on a factory floor, and this is where the real industrial application problems lie.

The point is that it must be recognized that in any computer-based system we are developing a total system. Thus, a totally integrated approach must be taken. We have not got anywhere toward truly matching the need for a flexible, knowledge-based approach to the handling of the image recognition problems, but we do see some light ahead. This clearly indicates that the division between high- and low-level processing is an artificial barrier that—despite the obvious advantages of a layered and modular structure (in terms of validation, testability, maintainability, etc.)—unless we are very careful, can result in highly inefficient systems. Our knowledge-based systems must be created and integrated into the *whole* processing system, from edge-detection and enhancement right thorough to advanced recognition. The knowledge must be acquired and represented accordingly.

8 HARDWARE FOR KNOWLEDGE-BASED COMPUTER VISION SYSTEMS

Producing the appropriate computing structures for computer vision systems has posed many fascinating research questions for many years. Now the approach is changing once again, when one considers the use of knowledge-based systems. As was mentioned earlier, serious problems emerge when one tries to bring together traditional low-level image-processing tasks, which might well be suitable for processing on highly parallelized, specialized architectures [such as that offered by the well-known CLIP environment (Fountain et al., 1988)], together with the high-level requirements calling upon expert systems or general knowledge-based structures. The temptation is to join together some of the low-level structures with a typical high-level, AI-oriented engine, such as, say, a Lisp machine or similar environment, which has been optimized for processing, perhaps, either a rule-based or a frame-based system. The way ahead, however, is still unclear, and there is much work to be done. I feel it is useful to provide here some background to the various routes that have been taken, in order to support the tutorial nature of this chapter.

There is, naturally, a whole world of special-purpose, highly parallel processing systems such as CLIP and other structures that call upon arrays of relatively unsophisticated processor elements, typically based on SIMD (single instruction, multiple data) architectures. At the other end of the spectrum, there are those approaches that attempt to use the inherently powerful, parallel-processing features of the MIMD (multiple instruction, multiple data) class of machines. A typical example, (Wu, 1989) utilizes the transputer in the Computing Surface Environment produced by the Meiko Corporation of the United Kingdom. The importance in this form of environment is that the individual processor elements have great processing power, equivalent to a state-of-the-art 32-bit microprocessor. Combined with this are the four high-speed interprocessor communication channels, which are supported by an inherent software-programming environment that permits very efficient parallel processing. Of interest here is the experience of my research group, which has shown that in many cases the raw processing power of the transputer combined with the ease of structuring pipelined architectures results in very efficient high-speed industrial vision systems—which, incidentally, call relatively lightly on the inherently parallel nature of the processors. One of the other keys, in the experience of this group and others exploring the transputer and similar environments, is that it is extremely important to choose the software environment correctly. The overheads incurred in resorting to the use of extensive AI language tools, such as Prolog and Lisp, cannot be tolerated, and in many cases one has to structure rule-based systems using the relatively primitive software environments of C (or indeed, for the transputer, OCCAM). Clearly, in software engineering terms, this is a retrogressive step, but it reflects the mismatch between tools and application problems.

Other particularly interesting processors that are being developed include the Philips system, which is a pipelined image analysis system based on customized IC circuits (Persoon, 1988). In many ways this is yet another processor-element-based approach, but it has been designed with the task of iconic image processing very much in mind. The custom ICs developed make it possible to realize at least four basic operations in (it is claimed) a highly effective way. These operations include primitive shape recognition, mask generation, and fundamental filtering. Preliminary results discussed in Persoon (1988) reveal very interesting prospects.

In specific areas of image processing, advanced structures are emerging that will allow specialized tasks to be undertaken. As was mentioned earlier, the well-understood and highly effective Hough transform still provides much interest, not only as a tool for finding simple lines and circles but also, increasingly, for general feature extraction. It is not surprising, therefore, to find various special-purpose architectures emerging that specifically handle the relative complexities of the Hough transform. A good example of this is the work from Fujitsu (Hanahara et al., 1988).

In summary, although one certainly finds much interesting work taking place in producing special-purpose architectures, industrial observers must reflect on the cost of purchasing highly expensive, dedicated hardware and relate this back to their real needs of online processing at reasonable (or acceptable) cost. Clearly, special chips using the great advantages offered by VLSI will play major roles in the future. The problem at this stage is that we have yet to define what procedures are actually required to be processed by that hardware, and this must be a reflection of the relative youth of the technology.

9 A BRIEF CASE STUDY: CLOSING THE MANUFACTURING LOOP

As has been emphasized, one of the major problems facing the potential industrial user of computer vision is the question of acquiring knowledge about the scene. In this section we will discuss a relatively simple example of how a priori knowledge can be used to provide a compact, high-speed solution to satisfy a requirement posed in completing a classic manufacturing loop. In addressing industrial problems there have been many recorded successes, but they tend to be in well-structured environments. However, even in areas in which little success is documented, one finds that the boundaries of a significant class of industrial parts are increasingly being described by combinations of straight-line segments and circular arcs! The point is that, as mentioned earlier, these simple features are used as the basic primitives in many CAD systems. Surprise, surprise! Some of the ideas on primitives mentioned above have been picked up and used by the designers of CAD databases. Therefore, in analyzing the results of, say, a machining operation, an accurate estimation of centers and radii of circular arcs can be used as direct feedback to the CAD database. Clearly, in this case study we will not discuss any internal feedback loops—say, to the illumination system—and we will assume that relatively well-structured lighting and environmental conditions can be obtained. However, the application described here is a real one, and one of the objectives has been to achieve acceptable speeds of operation.

In studying the problem of inspecting machine-produced components, it was rapidly realized that to achieve the accuracy necessary, two problems had to be solved: the accurate location of major points of discontinuity on the object boundaries (or so-called knot-points), where different primitive segments join, and an accurate determination of the parameters relating to each primitive segment. Approaches to the first issue, that is, finding the knot-points, could include either Gaussian filtering or angle detection. It had been noted, however, that in practice neither of these methods is capable of adequately locating the required joint points, but that a combination of both algorithms could provide a powerful tool. The advantage of the Gaussian-filter approach is that it allows a scheme to be adopted that finds instances of curvature change primitives at one scale even if they cannot be found at others. The disadvantage is that the process is computationally expensive. Angle-detection schemes have the advantage that their computational load is relatively low, and they give reasonably good locations of sharp corners. The procedure proposed here (Wu et al., 1988b) starts by using an angle-detection scheme [such as that described by Freeman and Davies (1977)] to locate the points with significant changes in curvature. Subsequently, based on prior observations, we choose an appropriate threshold to extract the major corner points—which will occur as joint points between a line and a line, or between a line and an arc, or between one arc and another. Following this, we use criteria as suggested by Wu (1989) to determine if the segment between the two knot-points forms a straight line, a circular arc, or a combination (or, in fact, if this is possible in terms of the knowledge gained from the CAD system that generates the components, any other primitive planar curve).

Following this second operation, if the segment is indeed a combination, a Gaussian-filter-based method is used to locate the internal joint points. This is necessitated by the precision now required because the points were missed during the first (and less accurate) pass. This is followed by an algorithm to determine the centers of arcs and their radii. Fairly conventional routines can be used here; however, because we are concerned about the computational time, short-cuts are necessary—for example, those described in Wu et al. (1988a) that *predict* the arc's center to within coarse limits and use this in the first iteration. This has been found to result in significant improvements in run time and to give results that are very robust.

In extending the above approach in other applications, such as the inspection of multiple components, different types of practical problems emerge, and this is where explicit knowledge of environments must be considered. Two frequent problems are worth mentioning here: The objects might touch each other, or they might be located on a background that is not the ideal always assumed by the theoreticians. (In this actual case, a special conveyor had a couple of bands running longitudinally, supporting the devices being inspected.) Clearly, the case of images overlapping presents major problems in the 100% inspection normally required for quality control. One cannot, of course, make any valid assumptions about the lower object, but it would be highly desirable to analyze the upper object, or, if the edges were just touching, the complete picture; bunched-up images often occur on conveyor systems. Of importance are the industrial realities: The situation is clearly an online one, and because each frame of the picture must be analyzed within a fraction of a second, this clearly precludes sophisticated operations to separate the touching objects. Therefore in designing the extraction algorithms, any lengthy and nondeterministic operation must be avoided. It is also critical that access to, say, a conventional expert system, with its unknown real-time performance, is out of the question.

The method adopted in this case consists of a broad-brush approach, which first of all locates the major objects in the scene. It then utilizes an intelligent, knowledge-driven, edge-boundary-follower routine, which simultaneously incorporates a binarization routine; the boundary follower works directly on grey-scale levels, but the output is a binary image. If a touching point is found (i.e., the boundary follower is not sure which path to follow), then processing is moved to a knowledge-based routine that makes a decision on which way the boundary should go! Clearly, backtracking might be necessary.

One of the keys in implementing such a system [as discussed in Wu (1989)] is that the algorithms developed must be highly modular so that they can be executed in either a pipelined or a parallel fashion depending on the processing time requirements. The broadly based algorithm used to detect the presence of basic objects can farm out subsequent processing to parallel processors. Indeed, an industrially acceptable solution has been developed owing to the use of a high-speed reconfigurable parallel environment. As reported in Rodd et al. (1989), relatively sophisticated scenes with multiple images can be analyzed in less than 0.2 seconds—directly matching line speeds in this particular application environment.

10 CONCLUSIONS

In this chapter we have addressed various aspects of knowledge-based computer vision systems. It is clear that computer vision is an extremely important area of artificial intelligence, no matter how one chooses to define that term. Clearly, computer vision is itself an area of great fascination for AI researchers. This chapter has attempted to take an extremely pragmatic view of computer vision as an important candidate for the solution of many unresolved instrumentation problems encountered in the hard, industrial environment in which cost and ruggedness rule the day.

The chapter has emphasized that there are many successful applications of computer vision but that most of them call upon fixed routines, operating either in dedicated hardware or on powerful computers, or at speeds of operation that are acceptable only in offline applications. However, a wide range of problems still await solutions and are beyond the comprehension and ability of our current generation of vision equipment. These problems are not currently being solved, primarily because the processing of the complex or unstructured nature of the scenes under observation is too slow or too expensive. There is no doubt that knowledge-based systems are extremely important as a methodology for the future. The question as to how much of the existing knowledge-based technology is immediately transferable must be assessed. Hopefully, this chapter has given some indication of the problems that lie ahead, paramount among which must be the tackling of the multifaceted problem of knowledge acquisition and representation.

ACKNOWLEDGMENTS

I am sincerely grateful for the assistance received in preparing this chapter from my colleagues Dr. Farzin Deravi, Qing-Ming Wu, James Powrie, and Cao Xing of the University of Wales and Professor Bao-Zong Yuan of the Institute of Information Science, Northern Territory University, Beijing, People's Republic of China.

REFERENCES

Asada, H., and Brady, M. (1986). The Curvature Primal Sketch. *IEEE Trans. PAMI* **8**(1):2–14.
Ballard, D.H. (1981). Generalising the Hough Transform to Detect Arbitrary Shapes. *Pattern Recog.* **13**:111–122.

Bartlet, S.L., Besl, P.J., Cole, C.L., Jain R., Mukherjee, D., and Skifstad, K.D. (1988). Automatic Solder Joint Inspection. *IEEE Trans. PAMI* **10**(1):31–34.

Berger, G.F.N. (1985). Software for Particle Size Analyser Based on Image Analysis Techniques. Dissertation, University of the Witwatersrand, Johannesburg, Republic of South Africa.

Brachman, R.J., and Smith, B.C. (Eds.) (1980). Special Issue on Knowledge Representation, *SIGART Newsletter,* February.

Canny, J.F. (1986). A Computational Approach to Edge Detection. *IEEE Trans. PAMI* **8**(6):679–698.

Cao, X., Rodd, M.G., Deravi, F., and Wu, Q.M. (1988). Detection of Multiple Circles Based on Adaptive Hough Transforms. *Int. J. Eng. Appl AI* **1**(2):97–101.

Chen, B.D., and Siy, P. (1987). Forward/Backward Contour Tracing with Feedback. *IEEE Trans. PAMI* **9**(3):438–445.

Deravi, F., and Pal, S.K. (1983). Grey Level Thresholding Using Second-Order Statistics. *Pattern Recog. Lett.* **1**:417–422.

Fischler, M.A., and Bolles, R.C. (1986). Perceptual Organisation and Curve Partitioning. *IEEE Trans. PAMI* **8**(1):100–104.

Fountain, T.J., Matthews, K.N., and Duff, M.J.B. (1988). The CLIP7A Image Processor. *IEEE Trans. PAMI* **10**(3):310–319.

Freeman, H., and Davies, L.S. (1977). A Corner Finding Algorithm for Chain-Coded Curves. *IEEE Trans Comput.* **26**:297–303.

Hanahara, K., Maruyama, T., and Uchiyama, T. (1988). A Real-Time Processor for the Hough Transform. *IEEE Trans. PAMI* **10**(1):121–125.

Haralick, R.M. (1986). Digital Step Edges and Zero Crossings of Second Directional Derivatives. *IEEE Trans PAMI* **6**(1):58–68.

Horn, B.K.P. (1986). *Robot Vision.* McGraw-Hill, New York.

Lin, W.-C., Weng, Y.-T., and Chen, C.-T. (1988). Expert Vision Systems Integrating Image Segmentation and Recognition Processes. *Int. J. Eng. Appl. AI* **1**(4):230–247.

Liu, H.K. (1977). Two and Three Dimensional Boundary Detection. *Comput. Graphics Image Process.* **6**:123–134.

Marr, D.C., and Hildreth, E.C. (1980). Theory of Edge Detections. *Proc. R. Soc. London* **207**:187–217.

Mokhtarian, F., and Mackworth, A. (1986). Scale-Based Description and Recognition of Planar Curves and Two-Dimensional Shapes. *IEEE Trans. PAMI* **8**(1):34–43.

Montanari, U. (1971). On the Optical Detection of Curves in Noisy Pictures. *Commun. ACM* **14**:335–345.

Nalwa, V.S., and Binford, T.O. (1986). On Detecting Edges. *IEEE Trans. PAMI* **8**(6):699–708.

Nazif, A.M., and Levine, M.D. (1984). Low-Level Image Segmentation: an Expert System. *IEEE Trans. PAMI* **5**:555–577.

Niemann, H., Bunke, H., Hofmann, I., Sagerar, G., Wolf, F., and Feistel, H. (1985). A Knowledge-Based System for Analysis of Gated Blood Pool Studies. *IEEE Trans. PAMI* **7**(3):246–259.

Ohta, Y. (1985). *Knowledge-Based Interpretation of Outdoor Natural Colour Scene.* Pitman Advanced Publishing Inc., New York.

Pao, Y.-H. (1986). Summary of Panel Discussions. *Proc. IFAC Symp. SOCOCO,* Graz. Austria, Pergamon Press, U.K.

Persoon, E. (1988). A Pipelined Image Analysis System Using Custom Integrated Circuits. *IEEE Trans. PAMI* **10**(1):110–116.

Powrie, J. (1989). A Review of Edge Detection Algorithms. Internal Report, University of Wales, Swansea, Image Processing Group.

Rao, A.R., and Jain, R. (1988). Knowledge Representation and Control in Computer Vision Systems. *IEEE Expert* **3**(1):64–79.

Rodd, M.G., and Deravi, F. (1987). Image Processing as a Practical Measurement Tool. *Proc. Int. Conf. Test & Transducers*, London, **2** Trident International, U.K.:85–96.

Rodd, M.G., and Wu, Q.M. (1989). Intelligent Machine Vision System for Inspection and Control. *Proc. IEEE Conf. on Image Processing*, Singapore.

Rosenfeld, A. (1977). Iterative Methods in Image Analysis. *Proc. IEEE Conf. on Pattern Recognition in Image Processing*, New York, pp. 14–20.
Sanz, J.L.C. (1988). Introduction to Special PAMI Issue on Industrial Machine Vision and Computer Vision Technology. *IEEE Trans PAMI* **10**(1):1–3.
Tenenbaum, J.M., and Barrow, H.G. (1977). Experiments in Interpretation Guided Segmentation. *AI* **8**:241.
Torre, V., and Poggio, T.A. (1986). On Edge Detection. *IEEE Trans. PAMI* **8**(2):147–163.
Tranowski, D. (1988). A Knowledge Acquisition Environment for Scene Analysis. *Int. J. Man-Mach. Stud.* **29**(2):197–214.
Witkin, A.P. (1983). Scale-Space Filtering. *Proc. 7th Int. Joint Conf. Artificial Intelligence*, Kaufmann, Palo Alto: p. 1019.
Wu, Q.-M. (1989). Fast Intelligent Boundary Extraction of Touching Objects. Internal Report, University of Wales, Swansea, Image Processing Group.
Wu, Q.-M., Rodd, M.G., and Deravi, F. (1988a). A New Technique for High-Speed On-Line Object Recognition. *Proc. IFAC Symp. SOCOCO*, Johannesburg, Republic of South Africa, Pergamon Press, U.K.
Wu, Q.-M., Rodd, M.G., and Cao, X. (1988b). Improved Algorithms for Boundary Segmentation and Curve-Fitting, and their Parallel Implementation on a Transputer Network. *Proc. COMPAR '88*, Manchester, IEE, London, U.K.

CHAPTER 9

LINGUISTIC KNOWLEDGE AND AUTOMATIC SPEECH RECOGNITION

STEVEN L. LYTINEN

1 INTRODUCTION

This chapter will review some of the recent efforts to develop automatic speech recognition (ASR) systems. The goal of an ASR system is to automatically convert a speech waveform into some sort of symbolic description of its content. In particular, I will focus on the use of AI techniques in these systems. These techniques address the need to apply many different kinds of knowledge during the analysis process, including *phonemic knowledge,* or knowledge about the building blocks of spoken words and how they interact with each other; *syntax,* the structure of a language; *semantics,* the meaning of words; and *pragmatics,* how language is used.

The use of linguistic knowledge in speech recognition systems poses many interesting challenges, not all of which have been solved. Some of the issues that arise in the application of this knowledge are the following:

1. How does linguistic knowledge interact with "lower-level" knowledge that is used for subtasks such as feature extraction and phoneme identification?
2. How is this linguistic knowledge represented?
3. What additional power is necessary to process at the phoneme level rather than at the lexical level?

Intuitively, it seems natural to try to utilize linguistic knowledge in speech recognition. Humans seem to use a great deal of their knowledge about language, and even about the world in general, to help them understand speech. There is much psycholinguistic evidence that this knowledge is essential in the understanding process (for example, see White, 1976). However, the focus of this chapter on linguistic approaches to ASR does not reflect the emphasis of the field in general. Many of the most successful efforts in ASR have been based purely on nonlinguistic techniques, involving low-level feature extraction, template matching, pattern recognition, and other statistical techniques. Much of the current research in ASR continues to develop these techniques. In addition, there has been a recent surge in the use of connectionist systems. This chapter will not discuss these nonlinguistic techniques; for surveys, see Jelinek (1976), Allerhand (1987), Lea (1980), Allen (1985b), and Lippmann (1989). I will also not attempt to argue for one approach over the other. However, given the inability of any speech recognition system to equal the performance of humans, and given the evidence that humans use knowledge a great deal to guide speech understanding, the linguistic approach is an interesting one, with the potential for improvements in performance.

The goal of developing an automatic speech recognition system has been pursued by researchers for more than 30 years, beginning in the early 1950s. Often, researchers have felt that they were on the verge of developing the technology for commercially viable systems, but, as has been the case in many other AI applications, that goal has not been achieved thus far.

Early ASR work included that of Davis et al. (1952), Dudley and Balashek (1958), Forgie and Forgie (1959), and Denes and Mathews (1960). Even at the beginning, the need to use linguistic knowledge was recognized (e.g., Fry and Denes, 1953; Peterson, 1961). As the notion of *generative grammar* was developed in linguistics (Chomsky, 1957), ASR researchers realized that grammatical analysis was potentially very useful for speech recognition systems. Lindgren (1965) advocated the use of grammars, as well as other constraints on "meaningful" word sequences, to limit the possible analysis of a speech signal.

In the 1970s, the Advanced Research Projects Agency (ARPA) undertook a major funding effort in speech recognition. Many systems were developed during this period, including HEARSAY-II (Erman et al., 1980), HARPY (Lowerre and Reddy, 1980), and HWIM (the Hear What I Mean project) (Woods et al, 1976). These projects will be discussed in more detail later in this chapter. Results of the ARPA project were mixed; the HARPY system, which obtained the best performance results, achieved 95% accuracy for multiple speakers on a small corpus of about 200 sentences. After the conclusion of the ARPA funding effort, resources available for speech recognition research were severely curtailed, and many of these efforts were terminated.

Currently, research in ASR in North America is continuing at many industrial sites, including IBM (Jelinek, 1985; Bahl et al., 1983) and Bell Labs (Levinson and Shipley, 1980), as well as academic sites, including MIT (Allen,

1985a), Carnegie-Mellon University (Lee, 1988; Young et al, 1989), and McGill University (Bengio et al., 1989; De Mori, 1983). Much of the current effort is concentrated on so-called pattern-matching techniques including template matching (e.g., Rabiner and Levinson, 1981) and hidden Markov models (e.g., Lee, 1988). However, some of these projects continue to investigate the use of higher-level linguistic knowledge (e.g., Young et al., 1989) and will be discussed in more detail in this chapter.

The chapter is organized as follows: First, we discuss the general way in which linguistic knowledge might be organized in a speech recognition system. Usually the general organization involves some sort of hierarchy of levels, with each level corresponding to a level of abstraction at which knowledge about speech can be expressed. We will also discuss some evidence that indicates that humans use linguistic knowledge to help understand speech. Next, we survey some of the approaches that have been used in recent systems for introducing linguistic knowledge into automatic speech recognition. Finally, we will discuss the issue of control: How can a system be designed that efficiently applies different levels of knowledge? As more and more knowledge is introduced into the system, the computational complexity generally increases greatly, as does the need to control the way in which knowledge is applied.

2 THE HIERARCHICAL NATURE OF SPEECH KNOWLEDGE

Spoken human language has properties that can be described at many different levels. At very low levels, we can characterize the waveforms that human vocal cords produce, as well as the variations in waveforms that can be caused by various movements of the throat and mouth. Next, we can describe a set of features of the waveform that carry the most information as to the words contained in the signal. Higher up, we can characterize the properties of particular phonemes in terms of these features, as well as the contextual effects of the surrounding waveform on phonemes. We can describe legal sequences of phonemes—those that are allowed in a particular natural language. Continuing, we can provide a dictionary of what sequences of phonemes map into what lexical items in the language. We can characterize legal syntactic constructions that constrain the sequences of lexical items allowed in the language. At still higher levels we can provide semantic information about how the meanings of lexical items can be combined. Finally, we can characterize knowledge about the world that language describes, as well as rules about discourse and other pragmatic constraints.

It is natural to think of these levels of description as being ordered. This is because a description at one level uses as its vocabulary the "output" of one or more levels below it. For example, the syntactic level characterizes the order of lexical items that can appear in a sentence; thus, the lexical level in some sense precedes the syntactic level.

This ordered set of descriptions has implications for speech recognition. First, each level provides constraints as to what a speech waveform is likely to look like. Thus, if we want to find the information in a speech input, the amount of processing we might need to do could be very large, because we need to produce a description of the waveform at each level in order to make sure that each level's constraints are applied in processing.

Further complicating the matter is the fact that typically the mapping from one level to the next is one-to-many, as displayed in Fig. 9-1. Speech input is very imprecise, due to variabilities across speakers, background noise, and even variations in speech produced by a single speaker. Thus, there are many ambiguities in the signal at each level of description. Often, it is not possible to resolve an ambiguity until we apply constraints from one or many levels further up the hierarchy. Thus, the search process can be very lengthy, with many interpretations pursued only to be invalidated several levels further along in the processing.

Different speech recognition systems have different goals as to their eventual output description. Some possibilities are a transcription of the sequence of phonemes in the waveform, a written transcript of the speech input, a representation of the meaning of the input, or even a translation of the input into another language. At first glance, one might think that the need to process at higher levels would vary depending on the level of the system's output. For example, unless the desired output is a representation of the meaning of the input, one might expect that semantic analysis would be unnecessary. However, since each level of description further constrains the waveform, deter-

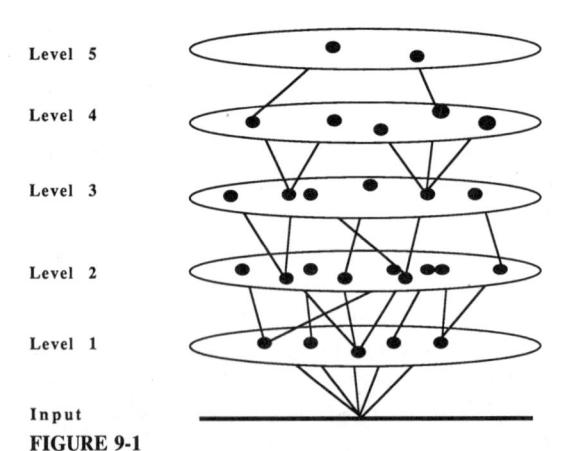

FIGURE 9-1
Multilevel processing. The initial input may cause several hypotheses to be asserted at the lowest level (level 1) of processing. Each of these hypotheses may in turn generate several possible hypotheses at the next highest level. At each level, some hypotheses may not map to the next highest level (represented by points with no line to the next level). Eventually, many hypotheses will be ruled out, leaving a few hypotheses at the highest level, representing those interpretations that are consistent with the constraints from all levels of knowledge.

mining the description of the waveform at a lower level may very well depend on processing at a higher one. This is in fact quite often the case. It is well known from natural language processing that many ambiguities in syntactic structure cannot be resolved without semantic or pragmatic processing [see, for example, Lytinen (1986)]. A common occurrence of this is prepositional phrase attachment, such as

>John ate the cake with a spoon.
>John ate the cake with chocolate frosting

Using syntactic information alone, it cannot be determined whether the prepositional phrase at the end of the sentence modifies "ate" or "cake." However, semantics can tell us which is correct, because of the fact that a spoon is an eating utensil, while chocolate frosting is an edible item that often appears on the top of cake.

The interaction of levels of linguistic information is one of the motivations for using higher-level knowledge in ASR. There is no reason to believe that this sort of interaction does not also cross the boundary between linguistic levels of analysis and lower-level waveform analyses. Perhaps the integration of these levels can improve the performance of ASR systems.

There is a great deal of evidence that lower-level speech processing in humans is affected by higher-level linguistic knowledge. For example, the "click" experiments of Fodor and his colleagues demonstrated effects of syntactic structure on auditory processing. Subjects listened to sentences in which a clicking noise was embedded and then were asked to identify where in the sentence the click occurred. They tended to place the click at boundaries of clauses, even when it occurred in the middle of a clause (Fodor and Bever, 1965). In another experiment, speech production errors such as spoonerisms were studied (Garrett and Shattuck, 1974). It was found that these errors almost always occurred exclusively within a single clause. Rarely did the errors cross clause boundaries. Again, this indicates the effect of higher-level knowledge on lower levels of processing (at least, in production).

Several "shadowing" experiments by Marslen-Wilson demonstrated that even semantic information comes into play very quickly in human speech understanding. In these experiments, subjects were asked to repeat spoken sentences played to them after as short a delay as possible. Despite the fact that some subjects were able to repeat the input with delays as short as one syllable, errors made by subjects were almost all syntactically and semantically "congruent," meaning that they were compatible with the syntax and semantics of the context (Marslen-Wilson, 1975). Given the extremely short delay between input and output, this would indicate that syntactic and semantic processing were occurring in tandem with lower-level processing of the speech input.

Several other experiments in which speech sounds were selectively masked with noise show that listeners use higher-level knowledge, including semantics and even pragmatics, to understand corrupted speech [see White (1976) for a survey].

At least two key issues arise in the use of hierarchical systems in ASR. First, what is the way in which knowledge is represented at each of these levels? Is the knowledge representation uniform, and if not, how do different levels communicate with each other? Second, how does control pass between levels? Is the process strictly "bottom-up," with all computation at lower levels preceding computation at higher levels, or is processing intermixed? These are crucial decisions in the design of a multilevel system. Much of the rest of this chapter will deal with these two issues. First, we will discuss the use of *grammars* to represent linguistic knowledge. Often, grammars are used to encode knowledge of many or all "linguistic" levels in ASR systems; that is, levels at which linguistic knowledge is encoded and used for computation. A means of communication between lower levels of processing and the levels of grammatical analysis then must be devised. We will discuss some approaches to this communication problem.

Second, we will discuss the issue of control. We will describe several different systems and their approaches to determining the order in which processing should occur. In particular, we will discuss the HEARSAY-II system, which used a blackboard architecture to enable explicit control knowledge to be encoded in the system, and HWIM, which used a dynamic programming approach.

3 GRAMMARS AND SPEECH RECOGNITION

3.1 Introduction

Many attempts to bring higher-level analysis to bear on ASR have involved the use of formal grammars. Briefly, a formal grammar is defined as a 4-tuple, $G(V_n, V_t, P, S)$, where V_n is a set of nonterminal symbols, V_t is a set of terminal symbols, P is a set of productions, or rewrite rules, and S is the grammar's start symbol.

A grammar generates a language L, made up of sequences of symbols in V_t. The grammar's productions, P, are a set of rules of the form

$$A \rightarrow B$$

where A and B are any sequence of symbols from $V_n \cup V_t$ and A must contain at least one symbol from V_n.

A string V, consisting of a sequence of symbols from V_t is in the language $L(G)$ defined by the grammar G if the grammar's start symbol S can be rewritten by applying a sequence of productions from P, resulting in V. Productions rewrite a string in the following way: If a string V_i consisting of symbols from $V_n \cup V_t$ contains a sequence of symbols that matches the left-hand side A of a production, then that sequence is replaced by the sequence B (the right-hand side of the production).

The *derivation* of a string V is the set of productions that must be applied to S in order to generate V. A *parser* is a program that determines if a string V is a member of L, and if so seeks to discover the derivation(s) of V.

An example will make this notion clearer. Consider the following grammar G1:

$$V_n = A, B$$
$$V_t = a, b$$
$$P = \{S \to AB$$
$$A \to a$$
$$A \to aA$$
$$B \to b$$
$$B \to bB\}$$
$$S = S$$

The language generated by G1 consists of all strings $a^n b^m$; $n, m \geq 1$. Any string of this form can be obtained by applying a sequence of the products P of this language to the start symbol S. For example, the string *aaab* can be obtained by applying rules in the following order:

String	Rule	Resulting String
S	S → AB	AB
AB	A → aA	aAB
aAB	B → b	aAb
aAb	A → aA	aaAb
aaAb	A → a	aaab

G1 is an example of a special type of grammar, called a *context-free grammar* (CFG). A CFG contains only productions whose left-hand sides consist of one symbol from V_n.

Context-free grammars are often used to describe natural languages, not necessarily because they are powerful enough to describe them,[1] but because of their computational characteristics. A string V consisting of n symbols from V_t can be parsed in the worst case in a time proportional to n^3. This is relatively efficient compared with the computational complexity of many other classes of grammars.

---

[1] There are many languages that CFGs cannot generate, such as the language consisting of all strings $a^n b^n a^n$.

3.2 Grammars and Speech Recognition

In the application of grammars to natural language processing, terminal symbols are usually associated with lexical items in the language. In ASR, the grammar is often extended to a lower level, with terminals corresponding to phonemes. There are (at least) two complicating factors in this extension.

First, speech systems cannot identify phonemes with 100% reliability. This means that the input to the parser will consist of a sequence of *sets* of elements from V_t, with each set representing the possible phonemes appearing at a particular position in the input.[2] The parser's job, then, is not only to find a structural description of the input, but also to choose which phonemes fit into that description. Since most techniques for extracting phonemes from the speech input also assign probabilities to each possible phoneme, the parser should take into account the likelihood that each phoneme actually appeared in the input in its decisions as to which phonemes should be included in the final parse. To do this, many systems use some sort of "probabilistic parsing" approach to incorporate uncertainty into the parsing process. Given probability values assigned to each possible phoneme, the parsing process finds the most likely parse.

Second, realizations of phonemes (called *allophones*) vary depending on their context. Because of these coarticulation effects, it does not seem possible to describe a natural language at the phonetic level with a CFG. There have been several attempts to deal with this problem by strengthening the power or CFGs in various ways to allow them to capture this contextual influence.

3.2.1 PROBABILISTIC PARSING. There are many possible models that we could use to calculate the "most probable" parse of a string. Most of these models assume that the likelihood of a phoneme appearing in a particular region of the speech signal is independent of its context; that is, it does not depend on the surrounding phonemes. This is not necessarily a valid assumption (see Section 3.2.2); however, for the sake of computational tractability, it is an important assumption to make.

One approach is to assign as "cost" to believing the existence of each phoneme in the speech signal. This cost is inversely proportional to the probability that the phoneme will appear in the input. Let us assume that the input to the parsing module is of the following form:

$$V_1 V_2 V_3 \cdots V_n; \text{ where } V_i = \{v_{i1}, v_{i2}, \ldots, v_{ij}\}; v \in V_t$$

Associated with v_{ij} is a cost $C_{ij} > 0$. This cost is inversely proportional to $\Pr[v_{ij} | t_{i-1}, t_i]$; that is, the probability that v_{ij} is the elements of V_t (i.e., the

---

[2] Actually, the input is still more complicated, because alternative words in the input may not have the same boundaries in the speech signal. For the purposes of this chapter, we will ignore this problem.

phoneme) that appears in the input signal between time t_{i-1} and t_i. We can characterize the "best" parse of V as $\hat{V}$ such that

$$C_{\hat{V}} = \min \sum C[v_i t_{i-1}, t_i]$$

It turns out that finding the best parse according to this criterion does not add to the computational complexity of the parsing algorithm [see Levinson (1985) for details].

Another approach is to use the notion of fuzzy subsets (Zadeh, 1975) to characterize the set of possible realizations for a given phoneme. In this approach, as described in Allerhand (1987), the number associated with each v_{ij} as defined above is the degree of belief that the signal from time t_{i-1} to t_i is a member of the fuzzy set v_{ij}. The degree of belief in a string V, conditioned on a sequence of observations O, is the logical intersection of the degree of belief in each terminal v_i; given observation O_i. Since the belief functions are defined as fuzzy sets, this means that

$$B_V = \min B_{v_i \mid O_i}$$

If each time sequence (t_{i-1}, t_i) can be interpreted in several different ways, then the "best" parse $\hat{V}$ is defined such that

$$B_{\hat{V}} = \max \min B_{v_{ij} \mid O_i}$$

Again, this approach is designed not to affect the complexity of context-free parsing. Dynamic programming can prune a great many possible parses, because a potential parse fails as soon as any component membership belief falls below the current maximum belief of derivations considered so far.

3.2.2 EXTENSIONS TO CONTEXT-FREE GRAMMAR.

There are several reasons to adopt a grammar formalism more powerful than a CFG. First, not even taking into account the added problems of processing spoken input, it is not at all clear that written natural languages can be specified by CFG (see Chomsky, 1965). As a result, in natural language processing research, many attempts have been made to use more powerful formalisms, such as augmented transition networks (Woods, 1970) and unification grammars (Shieber, 1986), to add to the expressiveness of the grammar.

Second, in ASR, it is impossible to describe coarticulation effects between allophones in CFGs. There have been several attempts to deal with this problem, by strengthening the expressiveness of CFGs in various ways to allow them to describe limited kinds of contextual influences.

Histories and expectations Allerhand (1987) describes a modification of the context-free formalism in which an important class of contextual dependencies can be expressed but that does not affect the efficiency of the parsing algorithm. In his approach, the grammar contains productions of the form

$$[A_1]A[A_2] \to \alpha$$

where $A \in V_n$, $A_1, A_2 \in V_n \cup V_t$. A_1 is a symbol that must appear in the *history* of A, and A_2 must appear in the *expectation* of A. The history and expectation of a nonterminal symbol are defined for top-down, left-to-right parsing algorithms, in terms of derivations that can "lead to" and "result from" that symbol, in some sense. Precisely, the history $H(A)$ of A is defined in terms of the longest derivation sequence that leads to the nonterminal symbol directly to the left of A. Let us assume that in top-down, left-to-right parsing, at some point in the derivation of a sentence the string $x_i A_i \beta_i$, where $x_i \in V_t^*$, $\beta_i \in (V_n \cup V_t)^*$, occurs. That is, at some point in the application of productions, the start symbol S has been rewritten to $x_i A_i \beta_i$, and x_i has been matched against the first n symbols in the input, where $|x_i| = n$. Then $H(A)$ is defined in terms of the longest derivation sequence whose rightmost symbol is the same as the rightmost symbol of x_i, denoted by $x_i^{[R]}$; that is,

$$H(A) = \gamma_1^{[R]}, \ldots, \gamma_m^{[R]}$$

where γ_i are defined in terms of the longest derivation sequence

$$\gamma_1 \to \gamma_2 \to \cdots \to \gamma_n; \gamma_n \in V_t^*$$

for which $\gamma_n^{[R]} = x_i^{[R]}$.

Similarly, the expectation $E(A)$ of A is defined as the set

$$E(A_i) = \beta_1^{[L]}, \gamma_1^{[L]}, \ldots, \gamma_m^{[L]}$$

where each γ_i is defined in terms of the derivation sequence

$$\beta \to \gamma_1 \to \gamma_2 \to \cdots \to \gamma_n; \gamma_n \in V_t^*$$

Again, this modification to CFGs does not affect the efficiency of the parsing algorithm [see Allerhand (1987) for details].

It is interesting to note that in encoding the interactions between phonemes using a context-sensitive extension such as the one described above, it is no longer possible in the grammar to specify higher-level characteristics of the language. The grammar becomes a grammar of what phonemes can possibly follow other phonemes. It is not possible to overlay syntactic information on top of this—that is, to overlay information about what words follow other words. A separate level of analysis is needed for this information. How to encode phonemic constraints into the *same* grammar as syntactic information still remains an open question.

Augmented transition networks Augmented transition networks (ATNs) are another extension of context-free grammars that allow the encoding of certain kinds of dependencies between constituents. More precisely, ATNs are an extension of recursive transition networks (RTNs), a formalism equivalent in expressive power to CFGs.

In an RTN, productions of a context-free grammar are encoded as finite-state graphs. Each transition in the graph corresponds to one of the symbols of the right-hand side of a production. A simple example of a finite-state graph for the rule S → NP VP can be found in Fig. 9-2.

In parsing, a transition can be traversed if a constituent is found in the appropriate place in the input that can be labeled with that symbol. If the label of a transition is a nonterminal, then the finite-state graph for that label is used for its subconstituents. The parse succeeds if the end of the sentence is reached when the parser is in an accept state.

If the grammar contains two or more productions whose left-hand sides are the same, they are merged into a single finite-state graph, with multiple transitions between some of the states. For example, Fig. 9-3 shows a graph for verb phrases constructed from the context-free rules shown. The grammar rules allow for either transitive verbs (those with a direct object) or a form of "to be." Since any type of verb phrase can have multiple prepositional phrases (PP) at the end, different paths converge to state 3, so they may all traverse the PP transition any number of times. State 2 must also have a transition labeled PP, so that verb phrases with no direct object may also have prepositional phrases.

An ATN extends the notion of an RTN by allowing each network to have a set of *registers*, in which arbitrary values can be stored. Registers are like local variables; whenever the parser begins to traverse a new network, a new set of empty registers is created. They can be set whenever a transition is made; each transition has associated with it an *action* that can set the value of one or more of the registers. In addition, transitions may also have *tests*, which are allowed to check values of registers. If the test of a transition fails, then that transition cannot be taken. Finally, each network has a *return value* associated with it, which is the value passed up to the next higher network in the parser when a subconstituent has been completed.

Typically, the values stored in registers are trees, which represent the presence or absence of certain properties of the constituent being parsed by a particular network. For example, the NP network might build a structure that contains information as to whether or not the NP contained an article, what noun appeared, and the number/person of the noun, such as the following structure for "the dogs":

```
(NP ART the
ROOT dog
NUMBER {3O})
```

Here, 3p stands for third person plural. This information can then be used in the S transition network, where a test on the VP arc would check to see that the NUMBER property of the NP (stored in one register) is identical to this property of the VP (stored in another).

The Hear What I Mean (HWIM) system (Woods et al., 1976) used a "pragmatic" augmented transition network grammar to encode syntactic, se-

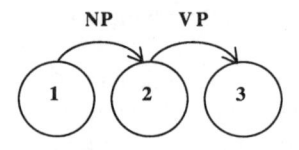

FIGURE 9-2
Accept: State 3   Finite-state graph for the production S → NP VP.

mantic, and pragmatic information. The approach was similar to the notion of a *semantic grammar*. That is, instead of the usual syntactic categories such as NP, VP, and PP, constituents in this system were semantic categories from HWIM's domain, travel budget management. Thus, categories such as "meeting," "trip," and "budget item" appeared in the system's ATN grammar. One reason for doing this was to increase the predictive power of the grammar, because the semantic grammar severely limited the possibilities of what could occur next in a sentence compared to a more typical syntactic grammar. The grammar's predictive power was useful in the interactions between the linguistic component and the system's lexical retrieval component.

Semantic grammars have been used by many other ASR systems to incorporate semantics and pragmatics into processing (e.g., Borghesi and Favareto, 1982; Kimball et al., 1986; Levinson and Shipley, 1980). An interesting variant of this approach is used in the MINDS system (Young et al., 1989). The philosophy behind MINDS is to use as much knowledge as possible to *predict* subsequent unprocessed input, so as to constrain the search at lower levels as much as possible. This is accomplished through constructing an *active lexicon* at each stage of processing the input, based on predictions from already processed portions. The active lexicon reflects the predictions that are made by combining syntactic, semantic, and pragmatic knowledge about the already processed portion of the input.

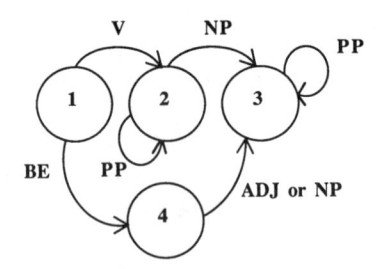

Accept: States 2 & 3

VP -> VP PP
VP -> V NP
VP -> V
VP -> BE NP
VP -> BE ADJ

FIGURE 9-3
Finite-state graph for VP productions.

MINDS uses a semantic grammar to construct its active lexicon, similar to HWIM. However, unlike HWIM, the semantic grammar is dynamically constructed from a syntactic grammar and knowledge from semantics and pragmatics. Semantic/pragmatic knowledge is overlaid onto the syntactic grammar, greatly restricting the choice of possible words that could follow. After the semantic grammar is constructed, it is applied to the lower levels of processing, which look at the input signal to try to confirm any of the predictions made by the semantic grammar.

The MINDS system achieved 96.5% accuracy on input of 200 sentences in a naval resource management domain from 10 different speakers, after being trained on a set of 20 sentences from each of these speakers. The system performs in real time, providing evidence that its use of semantics and pragmatics severely limits the possible interpretations that must be considered by lower levels of processing.

Unification grammar Another approach has been to use *unification grammar* to encode context-dependent effects. Unification grammars enable the grammar writer to express the same sorts of dependencies between constituents as ATNs, but in a more systematic way.

The data structure produced by a unification-based parser is a directed acyclic graph (DAG) consisting of labeled nodes and arcs. Linguistic knowledge is expressed using a set of equations, each of which constrains the DAG in some way. Constraints limit, for a class of nodes (i.e., any node with a particular label), the information that can be found at the end of a *path* (i.e., a sequence of arcs with particular labels). Each equation can constrain a path in one of two ways: Either it specifies the label that must be found on the node at the end of that path, or it specifies that two paths must lead to the identical node. Identity here is defined by the *unification* operation; if two paths must lead to the identical node, then the nodes at the ends of the two paths must unify.

We will illustrate by presenting a set of equations that force subject–verb agreement in very simple English sentences. First, we need equations that tell us the general makeup of a sentence and define its subject. This information comes in the form of a set of constraints (equations) that apply to all S nodes:

```
S:
(1) = NP
(2) = VP
(1 agreement) = (2 agreement)
```

This encodes the information that any node labeled S that it builds must have an arc labeled 1 that leads to a node labeled NP and an arc labeled 2 that leads to a node labeled VP. The labels 1 and 2 are arbitrary symbols that allow us to uniquely refer to the nodes at the ends of these arcs. They are used in the third equation to express that the agreement arcs from the NP and VP nodes must lead to identical nodes.

The actual values (or nodes) that are placed in the agreement properties of the NP and VP nodes are "passed up" from subconstituents of the NP and VP. To accomplish this, we need the following equations about noun phrases, verb phrases, nouns, and verbs:

```
NP:                                    V:
(1) = N                                (1) = sleeps
(agreement) = (1 agreement)            (agreement) = (1 agreement)

VP:                                    V:
(1) = V                                (1) = sleep
(agreement) = (1 agreement)            (agreement) = (1 agreement)

N:
(1) = John
(agreement) = (1 agreement)
```

In this simple grammar, an NP consists simply of an N, and the agreement property of the NP is the same as the agreement property of the N. We have encoded knowledge about one noun, namely, "John." The N node's agreement property is similarly passed up from the agreement property of "John." Similarly, VP's agreement property comes from the verb. We have included two verbs in our grammar, "sleeps" and "sleep." The two sets of equations about V nodes should be taken as a disjunction: All V nodes that are built must satisfy either one or the other set of equations.

Actual values of the agreement properties are specified in the "lexicon," which is the lowest level of equations:

```
John:                                  sleep:
(agreement number) = SINGULAR          (agreement number) = SINGULAR
(agreement person) = 3RD               (agreement person) = 1ST

sleeps;
(agreement number) = SINGULAR
(agreement person) = 3RD
```

We have defined the values of the agreement property as themselves being complex entities with number and person properties. Because both number and person agree for the words "John" and "sleeps," the above grammar would accept "John sleeps." However, "John sleep" would be rejected, because the (agreement person) paths from the nodes labeled John and sleep would not unify.

Another advantage of unification grammars is that simple semantic constraints can be expressed in the same way, bringing semantic knowledge into the ASR process. Lexical entries provide much of the knowledge, such as this entry for the word "eats":

```
eats:
    (head agreement number) = SING          (1)
    (head agreement person) = 3RD           (2)
    (head rep) = INGEST                     (3)
    (head rep through) = BODYPART           (4)
    (head rep through type) = MOUTH         (5)
    (head subj rep) = (head rep actor)      (6)
    (head dobject rep) = (head rep object)  (7)
```

According to this definition, "eats" requires a rep arc (denoting the semantic representation), which points to a complex structure representing the fact that it means ingest an object through the mouth (equations 3–5). Equations 6 and 7 specify mappings from syntactic to semantic dependencies. These are used in conjunction with equations about "world knowledge" to impose restrictions on the semantic properties of the subject of "eats." The relevant world knowledge is the following:

```
INGEST:
    (actor) = ANIMATE
    (object) = FOOD
    (through) = BODYPART
```

This is an encoding of the sort of case information that many people have proposed, such as Schank's conceptual dependency theory (Schank, 1975) or Fillmore's case grammar (Fillmore, 1968). Because of the mapping provided by "eats" between its subject and the actor of the INGEST, the restriction that this constituent's representation must be ANIMATE is propagated up to the NP that fills the subj role in the following, more complete version of the S rule:

```
S:
    (1) = NP
    (2) = VP
    (head) = (2 head)
    (head subject) = (1 head)
    (head agreement) = (head subject agreement)
```

For example, the representation of the word "John" can be linked to the INGEST as its actor if, using an is-a hierarchy, HUMAN is defined to be ANIMATE.

```
John:                                       HUMAN:
    (head agreement number) = SING              is-a (ANIMATE)
    (head agreement person) = 3RD
    (head rep) = HUMAN
    (head rep name) = *JOHN*
```

Similarly, the FOOD restriction on the object of an INGEST would propagate to the NP assigned as the direct object (dobject) of "eats," because of equation 7.

Unification grammars have been used by Tomabechi and Tomita (1988). They combined a unification-based approach encoding syntax and semantics similar to what is described here, with a spreading activation mechanism for pragmatics. Although they have reported no results, the approach seems promising in that it brings many sources of higher-level knowledge into the ASR process.

4 HIGHER-LEVEL KNOWLEDGE AND CONTROL

A major issue in multilayered systems is the order in which processing takes place at different levels. As we have said, a potential pitfall is that an interpretation that looks valid on one level may turn out to be invalid, but only after several more layers of processing. Thus, unless we are clever about the way in which levels interact, processing could potentially be highly inefficient.

One approach to this problem is to explicitly encode control information into the system, enabling it to make decisions during processing as to which level of information should next be allowed to proceed in the analysis of the input. This was the approach used in the the HEARSAY project. The general approach in this project was to build multiple modules, or *knowledge sources* (KSs), one for each level of processing. The KSs were embedded within the context of a *blackboard architecture,* which was responsible for enabling communication between modules as well as controlling the order in which modules did their processing.

The version of the system to receive the most attention was HEARSAY-II (Erman et al., 1980). This system constructed *multilevel partial solutions* in the course of analyzing a signal. These partial solutions consisted of a set of hypotheses, each hypothesis at a different *level* of the blackboard. A blackboard level corresponded to a level of abstraction of the speech signal such as phonemes or syllables.

Several competing partial solutions might be entertained by HEARSAY-II at the same time. However, each partial solution could contain at most only one hypothesis from any given level. Hypotheses had likelihood measures associated with them, representing the degree to which the system believed each hypothesis. These likelihood measures were used to determine which partial solution should be further investigated.

For each level of the blackboard, there was a KS responsible for constructing and manipulating hypotheses at that level. KSs were responsible for three main activities: hypothesis generation, hypothesis combination, and hypothesis evaluation. A KS could look at hypotheses constructed at other levels of the blackboard to decide what to do next on its own level. For example, it might look to the next lowest level to see if it could incorporate any hypotheses made at that level into a hypothesis at the current level. Or it might change the likelihoods of hypotheses according to information on other levels of the blackboard.

Each KS was a condition–action module, in the style of a production system. The condition component prescribed the situations in which the KS could be applied; that is, if the condition evaluated to True in a situation, then the KS could apply to that situation. The action component specified what action would be taken by the KS if it applied.

Control in HEARSAY-II was achieved via a *heuristic scheduler,* which examined the KSs that could apply in a situation and decided which one should execute its actions. This was achieved by the following three steps:

1. Estimate probable effects of potential KS actions.
2. Deduce global significance of an isolated action from its cooperative and competitive relationships with existing hypotheses.
3. Assess desirability of an action in comparison with other potential actions.

The desirability of an action was determined by assessing its numeric priority. Then the hueristic scheduler executed the waiting action with the highest priority.

Thus, much of the knowledge in HEARSAY-II was "metaknowledge," knowledge about how to decide what to do next. This metaknowledge consisted mainly of a set of heuristics about what actions were most promising in what situations and was used by the heuristic scheduler to calculate numeric priorities for potential KS actions.

HEARSAY-II recognized connected speech in a 1000-word vocabulary, with correct interpretations for about 90% of test sentences. It achieved this in close to real time, with average processing for a typical sentence of 85 MIPS [85 seconds on a 1-(MIPS) machine]. The control structure of the system was largely responsible for its ability to perform at this level.

Another approach to control was proposed by Woods (1982), based on the HWIM system (Woods et al., 1976). Woods proposed an *island-driven strategy,* in which partial hypotheses about the possible identity of an utterance were formed around initial "seed" words and were enlarged by gradually adding adjacent words. The process continued until islands grew larger and larger, eventually colliding and combining with each other, until the entire sentence was covered by a single hypothesis.

HWIM consisted of two modules: a *lexical access* module and a *linguistic* module. The lexical access component was responsible for matching words against the input signal. The linguistic component, which consisted of a "pragmatic" ATN grammar (see Section 3.2.2), verified the grammaticality of proposals from the lexical component, and made predictions to be verified by the other component. The control strategy determined precisely how the two components would interact during the analysis of a sentence.

The algorithm worked by first calling the lexical access module to determine the *n* best matches of words anywhere in the utterance, where *n* was an adjustable parameter. Each of these words served as a *seed* for an island. Each seed hypothesis was assigned a *priority* score that reflected the system's confidence in the hypothesis and was placed on an *event queue*.

The event queue selected a hypothesis to pursue next on the basis of the priority scores. To expand this hypothesis, the linguistic component was called to check the consistency of the hypothesis with the system's ATN grammar and to predict what words and/or word classes might occur adjacent to the hypothesis in the text. This resulted in a call to the lexical access component to select the *k* words that best verified these predictions. Islands grew as more words were verified and added to them. Eventually, islands would grow until they collided, in which case a "merge" event was placed on the queue. This event was responsible for making sure that the hypotheses were compatible. If they were not, then the system abandoned one or both of them and backtracked to the next most plausible hypothesis. This process continued until the entire input was accounted for.

5 OTHER KINDS OF LINGUISTIC KNOWLEDGE

Even in ASR systems whose primary emphasis is on nonlinguistic analytic techniques, linguistic knowledge can be relevant. In this section, we will examine more "pattern-matching"-oriented approaches, and see how even these systems take advantage of linguistic knowledge to improve their performance.

5.1 Hidden Markov Models

One popular approach to speech recognition is to use a hidden Markov model (HMM). Examples of HMM approaches include those of Baker (1975), Jelinek (1976), Levinson et al., (1983), and Lee (1988). They are probabilistic models based on a stochastic finite-state machine. There are two types of HMM models: discrete and continuous. We will describe discrete HMMs here.

An HMM is similar to a grammar in that it is a model of the language L to be recognized. However, unlike a grammar, a language in this model is not just a set of sentences but a frequency distribution of sentences. In other words, associated with a language is the set of sentences in the language and how frequently they occur. Thus, an HMM is a good model of the language *L* if it accurately predicts how likely it is for a speaker of *L* to utter any sentence *S* (including sentences not in *L,* which have zero probability of being uttered).

An HMM consists of a set of *N* states, $Q = \{q_1, \ldots, q_n\}$. Associated with each state is a set of possible outputs as well as a set of possible transitions to other states. At each time step, the model generates one of the outputs and then follows one of the transitions from that state, possibly changing states. Generation of outputs and the following of transitions are random events; that is, associated with each possible output and each possible transition is a probability that the output or the transition will be chosen at any given time step. Each state also has a probability of being the initial state, that is, the state of the model at time t_0. Thus, the model makes a prediction as to how likely it is for any sequence of symbols to occur.

We can rank an HMM as to how well it models a particular language L according to how accurately the probability that the model will generate any sentence S reflects the distribution of sentences in L. In theory, for any language L and a set of observations O from L, there will always exist a "best" HMM containing n or fewer states, that is, the HMM that has the highest probability of generating. O. As we increase the size of O, the best HMM for Q will approach the best model of L.

One of the virtues of statistical approaches to ASR is that statistical models can be *trained*. That is, one can define an algorithm to automatically adjust the parameters of the model so that it improves as it receives more observations. This is true for HMMs. We will not discuss learning algorithms for HMMs here, as they are beyond the scope of this chapter [see Allerhand (1987)]. Suffice it to say that since HMMs have a large number of parameters ($2n$, assuming a model with n states), the algorithms used are not guaranteed to converge on the optimal model. Thus, the performance of an HMM depends greatly on the initial parameters of the model that the system starts with before learning. The parameters include not only the probabilities for a given state of each output and each possible transition, but also the number of states in the model.

Thus, speech knowledge is used in HMM models in the selection of the initial model from which training begins. Depending on the level of outputs of the model, different kinds of knowledge can be encoded in the system. If the output is the set of allophones of a language, then initially knowledge about coarticulation effects on allophones can be encoded in the initial values of the parameters, with transitions with zero or low probabilities between states whose phonemic outputs are not compatible in sequence, and transitions with high probabilities between states whose outputs are compatible [see Allerhand (1987)]. If the outputs of the model are lexical items, then a priori knowledge about word frequency distributions or even local syntax rules of the language (e.g., nouns follow adjectives) can be encoded into the initial parameters [see Bahl et al. (1983)].

5.2 Partitioning of the Lexicon

Another useful source of knowledge for ASR involves the categorization or words by phonetic categories. The basic idea is to partition the lexicon according to relatively general, and thus easy to identify, phonetic characteristics, such as strong-fricative, vowel, or stop. Categories consist of sequences of these phonemes.

The first "pass" over the signal extracts these broad phonetic features, which are then used to identify what class of lexical items the signal falls in. This leaves the system with a small subset of words in the language from which to choose through more detailed phonetic analysis.

This approach has the advantage that many possible candidate words are eliminated from consideration by the rough first pass before more detailed analysis is performed. Zue (1985) reports that the broad phonetic analysis partitions the lexicon relatively evenly, with the following category distribution:

	Words Equally Weighted	Words Weighted by Frequency
Expected class size	22	34
Median class size	4	25
Maximum class size	223	223

After this general categorization of the input signal, a more detailed analysis is performed, exploring the particular characteristics of the equivalence class to discriminate among the candidate lexical items.

6 SUMMARY

We have explored the use of higher-level knowledge in automatic speech recognition (ASR) systems. Evidence exists that humans use knowledge about language as well as world knowledge in processing speech. This evidence, coupled with the inferior performance of machines compared to that of humans in speech understanding, provides motivation for the use of higher-level knowledge in ASR.

Several key issues arise in trying to use linguistic knowledge in ASR. First, the formalisms used for linguistic analysis in natural language processing were not designed for use with uncertain inputs. We have examined extensions to parsing algorithms to deal with uncertainty values without worsening the computational complexity of context-free parsing. Second, efficient parsing methods do not typically allow for the expression of contextual dependencies, such as coarticulation effects among allophones. We have seen how context-free grammars can be extended to allow for the encoding of some of these effects, again without adding to the complexity of parsing.

Linguistic knowledge has also been used, at least tacitly, in some pattern-matching approaches to ASR. In particular, a priori knowledge about speech is encoded in hidden Markov models in their initial parameters. We have also examined the use of knowledge about distributions of lexical items, with respect to certain broad phonological features, to eliminate possible candidate matches as well as to focus processing on those portions of the signal that discriminate the best among candidate words.

Finally, we examined the issue of control. We described three approaches to this problem: using "metaknowledge," using dynamic programming techniques, and using predictions from semantics and pragmatics to constrain the amount of search necessary at lower levels of processing. Control techniques are essential to multilevel systems, as the number of possible hypotheses for these systems to consider is enormous.

Several key issues remain to be solved in the application of linguistic knowledge to automatic signal recognition. First, constraints can come from many sources of knowledge. It is not clear in general when different constraints should be encoded together in the same representation and when they should not be. Often, it is not even possible to encode them together, even if the system designer decides it would be good to do so. For example, if allophonic constraints are encoded in a context-free grammar (or an extension of one), this precludes the encoding of syntactic information in the same grammar (see Section 3.2.2). Without the ability to encode many different kinds of constraints in the same set of rules, processing may become unnecessarily cumbersome.

Another issue is how to systematically encode semantic and pragmatic knowledge. We have seen many systems that apply semantic/pragmatic knowledge to ASR, but it is not clear that these systems have proposed any sort of principled approach to the encoding and application of the knowledge. Several systems used *semantic grammars* for this information; at best, semantic grammars seem quite ad hoc. It seems clear that semantic knowledge is different from syntactic knowledge, and attempts to encode the two into a single grammar are likely to cause problems. For example, doing so makes the system's entire grammar domain-dependent. In general, syntactic knowledge does not vary with domain (although there may be domains that are well suited for a sublanguage approach). Other approaches to encoding semantics and pragmatics seem equally unprincipled.

While the application of higher-level knowledge in speech recognition may be well motivated, so far these techniques have failed to perform better than statistical approaches. As more principled solutions to the problems mentioned above are developed, perhaps knowledge-based approaches will begin to live up to their potential. Whether or not this happens remains to be seen.

REFERENCES

Allen, J. (1985a). *From Text to Speech: The MITalk System*. Cambridge Univ. Press, Cambridge, U.K.
Allen, J. (Ed.) (1985b). *Proc. IEEE: Spec. Issue Man-Mach. Speech Commun.* 73, No. 11.
Allerhand, M. (1987). *Knowledge-Based Speech Pattern Recognition*. Kogan Page, London.
Bahl, L., Jelinek, F., and Mercer, R. (1983). A Maximum Likelihood Approach to Continuous Speech Recognition. *IEEE Trans. Pattern Anal. Mach. Intell.* 5(2):179–190.
Baker, J. (1975). Stochastic Modelling for Automatic Speech Understanding. In: *Speech Recognition* (R. Reddy, Ed.). Academic, New York, pp. 521–542.
Bengio, Y., Cardin, R., De Mori, R., and Merlo, E. (1989). Programmable Execution of Multilayered networks for Automatic Speech Recognition. *Comm. ACM* 32(2):195–200.
Borghesi, L., and Favareto, C. (1982). Flexible Parsing of Discretely Uttered Sentences. *Proc. COLING-82,* Prague, July 1982, pp. 37–48.
Chomsky, N. (1957). *Syntactic Structures*. Mouton, The Hague.
Chomsky, N. (1965). *Aspects of the Theory of Syntax*. MIT Press, Cambridge, Mass.
Davis, K., Biddulph, R., and Balashek, J. (1952). Automatic Recognition of Spoken Digits. *Acoust. Soc. Am.* 24:637–645.
De Mori, R. (1983). *Computer Models of Speech Using Fuzzy Algorithms*. Plenum, New York.

Denes, P., and Mathews, M. (1960). Spoken Digit Recognition Using Time-Frequency Pattern Matching. *J. Acoust. Soc. Am.* **32**:1450–1455.

Dudley, H., and Balashek, S. (1958). Automatic Recognition of Phonetic Patterns in Speech. *J. Acoust. Soc. Am.* **30**:721–739.

Erman, L., Hayes-Roth, F., Lesser, V., and Reddy, D. (1980). The Hearsay-II Speech-Understanding System: Integrating Knowledge To Resolve Uncertainty. *Comput. Surv.* **12**(2):213–253.

Fillmore, C. (1968). The Case for Case. In *Universals in Linguistic Theory*. (E. Bach and R. Harms, Eds.). Holt, Rinehart, and Winston, New York, pp. 1–90.

Fodor, J., and Bever, T. (1965). The Psychological Reality of Linguistic Segments. *Verbal Learning Verbal Behav.* **4**:414–420.

Forgie, J., and Forgie, C. (1959). Results Obtained from a Vowel Recognition Computer Program. *Acoust. Soc. Am.* **31**:1480–1489.

Fry, D., and Denes, P. (1953). Mechanical Speech Recognition. In *Communication Theory* (E. Cherry, Ed.) Butterworths, London, pp. 426–432.

Garrett, M., and Shattuck, S. (1974). An Analysis of Speech Errors. Quarterly Progress Report #113. Research Laboratory of Electronics, Massachusetts Institute of Technology, Cambridge, Mass.

Jelinek, F. (1976). Continuous Speech Recognition by Statistical Methods. *Proc. IEEE* **64**(4):532–556.

Jelinek, F. (1985). The Development of an Experimental Discrete Dictation Recognizer. *Proc. IEEE* **73**(11):1616–1624.

Kimball, O., Price, P., Roucos, S., Schwartz, R., Kubala, F., Chow, Y., Haas, A., Krasner, M., and Majhoul, J. (1986). Recognition Performance and Grammatical Constraints. Proc. DARPA Speech Recognition Workshop. Science Applications International Corporation Report Number SAIC-86/1546, pp. 53–59.

Lea, W. (Ed.) (1980). *Trends in Speech Recognition*. Prentice-Hall, Englewood Cliffs, N.J.

Lee, K. (1988). Large-Vocabulary Speaker-Independent Continuous Speech Recognition: The Sphinx System. Ph.D. dissertation. Department of Computer Science, Carnegie-Mellon University, Pittsburgh, Pa. Research Report CMU-CS-88-148.

Levinson, S. (1985). Structural Methods in Automatic Speech Recognition. *Proc. IEEE* **73**(11)1625–1650.

Levinson, S., and Shipley, K. (1980). A Conversational-Mode Airline Information and Reservation System Using Speech Input and Output. *Bell Syst. Tech. J.* **59**:119–137.

Levinson, S., Rabiner, L., and Sondhi, M. (1983). An Introduction to the Application of the Theory of Probabilistic Functions of a Markov Process to Automatic Speech Recognition. *Bell Syst. Tech. J.* **62**:1035–1074.

Lindgren, N. (1965). Machine Recognition of Human Language. *IEEE Spectrum* **2** (March-May).

Lippmann, R. (1989). Review of Neural Nets for Speech Recognition. *Neural Comput.* **1**(1).

Lowerre, B., and Reddy, R. (1980). The HARPY Speech Understanding System. In: *Trends in Speech Recognition* (W. Lea, Ed.). Prentice-Hall, Englewood Cliffs, N.J.

Lytinen, S. (1986). Dynamically Combining Syntax and Semantics in Natural Language Processing. Proc. 5th Nat. Conf. Artificial Intelligence, Philadelphia, August 1986, pp. 574–578.

Marslen-Wilson, W. (1975). Sentence Perception as an Interactive Parallel Process. *Science* **189**:226–228.

Peterson, G. (1961). Automatic Speech Recognition Procedures. *Lang. Speech* **4**:200–219.

Rabiner, L,, and Levinson, S. (1981). Isolated and Connected Word Recognition—Theory and Selected Applications. *IEEE Trans. Comput.* **29**.

Schank, R. (1975). *Conceptual Information Processing*. Lawrence Erlbaum Associates, Hillsdale, N.J.

Shieber, S. (1986). *An Introduction to Unification-Based Styles of Grammar*. CSLI, Palo Alto, Cal.

White, G. (1976). Speech Recognition: A Tutorial Overview. *Comp. Mag.* pp. 40–53.

Woods, W. (1970). Transition Network Grammars for Natural Language Analysis. *Commun. ACM* **13**(10):591–606.

Woods, W. (1982). Optimal Search Strategies for Speech Understanding Control. *AI* **18**:295–326.
Woods, W., Bates, M., Brown, G., Bruce, B., Cook, C., Klovstad, M., Nash-Webber, B., Schwartz, R., Wolf, J., and Zue, V. (1976). Speech Understanding Systems—Final Technical Progress Report. BBN Report 3438, Vols. I–V, Cambridge, Mass.
Young, S., Haptmann, A., Ward, W., Smith, E., and Werner, P. (1989). High Level Knowledge Sources in Usable Speech Recognition Systems. *Comm. ACM* **32**(2):183–194.
Zadeh, L. (1975). Calculus of Fuzzy Restrictions. In: *Fuzzy Sets and Their Application to Cognitive Decision Processes* (L. Zadeh, K. Fu, K. Tanaka, and M. Shimvra, Eds.). Academic, New York.
Zue, V. (1985). Speech Knowledge in Automatic Speech Recognition. *Proc. IEEE* **73**(11):1602–1624.

CHAPTER 10

KNOWLEDGE PROCESSING AND ITS APPLICATION TO ENGINEERING DESIGN

S. OHSUGA

1 INTRODUCTION

The computer is a tool to aid human problem solving. We expect computers to support our problem solving in all aspects. However, neither conventional computers nor existing expert systems are satisfactory in supporting human problem-solving activity because the mechanisms of these systems do not fit the requirements of problem solving.

It is necessary first to know what is needed for problem solving and then to develop an appropriate system. This chapter addresses the need to establish a new problem-solving style involving humans and machines and then to design knowledge-processing systems incorporating it.

There are different types of problems, and each type requires a specific problem-solving procedure. We use here the term "problem-solving structure" to clarify our idea of the need to discriminate these problem types. Typical problem types are analysis and synthesis. *Analysis* is the activity, given an object, of deriving its attribute, property, behavior, and function or relation with other objects, which we call functionality for short hereafter. *Synthesis* is the activity, given a set of requirements in the form of functionalities, of obtaining an object with the required functionalities. If computers cannot represent a problem-solving structure, then they cannot cope satisfactorily with that problem type. Ordinary von Neumann computers are suited for coping with analysis but not with synthesis.

Nowadays, real problems are becoming bigger and more complex, involving different types of problems. Typical engineering problems include computer-aided design (CAD) and computer integrated manufacturing (CIM), which require an integrated support by computers. What we wish, therefore, is to have a computer program that can manipulate various types of problems.

Current computer programs are not always satisfactory for supporting human total activities because the processing procedures those systems are based on are often suited for only specific types of problem solving and not for others we encounter in the real world.

Expert systems have been expected to improve the current situation (Hayes-Roth et al., 1983). There are good reasons to believe they can, because their inference mechanism, knowledge bases, and search methods seem to work effectively to solve problems differently than conventional information processing (Ohsuga, 1985). For example, it has been expected that expert systems would have the capability of processing declarative language. The modularity in representation that would be ensured by this language must enable incremental additions of information to the system and deletions from the system. This is the basic condition to enable trial-and-error activity. It is well known that this is an important technique for performing creative activities like engineering design. Hence it has been expected that expert systems could offer us a powerful means to build advanced CAD systems.

But existing expert systems have not always been shown to work satisfactorily in these problem domains. I think this is because existing expert systems are not designed to take into account the types of problems and problem-solving structures they require. Thus what we must do today is not to put real problems in the framework of existing expert systems but to design an expert system that is suitable for real problem-solving and, accordingly, is able to take part in human problem-solving as much as possible. It is necessary for this purpose (1) to classify the problem types by analyzing real problems and to make clear the problem-solving structure for each type, (2) to list the requirements for expert systems to cope with various types of problems, and finally, (3) to design an expert system that satisfies the requirements.

Thus in Sections 2 to 4 we analyze and formalize the problem-solving process and discuss briefly von Neumann computers and existing expert systems. Then we derive the requirements for a desirable expert system.

In Sections 5 to 8, we propose a system that is expected to satisfy these requirements. We have designed a system named KAUS (knowledge acquisition and utilization system) along these lines (Yamauchi and Ohsuga, 1985). This system has a multi-metalevel organization, with a basic single-level subsystem and a level manager. Any number of levels can be defined by accumulating the basic level subsystem under the control of the level manager. Before designing the basic subsystem, we analyzed the requirements for knowledge representation and developed a language to meet these requirements (Ohsuga,

1983, 1985). This is characterized by predicate logic plus data structure. Then an inference algorithm and other important system functions were developed based on this language. The basic subsystem has been implemented, and the level manager is in the process of being implemented. Even the basic subsystem alone has a large capability for model building and manipulating. The subsystem has been used as the object-level system and has been applied to various real problems in mechanical design, control-system analysis, airplane-wing design, and chemical compound structure estimation to check its applicability.

As the next step, we are preparing for various experiments on the higher-level functions that require a multiple metalevel system, including representation and control of the problem-solving process, ambiguous information handling, knowledge acquisition, and a more sophisticated human–computer interface.

2 PROBLEMS AND PROBLEM SOLVING

2.1 Problem Representation

In order to use computers for problem solving, it is necessary to represent the problem explicitly. In most cases representations of real problems are domain-specific and depend on the meanings of the terms specifically defined in each domain. As each problem originates from some object in which we are interested in the real world, the problem is represented in terms of the object information, which we call an *object model*. An object has various aspects, and the object model is composed of those that are directly concerned with problem solving. Thus, we define a problem as "to obtain information on some aspect(s) of an object we are interested in." This information is, as a matter of course, the solution. We define an object model as comprising (a) a description of an object structure and (b) a set of descriptions on attributes, properties, behaviors, functions, and so on, which we call functionalities. In computers, the former is represented by a data structure and the latter is represented in the form of a predicate that involves the data structure as a term. Functionalities are also dependent on the environment and/or conditions in which the object is placed. Thus, an object model may be represented formally by a set of formulas in the form

PREDICATE(OBJECT-STRUCTURE, ENVIRONMENT/CONDITION, VALUE)   (1)

ENVIRONMENT/CONDITION represents all quantities on environments and/or conditions other than those included in this formula. Then formally we can define different types of problems such as analysis, synthesis, environment-estimation, and knowledge acquisition depending on which predicate value or object structure or environment/condition or predicate type, respectively, is unknown.

For example, design is a typical synthesis operation. It is the activity of finding an object model that satisfies the given requirements presented in the form of functionalities. This is a nondeterministic problem, and ordinarily it is represented as a repetitive cycle of model analysis and evaluation and model modification. The first part is an analytic problem, and thus design is a compound process. Diagnosis is a different type of activity that, given a set of findings, forms a hypothesis that explains the findings. To form a new hypothesis is to generate a new predicate. It requires also a trial-and-error process, like a design process, of forming a hypothesis, examining it, and modifying the hypothesis. The hypothesis is based on the model. For some type of problems the time needed for problem solving is important. Real-time control is a typical example. The time requirements must be included in the ENVIRONMENT/ CONDITION.

In the following we focus our attention on the relation between the object structure and its functionalities in the formal expression. Therefore we abbreviate the above expression hereafter and use a shortened form to make the point clear. We pay much attention to design as a typical synthesis problem.

We represent an object model as a set of functionalities corresponding to different aspects of the problem. In computer programs the object model is represented as a combination of the data structure and a set of predicates. Since the data structure represents the object body to which predicates give functionalities, it must be of the form

```
Object Model; Predicate-i(Data-Structure x), i = 1,2,...,n      (2)
```

where predicates might be given to the complete object structure or to its substructures to represent their functionalities. We use x to represent all the other terms.

Note that this is not a specific model but gives a schema to represent various object models. A specific object model represented with this schema varies with the problem domain—a three-dimensional physical object in mechanical engineering, an electronic circuit in electronic engineering, a chemical compound in chemistry, and so on. The model representation depends also on the extent of our knowledge about the object. To know more about an object means to know the finer object structure and its functionalities. Some fields, such as organic chemistry, have their own ways of representing object structures precisely and their functionalities in relation to the structures. Research is being performed to find the structure–functionality relationships and to use these relations to develop new object structures with the required functionalities. Some other fields, such as metallurgy, on the other hand, have no way of representing an object structure precisely. Instead, an alternative method is used to define an object, for example, the list of component metals in a metal alloy together with the metallurgical process used to obtain the alloy.

When a domain is still in its infancy, the fine structure of the object is not known well and we must represent it with observational information, not in the form of a data structure but with the predicates in computer language. In this case we need to separate the predicates according to their role: those that are to be converted to data structure when more facts are found and those that substantially represent its functionalities. As the functionalities are dependent on the object definition, each predicate in the latter class must be dependent on the former set of predicates. Thus a very flexible modeling method must be provided to accommodate the variety of environments encountered by the computer systems.

2.2 Problem-Solving Process

The solution of a problem is, in many cases, embedded in the other information in the original model representation. Thus, problem solving is formalized as the process of transforming model representation from one form to another in order to obtain a model representation such that the solution, or, rather, the procedural program to derive the solution, is generated easily therefrom. That is,

$$\text{Problem Solving; Model-Description 0} \xrightarrow{KS1} \text{Model-Description 1} \xrightarrow{KS2} \cdots \xrightarrow{KSn} \text{Model-Description } n \tag{3}$$

where KSi ($i = 1, 2, \ldots, n$) denotes a knowledge source that, in the case of human problem solving, is in the human brain as a matter of course.

For the deterministic problems, this is an equivalent transformation in the sense that the models before and after each transformation represent the same object. Let us refer to this as EQ-trans to mean equivalency-preserving transformation. Figure 10-1 shows an example of the analysis of a feedback control system. This is typical of the problems that arise when we wish to know the behavior of an overall control system involving object processes such as that of a chemical plant or a vehicle. The system includes an object process and various equipment such as an actuator to control the object process.

Let us assume that the characteristic of each component of the system is represented in the form of a linear differential equation. Usually the characteristic is represented in the form of a Laplace transform including the transformation parameter s in imaginary space. Then an overall system is represented in the form of a block diagram. An expression such as G1 or G2 in the block represents the characteristic of a component in the system in the Laplace transform. This block diagram representation is a kind of model of the control system because it includes sufficient information to analyze the system and every control engineer can understand it.

In analyzing the system, the original object model in the form of a block diagram is first transformed into a signal flow graph, and then the sets of all local loops involved in the graph and all open paths from the input gate to the output gate are derived. The characteristic of each loop (or path) is obtained as the product of all characteristics of components included in the loop (path). A global transfer function of the control system can be obtained by applying a specific mathematical operation to the sets of characteristics for these loops and paths. A response function can be obtained, given an input function, and

KNOWLEDGE PROCESSING AND ITS APPLICATION TO ENGINEERING DESIGN **305**

G1=3/s
G2=1/(s+4)
G3=1/(4*s)
G4=4
G5=(s+2)/(s**2-8)
H1=-1
H2=-1

(a) Block Diagram

KB

(b) Signal Flow Diagram

KB

```
loop-set=((G3 G4 G5 B1 H2) (G1 G2 H2) (G4 G5 H1))
open-path-set=((B0 G3 G4 G5 B1) (B0 G1 G2))
```

(c) Local Transfer Function Set

KB

G(s)=(4*s+2)/(s**3+4*s**2+4*s+2)

(d) Global Transfer Function

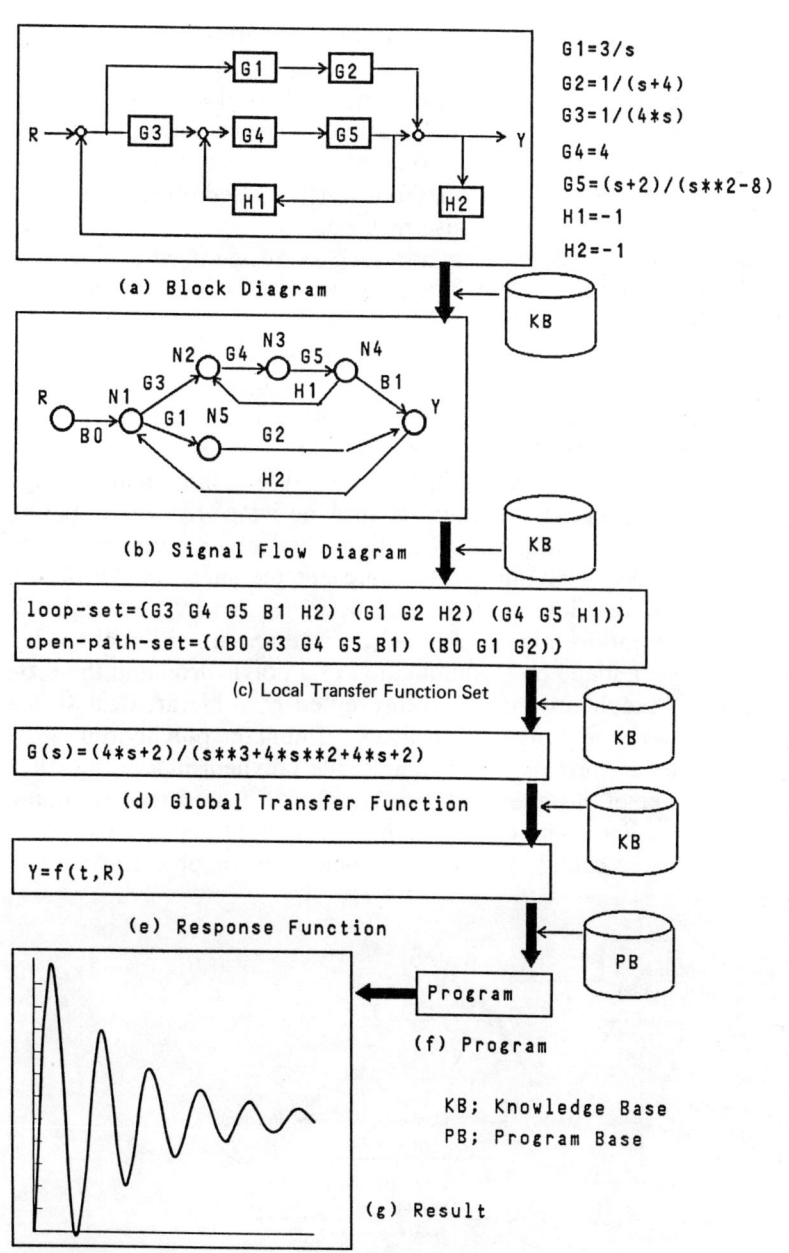

KB

Y=f(t,R)

(e) Response Function

PB

Program

(f) Program

KB; Knowledge Base
PB; Program Base

(g) Result

FIGURE 10-1
An example of an analysis process.

is transformed into a computer program. Then the program is executed to obtain the required quantity.

The specific problem-solving method known as Mason's method is used in this example. In each application field, various problem-solving methods have been studied and accumulated to derive characteristics of the given object for analysis and evaluation. These methods must be used effectively. The KSi in (3) denote the information on these methods.

On the other hand, synthesis problems such as design need a trial-and-error process. This is formalized as shown in Fig. 10-2. Given the requirements on the functionalities for the object, the designer makes an incipient model and then analyzes and evaluates it. This part is EQ-trans. If the model does not meet the requirements, then the designer modifies it. This transformation changes the current object model to one not equivalent to the original model. Let us refer to this transformation as NE-trans.

Figure 10-3 illustrates an example of NE-trans. We assume that this figure represents a design process to obtain an airplane wing with the required aerodynamic characteristics using a CAD system. First of all, we need to define a three-dimensional curved surface to represent the shape of the object wing. But as a three-dimensional surface can be generated by performing a specific procedural operation upon a polyhedron in three-dimensional space, we can define the object shape by a combination of a polyhedron and the procedure. Ordinarily, a polyhedron can be represented by a hierarchical structure composed of a polyhedron, a set of surfaces defining the polyhedron, a set of edge lines, and a set of vertices. For example, the polyhedron h in Fig. 10-3 is represented by a set of surfaces ($s1$–$s6$, $s31$, $s32$). Each surface is represented by a set of edge lines, and each edge line by a set of vertices (pij) in a similar way. Let this be called the skeletal structure of the object. Then the

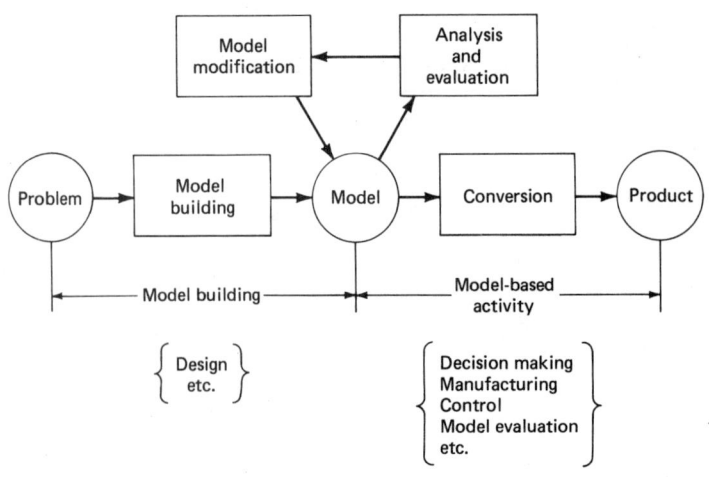

FIGURE 10-2
Problem-solving process.

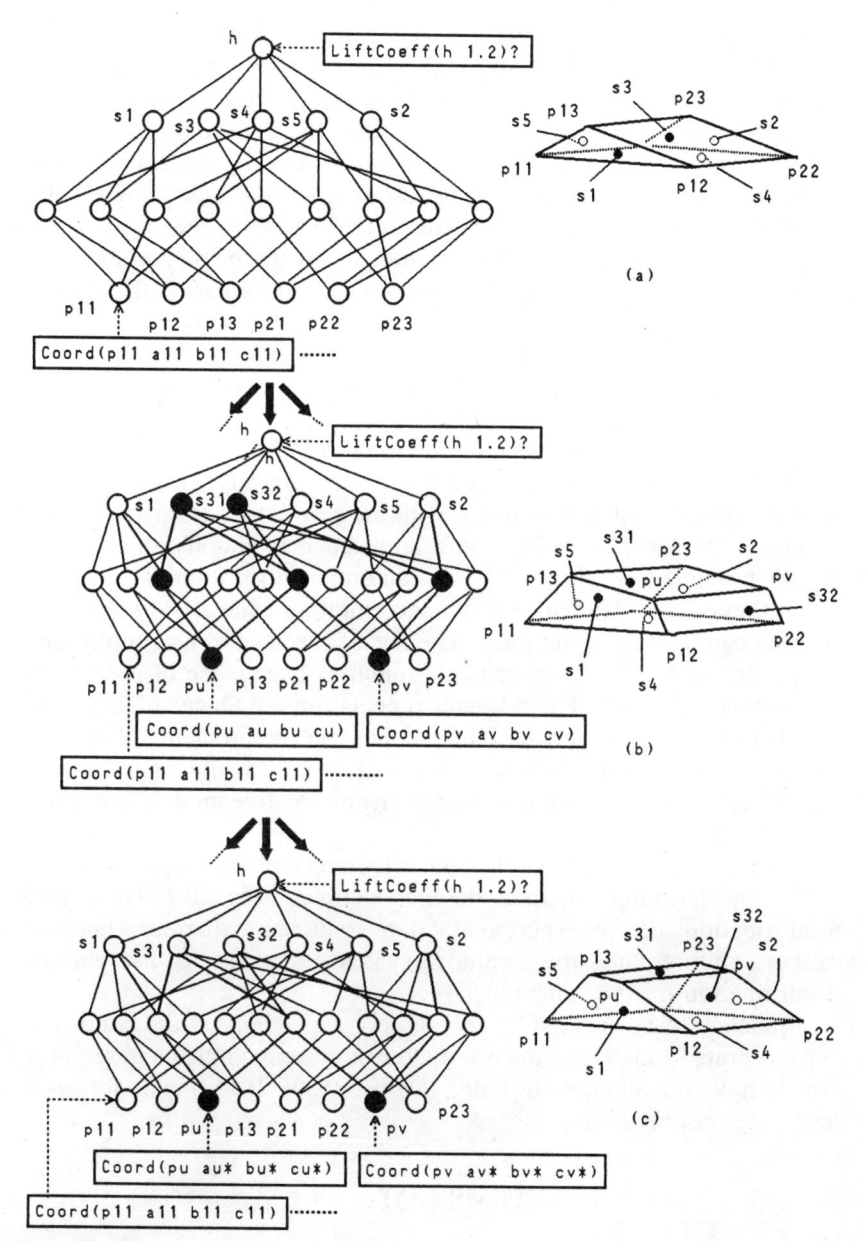

FIGURE 10-3
An illustration of a synthesis process.

object model is represented by a combination of the skeletal structure with an arbitrary number of descriptions on the structural constraints and/or the functionalities of the wing including a curved-surface generation function. The term `Coord(p11, a11, b11, c11)` signifies that the coordinates of vertex p11 are `(a11, b11, c11)`, and so on. These allow us to generate a curved surface. Then, by applying a specific program to analyze the air flow around the curved surface, we obtain an air-pressure distribution on the surface. We can then derive the aerodynamic quantities such as lift force and aerodynamic moment acting upon the wing in the given environment. Ordinarily, these aerodynamic characteristics of a wing are represented in nondimensional form such as with the lift coefficient denoted `LiftCoeff(h 1.2)` in Fig. 10-3. The transformation to obtain characteristics such as the lift coefficient, given the skeletal structure, is EQ-trans.

If the model is judged unsatisfactory on the basis of these characteristics, then the original skeletal structure is modified. This is an NE-trans. There can be an indefinite number of candidates for the new structure from which one must be chosen. If one can define some knowledge to modify the skeletal structure, it is possible to perform NE-trans automatically. Otherwise humans have to do it themselves. Human–machine cooperation is necessary here.

NE-trans can include some inconsistency between object structure and the existing functionalities and accordingly requires a sequence of operations to review the functionalities. The designer repeats the sequences of EQ-trans and NE-trans looking for the model that satisfies the requirements. This process is very similar to the assumption-based truth maintenance system (ATMS) (De Kleer, 1986). But, in real design, the alternative models cannot be restricted to the finite set.

There may be cases where neither the NE-trans nor the EQ-trans can be performed by the algorithmic method like the example of Fig. 10-1. Then other forms of information such as experimental data or human experience must be used together. This requires the computer system to be able to use various forms of information for the same purpose.

The efficiency of problem solving is largely dependent on the control to select a proper transformation. This is a matter of system control and requires the system to have metalevel knowledge (Davis, 1980). It also calls for good human–computer cooperation.

3 WHY ARE EXISTING SYSTEMS NOT ALWAYS EFFECTIVE?

The object model is represented originally in declarative form, and most problem domains have their own modeling schemes as discussed above. These representations are substantially different from programs in the procedural language of conventional computers. As the expressive powers of declarative language and procedural language are different and also differ in their conformity with the human manner of representation, there can be cases in which the real problem cannot be represented in programming language as it is. In a word, procedural language is suited for representing deterministic problem-solving processes where the transformations for obtaining the solution are defined in an algorithmic way.

Databases allow users a different approach to the use of computers (Date, 1981). Databases look like the declarative information, and if the object model is well represented by the data model of databases, then the subsequent processing can be performed by means of the facilities provided by the database system. The extent to which the databases can represent the object model depends on the data model (Tsichritzis and Lochovsky, 1982) of the database. Many attempts have been made to represent object models in conventional databases (Kemper and Wallrath, 1987). Many of these attempts have been unsuccessful because the expressive power of the current data model is rather low in comparison with what is required for representing an object model.

There are two reasons. One is the lack of capability to represent an object structure. As anticipated from the examples of modeling schemes mentioned above, an object model needs structural information as well as its functionalities. Recent research on object-oriented data models is aimed at solving the problem by extending the framework of the database to include a hierarchical structure [OBJ87]. There is, however, a second and more serious problem. Problem solving is a dynamic process to modify the original model representation to achieve goal representation. Hence, mere static representation of an object is not enough; its transformation process must also be represented. A model representation must be modified to another model, also represented in the declarative form, under the proper control. The information needed to guide this process must also be represented. This is beyond the capability of the database even with the object-oriented data model and requires very sophisticated operations. Research into deductive databases (Gallaire et al., 1984) is another important trend that is a closely related to this problem. But it is not the complete solution to this problem for the time being. Generally speaking, since the operations of the database system are confined to a set of predefined procedural programs, they can not enjoy fully the advantages of using a declarative system, such as flexibility, adaptability, and extendability.

Because of these limitations of conventional ways of computation in problem-solving, object-model information has been formed and retained in the human brain, and it remains the human's role to manage the problem-solving process, including the use of computer programs based on the object model. The effectiveness of computers remains at a rather low level in problem-solving. The more sophisticated the problems become, the less effective computers are in the problem-solving tasks.

Artificial intelligence (AI) has provided a new information-processing style based on an inference that operates on knowledge in the declarative form. There is a big difference between procedural and declarative language in terms of semantics. The semantics of declarative language is defined as the direct correspondence between the language and the things in the world being described—the entities and their functionalities—and each expression can be independent of others (context free). Consequently, declarative language has the following characteristics:

1. The unit of description is usually small; that is, the language keeps its modularity.
2. Expressions can be stored and used later.
3. Addition, deletion, and updating of information are easy.
4. The language can express things that are not necessarily known in detail in advance, and therefore it is possible to describe hypotheses.

We call information with these characteristics "knowledge."

The semantics of procedural language, on the other hand, is defined as the correspondence between language and the functions provided by computers. The meaning in the real world is not represented directly but only indirectly by writing down the way of achieving the goal the real problem requires. It does not have the same characteristics as declarative language. Its characteristics are:

1. The module of procedural description is long and context-dependent.
2. It is not easy for others to reuse the program.
3. Addition, deletion, and updating of information are not easy.
4. The program cannot express things that are not known in detail in advance.
5. The processing efficiency of a procedural program is better than that of knowledge processing.

Characteristics 1–4 of declarative language are required for some types of problem solving. Hence, if a knowledge representation language is designed to have these characteristics, then the system using that language is expected to meet the conditions of an intelligent problem-solving system. On the other hand, a new processing mechanism is necessary for declarative language to deduce a new expression from the set of given expressions. It is the inference mechanism that plays the key role in intelligent systems.

In reality, there are different types of inference including inductive inference, analogical reasoning, and deductive inference. They are different in the way new information is generated or deduced from the given premises. Deductive inference is the only type of inference that has been studied in detail for use as the general processing mechanism. Its function is to deduce information within the scope of meanings of the given expressions. This function has enabled us to use knowledge in computers and has opened a new era of knowledge processing.

It has been expected, consequently, that artificial intelligence with this mechanism would enable us to use computers more conveniently for problem-solving, and many expert systems have been developed as application systems. But it seems that people are not content with them. There are a number of reasons for this dissatisfaction. Here we present our views on this issue referring to two typical AI methods used in expert system shells: the production system and the frame system. The key issue is to ask whether these systems can process model information directly and as needed.

A production system has a simple organization composed of a knowledge base as a collection of if-then rules and an inference engine to derive a conclusion (or premise) based on pattern matching from some facts (or queries) and rules. This system replaces the program execution mechanism of conventional computers with the inference operation. But most of the system relies only on symbol manipulation. This is unsatisfactory for representing and manipulating object models for real problems because they need a complex combination of structure and functionalities, transformation rules, and control strategy.

A frame system introduces the concept of a frame to represent every conceptual entity in the world of interest and its structure. A frame includes a set of slots representing aspects of the entity represented by the frame. The class-instance relation with the inheritance mechanism forms a hierarchy of frames, and a message-passing mechanism is provided between frames. It seems possible to represent a problem structure with this mechanism, but not necessarily so. Some use this structure as a control structure to define the problem-solving process, while others use it for representing object structures. This reveals that we need at least two different structures to represent any problem-solving structure: an object structure and a process (control) structure. The latter must be able to manage the group of object-structure frames. In reality, we had better have more levels of structures. We will discuss this point in Section 6. Moreover, it seems that the frame system loses some of the advantages of declarative language. Thus, the frame system is not satisfactory either, and we need a different method or tool for our purpose.

4 REQUIREMENT FOR DESIRABLE EXPERT SYSTEMS

A human being forms a problem-solving process in his or her brain, makes a plan to control the process, and executes it. Computers participate in this problem-solving activity only in part (Fig. 10-4a). As long as we persist in this style of problem solving, we cannot expect very much support from computers in the total problem-solving activity. To improve the situation, we need to transfer most of the processing to computers so that they can undertake the workloads involved in the process as much as possible (Fig. 10-4b). For this purpose we need to represent explicitly in the computers (1) an object model, as the key concept of problem solving. But the representation of an object model as a static entity does not contribute directly to our purpose, because problem-solving is a dynamic process. Therefore, we also need to represent (2) model transformation rules, as components of the process. A model transformation rule is the description of the model representation. This is, however,

312 KNOWLEDGE ENGINEERING: APPLICATIONS

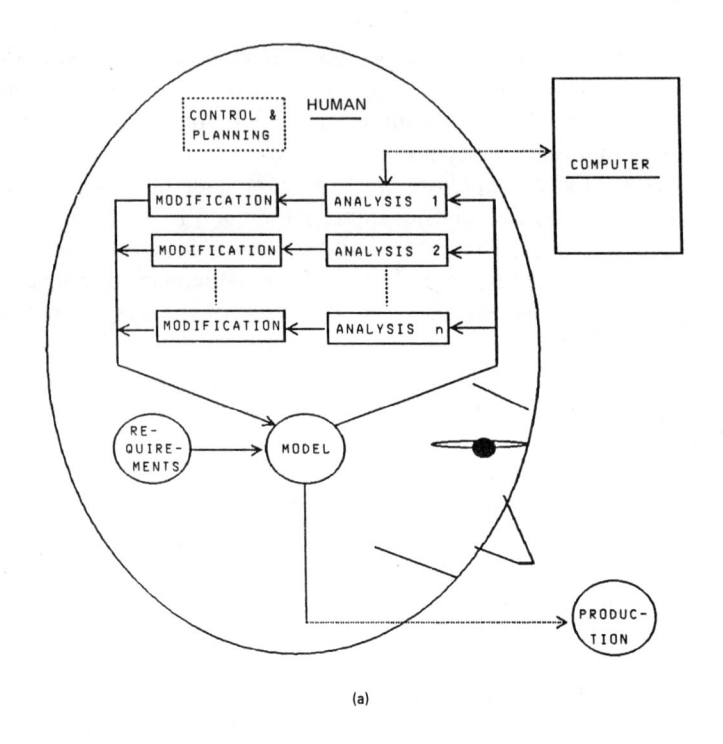

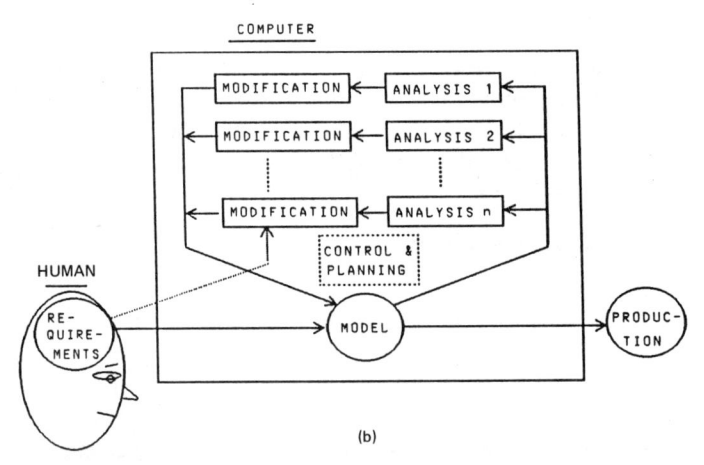

FIGURE 10-4
Human–computer relations.

still unsatisfactory, because there can be many rules, and a collection of these rules does not represent the process. We need further to write down (3) the problem-solving structure shown diagrammatically in Fig. 10-2 explicitly in the computer. To represent a problem-solving structure is to describe the way of using transformation rules. Hence this information must be located at a higher level than the transformation rules. Thus we need to define the level concept in the system.

In order to achieve this goal, various capabilities are required in the system. For example, every model must be represented in the system in such a way that various problem-solving methods developed in each problem domain and given to the system are directly applicable to the model. Very often different information and different methods must be combined to represent the model and also to achieve model analysis, evaluation, and modification in the same system. Different functions of the system must be integrated for the same purpose. For example, in order to represent a model involving a large amount of information, knowledge bases and databases with different data models may be used together. In order to solve the problem, human experience may be used in combination with theoretical methods and various databases.

In this new style of problem solving, the computer is the main body of problem-solving activity in the sense that the computer keeps the object model and also keeps track of its modification process. Humans, standing aside, direct and help the computer only if necessary. Among many conditions for achieving this goal, the following components are required:

1 *Model representation/transformation:* The system should be provided with a good modeling method suitable for representing a model not only as a static entity but also as the object of dynamic transformation. Each problem domain has its own modeling scheme, and the model differs from domain to domain. For a general-purpose system, the modeling method must be free from domain-specific conditions. This means that the system must have a good knowledge representation language that can express a wide range of models and their transformation rules.

2 *Model generation and hypothesis formation:* These are the most difficult but quite desirable functions with which to endow the system for the purpose of automating, at least partially, the processing cycle shown in Fig. 10-2. These capabilities are obtained in many cases through experience. Thus, the experience or engineering know-how must be represented in the form of knowledge as much as possible.

3 *User interface:* Problems arising in the real world should be given first to the computer. Then, during the problem-solving process, a human should be able to monitor the process and intervene in the process whenever he or she wishes. The system should be provided with a good user interface. This raises a number of problems. For example, a focus-tracking capability is required for the user interface to keep the main thread of discourse even if the user changes the subject temporarily (Fitter, 1979). We need more time to solve these problems, but it is essential to allow users to use various media such as pictorial expression, natural language, and mathematical expressions simultaneously, in order to describe problems as precisely as possible. Let us call these *external expressions*. The system must be able to accept these expressions and to transform them into a model/knowledge representation. This means that these ex-

pressions must be translated into the knowledge representation language, or that knowledge representation must be able to accommodate these mixed expressions. It is further desirable that the translation be performed by the knowledge based system.

4 *Use of various resources:* The system should be able to use information expressed in different forms in the computer, such as knowledge, data, and procedural programs. Let us call these *internal expressions*. An object has various aspects that each require a different operation. Information in one form or another is needed in each operation, depending on the extent to which we know that aspect of the object. If it is well studied and analyzed to such an extent that mathematical formulas and their solutions can be obtained to represent it, then a procedural program can be used. If our knowledge is not yet at such a level, then experimental data or human experience must be used alternatively. The extent to which different methods are used depends on the problem domain. But, to some extent, every problem domain combines information in different forms, and if there is a new discovery, it must be added to the system or an old method may be replaced by a new one in the computer system. Thus, the computer system must be able to explain itself. For these purposes, the system must be provided with a high-level language with which information in any form can be completely described and transformed into any one of these forms. This language is the knowledge representation language.

5 *Metalevel structure:* The problem-solving process must be well controlled to ensure efficiency. It is desirable that the control strategy and problem-solving structure be represented in the form of knowledge and processed by the inference mechanism. As both of them are descriptions of the object process, they must be in the metalevel (Davis, 1980). Sometimes the problem-solving structure and/or control strategy can be redesigned to improve the problem-solving process. Thus, it is desirable to have a meta-metalevel and so on. Managing these multiple metalevels is an important role of the management system. Other than these logical functions, the management system must be responsible for ensuring real-time operation, handling ambiguous information, and other characteristics.

6 *Model management:* In the mode-based method of problem-solving, model analysis and evaluation are the operations to derive a requested functionality of the given model. The functionality must be consistent with the model structure in the sense that the structure has the functionality. Thus the analysis is the operation directed at making the model consistent. On the other hand, model modification is the operation of modifying either the structure or some functionalities of the consistent model. It breaks the consistency of the model and asks the human user or the system to recover the consistency. A single modification can propagate along the model structure and may induce a sequence of analyses and evaluations to recover the consistency for the modified model.

It should be noted that there are three different languages—external language, knowledge representation language, and internal language—each of which plays a unique role in the system to adapt to the real environment. The advanced system must be able to integrate systems functions carried out by these languages toward the solution of the problem.

These requirements must be analyzed and translated further into the requirements for the system and its component design. There is a system design step such as that shown in Fig. 10-5. The key concepts are the knowledge representation language and the system architecture. Then the inference mechanism and the management system must be designed correspondingly. The functions discussed above can then be defined.

5 KNOWLEDGE REPRESENTATION AND SYSTEM ARCHITECTURE

From the discussion so far the requirements for knowledge representation and system architecture are derived. We cannot discuss them independently because the representation of the problem-solving process is related to the system architecture. As pointed out in the last section, three concepts must be represented explicitly: (1) object model, (2) model transformation rules, and (3) problem-solving structure. Each of these requires a different level of representation. Thus we need to combine the knowledge representation language with the representation level concept.

In this section we first list the minimum necessary set of requirements for a knowledge representation language. Then we focus our attention on the modeling issue.

5.1 Knowledge Representation

From the discussions so far, we can extract the requirements for knowledge representation, as listed in Table 10-1. We elaborate on each requirement in the following paragraphs.

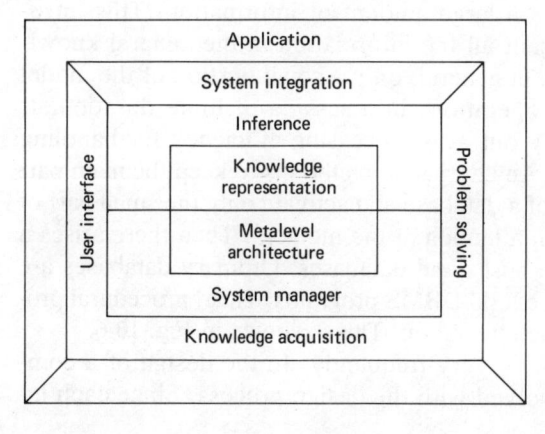

FIGURE 10-5
Function layer of knowledge-processing systems.

TABLE 10-1
Requirements for Knowledge Representation

1. Complex model representation
2. Easy addition/deletion of information
3. Dynamic model building/transformation
4. Complete deductive inference
5. Handling of a large amount of data
6. Automated consistency check
7. Conversion to internal expression
8. Conversion from external expression

1 In many real-world cases the object model has a complex structure with various structural constraints. Each component or assembly has various functionalities. Knowledge representation language needs to have great expressive power for both data structure and functionalities.

2 The model-based method is a process of reaching the final goal by adding or deleting pieces of information incrementally and independently of each other. This means that modularity must be ensured in the knowledge representation language.

3 It is desirable for problem-solving systems to represent operations for building and manipulating the model in the knowledge form as much as possible. As each operation is to build or modify a part of the structure so that the whole structure will tend to satisfy the given requirements, the language must be such that knowledge can be expressed as an amalgamation of the structure and functionality. That is, the data structure and the functionality description must be integrated in the knowledge representation.

4 In using knowledge, the completeness of deductive inference must be ensured in order to keep the results always sound. It is especially important in the cases where not only the model analysis methods but also the model modification methods can be expressed explicitly and the model analysis–evaluation–modification loop can be repeated autonomously.

5 An object model involves a large amount of information. This introduces a new problem. To represent all the information in the general knowledge form is inefficient, because, in general, only a small portion of the model information undergoes dynamic operations in a session of finite duration. It loses not only memory efficiency but also processing efficiency for handling large amounts of data as a whole. An alternative method is to keep the main part of model information in the form of a database and activate only the small part of the information that is being given attention at the moment. Then there arises a problem of integrating knowledge bases and databases. Ordinary databases are managed and manipulated by procedural DBMS programs. Thus, procedural programs must also be involved in the integration. This is shown in Fig. 10-6.

6 An object model is modified very frequently. In the design of a complex object, many people are involved with the design process. Since each in-

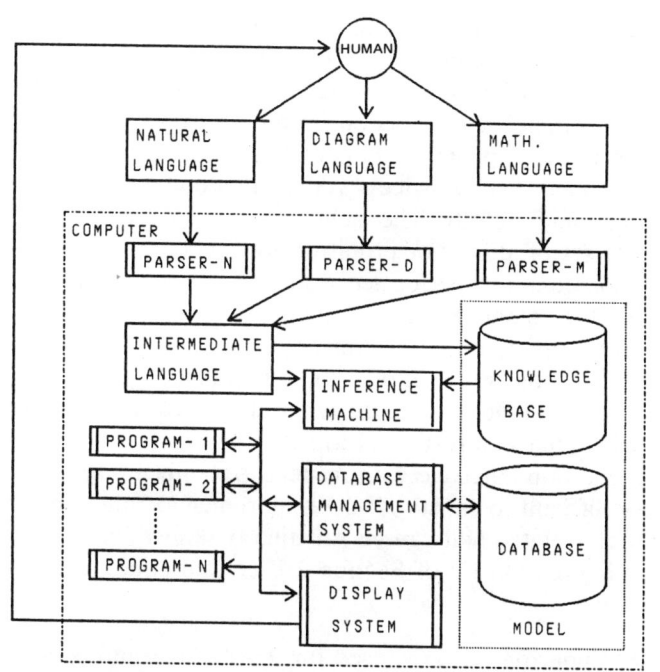

FIGURE 10-6
Knowledge-based system organization.

dividual manipulates the model independently, it becomes necessary to check the consistency of the model. This is probably the most difficult requirement to meet. At present, we have to rely upon human capability to maintain consistency. But consistency checks are becoming more difficult even for human beings, and the system must be able to take part in the task as much as possible. Consistency is a characteristic not of the individual knowledge representation but of knowledge as a whole, the knowledge base. In other words, all modularized expressions in the knowledge base must keep such relations that ensure overall consistency. This means that there must be a theory at the foundation of knowledge representation, based on which each expression can be examined when it keeps consistency with the other expressions.

7 Conversion to internal representation is necessary because many engineering problems need procedural programs in parallel with experiential rules as we have discussed. The knowledge processing part must be able to tailor the existing procedural programs to the current model. Let us return to the problem shown in Fig. 10-1. A specific set of procedural programs is used here for the model. But if the model is modified to include nonlinear elements, then the analysis method must also be changed and a different set of procedures must probably be used. Thus, planning at the knowledge processing level and then transforming to the procedural processing part must be done smoothly.

8 A desirable CAD system must be able to ensure a convenient external language so that the human designer can express his or her idea conveniently. This is, in reality, the problem of knowledge representation language design. What is required of the system at the conversion from external expression to knowledge representation is the capability to understand the user's idea expressed in the external language. The knowledge representation language must be able to express the meaning faithfully. The meaning of the external expression is decomposed into a set of atomic or primitive concepts and their relationships. These decompositions are performed according to the morpheme and syntax, respectively, of the language. If the knowledge representation language is designed to comprise every primitive concept included in the external language and its syntax corresponds to that of the external language, then the conversion is achieved by syntactic translation without loss of meaning. In other words, the external language is restricted to those that can be accepted by the knowledge representation language with respect to the meanings.

It seems to be very difficult to satisfy all the requirements. But some of them are, in reality, closely related and can be satisfied by knowledge representation in the form of expression (2) of Section 2 if certain conditions are met. These conditions are:

1. The logical predicate (Enderton, 1972) is used for `Predicate` and is combined with `Data-Structure`.
2. This data structure is designed to represent all structures that can be involved in different expressions (external expressions, modeling scheme, and internal expressions).

We will not go into the details of all the issues listed in Table 10-1 but will pay attention specifically to the part related to the representation of a model-based problem-solving process.

6 METALEVEL SYSTEM

The modeling knowledge we have discussed so far is concerned mainly with an object and its transformations. Let us call it object-level knowledge or simply object-knowledge. In order to solve real-world problems most automatically and efficiently, it is necessary to represent the problem-solving structure and a control strategy. These are the descriptions on the object-level operation and, therefore, are the higher-level information. As the general notion of knowledge processing, there are many other functions such as knowledge acquisition and maintenance and ambiguous information handling that also need a higher-level description system, which we call the metalevel system in contrast to an object-level system. Knowledge at the metalevel is metalevel knowledge or is called simply metaknowledge. We will not enter into a general discussion on metalevel problems but restrict ourselves to discussing aspects of model-based problem solving. Thus, we assume that the role of the metalevel system is as follows:

1. To represent control strategy and the problem-solving structure.
2. To define arbitrarily the local worlds in the object level, where a local world is a chunk of knowledge in the global knowledge base, so as to (i) accelerate the inference operation by restricting the scope of searching the relevant knowledge or by specifying the application order of formulas in this scope, and (ii) ensure that the system has the capability of checking consistency of every knowledge source by restricting the scope of checking to the small finite set of rules.

For discussing the metalevel system, the other components of the system must be made clear. We therefore defer further discussion on the details of the metalevel system to Section 8.

7 MODEL, MODEL TRANSFORMATION, AND PROBLEM-SOLVING STRUCTURE

7.1 Model Representation

Object-model representation must be such that the object structure and functionalities are amalgamated so that both EQ-trans and NE-trans are represented in the same modeling schema. For the application shown in Fig. 10-3, the form shown in Fig. 10-7 is appropriate. This is the same as that of Fig. 10-3, representing a model shape by the skeletal structure composed of a polyhedron (h), a set of surfaces ($s1$–$s6$), a set of edge lines (label abbreviated), and a set of vertices ($p11$–$p23$). The object model is the combination of the skeletal structure and descriptions of the whole structure or its components.

7.2 Model Transformation Rule

With this modeling scheme and following the discussions so far, the basic form of knowledge representation on model transformation must be as follows:

```
Knowledge Representation;
  (Object Model Representation 1 → Object Model Representation 2)
    = Predicate-1(Data-Structure1 x1) ∧ ----- ∧
        Predicate-m(Data-Structure1 xm) ∧
        Change(Data-Structure1, Data-Structure2)→ Predicate(Data
        Structure2 y), i = 1, 2, ..., m.                      (4a)
```

which means that by changing the structure (`Data-Structure1`) of the current model, represented as the compound of the data structure and a set of predicates (`Predicate-1` through `Predicate-m`), to the other structure (`Data-Structure 2`), a new model, `Data-Structure2`, is obtained with accompanying functionality (`Predicate`). Or, introducing variables,

```
    = Predicate-1(s x1) ∧ --- ∧ Predicate-m(s xm) ∧ Change(s t)
                        → Predicate(t y)                     (4b)
```

320 KNOWLEDGE ENGINEERING: APPLICATIONS

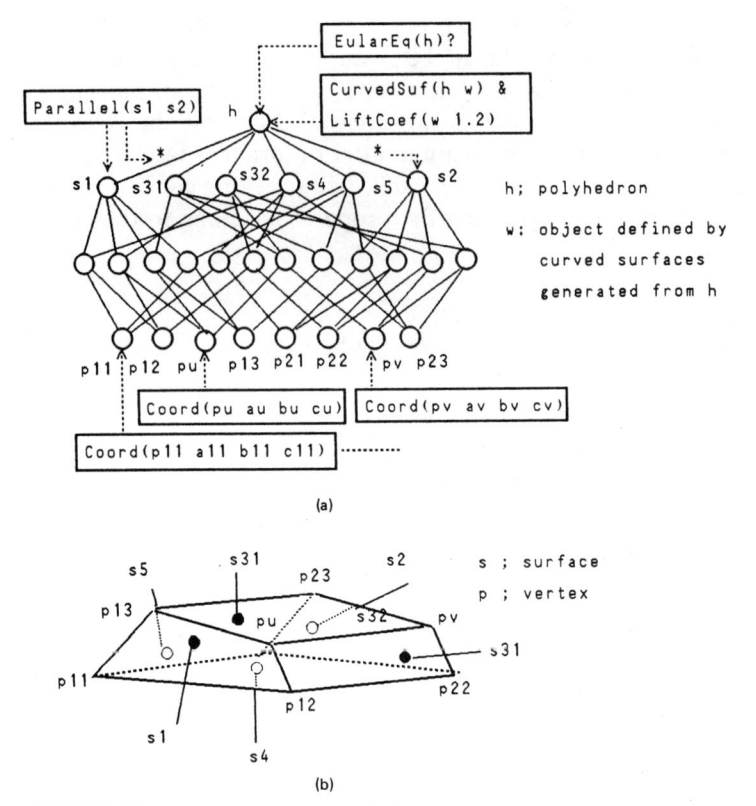

FIGURE 10-7
An example of object-model representation.

can be used where *s* and *t* are the variables defined over the set of all possible structures and `Change(s t)` means to change *s* to *t*. The variables *xi* and *y* represent all the other terms included in the predicates. For a more generalized case, it is better to use `Change(s s' t' t)` instead of `Change(s t)` to mean to change a substructure *s'* of *s* to *t'* resulting in a new structure *t* including *t'* as a substructure. We denote in this chapter the logical AND and OR by the symbols $\wedge$ and $\vee$, respectively.

Formula (4b) includes a special predicate, `Change`. Ordinarily a predicate is evaluated by following the method of pattern matching with the other predicate. But in this case, it is better to use an algorithmic method of evaluation because it must perform the modification of the structure. There are many other predicates similar to `Change`, and it is necessary to link them with the procedural programs for evaluation. This is the way to integrate knowledge processing with conventional ways of processing.

7.3 Representation of Problem-Solving Structure

We can also represent the problem-solving structure by using metaknowledge. Let us represent the process model of Fig. 10-2. It is to be noted that this process is an example only, and there can be other process models as well. System users may wish to represent their own process models. What is important for AI systems is the capability to represent any process model. A process model is represented in the metalevel in the same way as any object model is represented in the object level. The process model of Fig. 10-2 can be represented as

```
AnalExam(Req-i, Model) ∨
    (Modify(Model, Model') ∧ Satisfy(Req-i, Model'))
                      → Satisfy(Req-i, Model)                    (5a)
```

where `Satisfy(Req-i, Model)` and `AnalExam(Req-i, Model, w)` mean "the model satisfies the ith requirement" and "analyze and examine if the model meets the ith requirement," respectively. Thus, the formula says, "First analyze the model and examine if it meets the requirement. If it is the case, the model satisfies the requirement, but if not, then modify the model to a new one and test again for the new model."

As there can be more than one requirement, it is represented by introducing variables, as

```
(For all requirements),
  [AnalEval(x, Model) ∨ (Modify(Model, Model') ∧ Satisfy(x,
       Model')) → Satisfy(x, Model)]                             (5b)
```

This is only the skeletal framework of the process and is not sufficient, because it does not include any mechanism for controlling the process. `Modify` is the same as `Change` in (4) and is included in an object-level transformation rule like (4). Let it be referred to as rule i. Then it may be better to refer to the object rule to avoid redundancy in representation. Moreover, instead of referring to the rule directly, it is better to add some rule-selection strategy. Thus we can include the rule for selecting a transformation rule as follows:

```
(For all requirements x and rules u),
    [AnalEval(x, Model, w) ∨
       (SelectRule(u, x, Model, w) ∧ Apply(u, Model, Model') ∧
              Satisfy(x, Model')) → Satisfy(x, Model)]           (5c)
```

Each predicate in this formula is linked to the related set of rules in the system, after being resolved with the given query of the form "`(For all requirements x), Satisfy(x, Model)?`." As an example, let us assume that there is a set of rules in the form of distributed knowledge sources for the problems of feedback control systems shown in Fig. 10-1. Then `AnalEval(x, Model)?` is issued to this system to analyze and obtain the result and to examine whether the current model satisfies the requirements. Similarly, the system must be provided with a set of rules to make a decision on the selection of the transformation rules that is evoked by `SelectRule`. This is shown in the next section.

7.4 Control of Model Modification

Controlling the problem-solving process presents another problem. Generally speaking, control is a concept closely related to sequential operations. But in the case of knowledge-based problem solving, to control is to select the transformation rules in the optimal way to solve the problem in hand. There are two ways of specifying the rule in the global knowledge base: (1) Directly specify the scope of search by introducing the concept of the set of rules and (2) indirectly specify the rule through the control predicate, giving the condition of rule selection.

The first method is very effective but is possible only when a selection strategy is known in advance. Real control is thus the combination of these two—that is, to select a rule dynamically by the second method within the scope of the set specified by the first method. We show the first method in Section 8 in reference to a real system, and we discuss only the second method here.

Let us think of model modification operations in synthesis-type problem solving. The operations must be guided by some knowledge. Basically, it may be represented in the form "if the model has a `Structure1` and is `Changed` to `Structure2`, then the jth property (`Predicate-j`'s value) becomes greater." As `Change` is included in some object-level transformation rule, it may be represented as

```
Apply(Rule-i, Model)
        → Increase-value(Rule-i, Predicate-j, Model)            (6a)
```

This rule means that the application of rule i to the object model increases its characteristics denoted by `Predicate-j`. It can be generalized by using a variable defined over the set of formulas KS (knowledge source) in the object level, each member of which contributes to increase the value of `Predicate-j`, as

```
(For all rules u in KS),
     [Apply(u, Model) → Increase-Value(u, Predicate-j, Model)]   (6b)
```

Note that these expressions are presented only for the purpose of showing the necessity for the metalevel in representing such a basic concept as the problem-solving structure. These expressions are not precise enough for an actual implementation. In reality, the representation of the problem-solving structure and its control is not so easy as shown here. For example, `AnalExam` and `SelectRule` in (5c) are dependent on the requirement and cannot be dealt with separately. There is also the problem of linking formula (6) with formula

(5c). We need to make the metalevel organization more concrete in order to discuss this issue in more detail. We discuss it in the next section with respect to a realistic system.

8 FEASIBILITY OF ADVANCED EXPERT SYSTEMS

Before closing we need to discuss the feasibility of this idea. Here we show it by a system we are developing, named KAUS (Knowledge Acquisition and Utilization System) (Yamauchi and Ohsuga, 1985). In this system, a knowledge representation language has been designed along the line of thought discussed so far. This language is based on predicate logic and is enhanced to include data structure. Then an inference algorithm, integration with the procedural program, integration with databases, user interfaces, and metalevel structure have been developed on the basis of this language. (Fig. 10-5). The system has been used in various applications (Ohsuga, 1983, 1984, 1987a, 1988; Ohsuga and Yamauchi, 1985). As our objective is to show the feasibility of the idea, we describe the system briefly.

8.1 Predicate Logic Plus Data Structure as Knowledge Representation Language

A knowledge representation language has been designed to satisfy the requirements listed in Table 10-1. It is to be noted that first-order predicate logic can almost satisfy, or at least is nearest to satisfying, items 2 and 4 to 8. It is declarative and modular in expression (items 2 and 8), it is based on a solid theoretical foundation (item 5) (Enderton, 1972), and a complete deductive inference algorithm exists (item 6) (Chang and Lee, 1972). Moreover, it has been proved that it can represent the procedural program to some extent (item 7) (VanEmden and Kowalski, 1976). This enables us to integrate knowledge processing and conventional processing. It has closely related to relational databases (item 4) (Gallaire et al., 1984). In order to satisfy the remaining requirements (1, 3) for modeling, however, it must be expanded to include the capability to represent various data structures.

Since an object model is included as a term in predicate language, we need to expand the definition of "term" to include data structure and that of "predicate" to include the expanded terms as arguments. This can be achieved in two steps: First define the data structure (type) and then introduce it into predicate logic. The language thus expanded can express knowledge in the object-oriented way; that is, the object structure is defined and descriptions are given to this object.

8.2 Data Structure as a Generalized Set

In order to define such a language it is necessary to make clear the concept of data structure in a declarative language. Any data structure defined in a declarative language must correspond to some real structure. As such a data structure, we introduce the idea of axiomatic (Zermelo-Fraenkel; ZF) set theory (Krivine, 1971). This theory states that a set of entities large enough to represent every mathematical concept but free of any contradiction must be defined in a constructive way by using a finite set of primitive constructors (defining too large a set causes contradictions known as Russel's paradox). The term "set" is almost equivalent to "data structure" from the viewpoint of information processing.

A set of primitive structural relations including "element-of" ($\in$), "component-of" ($\triangleleft$), "power-set-off" (*), "product-set-of" ($\times$), "union-of" ($\cup$), "intersection-of" ($\cap$), and "pair-of" ($\langle\rangle$) are provided in KAUS. These structural relations are at the same time structure constructors if one of the entities necessary in the given relation is not yet defined. This set of constructors has been chosen in KAUS with reference to ZF theory but with slight modifications. This modification is necessary because ZF theory is restricted to the mathematical world and "set" is defined as a purely mathematical concept. A set represents an entity in the real world translated into mathematical terms. On the other hand, knowledge processing deals with every real entity as it is. Sometimes different structural relations in the real world can be transformed into the same relation in mathematics. For example, "component-of" is included in the KAUS data structure for the purpose of representing a hierarchical structure in the real world with no property inheritance (Ohsuga, 1984). It is represented in the mathematical world by a special type of "element-of" relation. The "component-of" relation is necessary for representing a real entity as it is. Then it can be translated into a mathematical structure if necessary in the system.

Any compound structure constructed from these relations is also allowed in KAUS. For example, a set *n X is obtained by applying the power-set constructor repeatedly n times to the given set X, that is, *n X = *(*n − 1 X). This represents a set of all n-level hierarchical structures that can be constructed from the given set X. Any specific hierarchical structure constructed from X is an element of the set. Similarly, any structure—for example, a graph or a table—can be defined. The set of all entities including the given primitives and those that can be generated from them forms the universe. Hence the universe of KAUS includes every structure that can appear in mathematics as well as the hierarchical structures in the real world. These structures, both primitives and compounds, can be represented directly using pointers as well as in the ordinary predicate form. The definition of these set constructors is presented in Table 10-2.

8.3 Multilayer Logic as Predicate Logic Including Data Structure

As the next step, the syntax of first-order predicate language is expanded to include the structures thus defined so that a functionality on a structured ob-

TABLE 10-2
A Set of Primitive Structural Relations/Constructors

Constructor	Symbol	Definition
1. Element-of	∈	$x \in X$ means that an entity x is an element of a set X.
2. Component-of	◁	Let X be assembled of the parts $y1, y2, \ldots, yn$. Let Y be the set of the parts, that is, $Y = \{y1, y2, \ldots, yn\}$. Then, $X \triangleright Y$.
3. Power-set-of	*	$Y = *X$ denotes that Y is the set of all subsets of a set X.
4. Product-set-of	×	$Y = X1 \times X2 \times \ldots \times Xn = \times_i$; X_i denotes a Cartesian product of X_i, $i = 1, 2, \ldots, n$.
5. Union-of	∪	$Y = X1 \cup X2 \cup \ldots \cup Xn = \cup_i X_i$ denotes a union set of Xi, $i = 1, 2, \ldots, n$.
6. Intersection-of	∩	$Y = X1 \cap X2 \cap \ldots \cap Xn = \cap_i X_i$ denotes an intersection of Xi, $i = 1, 2, \ldots, n$.
7. Pair-of	⟨⟩	When $X1$ and $X2$ are the sets, then $y = \langle X1, X2 \rangle$ is an allowable entity.

ject represented by this generalized data structure is described by the predicate. We call it multilayer logic (MLL) (Ohsuga, 1983; Ohsuga and Yamauchi, 1985). MLL satisfies most of the requirements for knowledge representation and is very convenient not only to define any structured object and its transformation but also to meet the conditions for human–machine communications. Moreover, it is possible to describe and to link it to existing programs and databases, as will be discussed in Sections 8.5 and 8.6.

Data structure is included in predicate logic by expanding the syntax of predicate logic. We start from many-sorted logic (MSL), a branch of ordinary first-order predicate logic (Enderton, 1972). MSL includes the concept of type as a domain set in its syntax. With this logic a predicate is represented in the form (Ax/X)F(x) or (Ex/X)F(x), where X is a set in the universe and x/X denotes $x \in X$. A and E denote the quantifiers in the ordinary sense. (Ax/X)F(x) and (Ex/X)F(x) are read "for all x in X, $F(x)$" and "for some x in X, $F(x)$," respectively. These expressions are equivalent to expressing $(Ax)[x \in X \rightarrow F(x)]$ and $(Ex)[x \in X \land F(x)]$, respectively, in ordinary predicate logic. For example, "Man is mortal," which is represented in ordinary logic as $(Ax)[\text{man}(x) \rightarrow \text{mortal}(x)]$, is represented in this syntax as (Ax/man)mortal(x). "Man" in the ordinary logic expression is the predicate name, while in the expanded syntax expression it is the set name.

In the expressions above, X can be any set and therefore it can be the generalized set defined in the last section. Thus x can be an individual structure, and the predicate gives an expression on the structured object x (Ohsuga, 1983; Ohsuga and Yamauchi, 1985). This is multilayer logic. MLL is the predicate logic involving the object-oriented data type. It is possible to represent functionalities on any hierarchical object or its components. As an example, let us think of the expression (Ex/X)(Ay/x)F(y), where x is an element of a given set X and at the same time is a set itself. The variable y represents x's element. The sequence of "element-of" relations comes from the mathematical interpretation of a hierarchical structure. Then this expression states that there is some element x of the node X, of which every element y has the functionality F. Or, let us assume the case of X being a power set of the given set W. Then (Ex/*W)(Ay/x)F(y) requires the system to obtain a subset x of W such that every element y of x satisfies $F(y)$. Here *W denotes a power set of W. Then its element is a subset of W. This is the basic form to take the set X out of W with such elements x that meet the given condition, by giving a constraint to the base set W.

As an example expression, let P be the set of points in three-dimensional space. Then

$$(Az/*3\ P)[EulerEq(z) \wedge (Ay/z)\{ElemCycle(y) \wedge (Ax/y)Count(x\ 2)\} \rightarrow ConvPolyhedron(z)] \qquad (7)$$

gives a condition that a three-level hierarchical structure composed of the set P as a base set represents the convex polyhedron where EulerEq(z), ElemCycle(y), Count(x 2), and ConvPolyhedron(z) are the predicates meaning "z satisfied the Euler equation" (a relation holding among the number of points, lines, and surfaces), "y is an elementary cycle," "x is a set with two elements," and "z is a convex polyhedron," respectively. Then it is possible, by making use of this rule, to generate polyhedra using the given points as the vertices. Note that this example is for the purpose of explanation. In real-world applications, additional predicates are necessary such as (Ay/z)Coplanar(y) meaning that every y is coplanar (a set of edge lines is on the same plane).

8.4 Inference

A specifically designed inference algorithm has been developed for MLL that is different from the one used in most conventional expert systems based on string matching. This algorithm uses the set-theoretic relation between domain sets of variables included in the predicates for deriving implicative relations according to the following equivalence rule:

$$\begin{array}{lll} X \supset Y & \leftrightarrow & [(Ax/X)F(x) \rightarrow (Ax/Y)F(x)] \\ X \subset Y & \leftrightarrow & [(Ex/X)F(x) \rightarrow (Ex/Y)F(x)] \\ X \cap Y \neq \emptyset & \leftrightarrow & [(Ax/X)F(x) \rightarrow (Ex/Y)F(x)] \end{array} \qquad (8)$$

Any relation between compound sets is decomposed into the set of these primitive relations. A part of the unification by symbol manipulation can be replaced by the test for set-theoretic relations between domain sets. Since the problem is to know either the object structure or its functionalities on the basis of their relations, this is the basis of problem solving.

To aid the test for the set-theoretic relation between sets, a conceptual entity network is formed. All entities defined in the system are linked by the primitive structural relations of Table 10-2 to fabricate a conceptual entity network (Ohsuga, 1983; Ohsuga and Yamauchi, 1985). Then the test is performed by traversing the network in a specific way. Every logical predicate is embedded in the network in such a way that a predicate including a term (entity) is linked to the node representing this entity in this network. This forms a knowledge structure.

8.5 Integration with Procedural Programs

As we have seen in formula (4) in Section 6.3, there are a number of predicates such as Change for which the procedural method of evaluation is much better. These are data-structure manipulation, input and output operations, Boolean operations, and numeric calculations. A part of the model information might be represented in a database as well. The inference mechanism must be combined with conventional information processing in this way.

The integration became possible basically by providing KAUS with the mechanism to link with built-in procedures. For example, two types of predicates can be defined in advance; one is the ordinary predicate, and the other is the predicate that corresponds to a procedure to evaluate the predicate. The latter is called the *procedural type atom* (PTA for short). For each PTA, the inference mechanism evokes the corresponding procedure if a certain condition is met during the inference operation and executes it to return the value(s) of some variable(s) as the result. Each PTA is represented by the procedure name followed by the input and output variables included in the program. KAUS is ready to accept any kind of procedures defined by the user through its PTA.

However, only programs specifically written for KAUS can be used with this method. In order to use existing, independently developed programs with KAUS, another way of transferring the control between the knowledge-level operation and the programs is provided. A KAUS version running under the UNIX system uses a fork-and-execute mechanism. A specific PTA named Exec contains the procedure name to evoke as an argument. It evokes a specified program, activates the UNIX function to move control to the specified program, and receives the result. Thus it is possible, in principle, to use every program working under the UNIX system. A set of these programs forms the program base.

8.6 Integration with Databases

Integration of knowledge base and databases is an especially important issue (Gallaire et al., 1984). KAUS is provided with two types of coupling with databases: tight coupling and loose coupling. For the former, any access method can be defined at the knowledge level and executed by the inference mechanism incorporated with the PTA mechanism. The data model is expanded so as to represent complex data objects. Its structure is represented by the KAUS data structure. KAUS can obtain information referring to this structure on the way of handling databases.

This data structure is also used to communicate with commercial databases. As the existing DBMS cannot be modified for the purpose of integration, the loosely coupled method becomes necessary. KAUS generates the access commands to these databases. KAUS can refer to the data structure to identify the relation schema and the database schema of the database and then generate an intermediate code using this information. Then the code is translated into the commands each DBMS requires. Now KAUS is able to access two different DBMSs. In either method of communication, KAUS is the master and the DBMS is the slave.

8.7 Model Representation

An example of a model representation in MLL is shown in Fig. 10-7 assuming the case of design discussed in Section 3. A predicate includes the hierarchical structure or its substructure as a term that is represented by the node. In this case the predicate is linked to the node. On the other hand, the structure includes the predicates linked to any subnode as the constraints or the description of functionalities to define the model in more detail. Thus structure and functionality description can be amalgamated in this model representation. The predicates are related to each other indirectly through the structure. This facilitates the handling of the constraint propagation. This mutual inclusion relation between predicates and structure is essential for problem representation. The model is a part of the knowledge structure.

8.8 User Interface

A user interface has been implemented in KAUS to allow the mixed use of various media such as the subset of natural language, mathematical formulas, and picture drawing on the multiwindow system. Figure 10-8 is a sample display of the interface used in the example of Fig. 10-1. A block diagram to define a model of a feedback control system and a result of the analysis are shown in separate windows. The upper-left window shows a root locus of the given block diagram (upper right and behind), a special way of analyzing the block diagram.

8.9 Control Structure in the Metalevel

The domain KS of the variable x in expression (6b) is a subset of the set of all transformation rules in the object level. It is a knowledge source that is effective for achieving a specific objective. It can be represented by a simple tree in

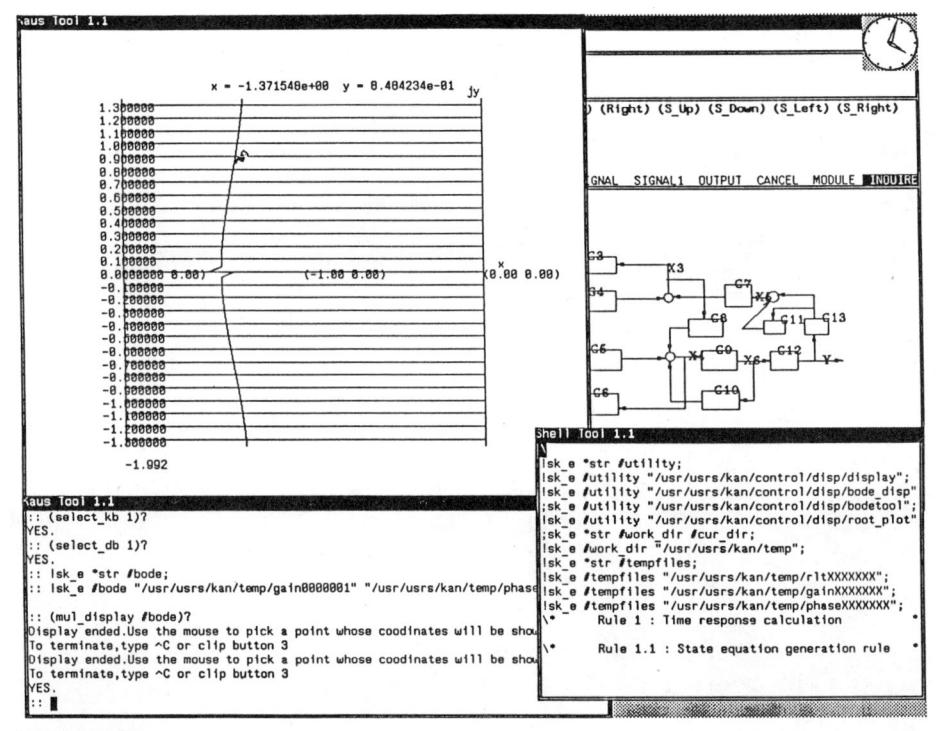

FIGURE 10-8
An example of human–machine interface.

the metalevel, composed of a single root node and the terminal leaves, where the root node is attached to the knowledge source (KS) while each terminal node is attached to an object-level rule number. It is possible to make the tree a more complex hierarchical structure to represent the finer control rule. For example, it is possible to represent the order of rule applications in the form of a tree structure.

As an example, let us consider the sequence of transformation shown in Fig. 10-1. Each knowledge source (KS) is a set of rules and is used at different stages of transformation. Generally speaking, the more we know about the problem, the finer we can make the structure even within each knowledge source. As a typical case, there can be a linear order of applying individual rules in the knowledge source to the model. Let us assume first that there is no information on the order and that a problem is solved by repeatedly backtracking in the inference mechanism. This is a very inefficient process, but as we learn more about the problem we can modify the control structure as shown in Fig. 10-9, where $R1$–Rn represent the individual formulas given at the object level. We introduce here a convention for interpreting the structure: If the lower-level node is linked by the "component-of" relation ($\triangleleft$) to the upper node, the order of processing is from left to right. For example, if $X \triangleright Y$ is to

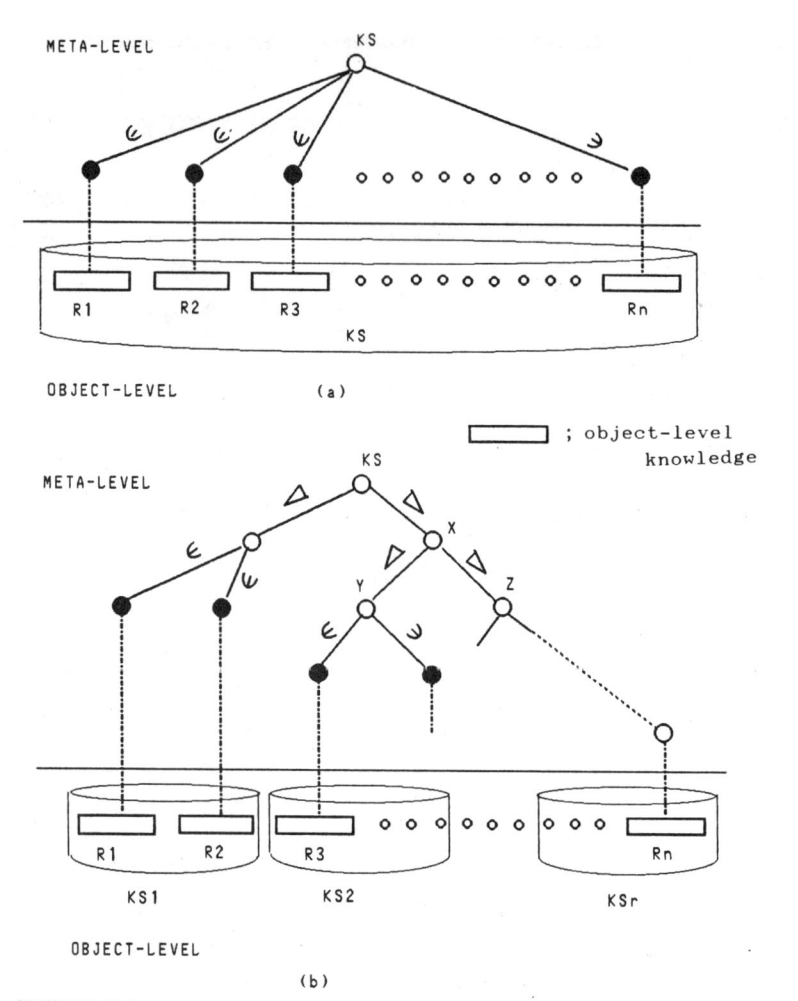

FIGURE 10-9
Metalevel control structure.

the left of $X \triangleright Z$, then Y precedes Z. Otherwise, these elements are interpreted to form a simple set to the upper nodes. This convention is used only when the structure is interpreted as a control structure.

The control structure is an entity in the metalevel, and it is possible to give descriptions to this structure in the same way as we give descriptions to the object structure in the object level. For example, the metarule of the form (6b) is linked to the node. Thus metalevel knowledge is also represented as a combination of data structure and predicates, the same as object knowledge. In KAUS, the same structuring scheme and MLL can be used to represent metalevel knowledge. The difference is in the meaning; that is, the data structure of the object level represents an object, while that of the metalevel represents a control structure.

To specify a subset of rules in the object level as a knowledge source is to define a local world at the object level that is a unit of activation of knowledge. It is possible to define any number of local worlds, and a rule can belong to a number of worlds. One local world can be defined within the scope of another local world. These relationships between local worlds are represented by the control structure at the metalevel. It is also possible to use this mechanism to define the scope within which logical consistency is ensured.

The control structure given in advance for some problems is not always optimal, but it can be improved. This is due to the design of the control algorithm. To improve the process, the control structure can be modified at the metalevel. This operation is performed in the same way as the modification of the object structure at the object level.

In order to improve the control structure, it is necessary to evaluate and modify the control tree on the basis of a certain evaluation function defined in advance. Let us assume that we can write down some rules for modifying the control tree at the metalevel in the same way as transformation rule (4) at the object level. Then, there arises the problem of selecting one of these rules, and it is possible to write down other rules for selecting one. This rule must be put in a higher level than the control level, the metametalevel. More levels may be necessary for achieving more sophisticated operations.

The knowledge representation scheme defined in the object level can also be used to define the other levels. Thus we can define a multilevel system in which each level has the same subsystem.

The data structure included in KAUS is used very effectively to define a many-world, multilevel system. Every function involved in KAUS's object-level subsystem is used to form a basic package, and these packages are accumulated to form multi-metalevels. As metalevel knowledge can be represented by the same language as the object-level language, metalevel operations are performed by the same mechanism as the object-level operations. This multilevel mechanism is managed by the level manager.

8.10 Interlevel Communication

The relation between adjacent levels must be very close from the viewpoint of enabling the fine control, but at the same time it is desirable that the relation be very simple from the viewpoint of system design and implementation.

KAUS has three routes for connecting different levels. First, the inference mechanism bridges adjacent levels. Generally speaking, an inference operation is decomposed to (1) the search for relevant knowledge and (2) the resolution operation with the selected knowledge. Let us assume that the object-level inference mechanism is located between the metalevel and the object level as shown in Fig. 10-10. The searcher, receiving the node name KS of the

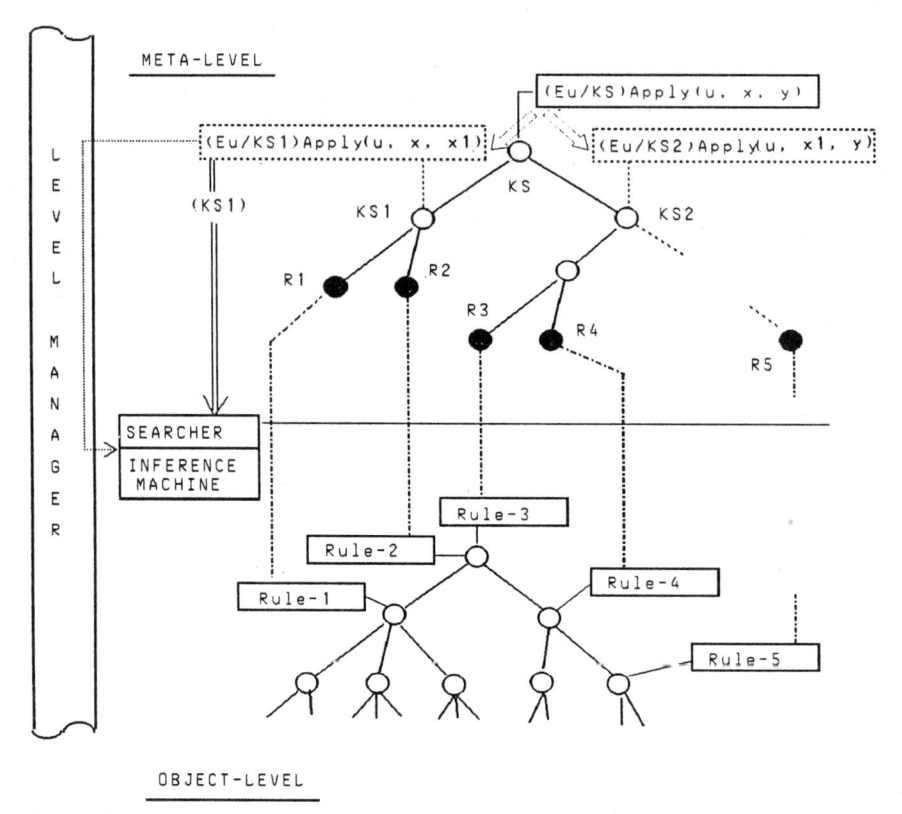

FIGURE 10-10
Interlevel communication.

control structure, confines the scope of searching for the relevant knowledge to the substructure of this node in its inference operation. If the node is in the set of nodes linked by the component-of relation, then the left component must be sent to the searcher first.

The second way of linking different levels is necessary for the transfer of control. This is the role of the level manager. We explain its role by keeping the problem-solving process of Fig. 10-1 in mind as an example.

Let us assume that the control structure KS as shown in Fig. 10-9a is given and to this structure is added the metarule (6b) but represented in the form of a KAUS rule,

(Au/KS)[Apply(u, Model, Model')
 → Increase-Value(u, Predicate-j, Model, Model')]   (6c)

where Model' is included in IncreaseValue to mean precisely that the value of Predicate-j increases by modifying the current model (Model) to the new one (Model'). In fact, both Model and Model' are replaced by the variables.

Assume also that the request "Increase the value of the jth predicate of the current model by modifying to the new model" is issued to the metalevel. Then the system begins to solve this problem at the metalevel and deduces `(Eu/KS)Apply(u, Model, Model')` by means of (6c). Evaluation of this predicate must be done in cooperation with the object-level subsystem because the objective is to apply the object rule specified by the control structure to the model in the object level.

In the case of the KS being a simple unordered set of nodes, the node name KS is sent by `Apply(u, Model, Model')` in the metaknowledge to the searcher. `Apply` is a PTA and corresponds to a procedure that sends the node name KS to the searcher of the object-level inference mechanism. The searcher confines the scope of search to this set of rules in the object-level operation.

In general, however, the control structure is not so simple as this but can be a hierarchy with many levels as shown in Fig. 10-9b. In this case the predicate is expanded to the components following the control structure and must be evaluated by each component, each time waiting for the result of the preceding operation in the object level. Every evaluation of a component generates an interim model. To represent this situation, we need to use the variables x and y for `Model` and `Model'` in the expression of `Apply`. Let KS be decomposed to (KS1, KS2,...KSn). Then the query `(Eu/KS)Apply(u, x, y,)` is expanded to a set of queries,

`(Eu/KS1)Apply(u, x, x1)`
`(Eu/KS2)Apply(u, x1, x2)`

$$\vdots$$

`(Eu/KSn)Apply(u, xn - 1, y)`

and each one is linked to the related node. These queries are then processed one by one. This is shown in Fig. 10-10. `(Eu/KS1)Apply(u, x, y,)` is linked to node KS of the control structure and then decomposed to `(Eu/KS1)Apply(u, x, x1)` and `(EU/KS')Apply(u, x1, y)`, where KS' denotes the set (KS2, KS3,..., KSn). The second of these expressions is decomposed again to `(Eu/KS2)Apply(u, x1, x2)` and the remainder. This process continues until the decomposition is complete.

Let us assume, in this example, that this first query is evaluated. A procedure corresponding to `Apply` is called again and sends KS1 to the searcher. Then the metalevel operation suspends itself and asks the level manager to activate the object-level operation by transferring control to the object-level inference mechanism. On the other hand, the object-level subsystem, after finishing the operation using the rules in KS1, returns control to the metalevel through the level manager with the truth value denoting success or failure. If it ends in success, the evaluation of `(Eu/KS1)Apply(u, x, x1)` also ends in success at the metalevel. Then the next query is selected for evaluation. Thus the problem-solving process is performed automatically and sequentially by the control of metaknowledge. This type of query evaluation by expansion is necessary at every level.

In reality, metaknowledge sends mode assignment to the searcher as additional information. It specifies the operation at the lower level. The *execution mode* instructs the lower level in normal problem solving as in the above example. The *trace mode* requires the lower level to keep track of the rules used to achieve the goal during the problem solving. This information is used to redesign the control structure at the metalevel, to design the procedural program, and for other purposes. The *interpretive mode* directs the lower level to do a one-step inference operation and return the result. We intend to use this mode for software design also.

It is necessary to provide the system with still another route to transfer the control from the lower level to the higher level that can be activated by the lower-level knowledge. This is the third route. The demand for this type of transfer is rather special and belongs to the system's function. Thus, in order to ensure the maintainability of the system, the use of this route is dedicated to the system and privileged users by means of the special PTA through the level manager. The PTA generates the query, on the basis of the transfer request, and issues the query to the level manager.

It is important to note that even though high-level operations are performed at the higher levels, every high-level system behaves formally like the first-order system within the level and enjoys all its characteristics such as completeness. It is also important to note that the system manages every transfer route. In this system, the scope of information activated for an operation can be confined to a small set of formulas under the control of the management system. It is desirable to define the set of formulas to be concerned as directly as possible with the objective of the operation. Let us call such a set a *local world* or simply a *world*. It is possible to define any number of worlds, and it is also possible to ensure the logical consistency of every world. The relationship between worlds in the object level (the object-level world) can be managed at the metalevel. A set of metalevel formulas forms a metalevel world in the same way. The logical consistency of the metalevel world can also be ensured. It is expected that this system framework will ensure correct operation even when the system is greatly expanded.

8.11 Representing a Problem-Solving Structure

The representation of a problem-solving structure shown in Section 6 is not satisfactory for real-world problems. As the operations for both `AnalEval` and `SelectRule` are dependent on the requirements, the system must be provided with the knowledge that links them. A linking formula is necessary for each different form of requirement, and since there are a finite number of different forms of requirements, we can provide these formulas.

In the following we assume for simplicity that any requirement is represented as a condition on the value of a predicate in the object model. In the example of airplane wing design, the predicate was `LiftCoeff(wing, x)` and a condition such as `GreaterEqual(x, a)` was imposed on the value x with respect to the designated quantity a. The requirements are different if their condition parts are different—`Equal, LessEqual, LessThan, GreaterEqual, GreaterThan`, and so on. Let the type of these requirements be A, B, C, D, E, and so on, respectively. It is possible to expand the types of requirements to a wide class if necessary.

Let the kth requirement (referred to as `Requirement-k`) be represented as `Predicate-k(Model, w)` ∧ `LessThan(w, a)`. The requirements are given at the object level, and each requirement is given an identify designator (I.D.). At the metalevel the structure named `REQ` is formed with all I.D.'s as terminal nodes. Then the link between `AnalEval` and the requirements is made in the form

(∀x/REQ)(∀w, a/real)[Ask(x, Model, w, a)
    → AnalExam(Model, x, w, a)]   (9)

where `Ask(x, Model, w, a)` is the special PTA at the metalevel similar to `Apply`. But in this case the formula corresponding to a node in `REQ` of the object level is used as the query issued to the model. A set of additional variables w and a is included for the purpose of transferring the quantities included in the requirement through `AnalExam` to the other part of the formula representing the problem-solving structure. As in the case of `Apply`, this is system knowledge, and the user does not need to know about it. In effect, we can write equivalently

(∀w, a/real)[Predicate-j(Model, w) ∧ LessThan(w, a)
    → Requirement-k(Model, w, a)]   (10a)
(∀w, a/real)[Requirement-k(Model, w, a)
    → AnalExam(Model, Requirement-k, w, a)]   (10b)

Next, let us assume that evaluation of `AnalEval` ends in failure. Then model modification is necessary. But the operation is different for every requirement type. Let, for example, the requirement be of type C. That the valuation ended in failure means that the value of `Predicate-k` of the current model is greater than the specified value a and the model modification operation must be such as to decrease the value. It is therefore necessary to provide different formulas for different types of requirements. In order to link the formula with that of the problem-solving structure, we need another special PTA here: `TypeReq(Requirement-k, x)`. This checks what type of requirement is being processed currently and substitutes the type code for x. Thus, we need the following set of formulas:

(∀x/REQ)(∀u/KS)(∀w, a/REAL)
[AnalExam(Model, x, w, a)∨
  ((TypeReq(x, A) ∧
    (GreaterThan(w, a) ∧ DecreaseValue(u, Predicate-j, Model, Model'))

```
       ∨(LessThan(w, a) ∧ IncreaseValue(u, Predicate-j, Model, Model')))
                       ∧ Satisfy(x, Model') → Satisfy(x, Model)]
(∆x/REQ)∆u/KS)(∆w, a/REAL)
[AnalExam(Model, x, w, a)∨
  (TypeReq(x, B) ∧
  (DecreaseValue(u, Predicate-j, Model, Model')))
                       ∧ Satisfy(x, Model') → Satisfy(x, Model)]
```
(11)

and so on. In fact, `Model`, `Model'`, and `Predicate-j` are replaced by the variables.

The ideas discussed in this section are still in the preliminary stage. The level manager is being implemented and is not yet complete. Note that with this framework, sophisticated operations other than those discussed here become possible. For example, it may be possible to form still another hierarchical structure at the meta-metalevel, the terminal nodes of which are the I.D.'s of formulas (11). We can provide the system with a meta-metaformula that selects one of the formulas for the model depending on the type of requirement.

It is also possible, with this framework, to link the users' requirement directly to the system's operation. Any requirement, after being parsed, is entered into the `REQ` tree and can then be used immediately.

8.12 Examples and Current State of KAUS

KAUS is now being implemented. Currently only the object-level subsystem including the following components is running.

KAUS (Object-Level subsystem)

- MLL as knowledge representation
- Inference based on MLL
- Knowledge–database integration

  loose coupling

  tight coupling

- Knowledge–procedure integration
- Multimedia interface

The extension of KAUS to include multi-metalevel systems is under way. The basic part of the metalevel operation has been tested.

We are applying KAUS to various problems including electronic circuit analysis, feedback control system design (Guan, 1983), mechanical design (Han et al., 1987), airplane wing design, and the estimation of chemical compound structure to test its applicability. Figure 10-8 is an output of a control system design developed by J. B. Guan of our laboratory. A designer makes a tentative model in the form of a block diagram on the display using pictures and mathematical formulas. The block diagram represents an object model in this application. Then the object model is transformed, successively producing the signal flow graph, the sets of local loops and open paths, and the global transfer function, to the procedural program to calculate the input-output relation. Now the model modification rules are being added to the system to form the synthesis process.

In these applications the empirical rules and the established analytic methods are combined. In every application the object-model structure is stored in the database. But as the metalevel system is not yet complete and accordingly the problem-solving structure is not yet represented, the human user must perform these roles for the time being. For example, in the case of the feedback control system problem of Fig. 10-1, the user must tell the system what knowledge source to use next after each stage of transformation ends. If we wish to classify knowledge into different knowledge sources, the control system must be prepared to control the use of these knowledge sources. As this classification is not fixed but must be changed dynamically, the control system must be very flexible and expandable. Nevertheless these applications have revealed that the idea discussed in this chapter is quite successful. Once the metalevel system has been implemented, the longer sequence will be performed automatically.

9 CONCLUSION

We have discussed in this chapter our idea on the use of an expert system for problem solving, especially for engineering problems. We have shown first that conventional computer programs are not satisfactory in supporting human problem-solving activities because the mechanisms of current computer programs do not accommodate well the requirements of problem solving. Therefore it is first necessary to identify these requirements.

In the first half of the chapter we analyzed and formalized the problem-solving process and then derived a set of requirements that an expert system should satisfy. In the last half, we presented a system developed along this line of thought. This system, named KAUS for knowledge acquisition and utilization system has shown great potential capability for processing information that cannot be handled by conventional CAD systems.

This system is being tested for applicability to real-world problems such as mechanical design, feedback control system design, airplane wing design, and chemical compound structure estimation. These applications have been performed using only the object-level subsystem. This object-level subsystem is used as a package and a multi metalevel system is organized by accumulating subsystems. The metalevel system and its management system including metalevel control and many-world control is being implemented.

ACKNOWLEDGMENTS

I would like to acknowledge the contribution of Mr. H. Yamauchi, who has implemented KAUS, and those of Mr. R. Akutsu, Mr. A. Takasu, Mr. Futatsugi, Dr. G. Han, and Mr. J. B. Guan, who have applied KAUS to various problems in our laboratory. I also thank Professor J. Sato at the University of Tokyo, who developed the program for wing analysis and permitted us to use it in our system.

REFERENCES

Berztiss, A. T. (1971). Data Structure. In: *Theory and Practice*. Academic, New York.
Chang, C. L., and Lee, R. C. T. (1972). *Symbolic Logic and Mechanical Theorem Proving*. Academic, New York.
Date, C. J. (1981). *An Introduction to Database Systems,* 3rd ed. Addison-Wesley, Reading, Mass.
Davis, R. (1980). Meta-Rules (1980); Reasoning about Control, *AI* **15**(3):179–222.
De Kleer, J. (1986). An Assumption-Based TMS. *AI* **28**(2):127–162.
Enderton, H. B. (1972). *Mathematical Introduction to Logic*. Academic, New York.
Fitter, M. (1979). Towards More Natural Interactive Systems. *Int. J. Man-Mach. Stud.* **11**:339–350.
Gallaire, H., Minker, J., and Nicolas, J.M. (1984). Logic and Databases: A Deductive Approach. *Comput. Sur.* **16**(2):
Gene, H. H., et al. (1982). *Design of Feedback Control Systems*. Holter-Saunders,
Guan, J., and Ohsuga, S. (1988). An Intelligent Man-Machine System Based on KAUS for Designing Feedback Control Systems. In: *Artificial Intelligence in Engineering Design* (J. S. Gero, Ed.) Elsevier, New York, pp.
Han, G., Ohsuga, S., and Yamauchi, H. (1987). The Application of Knowledge Base Technology to CAD. In: *Expert Systems in Computer Aided Design* (J. Gero, Ed.). North Holland, Amsterdam, pp. 25–55.
Hayes-Roth, F., et al. (1983). *Building Expert Systems*. Addison-Wesley, Reading, Mass.
Kalay, Y. E., Swerdloff, L. M., and Harfmann, A. C. (1987). A Knowledge-Based Computable Model of Design. *Preprints,* Working Conf. W.G.5.2. on Expert Systems in Computer-Aided Design.
Kemper, A., and Wallrath, M. (1987). An Analysis of Geometric Modeling in Database Systems. *ACM Comt. Sur.* **19**(1):
Krivine, J. L. (1971). *Introduction to Axiomatic Set Theory*. D. Reidel, Dordrecht, Holland.
Ohsuga, S. (1983). A New Method of Model Description—Use of Knowledge Base and Inference. In: *CAD System Framework* (K. Bo and F. M. Lillehagen, Eds.). North-Holland, Amsterdam, pp. 285–312.
Ohsuga, S. (1984). A Consideration to Knowledge Representation—An Information Theoretic View. *Bull. Inform.Cybern.* **21**(1-2):121–135.
Ohsuga, S. (1985a). Introducing Knowledge Processing to CAD/CAM, Finite Elements. *Anal. Design* **1**:255–269.
Ohsuga, S. (1985b). Conceptual Design of CAD Systems Involving Knowledge Base. In: *Knowledge Engineering in Computer-Aided Design* (J. Gero, Ed.) North Holland, Amsterdam, pp. 29–56.
Ohsuga, S. (1987a). Problem Solving System Based on Intelligent Model Building Method. *Trans. Inst. Electron. Commun. Eng. Jpn.* **J69-D**(7):1009–1024 (in Japanese).
Ohsuga, S. (1987b). The Application of Knowledge Base Technology to CAD. In *Expert Systems in Computer Aided Design* (J. Gero, Ed.) North Holland, Amsterdam, pp. 25–55.

Ohsuga, S. (1989). Knowledge Processing System Design—Principles and Practice. In: *Machine Intelligence* Vol. 12 (D. Michie, Ed.), to appear.
Ohsuga, S., and Yamauchi, H. (1985). Multi-Layer Logic—A Predicate Logic Including Data Structure as Knowledge Representation Language. *New Generation Computing,* Vol. 4 (Special Issue on Knowledge Representation). Ohmsha, Ltd. and Springer-Verlag, Berlin.
Tsichritzis, D. C., and Lochovsky, F. H. (1982). *Data Models*. Prentice-Hall, Englewood Cliffs, N.J.
Van Emden, M. H. and Kowalski, R. A. (1976). The Semantics of Predicate Logic as a Programming Language. *J. ACM* **23**(4):
Yamauchi, H., and Ohsuga, S. (1985). KAUS as a Tool for Model Building and Evaluation. Proc. 5th Int. Workshop on Expert Systems and Their Applications, Avignon, France, May 13–15.

NAME INDEX

Agee, M. H., 210
Aggarwal, J., 158
Alayan, H., 188, 206
Albus, J., 128, 157, 159
Alexander, S. M., 168, 206
Al-Jaar, R. Y., 188, 206
Alla, H., 210
Allen, J., 96, 114, 278, 297
Allerhand, M., 278, 285–286, 295, 297
Altenhein, A., 170, 211
Ambler, A. P., 183, 206
Ambriola, V., 243
Anderson, D. C., 166, 207, 209
Andersson, R., 114
Andreasen, M. M., 165, 206
Andresen, F., 145, 157
Appleton, D. S., 162, 206
Apt, K. R., 4, 24
Arbib, M., 120, 157
Aristotle, 177
Arkin, R., 120, 123–125, 127, 129, 131, 136–137, 140–143, 150–153, 157–158
Asada, H., 254, 274
Atabakhche, H., 212
Atkinson, D., 114
Ayache, N., 126, 136, 158

Bach, E., 298
Bahl, L., 278, 297
Baker, J., 294, 297

Balashek, J., 278, 297–298
Ballard, D. H., 264, 274
Balzer, R., 216, 242–243
Barash, M. M., 207
Barghouti, N. S., 243–244
Barr, A., 163, 206
Barrow, H. G., 206, 265, 276
Bartholet, S., 148, 158
Bartlet, S. L., 268, 275
Bates, M., 299
Beck, C. L., 188, 207
Bedau, H. A., 55
Bel, G., 194, 209
Benayad-Cherif, F., 159
Bengio, Y., 279, 297
Berenji, H. R., 181, 207
Berger, G. F. N., 255, 264, 275
Bernold, T., 211
Berztiss, A. T., 338
Besl, P. J., 275
Bever, T., 281, 298
Biddulph, R., 297
Binford, T. O., 262, 275
Bisiani, R., 229, 243
Blair, H. A., 24
Bledsoe, W. W., 74, 82
Blidberg, D. R., 128, 157
Bo, K., 209, 338
Boddy, M., 96, 114
Bolles, R. C., 253–254, 275

341

NAME INDEX

Bond, D. C., 210
Bonissone, P., 48, 54
Boothroyd, G., 183, 207
Borghesi, L., 288, 297
Borne, P., 212
Bourey, J. P., 188, 190, 194, 209
Bourne, D. A., 182, 207
Boyer, K. L., 209
Boyer, R. S., 72–74, 79, 82
Boyle, J., 83
Brachman, R. J., 266, 275
Brady, M., 158–159, 254, 274
Bratko, I., 172–173, 207
Broadbent, D. E., 28, 54
Brodie, M., 25
Brooks, R., 110, 113–114, 120, 125–127, 129, 136–137, 147–148, 150, 158–159
Brooks, S. L., 209
Brown, C. M., 206
Brown, D. C., 180, 207
Brown, G., 299
Brown, H., 160
Browne, J., 187–188, 203–205, 208, 210
Broy, M., 216, 243
Bruce, B., 299
Bruell, P., 74, 82
Bruno, G., 182–183, 194, 207
Bry, F., 11, 24
Buchanan, B. G., 34–35, 38, 45, 54
Bundy, A., 173, 207
Bunke, H., 275
Bürle, G., 173–174, 207
Burlinger, H. J., 209
Burns, J., 135, 144, 158
Burstall, R. M., 206
Butala, P., 211

Canny, J. F., 262, 275
Cao, X., 264, 274–276
Carbonell, J. G., 210
Cardin, R., 297
Cardoso, J., 212
Carringer, R., 167, 207
Carson, D., 83
Cassidy, G., 210
Castelain, E., 194, 207
Castles, F. G., 28, 54
Ceri, S., 24
Chakravarthy, U. S., 6, 11, 15, 24
Chandrasekaran, B., 180, 207
Chandru, V., 209
Chang, C. L., 3, 7, 24, 323, 338
Chang, K. H., 183, 201–203, 207

Chang, T. C., 167, 182, 207, 209–211
Chapman, D., 96, 114
Chappell, S., 128, 158
Charniak, E., 105, 114
Chatila, R., 114, 123, 158
Chattergy, R., 131, 158
Cheatham, T., 216, 244
Chechile, R. A., 55
Cheeseman, P., 33, 54, 126, 160
Chen, B. D., 263, 275
Chen, C. H., 209
Chen, C.-T., 275
Chepponis, M., 160
Chisholm, G., 74, 82
Chiu, M. Y., 170, 207
Choi, B. K., 166, 207
Chomsky, N., 278, 285, 297
Choudhry, J. V., 210
Chow, Y., 298
Christopherson, P. D., 177, 209
Chung, J. C. H., 210
Churchman, L., 210
Clancey, W., 40, 54
Clark, D. A., 48, 54–55
Clocksin, W. F., 90, 114
Cochrane, J. L., 55
Cohen, D., 242, 244
Cohen, P., 48, 50, 54
Cohen, P. R., 206, 208
Cole, C. W., 275
Connell, J., 129, 136, 150, 158
Connor, D. E., 163, 207
Conterno, N., 168, 208
Cook, C., 299
Coolahan, J., 188, 208
Corbeel, D., 188, 190, 194, 208, 209
Courtney, J., 143, 158
Courvoisier, M., 212
Craye, E., 207
Crochetiere, W. J., 55
Crowley, J., 123, 158
Cuppens, F., 20, 24

Dahl, V., 24
Daniel, L., 172, 208
Darbyshire, I., 182, 208
Date, C. J., 309, 338
Davies, E. J., 182, 208
Davies, L. S., 272, 275
Davis, E., 110, 115
Davis, K., 278, 297
Davis, L., 124, 140, 145, 157–158, 160
Davis, R., 308, 314, 338

Davis, R. P., 169, 210
Dean, T., 84, 96, 113–114
Dechter, R., 173, 208
Decker, H., 24
de Dombal, T., 28, 54
De Kleer, J., 308, 338
Demolombe, R., 24
De Mori, R., 279, 297
Denes, P., 278, 298
Deravi, F., 246, 264, 274–276
de Saussure, G., 160
Descotte, Y., 181, 208
Desrochers, A. A., 188, 206
Dewhurst, P., 183, 207
De Winter, D., 208
Dickmanns, E., 140, 149, 158, 160
Dillmann, R., 161, 168, 183, 208, 211
Dixon, J. R., 166, 179–180, 208
Doll, T. J., 185, 208
Dorst, L., 131, 158
Doshi, R., 114
Doyle, R., 113–114
Drumheller, M., 145, 158
Dubois, D., 54–55
Dudley, H., 298
Dufay, B., 173, 208
Duff, M. J. B., 275
Duggan, J., 187–188, 203–205, 208
Dungern, O. V., 170, 208
Dunlay, R. T., 159
Dunn, M. S., 167, 208
Dym, C. L., 166, 208, 210

Elfes, A., 126, 145, 158
Elia, A., 207
Enderton, H. B., 3, 24, 318, 323, 325, 338
Endsall, A. C., 211
Erman, L., 278, 292, 298
Ernst, G. W., 172, 208
Estensen, L., 209
Eversheim, W., 167, 208, 212

Fagan, L. M., 55
Falster, P., 209
Farah, B., 194, 208
Farber, H. B., 184, 208
Faugeras, O., 126, 136, 158
Favareto, C., 288, 297
Feder, A., 167, 208
Feigenbaum, A., 206
Feiler, P. H., 242, 244
Feistel, H., 275

Fellenstein, C., 181, 208
Ferrate, G., 212
Ferreira, P. M., 179, 209
Fikes, R. E., 172, 209
Fillmore, C., 291, 298
Firby, J., 127, 158
Fischler, M. A., 253–254, 275
Fischoff, B., 28, 33, 55
Fisher, E. L., 163, 184–185, 208–209
Fisher, H. G., 179, 181, 198–200, 210
Fitter, M., 313, 338
Flynn, A., 158
Fodor, J., 281, 298
Forgie, C., 278, 298
Forgie, J., 278, 298
Forsyth, D. A., 275
Forsyth, R., 174, 209
Fountain, T. J., 270, 275
Fox, J., 48, 54–55
Fox, M. S., 182–183, 207, 209
Frank, P., 212
Franklin, A., 159
Franklin, B., 28
Freeman, H., 216, 275
Freeman, P., 244, 272
Friesen, O., 82
Fry, D., 278, 298
Fu, K., 299
Fuchs, H., 208
Fukui, I., 143, 145, 158

Gairola, A., 165–166, 209
Gal, A., 20, 23–24
Gallaire, H., 3, 24, 309, 323, 327, 338
Gams, M., 211
Garrett, M., 281, 298
Gene, H. H., 338
Gentina, J. C., 188, 190, 194, 207–209
Gerencser, M., 163, 209
Gidwani, K. K., 177, 209
Gilmore, J., 159
Giralt, G., 123, 158
Gliviak, F., 182, 209
Glowinski, A. J., 54–55
Goitein, B., 55
Goldberg, A. T., 216, 244
Golshani, F., 82
Good, D. I., 73, 82
Gordon, J., 55
Gordon, S. J., 275
Gossard, D. C., 183, 210
Goto, Y., 150, 159
Grant, J., 24

NAME INDEX

Green, C. O., 208
Gremban, K., 160
Griffin, T., 28, 55
Guan, J., 336, 338

Haas, A., 298
Hajnal, S., 54
Hammer, M. M., 14, 24
Han, G., 336, 338
Hanafusa, H., 160
Hanahara, K., 271, 275
Hanson, A., 158
Haptmann, A., 299
Haralick, R. M., 262, 275
Harfmann, A. C., 338
Harms, R., 298
Hart, P., 209
Hart, P. E., 130, 159
Hawkinson, L. B., 210
Hayes, J., 207
Hayes-Roth, F., 174, 209, 298, 301, 338
Hebert, M., 160
Hein, E., 167, 211
Henderson, M. R., 166, 209
Henderson, P., 244
Hennessy, S., 150, 159
Heragu, S. S., 169–170, 178–179, 209–210
Herman, M., 128, 159
Hildreth, E. C., 262, 275
Hill, P. H., 26, 28, 34, 55
Hillel, G., 159
Hindi, K., 208, 211
Hofmann, I., 275
Hogarth, R., 28, 55
Hollerbach, J., 159
Hollinger, D., 194, 209
Holloway, G., 244
Horn, B. K. P., 247, 275
Howe, A., 208
Huber, P., 188, 209
Huff, K. E., 229, 244
Hunt, W., 74, 82
Hunter, J., 55

Igarashi, S., 73, 82
Inoue, H., 160
Isik, C., 159
Iyengar, S., 124, 159

Jagannathan, V., 168, 206
Jain, R., 246, 260, 267, 275
Janas, J. M., 24

Jaswinder, S. A., 188, 191, 209
Jelinek, F., 278, 294, 297–298
Jensen, A. M., 209
Jensen, K., 209
Jepsen, L. O., 209
Johnson, T., 159
Jorgensen, C., 159
Jozefowicz, W., 183, 209

Kabat, W., 82
Kadonoff, M., 129, 159
Kaemmerer, W. F., 177, 209
Kahler, S., 206
Kahn, P., 141, 159
Kahneman, D., 28, 55
Kaiser, G. E., 218, 230, 242, 244
Kak, A. C., 183, 209
Kalay, Y. E., 338
Kamath, M., 185–186, 209
Kambhampati, S., 159
Kammer, D., 160
Kanal, L. N., 55
Kanazawa, K., 113–114
Kaplan, J., 20, 24
Kaplanski, E., 182, 211
Kapusta, M., 209
Karabinosova, E., 209
Kedzierski, B. L., 216, 244
Keininger, G. G., 210
Keirsey, D., 124, 127, 130, 159
Kellerman, B. L., 55
Kelly, B., 55
Kemper, A., 309, 338
Kerschberg, L., 24
Khoshnevis, B., 181, 207
Kimball, O., 288, 298
King, J. J., 14, 24
King, M. S., 163, 209
Kitchen, L., 135, 144, 158–159
Kljaich, J., 74, 82
Klovstad, M., 299
Knickerbrocker, C. G., 210
Koch, E., 127, 130, 159
Kochar, B., 209
Komanduri, R., 209
Komoriya, K., 125, 160
Koren, Y., 161, 210
Kotik, G. B., 244
Kowalski, R., 11, 25, 323, 339
Krasner, M., 298
Krause, F.-L., 167, 211
Krivine, J. L., 324, 338

Krogh, B., 124, 149, 159
Krogh, B. H., 188, 207
Kuan, D. T., 125, 159
Kubala, F., 298
Kubis, J., 209
Kuipers, B., 110, 114
Kulikowski, C., 212
Kushner, T., 158, 160
Kusiak, A., 163, 169–170, 178–179, 209–210

Laface, P., 207
Laird, J., 55
Langlotz, C. P., 55
Latombe, J. C., 173, 181, 208
Laumond, J.-P., 114, 146, 159
Lauritzen, S. L., 55
Lavrac, N., 207, 211
Lea, W., 298
Lecouat, F., 243
Lee, K., 183, 210, 279, 294, 298
Lee, R. C. T., 3, 7, 24, 323, 338
Lee, T., 148, 159
Lemaire, T., 212
Lemmer, J. F., 55
LeMoigne, J., 158, 160
Lenat, D., 209
Lesser, V. R., 229, 244, 298
Levine, M. D., 259, 275
Levinson, S., 278–279, 285, 288, 294, 298
Levitt, T., 114
Liang, E., 160
Libardi, E. C., 208
Lillehagen, F. M., 338
Lin, W.-C., 255, 259, 265–266, 275
Lindgren, N., 278, 298
Lindley, D. V., 28–29, 31, 44, 55
Link, C. H., 167, 210
Lippmann, R., 298
Litt, M., 183, 210
Liu, C. R., 209, 211
Liu, H. K., 263, 275
Lloyd, J. W., 11, 24
Lochovsky, F. H., 309, 339
London, R. L., 82
Looney, C. G., 188, 192–193, 210
Loveland, D., 3, 24
Lowe, D., 144, 159
Lowerre, B., 278, 298
Lozano-Perez, T., 110, 114, 125, 159
Luby, S. C., 208
Luckham, D. C., 73, 82
Lumia, R., 157

Lund, T., 206
Lusk, E., 74, 80, 82–83
Lyons, D., 130, 159
Lytinen, S., 281, 298

Mackworth, A., 254, 275
McCain, H., 157
MacCrimmon, K. R., 29, 55
McCune, W., 79–80, 82
McDermott, D., 96, 105, 110, 114–115
McGlennon, J. M., 184, 210
McSkimin, J. R., 14, 24
Maddox, J., 159
Magee, M., 158
Maier, D., 90, 115
Maimon, O. Z., 185, 209
Majhoul, J., 298
Malmborg, C. J., 184, 210
Mamdani, E. H., 55
Mann, S., 167, 208
Manthey, R., 24
Marchetto, G., 194, 207
Marill, T., 158
Marquina, N., 159
Marr, D. C., 262, 275
Marra, M., 159, 160
Marslen-Wilson, W., 281, 298
Martinez, J., 188, 193, 210
Maruyama, T., 275
Mason, M., 159
Mathews, K. N., 275
Mathews, M., 278, 298
Mathies, L., 126, 160
Matsushima, K., 167, 181, 197, 210
Meister, A., 167, 210
Mellish, C. S., 90, 114
Meltzer, B., 82
Mendelson, E., 3, 24
Mercer, R., 297
Merlo, E., 297
Meyer, R. J., 210
Meystel, A., 128, 159
Michalski, R. S., 173, 210
Michie, D., 82, 173, 207–208, 211, 339
Mikovsky, A., 209
Milačič, V. R., 182, 210
Mill, F. G., 182–183, 210
Miller, D., 124, 159
Miller, D. M., 169, 210
Minker, J., 1, 14, 20, 23–25, 338
Minsky, M., 177, 210
Minsky, N. H., 242, 244

NAME INDEX

Missikoff, M., 24
Mitchell, J., 124, 130, 159
Mitchell, T., 210
Mittal, S., 180, 210
Mittelstaedt, H., 120, 160
Mokhtarian, F., 254, 275
Montanari, U., 263, 275
Moore, J. S., 72–74, 79, 82
Moore, R. L., 177, 210
Moravec, H., 117, 120, 126, 136, 159–160
Morgenthaler, D., 159–160
Morisio, M., 194, 207
Morjaria, M., 210
Mouleeswaran, C. B., 179, 181, 198–200, 210
Mozetik, I., 207
Mukherjee, D., 275
Muller, L., 159
Muro, P. R., 210
Murphy, T., 174, 210
Murray, D. J., 54
Mylopoulos, J., 25
Mysliwetz, B., 148, 160

Nalwa, V. S., 262, 275
Narahari, Y., 188, 212
Nash-Weber, B., 299
Nau, D. S., 182, 210–211
Nazif, A. M., 259, 275
Neisser, U., 120, 160
Nevins, J. L., 163, 178, 211
Newcomb, R. W., 188, 206
Newell, A., 55, 172, 208
Nicolas, J.-M., 11–12, 24, 338
Niedermayr, E., 170, 207
Niemann, H., 259, 275
Nillson, N., 172, 209
Nilsson, N., 116, 123, 136, 160
Nilsson, N. J., 159
Ning Cai, Z., 188, 212

Ohsuga, S., 301, 323–325, 327, 338–339
Ohta, Y., 265, 275
Okada, N., 210
O'Keefe, R., 174, 211
O'Neil, M., 54–55
Ounjian, D., 55
Overbeek, R., 74, 80, 82–83

Pal, S. K., 264, 275
Palmer, L. M., 208
Pao, J. H., 207

Pao, Y.-H., 269, 275
Parodi, A. M., 124, 131, 150, 160
Parrello, B., 76, 82
Patton, R., 212
Pauker, S. G., 55
Pauker, S. P., 55
Paul, R., 159
Payton, D., 127, 129, 159–160
Pearl, J., 55, 113, 115
Pepper, P., 216, 243
Perry, D. E., 242, 244
Persoon, E., 271, 275
Peterson, G., 278, 298
Peterson, J. L., 185, 211
Petri, C. A., 185–195, 211
Plander, I., 209
Poggio, T. A., 261–262, 276
Popovich, S. S., 244
Potter, D. C., 54
Powrie, J., 262, 274–275
Prade, H., 54–55
Pratt, T. W., 212
Preiss, K., 182, 211
Preyss, E., 159
Price, P., 298
Priestley, J., 28
Przymusinski, T. C., 5, 25

Quinlan, J. R., 173, 211

Rabiner, L., 279, 298
Raibert, M., 148, 160
Ranky, P., 161, 169, 211
Rao, A. R., 246, 260, 267, 275
Rao, S., 159
Raphael, B., 159
Rayson, P. T., 163, 211
Rector, A., 55
Reddy, D., 298
Reddy, R., 278, 298
Reitman, W., 207
Rembold, U., 161, 183, 211
Reps, T., 242, 244
Rich, C., 216–217, 244
Rich, E., 163, 211
Rillo, M., 188, 191, 194, 211
Riseman, E., 158–159
Robinson, G., 82–83
Robinson, J., 60, 82
Rodd, M. G., 246, 274–276
Rolstådas, A., 168, 211

NAME INDEX

Rosen, C., 116, 160
Rosenbloom, P., 55
Rosenfeld, A., 263, 275
Roucos, S., 298
Roussopoulos, N., 188, 208
Rubin, J. Z., 55

Sacerdoti, E., 105, 115
Sacerdoti, E. D., 172, 211
Sadri, F., 11, 25
Saffiotti, A., 48, 55
Safranek, R. J., 209
Sagerar, G., 275
Saint-Dizier, P., 24
Salassa, D., 212
Sanz, J. L. C., 248, 276
Sata, T., 210
Sato, J., 25
Schaefer, R. M., 209
Schaffer, G., 167, 211
Schank, R., 291–298
Schmidt, G., 207–208, 211–212
Schmidt, G. K., 170, 208
Schmidt, J. W., 24
Schmidt-Streiter, U., 170, 211
Schneider, J. J., 163, 211
Schwanke, R. W., 244
Schwartz, R., 298–299
Schwartz, S., 28, 55
Seida, S., 159
Sert, B., 159
Shafer, S., 126, 150, 160
Shah, J. J., 180, 211
Shalla, L., 83
Shannon, C. E., 31, 55
Shapira, Z., 55
Shapiro, S. C., 54
Shattuck, S., 281, 298
Shen, H., 150, 160
Shepherd, B. A., 173, 211
Shieber, S., 285, 298
Shih, C., 148, 159
Shimvra, M., 299
Shipley, K., 278, 288, 298
Shoham, Y., 96, 115
Shortliffe, E. H., 55
Shriver, B. D., 243
Signarowski, G., 150, 160
Sikic, B. I., 55
Silva, M., 210
Simmons, M. K., 180, 208
Simons, G. R., 210

Singh, M., 170, 207–208, 211–212
Siy, P., 263, 275
Skifstad, K. D., 275
Slovic, P., 55
Sluga, A., 182, 195–197, 211
Smetek, R., 163, 209
Smets, P., 55
Smith, B., 74–75, 82
Smith, B. C., 266, 275
Smith, B. M., 167, 211
Smith, B. T., 82
Smith, D. R., 216, 244
Smith, E., 299
Smith, R., 126, 160
Smith, R. G., 34–35, 38, 45, 54
Smith, S. F., 182–183, 209–210
Snyder, R. A., 163, 211
Sokolsky, M., 243
Sondhi, M., 298
Sonenberg, E. A., 24
Spiegelhalter, D. J., 55
Spraggett, S., 182–183, 210
Spur, G., 167, 211–212
Srinivasan, B., 160
Stallman, R. M., 216, 244
Steering, W. P., 275
Stentz, A., 150, 159–160
Stoll, H. W., 165, 212
Stotts, P. D., 212
Sussman, G., 105, 115
Swerdloff, L. M., 338
Szenes, K., 182–183, 212

Tachi, S., 125, 160
Tanaka, K., 299
Teitelbaum, T., 242, 244
Tenenbaum, J. M., 265, 276
Thorpe, C., 124, 131, 136, 159–160
Tomabechi, 292
Tomita, 292
Topor, R. W., 24
Torre, V., 261–262, 276
Townley, J., 244
Tranowski, D., 269, 276
Trovato, K., 131, 158
Tsichritzis, D. C., 309, 339
Tsihrintzis, G., 184–185, 212
Tu, S. W., 55
Tulkoff, J., 167, 212
Turk, M., 141, 150, 160
Turkiyyah, G., 160

Turner, D. A., 77, 82
Tversky, A., 55
Tzafestas, S., 163, 169–170, 179, 184–185, 207–208, 211–212

Uchiyama, T., 275
Urbanski, A., 183, 209
Urosevič, M., 182, 210

Vaghul, M. V., 208
Vaisset, M., 158
Valavanis, K. P., 188, 191, 209
Valette, R., 195, 212
Van Brussel, H., 183, 208
van Caneghem, M., 212
Vancza, J., 182, 212
van Gelder, A., 5, 25
Van Emden, M. H., 323, 339
Vercauter, C., 208
Victor, K., 167, 208
Villaroel, J. L., 210
Viswanadham, N., 185–186, 188, 209, 212

Waldron, K., 148, 160
Walker, A., 24, 181, 208, 212
Wallace, R., 140–141, 160
Wallrath, M., 309, 338
Ward, W., 299
Warman, E. A., 163, 209, 212
Warnecke, H. J., 209
Warren, D., 90, 115
Warren, D. H. D., 172, 212
Waterman, D., 209
Waters, R. C., 216–217, 244
Waxman, A., 140, 158–160
Weaver, W., 31, 55
Webber, B., 20, 25
Wee, W. G., 183, 201–202, 207
Weill, E., 167, 212

Weisbin, C., 126, 159–160
Wellington, J., 167, 211
Weng, Y.-T., 275
Werner, P., 299
Westfold, S. J., 244
White, G., 278, 282, 298
Whitney, D. E., 211
Whittaker, W., 138, 160
Wilkins, D., 105, 113, 115
Wilkins, D. E., 172, 212
Williams, T. J., 168, 212
Witkin, A. P., 254, 262, 276
Wojcik, A., 74–75, 82
Wolf, F., 275
Wolf, J., 299
Wolfe, W., 159
Wolz, U., 218, 243–244
Woo, T. C., 166, 212
Woods, W., 278, 285, 287, 293, 299
Wos, L., 56–57, 59–61, 63, 68, 71, 75, 79–83
Wu, Q.-M., 246, 255, 260, 266, 269, 271–273, 275–276
Wyler, D. J., 208
Wysk, R. A., 167, 207

Yamauchi, H., 301, 323, 338–339
Yang, H. S., 209
Yeh, C., 159
Young, S., 279, 288, 299
Yuan, B. Z., 274

Zadeh, L., 285, 299
Zamiska, J., 159
Zapp, A., 140, 149, 158
Zdonik, S. B., 14, 24
Zeleny, M., 55
Zenie, A., 188, 192, 212
Zons, K. H., 208
Zue, V., 296, 299

SUBJECT INDEX

A* algorithm, 130–131
Ada, 216
Agora, 229
AI planning (see Planning)
ASR (see Speech recognition)
AURA, 75
AuRA, 120, 151–153
Automated reasoning, 56–81
  applications, 72–77
    assembly line scheduling, 76–77
    circuit design and validation, 74–75
    program verification, 72–74
  combinatory logic, 77–79
  demodulation, 68–70
  future of, 80–81
  history of, 58–59
  inference rules, 63–67
  objectives of, 57–58
  portable programs, 79–80
  programming languages, 77–79
  proof by contradiction, 71–72
  representation, 61–62
  review of, 59–72
  strategy, 67–68
  subsumption, 70–71
Automatic learning (see Learning)
Automatic programming, 213–243
  CIP, 216
  FSD, 216
  Genie, 217–229

Automatic programming (Cont.):
  Marvel, 217, 229–242
  PDS, 216
  Refine, 216
Automatic speech recognition (ASR) (see Speech recognition)
Autonomous Land Vehicle (ALV), 117
Autonomous Robot Architecture (see AuRA)

Backward chaining, 176, 181, 234
Bayes' rule, 30–31, 40–41
Binary resolution, 59, 63–64
Boolean algebra, 59
Breadth-first search algorithm, 116

CAD (see Engineering design)
CIM (see Manufacturing)
Classical decision theory, 28–34
Clause language, 59, 61
Combinatory logic, 59–60, 77–79
Computer-aided design (see Engineering design)
Computer-aided manufacturing (see Manufacturing)
Computer vision, 126, 132–133, 136–139, 156, 245–274
  edge detection, 260–262
  hardware, 270
  high-level image processing, 251–253
  knowledge representation, 266–270
  low-level image processing, 250–251

Computer vision (*Cont.*):
  scene recognition, 253–255
  segmentation, 260, 262–266
    edge detection extension algorithm, 263–264
    region extraction, 265–266
    thresholding, 264–265

Database:
  deductive, 1–3, 11, 15, 61, 309
  extensional, 5
  geometric, 2
  relational, 11, 14–15, 181
Decision theory (*see* Classical decision theory)
Deductive database (*see* Database)
Demodulation, 57, 59–60, 68–70
Depth-first search strategy, 172
Design (*see* Engineering design)
Digitization bias, 124
Dynamic programming, 131, 263

EMYCIN, 176
Engineering design, 300–338
Equivalential calculus, 59
Expert system shells, 176

First-order logic, 2–23
Forward chaining, 176, 234
Frames, 27, 177–178, 182, 311
Fuzzy sets, 192–193, 285

Genie, 217–229, 243
GPS (General Problem Solver), 172, 181
Grapple, 229
Gypsy Verification Environment, 73–74

HARPY, 278
HEARSAY-II, 278, 282, 292–293
HERMIES, 124
Hidden Markov Models, 294–296
HILARE, 123
Holonomic robots, 145–146
Horn clause, 4–5, 18, 90
Hough transforms, 264, 271
HWIM, 278, 282, 288–289, 293

Inference rule, 27, 57, 63–67
  binary resolution, 63–64
  paramodulation, 63–67
Inscape, 242
Instantiation, 63–64, 66
Integrity constraints, 1–24

Intelligent sensing, 131–145
  computer vision, 132–133, 136–138
  dead reckoning, 134
  laser scanners, 133–134
  ultrasonic sensing, 133
ITP, 74–76, 80

Kalman filtering, 86–87, 126
KAS, 176
KAUS (knowledge acquisition and utilization system), 301, 323–337
KBQP, 14
KEE, 177–178
Knowledge-based query process, 14

Lambda calculus, 14
Learning, 172–173, 182
Legged robots, 146–148
Linguistic knowledge, 277–297
LISP, 27, 79, 176–177, 179, 181–182, 185, 194, 214, 216, 270
Locomotion systems, 145–149
  dynamic performance, 148–149
  holonomic vehicles, 145–146
  legged locomotion, 146–148
  nonholonomic vehicles, 145–146
LOOPS, 177–178

M1, 176, 184
Machine learning (*see* Learning)
Machine vision (*see* Computer vision)
Manufacturing, 161–206
  assembly operation, 183–185
  automatic learning, 172–173
  automatic planning, 171–172
  CAD/CAM, 165–167
  design for assembly, 164–166
  dynamic simulation, 168–169
  equipment selection, 169, 183–185
  examples of CIM expert systems, 195–206
    expert-system-based simulator of Petri nets, 203–206
    operation sequence planning expert system (OPEX), 195–197
    planning expert system for mechanical assembly, 201–203
    process planning expert system (PROPLAN), 197–201
  facility layout, 170–171
  fault diagnosis, 169–170
  feedback control, 167–168
  Petri nets, 169, 185–195, 203–206
    basic concepts, 186–188

SUBJECT INDEX

Manufacturing: Petri nets (*Cont.*):
   drawbacks, 186
   features, 185
   generalized, 188–193
   merging with knowledge-based techniques, 193–195
  process planning, 167–168, 181–183
  product design, 164–166, 179–180
  qualitative modeling, 173–174
  quality assurance, 171
  scheduling, 167–168, 181–183
Marvel, 217, 223, 229–242
Marvin, 242
Meadow maps, 122–123
Meldog, 125
Metalevel reasoning, 35, 47
Metarule, 5
MINDS, 288–289
Mobile robots, 116–160
  cartographic knowledge, 121–126
   long-term memory representation, 122–125
    automaton representation, 125
    generalized cylinders, 125
    meadow maps, 122–123
    potential fields, 124–125
    regular grids, 123–124
    vertex graphs, 125
    Voronoi diagrams, 124
   short-term memory representation, 125–126
  intelligent sensing, 131–145
   computer vision, 132–133
   dead reckoning, 134
   laser scanners, 133–134
   perceptual tasks, 135
   ultrasonic sensing, 133
  knowledge representation, 121–127
  locomotion systems, 145–149
   dynamic performance, 148–149
   holonomic vehicles, 145–146
   legged locomotion, 146–148
   nonholonomic vehicles, 145–146
  navigational planning, 127–131
   hierarchical planners, 127–129
   parallel planners, 129–130
   route planning, 130–131
  obstacle avoidance, 135–139
   computer vision, 136–138
   laser rangefinders, 138–139
   ultrasound, 136
  perception, 119–121
  plan representation, 126–127
  survivability, 149–150
Monte Carlo technique, 126
MYCIN, 27, 35, 46

NASREM, 128
Natural language processing, 23, 284, 296
NOAH, 172
Nonholonomic robots, 145–146

OPS5, 176, 184–185, 203–204
OTTER, 80

Parallel planners, 129
Parallel processing, 80–81, 121–122, 270–271
Paramodulation, 59, 63–67
Parser, 283–285, 289, 296
Parsing algorithm (*see* Parser)
Petri nets, 169, 185–195, 203–206
  basic concepts, 186–188
  drawbacks, 186
  expert-system-based simulator of, 203–206
  features, 185
  generalized, 188–193
  merging with knowledge-based techniques, 193–195
Planning, 171–172
Predicate logic, 27, 38, 318–326, 335–336
Production system, 174–177, 311
Program verification, 72–74, 79
Programmer's Apprentice, 216–217
Prolog, 4, 80, 90, 92–93, 105, 176, 181, 184, 196, 271
Props2, 35, 38–39, 41, 44
PROSPECTOR, 35, 176

Quadtree representation, 124
Query improvement through semantic transformation (*see* QUIST)
Query optimization, 2, 14–19, 23
QUIST, 14

Reasoning about space, 105–110
Refine, 216
Regular grid representation, 123–124
Relational databases, 11, 14–15, 181
Rivest-Shamir-Adleman algorithm, 73
Robot problem solving, 84–115
  control, 110–113
  feedback, 110–113
  generating plans of action, 96–105
  reasoning about space, 105–110
  reasoning about time and change, 90–96
  sensing, 110–113
Robot Rover, 117
Robots:
  holonomic, 145–146
  legged, 146–148

Robots (*Cont.*):
    nonholonomic, 145–146
    (*See also* Mobile robots)
ROSIE, 176
Rule-based system (*see* Production system)
Rule instantiation (*see* Instantiation)

Semantic compilation, 6, 10–12, 18
Semantic network, 14, 27, 177
Semantic query optimization, 14–19
Shakey, 116–117, 123–124
SIPE, 172
Skolem function, 62
Speech recognition, 277–297
    grammars, 282–292
    hidden Markov model, 279, 294–295
    hierarchical nature, 279–282
    higher-level knowledge, 279, 292–294
Stanford Verifier, 73–74
STRIPS, 116, 172

Subsumption, 6–8, 57, 60, 70–71, 129
Syllog, 181
Symbolic decision procedures, 26–28, 38–54

TEMPLOG, 92–95, 98, 100–101, 103–104
Temporal reasoning, 90–96
Theorem proving, 3, 11, 38, 58, 60, 72–74, 81
Transputer, 271
Turing machine, 77

Update validation, 2, 11–14, 23

Vision (*see* Computer vision)
Voronoi diagrams, 124

WARPLAN, 172

XCON, 176